Exploration of AI in Contemporary Legal Systems

Halim Bajraktari
University "Ukshin Hoti" Prizren, Kosovo

IGI Global
Scientific Publishing
Publishing Tomorrow's Research Today

Vice President of Editorial Melissa Wagner
Managing Editor of Acquisitions Mikaela Felty
Managing Editor of Book Development Jocelynn Hessler
Production Manager Mike Brehm
Cover Design Phillip Shickler

Published in the United States of America by
IGI Global Scientific Publishing
701 East Chocolate Avenue
Hershey, PA, 17033, USA
Tel: 717-533-8845
Fax: 717-533-8661
E-mail: cust@igi-global.com
Website: https://www.igi-global.com

Library of Congress Cataloging-in-Publication Data

Library of Congress Cataloging-in-Publication Data

Names: Bajraktari, Halim, 1983- editor.
Title: Exploration of AI in contemporary legal systems / edited by Halim Bajraktari.
Other titles: Exploration of artificial intelligence in contemporary legal systems
Description: Hershey, PA : IGI Global, 2025. | Includes bibliographical references and index. | Summary: "This book aims to present the most recent empirical research findings and pertinent theoretical frameworks about AI's effects on legal systems"-- Provided by publisher.
Identifiers: LCCN 2024049410 (print) | LCCN 2024049411 (ebook) | ISBN 9798369372050 (hardcover) | ISBN 9798369372067 (paperback) | ISBN 9798369372074 (ebook)
Subjects: LCSH: Artificial intelligence--Law and legislation .
Classification: LCC K564.C6 E95 2025 (print) | LCC K564.C6 (ebook) | DDC 340.0285/63--dc23/eng/20241023
LC record available at https://lccn.loc.gov/2024049410
LC ebook record available at https://lccn.loc.gov/2024049411
ISBN:979-8-3693-7205-0
eISBN:979-8-3693-7207-4

British Cataloguing in Publication Data
A Cataloguing in Publication record for this book is available from the British Library.

Table of Contents

Detailed Table of Contents

The idea of artificial intelligence first surfaced at the turn of the 20th century, with the goal of enabling machines to carry out tasks that resemble those performed by humans. Since then, a number of theories have been proposed regarding the extent to which mistakes made by artificial intelligence entities and systems may be held accountable, particularly in the area of criminal law. This chapter seeks to clarify this matter by discussing the legal obstacles that surround the question of criminal responsibility for artificial intelligence's actions. It also offers concepts, justifications, and factors that tackle this problem by using a comparative analytical and descriptive methodology. The chapter concluded with a proposal for international cooperation to develop a legal and ethical framework for the worldwide use of artificial intelligence. Given the anticipated widespread use of this technology in the future, governments could use this framework as a reference.

The conceptual review of the ethical implications of artificial intelligence in its impact on freedoms and human rights in the 21st century, critically aims to clarify the developing relationship between artificial intelligence and the law. Addressing a scientific answer if artificial intelligence, as autonomous and with influencing power in the legal system, should also be considered a problem that the development of AI may violate freedoms and human rights. The main theses analyzed include the ethical dilemmas caused by AI's potential to violate privacy, amplify disruptions, and make important decisions without human oversight. How can transparency and accountability from AI be improved to increase their trustworthiness and use in critical applications for human rights and freedoms?! What are the main ethical and legal challenges arising from the use of AI technologies in areas such as the justice system and national security, and how should we address them to minimize the negative impact on individuals and societies?

The proliferation of online hate speech has emerged as one of the most pressing global concerns today, corroding digital communication and undermining security within various communities. This paper broadens the context to understand computers from legal perspective, and more specifically Explainable Artificial Intelligence (XAI), can be amalgamated using a new host of detecting tools against online hate speech. This chapter is significant because of its potential to inform policies and regulations aimed at reducing the toxicity while preserving freedom using a well-rounded multidisciplinary approach. The goal is to pinpoint specific problems and suggest ways in which these issues might be addressed (if at all), while also exploring questions about the best most just or perhaps least unjust ethical frameworks for new methods of addiction detection and regulation on online platforms.

In recent years, owing to significant advancements in deep learning technology, artificial intelligence (AI) has started to replace human content creators and produce quality creative works on a wide scale. By the end of the decade, it is probable that a substantial quantity of art, literature, music, software, and online material will be generated by AI instead of conventional human creators. However, the law is not keeping pace with this technical advancement since it now prohibits granting copyright protection to works created by artificial intelligence. The aim of this chapter is to examine the intricacies of this expanding artistic field, specifically examining the modern techniques used by those who utilize AI to augment and amplify their creative pursuits.

Context/Background -Today, the global world is moving in a challenging and leading direction with AI technology. Artificial intelligence (AI) has the potential to address some of the biggest challenges in education in order to define innovative teaching and learning practices. Rapid technological developments undoubtedly inevitably bring great challenges and opportunities. How are studies being conceived and prepared with this new trend in society, how much will we have such an increase in technology versus the possibility of classic studies with modern ones, how will we see these approaches for use in study permit formats. Which will be the limits on which the next generation will build their academic levels, how many risks are presented in the implementation or non-implementation of a future without sufficient and proper assessment of AI, how should we face such a demanding and challenging trend for society and the academic world in the country. These will be some of the questions that will be addressed in this paper.

Access to justice and legal services remains a critical issue in many societies, often hindered by high costs, complex procedures, and limited availability of legal professionals. This chapter explores the transformative potential of Artificial Intelligence (AI) in addressing these barriers and enhancing access to justice for all. AI technologies, including machine learning, natural language processing, and intelligent automation, are increasingly being integrated into legal systems to streamline processes and provide affordable legal assistance. It highlights key AI applications, such as AI-driven legal research tools, virtual legal assistants, and online dispute resolution platforms, which democratize legal knowledge and services. These tools empower individuals with limited resources to understand their legal rights, receive preliminary legal advice, and navigate legal systems without the need for costly professional services.

As Artificial Intelligence (AI) continues to reshape the legal landscape, it is essential to address the accompanying ethical and regulatory considerations. This chapter investigates these critical dimensions, focusing on the ethical concerns of bias, transparency, accountability, and privacy within AI adoption in legal systems. It provides an in-depth analysis of the current regulatory landscape, including existing laws, guidelines, and international standards, and examines the challenges and opportunities in crafting effective regulatory frameworks. The chapter emphasizes the necessity of balancing innovation with ethical and social responsibility to ensure public trust and confidence in AI applications. It concludes with best practices and recommendations for legal professionals, policymakers, and industry stakeholders, aiming to foster responsible AI adoption in legal systems. Through this exploration, the chapter contributes to the ongoing discourse on the integration of AI in law, offering insights and guidelines to navigate the complex ethical and regulatory terrain.

This chapter explores the impact of predictive analytics and AI on judicial decision-making, tracing the evolution of technology in law from early data analysis to advanced AI techniques. It covers core concepts and applications, such as case outcome predictions, sentencing, and AI-powered legal research tools. The benefits of AI—enhancing accuracy, efficiency, and consistency in legal decisions—are highlighted, along with ethical concerns like bias, accountability, and privacy. The chapter includes case studies demonstrating AI's global impact on legal systems and addresses challenges such as technical limitations and resistance to technology adoption. It concludes by discussing future trends, emerging technologies, and the need for ethical guidelines to create a more just, data-driven legal framework.

Preface

As editors of ***Exploration of AI in Contemporary Legal Systems***, we are proud to present a comprehensive examination of how artificial intelligence (AI) is reshaping the fabric of legal frameworks and the justice system worldwide. This book is a culmination of rigorous research and thoughtful analysis aimed at illuminating the multifaceted role of AI within modern legal contexts.

The integration of AI technologies into legal systems marks a transformative period in the way justice is administered and how legal practitioners engage with the complexities of law. Our contributors, experts from various fields, delve into the myriad ways AI influences not only the efficiency and effectiveness of legal processes but also the underlying principles of fairness, accountability, and transparency. As AI continues to evolve, it prompts both challenges and opportunities that demand our attention, particularly regarding the ethical and practical implications of its application in legal settings.

In an era where technology rapidly advances, the dialogue around the intersection of AI and law is more critical than ever. This volume addresses pressing questions: How can we harness AI to improve legal practices while safeguarding human rights? What are the implications of predictive analytics on legal decision-making? How can we ensure that the implementation of AI in legal systems is fair and equitable? Our contributors provide a thorough exploration of these themes, contributing valuable insights that enrich the ongoing discourse surrounding AI in law.

The growing advent of AI has opened new horizons in scientific, academic, and technological publishing, sparking deep debates on its effects on the integrity of research and the study. This book weaves the possibilities of exploring AI into the contemporary legal system to unravel the dark conundrums of the present and the bright discoveries of the future that AI will bring. Key themes include predictive justice in criminal proceedings, the role of AI as both a right and a potential violation of human rights, and the opportunities and challenges in legal and business decision-making.

Moreover, the book highlights the critical need for AI to be seen as an empowering force in combating injustices and abuses, especially in the fight against human trafficking and other societal ills. The themes of accountability and ethical considerations are paramount as we explore the implications of AI's role in shaping legal outcomes. The need for comprehensive legislative frameworks that define the rights and roles of AI is underscored, enabling the protection of individual rights and promoting transparency in how AI makes decisions that affect people's lives.

We also emphasize the necessity of integrating AI knowledge into legal education, ensuring that future generations of legal professionals are equipped with the skills necessary to navigate an increasingly complex legal landscape. This integration will prepare young professionals to utilize advanced AI technologies effectively and ethically.

We intend for this book to serve as a resource not only for legal professionals and policymakers but also for researchers, educators, and students interested in understanding the evolving landscape of AI in legal contexts. By presenting empirical findings alongside theoretical frameworks, we hope to equip our readers with the knowledge needed to navigate this complex intersection of technology and law.

In crafting this collection, we have strived to create a balanced and inclusive dialogue about the role of AI in legal systems, ensuring that diverse perspectives are represented. Our aim is to foster a rich and sustainable conversation about the responsible use of AI in justice, illuminating its potential while critically examining the associated risks. This exploration is not just about adapting to change but actively shaping a future where AI and the law work symbiotically for the betterment of society.

Chapter Overview

In **Chapter 1**, we explore the historical evolution of artificial intelligence (AI) and its implications for criminal responsibility. The chapter examines the legal challenges surrounding accountability for AI entities and systems, particularly in criminal law. Using a comparative analytical and descriptive methodology, it clarifies the complexities of assigning responsibility for AI actions, ultimately proposing an international framework for ethical and legal standards as AI technology continues to advance.

Chapter 2, delves into the ethical implications of AI on freedoms and human rights in the 21st century. It critically examines the growing relationship between AI and law, questioning whether AI's autonomous capabilities pose risks to individual rights. Key ethical dilemmas, such as privacy violations and unchecked decision-making, are addressed, alongside discussions on enhancing transparency and accountability in AI systems to bolster trust in their applications within the justice system and national security.

In **Chapter 3**, we focus on the alarming issue of human trafficking, examining how AI can serve as a powerful tool in combating this crime. The chapter discusses various applications of AI, including data analysis and victim identification, highlighting its potential to disrupt trafficking networks and assist investigations. Ethical considerations are also addressed, emphasizing the importance of human oversight in the deployment of AI technologies in this sensitive area.

Chapter 4, examines the transformative potential of AI in corporate law practices, particularly regarding the drafting of legal documents. The chapter discusses the advantages AI brings, such as increased efficiency and accuracy, while also addressing concerns related to data privacy and the evolving role of legal professionals. It offers recommendations and best practices for effectively integrating AI-generated documents into corporate law firms, highlighting both opportunities and challenges in this technological transition.

In **Chapter 5**, we tackle the pressing issue of online hate speech and the role of Explainable Artificial Intelligence (XAI) in addressing this challenge. This chapter emphasizes the need for innovative detection tools to combat hate speech while preserving freedom of expression. By offering a multidisciplinary approach, it identifies critical issues and suggests ethical frameworks for developing just methods of detection and regulation on digital platforms.

Chapter 6, investigates the implications of AI-generated creative works in the realms of art, literature, and music. As AI begins to produce quality content at an unprecedented scale, this chapter addresses the current legal frameworks surrounding copyright protection for AI-generated works. It examines the challenges and complexities of this new artistic landscape, considering how human creators can leverage AI to enhance their creative endeavors.

In **Chapter 7**, the focus shifts to the educational landscape, where AI technology presents both challenges and opportunities. This chapter explores how AI can revolutionize teaching and learning practices while also assessing the risks of overreliance on technology. It raises critical questions about the balance between traditional education methods and modern technological advancements, emphasizing the importance of thorough assessment in navigating these new educational paradigms.

Chapter 8, addresses the critical issue of access to justice and the role AI can play in enhancing legal services. By integrating AI technologies into legal systems, the chapter highlights how tools such as virtual legal assistants and online dispute resolution platforms can democratize access to legal knowledge. It explores the potential for AI to overcome barriers and provide affordable legal assistance, empowering individuals with limited resources to navigate complex legal landscapes.

In **Chapter 9**, we explore the ethical and regulatory considerations accompanying AI's integration into legal systems. This chapter provides an in-depth analysis of issues such as bias, transparency, and privacy, as well as the existing regulatory landscape. It emphasizes the need to balance innovation with ethical responsibility, offering best practices and recommendations for legal professionals and policymakers to ensure responsible AI adoption.

Chapter 10, examines the impact of predictive analytics and AI on judicial decision-making processes. The chapter traces the evolution of technology in law, highlighting core applications such as case outcome predictions and AI-powered legal research tools. It discusses the benefits of AI in enhancing legal accuracy and consistency while addressing ethical concerns related to bias and privacy, ultimately calling for the establishment of ethical guidelines to navigate this complex terrain.

In **Chapter 11**, we investigate the role of AI and jurimetrics in criminal proceedings, focusing on their potential to improve predictive justice. The chapter defines predictive justice and reviews various AI tools used in law enforcement and court systems. It critically assesses the challenges of bias and transparency, emphasizing the importance of trust and stakeholder engagement in the responsible adoption of AI technologies within the legal framework.

Finally, **Chapter 12**, discusses the significance of feature selection in machine learning, particularly within the context of information retrieval (IR) 5.0. This chapter outlines the importance of selecting relevant features for model construction, emphasizing the need for dimensionality reduction in a landscape marked by unprecedented complexity. It underscores how effective feature selection can enhance learning performance and accuracy in AI applications.

Chapter 13, concludes with an exploration of the effects of digitalization and AI on prison administration and the reintegration of elderly convicts. Drawing from international research, this chapter highlights the challenges faced by aging prison populations and identifies strategies for their successful societal reintegration. Through qualitative and quantitative analysis, it emphasizes the need for equitable support systems to address the unique post-release challenges encountered by older offenders.

Through these diverse chapters, we hope to provide a comprehensive understanding of the transformative impact of AI on various aspects of the legal system, stimulating critical dialogue and encouraging responsible innovation in the field.

We extend our heartfelt gratitude to all the contributors for their dedication and insight. We also acknowledge the support of our institutions, particularly the University "Ukshin Hoti" in Prizren, Kosovo, which has provided a nurturing environment for research and collaboration.

Together, we embark on this exploration of AI in contemporary legal systems, seeking to understand how we can leverage these advancements for the betterment of our legal frameworks and society as a whole.

CONCLUSION

As we conclude this volume, it is clear that the exploration of Artificial Intelligence (AI) in contemporary legal systems represents an important development in the field of justice. Through the input of various experts, we have examined the profound consequences of AI on traditional legal principles, highlighting its transformation potential. Each chapter provides a detailed analysis of innovative applications of AI in legal practice, from predictive justice to the ethical concerns that accompany this use. The integration of AI technologies is increasing transparency, efficiency and access to legal services, with the goal of creating a fairer system.

Moreover, the discussions presented illuminate the challenges and opportunities that lie ahead. Regulations, ethical dilemmas, and the need for education in the use of AI are essential to the responsible growth of these technologies. We are encouraged by insights into how AI can help fight injustice and improve access to justice. In conclusion, this volume represents a collaborative effort that underscores the importance of interdisciplinary approaches to understanding the role of AI in justice. We hope that the insights shared here will serve as a valuable resource for researchers, practitioners, and policymakers, guiding future advancements in the interaction of AI and legal systems.

Halim Bajraktari
University "Ukshin Hoti" Prizren, Kosovo

Chapter 1
Challenges of Criminal Liability for Artificial Intelligence Systems

Ramy El-Kady
https://orcid.org/0000-0003-2208-7576
Police Academy, Egypt

ABSTRACT

The idea of artificial intelligence first surfaced at the turn of the 20th century, with the goal of enabling machines to carry out tasks that resemble those performed by humans. Since then, a number of theories have been proposed regarding the extent to which mistakes made by artificial intelligence entities and systems may be held accountable, particularly in the area of criminal law. This chapter seeks to clarify this matter by discussing the legal obstacles that surround the question of criminal responsibility for artificial intelligence's actions. It also offers concepts, justifications, and factors that tackle this problem by using a comparative analytical and descriptive methodology. The chapter concluded with a proposal for international cooperation to develop a legal and ethical framework for the worldwide use of artificial intelligence. Given the anticipated widespread use of this technology in the future, governments could use this framework as a reference.

INTRODUCTION

With the dawn of artificial intelligence, society is on the cusp of a digital revolution that is expected to change the face of human life significantly. The world is on the brink of a new era, the fourth industrial revolution and digital transformation (Ghaitas, 2017). The term "Fourth Industrial Revolution" was coined at the World

DOI: 10.4018/979-8-3693-7205-0.ch001

Economic Forum in Davos, Switzerland, in 2016, during the final installment of the ongoing Industrial Revolution series. Prof. Klaus Schwab, "the President of the Davos Economic Forum," highlights three factors that support the notion of a fourth industrial revolution. This revolution is characterized by the rapid advancement of the current revolution and its dependence on a digital revolution that integrates various technologies, resulting in unprecedented transformations in the economy, business, and various systems. Throughout the globe, in various organizations, disciplines, and communities (Schwab, 2017).

Given these advancements, updating and creating laws and regulations that align with this new reality is imperative. The fourth industrial revolution has brought remarkable technological advancements such as AI, robotics, the Internet of Things, self-driving vehicles, 3D printing, nanotechnology, biotechnology, materials science, government computing, Blockchain, and others. These breakthroughs will usher humanity into a new era. Developing a comprehensive legal framework is necessary to regulate these new applications. It is crucial to have a realistic understanding of the uses of AI, their impact on human and social behavior, and the legal interests that should be protected (El-Kady, 2021).

Significance of the Study:

AI approaches are highly significant for criminal law jurists as they build robots that exhibit intelligent behaviors while interacting with people. Consequently, it becomes necessary to establish legal regulations appropriate for this technology's characteristics, which is anticipated to have a global impact. For instance, there have been suggestions to revise the European Convention on Cybercrime to establish legal regulations that govern advancements in information technology (Khalifa, 2018).

The study seeks to introduce AI applications, delineate their respective domains, elucidate their advantages, and forecast their anticipated impact in the forthcoming phase. Furthermore, it aims to underscore the suggested criminal law regulations that govern the utilization of AI and scrutinize the suitable penalties proposed to be imposed on AI entities.

Methodology:

The chapter will employ a comparative analytical methodology to elucidate, examine, and assess the research topic from multiple perspectives and dimensions to attain a lucid understanding of criminal liability for offenses arising from using AI and surveillance. The chapter examines the complexity of the subject matter, which involves very contemporary themes that lack adequate legal restrictions. However, certain matters are still under the jurisdiction of jurisprudence, which aims to define new legal principles appropriate for these new technologies (LEEMANS & JACQUEMIN, 2017), notwithstanding the scarcity of references addressing this topic. Consequently, the absence of legal control for AI applications raises research challenges. Consequently, the researcher was motivated to tackle this issue and provide insight into the appropriate criminal regulations for addressing it.

Chapter Plan:

The chapter will examine the study by clearly defining AI, outlining its key features and benefits, discussing its visual representations, exploring its connection to criminal law, and exploring the legal principles jurisprudence advocates to establish rules for holding AI accountable for criminal acts. This will involve examining the responsibility of the AI program itself and the responsibility of the operator, manufacturer, programmer, and any relevant third parties. The topic of discussion is divided into three parts: interference in the AI program and punishment for crimes committed by AI.

PART ONE- UNLOCKING THE FUTURE: A COMPREHENSIVE INTRODUCTION TO AI:

Definitions of AI:

The phrase "artificial intelligence" was coined by John McCarthy during a conference in Dartmouth in 1956. AI is a field of computer science and emerging technology that aims to replicate human cognitive abilities and methods of operation. AI is commonly defined as the capacity of digital technologies and computers to imitate and replicate the cognitive abilities of intelligent humans, including tasks like thinking, learning from past experiences, and performing mental processes (Mohamed, 2020).

Russell and Norving (2009) and Ibrahim (2020) define AI as a software system that can mimic human thinking using a computer or other device. It is a computer-based simulation of human behavior and cognitive processes. Therefore, it is evident that AI aims to equip computers with programs and abilities that resemble human intellect, allowing them to carry out intelligent tasks (Pham et al., 2020). The researcher recognizes the significance of collaborative international endeavors to establish a cohesive definition of AI, given the existence of multiple definitions. (see Figure 1)

Figure 1. Multifaceted AI

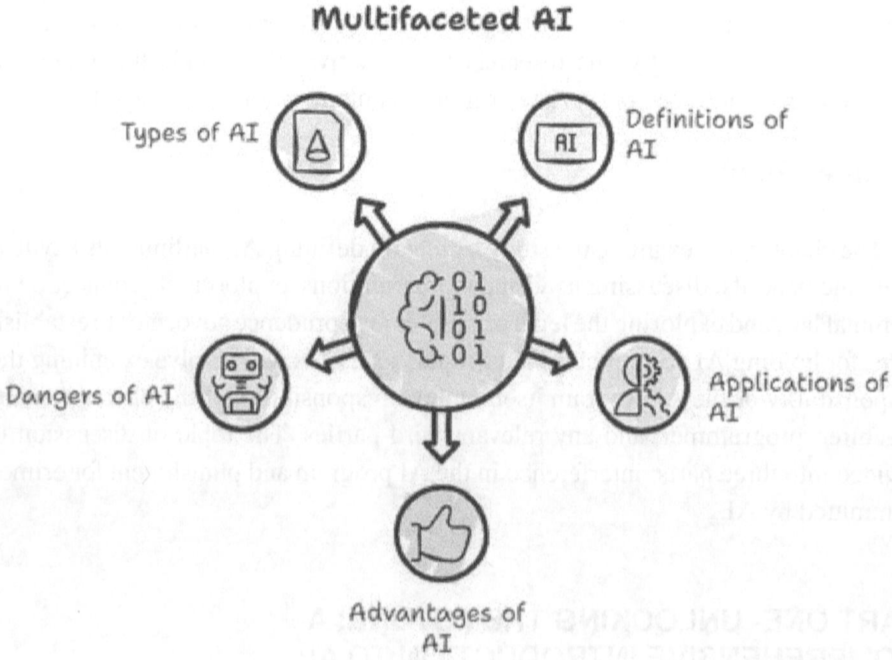

Characteristics and Fields of AI:

AI programs have several distinctive features, the most notable being the capacity to acquire knowledge, deduce logical conclusions, and respond to unforeseen circumstances not explicitly built into the system. AI applications have expanded across various sectors, including commerce, economics, and industry. The use of industrial robots in various industrial projects and the healthcare sector, such as medical robots performing intricate surgeries, demonstrates the growing application of AI in surgical procedures.

Although evidence of AI tools specifically for surgical operations was not found, the speed at which these operations can be performed suggests the potential for expansion. However, it is essential to note that there may be instances where the robot is not entirely responsible for the outcome of surgery (POIROT-MAZERESDU, 2013). AI is anticipated to significantly impact various areas of human life, including education, transportation, communications, traffic, environment, security, military, and social networking sites (WENG et al., 2015).

In Egypt, AI is being applied in various fields. One notable application is in the societal domain, where it is used to search for missing persons by comparing images of missing children with pictures of homeless children using face recognition technology. Another application is in tourism and antiquities, specifically in the Grand Egyptian Museum. Here, face recognition technology is used to display antiquities based on the characteristics of the interested public. In the security field, AI is used to determine the personality of suspects by analyzing crime data, timing, geographical location, and the database of accused, wanted, and convicted individuals. This facilitates the swift detection of crimes. Additionally, AI is employed in agriculture, where satellites assess crop quality and estimate the required amount of water for optimal growth (IDSC, 2020). (see Figure 2)

Figure 2. An Overview of AI

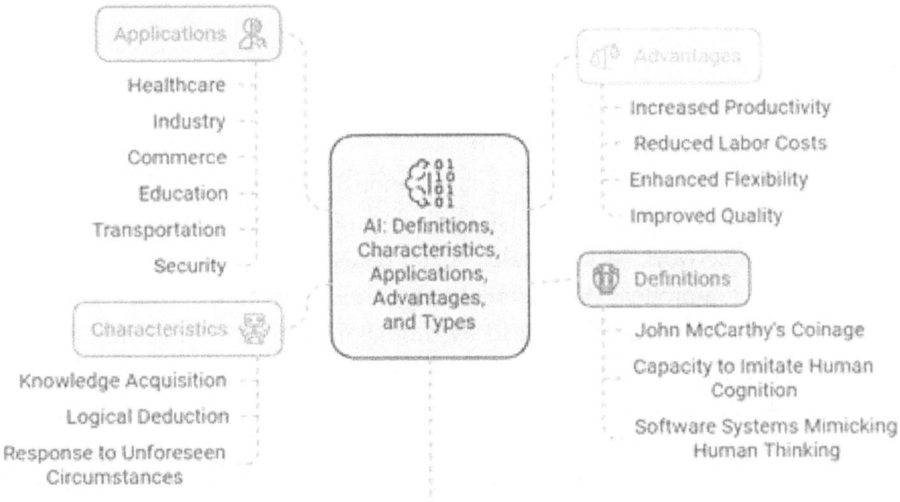

Advantages and Dangers of AI:

Advantages of robots include increased productivity, efficient use of equipment, reduced labor costs, enhanced flexibility, faster completion of work, ease of programming, ability to operate in hazardous conditions, improved workplace and production quality, and the ability to move freely in three-dimensional space (Khalifa, 2018).

Contrary to AI's positive characteristics, several estimations suggest that it also has a negative side, which makes it a fertile ground for the emergence of new forms of criminal activities. AI will enable malware and viruses to comprehend the context in which they operate. This has led the Executive Director of the European Police to emphasize the importance of anticipating the consequences of emerging technologies that criminals may exploit to safeguard the well-being of European Union citizens.

The European police have warned about the potential for AI to facilitate new methods for criminals, hackers, and attackers to carry out malicious activities. This includes using AI to enhance the effectiveness of phishing attacks by creating deceptive emails and negative responses. AI has the potential to facilitate criminal activities. Cybersecurity is more accessible for inexperienced criminals, allowing them to carry out advanced and hazardous attacks.

A highly significant domain in this research is the extensive manipulation of visual or auditory content, known as profound falsification, employed to execute widespread disinformation campaigns. Certain criminals have begun utilizing video and audio recordings to assume the identity of CEOs and deceive institutions and organizations for fraudulent purposes.

According to Darktrace experts, AI will enable malicious programs to be aware of the specific context in which they operate. This includes identifying whether the environment is a Windows operating system, a Linux application, a mobile application, or a network. Based on this understanding, the malicious program will then be able to make decisions independently.

Subsequently, it has the potential to autonomously reproduce and utilize any security weakness that becomes known to take advantage of interconnected computer systems inside a network. Additionally, it can delay the assault to acquire further knowledge and comprehension. Alternatively, it can initiate the attack discreetly and gradually, making it go unnoticed by mimicking the transfer of multiple uncomplicated files and data to the individuals operating it.

Europol and Dark Trace have issued warnings stating that law enforcement agencies must rapidly increase innovation, creativity, dynamism, and modernization. They must work diligently to keep up with imminent criminal threats, which are expected to become even more dangerous with emerging technologies (Europol, 2019). (see Figure 3)

Figure 3. Balancing AI's benefits and risks

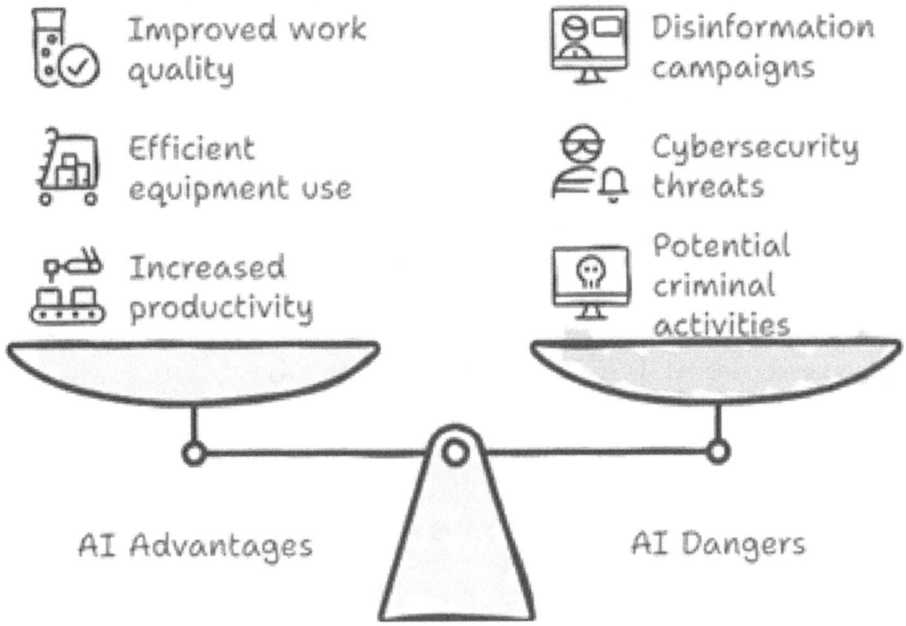

Types of AI:

There are three distinct categories of AI: Specialized AI, General AI, and Super AI. Specialized AI refers to AI systems capable of carrying out specific tasks, such as operating self-driving cars, recognizing speech or images, or playing chess on smart devices. This type of AI is widely used and readily accessible today.

General AI refers to an AI capable of performing tasks at a level comparable to human abilities. Regarding cognition, it centers on enabling machines to engage in autonomous thinking and planning, analogous to human cognition. However, there are no tangible instances of this nature yet. All existing entities are currently working on research projects that require substantial effort to transform into tangible realities.

Super AI, potentially surpassing human intelligence, can outperform specialized and knowledgeable individuals in various tasks. This type of AI must possess several essential characteristics, including learning, planning, communicating autonomously, and making informed judgments. The notion of superior AI is a theoretical construct not currently present in our contemporary epoch (Mohamed, 2020).

The significance of addressing these specific forms of AI underscores the potential that AI applications may achieve in the future and the degree to which the principles of criminal law are believed to be applicable. We note the inclination of numerous nations to implement measures aimed at augmenting the use of AI. Egypt has formed a national council for AI and multiple institutions dedicated to studying AI. There are some countries, including the United Arab Emirates. The United Nations has endeavored to develop a Ministry of AI to fulfill the UAE's objective of integrating AI across all sectors (Dahshan, 2020).

In 2016, the Science and Technology Committee of the English Parliament suggested the creation of a permanent committee on AI. The organization aims to examine the subject's impacts, define fundamental rules for its advancement, and establish a legal structure (UK Parliament, 2016). The United Nations Interregional Institute for Crime and Justice Research has created a center in The Hague that focuses on AI and robotics. This institute aims to serve as a global authority on subjects concerning AI (UNCCPCJ, 2020). (see Figure 4)

Figure 4. Types of AI

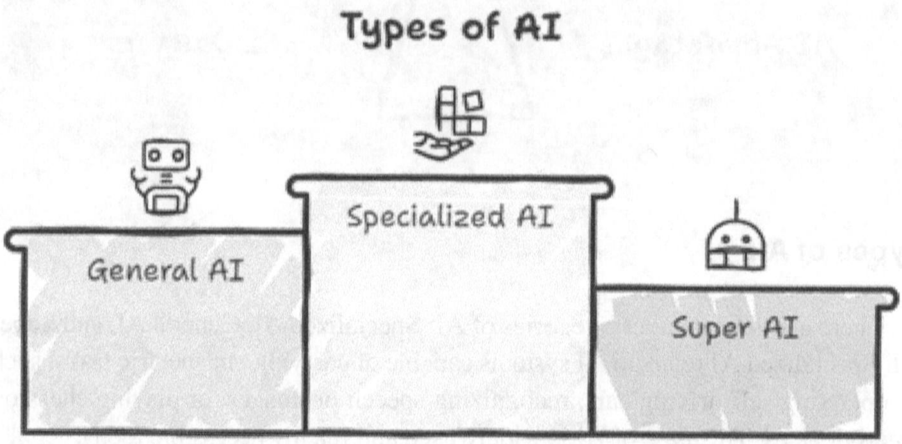

PART TWO- NAVIGATING THE FUTURE OF AI: RESPONSIBILITY AND REGULATION:

Between regulation and non-regulation, there has become an urgent necessity for an international framework regulating the uses of AI in light of regional and international movements to fill the void. The rapid advancements in AI, heralding the possibility of this technology taking over, have sparked significant interest among many individuals.

However, these developments also bring forth potential risks that must be addressed. All aspects of life, from applied science, aim to provide the computer with programs and capabilities similar to human intelligence to make it capable of performing intelligent operations. AI is moving to conquer the world in light of the close connection between this new science, algorithms, machine learning, and deep learning, leading to Generative AI (El-Kady, 2024). (see Figure 5)

Figure 5. Comprehensive AI Regulation Framework

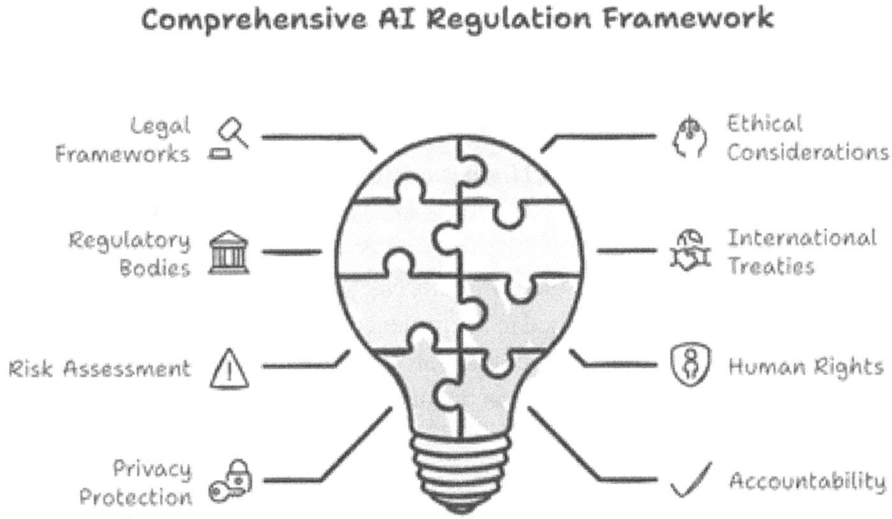

For a very recent period, there has been a great debate among legal circles about the extent of the need to establish legal regulation for the uses of AI between two trends: The first sees the necessity of not restricting the scope of innovation and development in the field of AI through legal regulation, as the expected legal restrictions on developing companies may push the field of AI calls for limiting investments in this field in a way that will negatively affect the development of this technology.

Another side of the jurists sees the necessity of having a legal framework regulating the uses of AI in all aspects and inaugurating an ethical framework regulating those uses to prevent its misuse in ways that harm humans. And humanity. This debate underscores the ethical considerations that must be at the forefront of our discussions, invoking a sense of responsibility. (see Figure 6)

Figure 6. Balancing AI Innovation and Regulation

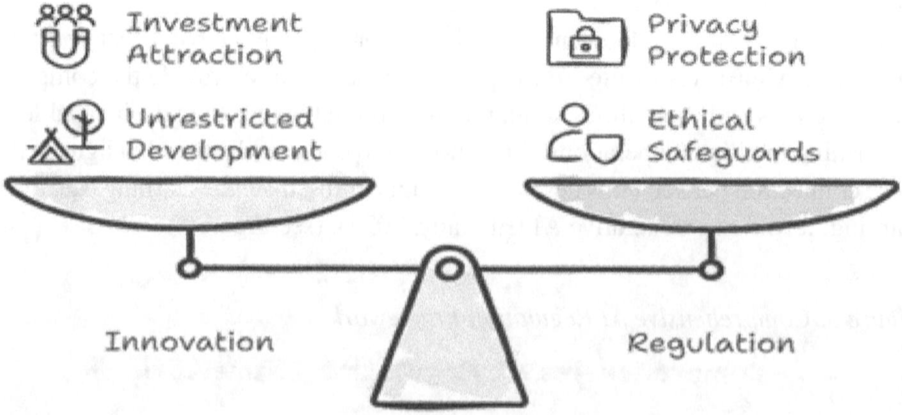

The importance of having a legal framework regulating these uses also highlights the fact that there are real concerns that the expansion of the use of AI technologies and making them available within the framework of processing individuals' data would constitute a violation of the right to privacy, in addition to the fact that the expansion of these uses has resulted in the presence of new people in the framework of the rules of criminal, civil, and administrative legal liability relates to examining the responsibility of programmers, manufacturers, developers, operators, users, and owners of these technologies and the legal limits of their responsibility for damages resulting from using them (El-Kady, 2022).

Moreover, the extent of the need to grant AI entities and systems legal personality. These topics require a regulating legal framework that governs these uses and their damages. The European Union was a pioneer in this field, and these issues were at the forefront of its experts, as the European Parliament's resolution issued on 10/6/2021 regarding the use of AI in the field of criminal law and law enforcement indicated the inevitability of having a transparent legal model for determining responsibility. Criminal liability for the potentially harmful effects of AI systems provided that the regulatory provisions for this liability preserve the determination of the natural person's responsibility for the damages resulting from these applications. The efforts of the European Union ultimately resulted in the launch of the first international treaty regulating this issue. Your role as legal professionals and scholars is crucial and empowering in shaping these regulations and ensuring they are fair and effective. (see Figure 7)

Figure 7. Debate on AI Regulation

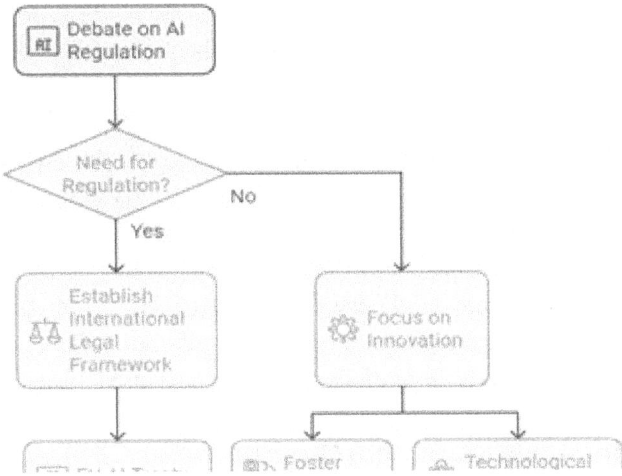

The European Union is Entering a New Phase in the Era Of Legal Regulation of AI:

During the 133rd Ministerial Meeting in Strasbourg on May 17, 2024, the Council of Europe adopted the first international treaty on AI, Human Rights, Democracy, and the Rule of Law. This treaty consisted of 36 items. The treaty establishes a legal framework based on risk assessment (Risk and impact management framework), and Paragraph (1) of Article (1) of the treaty specifies that it aims to ensure complete compatibility between all activities included in the Entire Lifecycle of the AI System (industry, programming, application, and operation).

Moreover, human rights, democracy, and the rule of law, so that the risks, such as job displacement and privacy breaches, raised by each stage are governed to reduce the overall adverse effects, such as social inequality and loss of personal autonomy, on fundamental rights and the rule of law without sacrificing the need to encourage creativity, but all that matters is that this creativity should be responsible creativity that cannot be unleashed without any control or link.

Chapter Two of the Treaty includes two articles, which represent general obligations on states parties regarding adopting the necessary measures to ensure that AI systems respect human rights (Article 4), as well as that AI systems are not used to undermine the integrity, independence, and effectiveness of institutions and the democratic process, and the necessity of respecting the sovereignty of the judiciary, access to justice, and the ability to Individuals can freely form their opinions (Article 5).

Chapter Three also includes a set of obligations related to the most prominent violations raised by AI applications and technologies. For example, Article (7) relates to each State Party taking the necessary measures to respect human dignity and individual autonomy, and Article (8) relates to taking all necessary measures to respect human dignity and individual autonomy. A State Party takes the necessary measures to consider transparency and oversight. Article (9) relates to each State Party taking measures to ensure accountability and responsibility, and Article (10) relates to each State Party taking the necessary measures to ensure Equality and non-discrimination. Article (11) relates to each State Party taking the necessary measures to protect privacy and personal data. Article (12) relates to each State Party taking the necessary measures to ensure the reliability of AI systems. Reliability. Article (13) relates to each State Party taking measures. Necessary for safe innovation.

The AI Office Within the European Commission:

In a related context to the issuance of the first international treaty on AI, the establishment of the AI Office within the European Commission was announced. This office, which serves as a central hub for AI-related activities within the EU, aims to enable future AI development, dissemination, and use to enhance social and economic benefits and innovation while mitigating risks. The office will be vital in implementing the AI Act, a comprehensive regulatory framework for AI, especially in general-purpose AI models. It will also promote trustworthy AI research and innovation and position the EU as a global discussion leader. The Office of AI is headed by a Chief who works under the guidance of a Chief Scientific Advisor to ensure scientific excellence in evaluating innovative models and methods and an Advisor for International Affairs to follow up on our commitment to working closely with international partners in the field of trustworthy AI.

Structure of AI Office:

The Office of AI consists of several units:

- **The Regulatory and Compliance Unit** coordinates the regulatory approach to facilitate uniform application and enforcement of AI law across the Union, working closely with Member States. The unit will contribute to investigations and potential violations and administer sanctions.
- **The AI safety Unit** identifies systemic risks for competent general-purpose models, possible mitigation measures, and evaluation and testing methods.
- **The AI and Robotics Excellence Unit** supports and funds research and development to foster an excellent ecosystem. It coordinates the GenAI4EU

initiative, stimulating the development of models and their integration into innovative applications.

- **The AI for Societal Good Unit** will design and implement the AI Office's international engagement in AI for Good, such as weather modeling, cancer diagnosis, and digital twins for reconstruction.
- **The AI Innovation and Policy Coordination Unit** oversees the implementation of the EU AI Strategy, monitors trends and investment, stimulates the uptake of AI through a network of European digital innovation centers and the establishment of AI factories, and strengthens the innovative ecosystem by supporting regulatory sandboxes and real-world testing.

In summary, it is clear to the reader the extent of the interest that the European Union attaches to AI in particular and the necessity of developing an integrated framework to regulate it in anticipation of expected developments in its use. These legislative efforts constitute a pioneering model that will undoubtedly contribute to advancing AI's innovation and development movement from a clear legal perspective that shows the legal limits for using this rapidly developing technology. (see Figure 8)

Figure 8. European AI Office

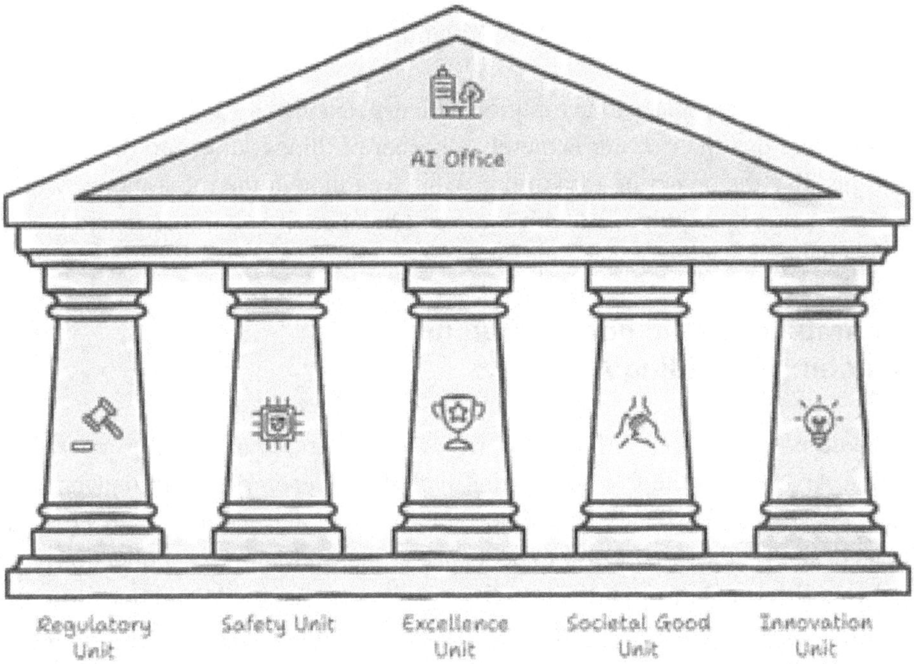

The Theory of "the responsible human representative":

European Parliament experts have previously worked hard to establish the "theory of the responsible human representative" to regulate European civil law rules on robots, which the European Union Legal Affairs Committee issued in February 2017. Through this theory, it is possible to impose responsibility for operating the robot on a group of people according to the extent of their error in manufacturing or exploiting it. The extent of their negativity in avoiding the actions expected from the robot, without assuming error or considering the robot as a thing, as the robot is an obedient servant to the human being, but it is not a thing or a being. An inanimate object that does not make sense but rather an automatic being with a beginner's human logic capable of development and reason. This results from imprinting on the human mind as a matter of technological imitation (El-Kady, 2024).

The European Union has introduced the concept of 'the human representative' to be responsible for the actions of automated robots. The European Robot Law acknowledges the impossibility of establishing the robot's responsibility for the damage it may cause to a third person. Therefore, the responsibility for the actions and omissions of the robot rests on a human representative. The European legislator has also made a forward-thinking promise regarding the future legal status of robots. With the emergence of new generations of robots, the European Union envisions a legal electronic personality for robots, granting them rights and imposing obligations on them.

The new theory replaced the traditional theory that views AI systems and robots as things and that their owner is merely a keeper of things subject to the assumed error, just like the owner of a traditional car. Even though the robot moves with a quasi-human mental judgment with logic and balance, it is not a controlled, submissive being like a deaf machine called "The Thing."

The Arab League is not Far Behind by Launching a Guiding Arab law:

We do not forget to point out the efforts of the Arab Parliament to develop a guiding Arab law in the field of AI that includes a general legal framework and integrated regulation of this new field based on its interest in the subject of AI and its desire for the Arab world to be a partner in developing AI applications and localizing them in Arab countries. In light of the increasing global interest in this subject, the law comprises six chapters that include (43) articles. The first chapter includes definitions and general provisions, which are contained in eight articles. The law's first article above defines AI, its applications, and the algorithm. The second article also refers to the localization of AI technology, and national plans for priorities for its application (Art. 3), physical and technical assets (Art. 4), keeping pace with global digital changes (Art. 5), and governance of AI technology (Article 6), obligations and duties (Art. 7), and scope of application (Article 8).

Chapter Two of the Law on AI Controls and Standards, which contained ten articles, referred to national controls and standards for AI (Art. 9), accreditation and authorization (Art. 10), respect for national sovereignty (Art. 11), respect for human dignity (Art. 12), protection of human rights (Art. 13), and protection of... Privacy (Art. 14), prohibition of discrimination (Article 15), gender equality (Art. 16), justice and equity (Art. 17), protection of property rights (Article 18), and ensuring cybersecurity (Art. 19).

The third chapter on supporting capacity building in the field of AI, which was contained in six articles, dealt with the obligations of countries that develop national strategies to support AI and its applications (Art. 21), enhancing the role of scientific research in the field of AI (Art. 22), and building qualified human competencies in the field of intelligence. AI (Art. 23), spreading awareness among citizens about enhancing the benefits of AI and confronting the negatives, establishing an independent national authority for AI (Art. 25), and establishing specialized technical departments for technical support and others for judicial control (Art. 26).

The fourth chapter also reviewed cooperation at the Arab and international levels in supporting research and applications of AI, which was contained in five articles on the exchange of experiences and information (Art. 27), the establishment of an Arab center to support and enhance Arab experiences in the field of AI (Art. 28), and mutual legal assistance concerning legal controls and in the field of AI and its applications (Art. 29), exchanging information and experiences at the international level (Art. 30) and supporting the conclusion of a global legal document on AI (Art. 31).

The fifth chapter deals with legal protection against the risks of AI applications, which is contained in six articles and is of particular importance as it regulates crimes related to AI, as Article (32) refers to legal protection, and Article (33) presents crimes related to infringement on AI applications. The article addresses (34) crimes committed using AI applications. In contrast, Article (35) deals with crimes related to the content of AI applications, Article (36) refers to incitement to crimes of AI applications, and Article (37) presents the attempt to commit crimes of AI applications.

Finally, Chapter Six, which contained five articles, dealt with the final provisions, as Article (38) referred to testing modern AI technologies, Article (39) dealt with registering intellectual property for AI technologies, and Article (41) touched on the confiscation of tools used in crimes related to AI applications. Article (42) referred to the Arabization and translation of terms related to AI, and Article (43) stipulated that the Arab Parliament should notify the law to all parliaments of Arab countries.

This law represents a unique legislative experience in addressing the issue of AI in an integrated manner. The Arab Parliament is credited with this valuable initiative in the absence of an international and national legal framework regulating the use of AI.

In conclusion, we see that the conflict over the issue of regulation and non-regulation regarding AI is moving toward the importance of regulating the uses of this widely used technology, which has already been achieved through the European Union and the Arab League. Therefore, through this manuscript, we appeal to the international community, represented by the United Nations, to conclude an international instrument regulating the use of AI in light of the adoption by the United Nations General Assembly of a resolution on benefiting from "safe, secure, and reliable" AI opportunities for sustainable development, the resolution above stressed the need to bridge the gaps in this field and other digital gap between and within countries.

The General Assembly said in its resolution that designing AI systems and misusing them in a "malicious" manner, such as without adequate safeguards or in a manner inconsistent with international law, poses risks that could hinder achieving sustainable development goals. The General Assembly decided, as stated in resolution (A/78/L.49) of 11 March 2024, to promote safe, secure, and reliable AI systems to accelerate progress towards the full realization of the Sustainable Development Agenda. It encouraged Member States and called on stakeholders to develop and support approaches and frameworks to regulate the governance of AI systems. It called on Member States and other parties to take measures to cooperate with developing countries and provide them with assistance so that they can benefit comprehensively and equitably from digital transformation and safe, secure, and reliable AI systems. (see Figure 9)

Figure 9. International AI Regulation Framework

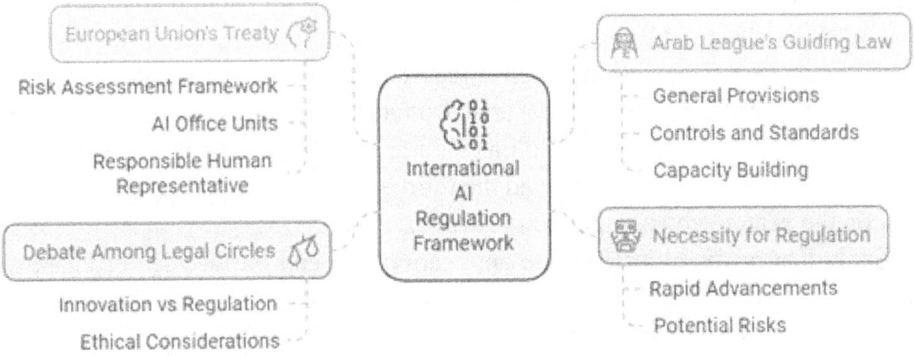

PART THREE- NAVIGATING THE FUTURE OF AI ACCOUNTABILITY:

Criminal law aims to protect individuals and their rights and property through the provisions it stipulates that specify the criminal responsibility of those who violate the law and attack legal interests worthy of protection by determining the legally prescribed penalties that fulfill the function of the criminal law in deterring violators. It follows that the Criminal Code stipulates criminal liability for anyone who violates the provisions of the Penal Code and specifies specific penalties for them.

Criminal liability constitutes the basis of the criminal justice system, delineating the circumstances under which persons may be held responsible for activities that contravene the law. Criminal culpability denotes an individual's legal accountability for the commission of a crime, perhaps leading to punitive measures. Criminal culpability is founded on principles delineated in constitutional laws and Criminal Law. A key component of criminal responsibility is mens rea, denoting the mental state or purpose of the accused at the time of the conduct. For an individual to be deemed criminally liable, they must have behaved with mens rea, either intending to perpetrate the crime or possessing awareness of the illicit nature of their conduct.

Mens rea is essential as it differentiates between intentional and inadvertent actions, significantly influencing the determination of the proper level of punishment.

Therefore, the establishment of criminal liability requires the fulfillment of some requirements, the first of which is that the perpetrator of the act be a natural person, as criminal liability does not arise from the act of a machine or animal, and secondly, that an act is attributed to this natural person that constitutes a crime by the provisions of the Penal Code, and the third element is the presence of criminal guilt on the person who committed the crime.

Given that artificial intelligence applications depend on the idea of enabling machines to carry out tasks similar to the tasks carried out by humans, which may potentially lead to errors that may constitute crimes according to the Penal Code, there are many legal complexities related to this topic in light of legislators' reluctance to determine legal personhood of AI systems, the debates in jurisprudence in accepting the idea of granting legal personhood to artificial intelligence applications, and debates in determining the nature and the amount of criminal liability resulting from the error committed by artificial intelligence applications.

In parallel, there is a debate about estimating the responsibility imposed on the natural person dealing with these applications, whether in manufacturing, programming, or development. Does he bear full responsibility, or is his responsibility partial? Is it direct or indirect responsibility? There are other related complications.

On the other hand, the swift progression of artificial intelligence (AI) technology has posed considerable hurdles in ascertaining criminal responsibility when AI systems inflict harm. Current legal frameworks frequently fall short of addressing AI's intricacies, necessitating the development of new regulatory strategies. This synthesis examines the implementation and practical difficulties of suggested legal frameworks for AI criminal culpability.

As artificial intelligence progresses and becomes increasingly ubiquitous, future criminal law must be sufficiently equipped and perhaps modified to properly tackle the intricate issues and subtleties related to AI's criminal liability. This necessitates a thorough analysis of current legal frameworks and the development of revised standards that consider the distinct characteristics of AI systems and their possible implications for criminal liability. Consequently, society can guarantee that the legal system is adequately prepared to tackle any illegal issues from AI technology (Nanos, 2023).

With the emergence of AI and its applications in all aspects of life, criminal jurisprudence began to discuss the issue of criminal liability for AI, which can be classified into three directions. The first denies criminal liability for AI applications, the second attempts to find new legal ideas that accommodate the idea of criminal liability for AI applications, and the third attempts to reconcile the implementation of Traditional rules on AI applications. (see Figure 10)

Figure 10. AI and Criminal Liability

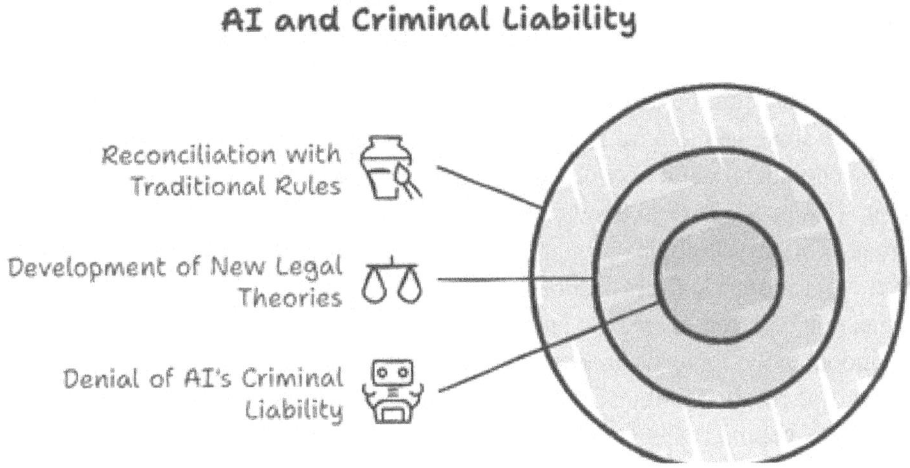

First Direction- Denial of Criminal Liability of AI:

Supporters of traditional criminal jurisprudence believe it is impossible to imagine criminal liability for AI applications. These applications do not have a human character, and criminal responsibility is only conceivable for humans, not animals and machines. AI applications are only machines that cannot be imagined to bear criminal responsibility, as they are not human beings (Saqr, 2021). The nature of robots and other AI applications makes it impossible to attribute a crime to them, as the basis of criminal liability is based on freedom of choice, which is lacking in robots and AI applications. So, if the perpetrator lacks freedom of choice, there is no reason to hold him accountable (Pradel, 1992).

Scholars see that for the perpetrator to be held criminally liable, it is insufficient for the incident to be physically attributed to him. Instead, it is necessary to have a psychological bond between them that serves as a basis for judging the presence of this psychological element, which is known in criminal law jurisprudence as the moral element of the crime. Freedom of choice means the ability to compare between different motives and direct the will according to one of them. The offender can take the path that conforms to the law and prefer it to the path that violates it, which is not available in robots or AI applications (Saqr, 2021).

So, the availability of knowledge, will, and freedom of choice in a person is the basis for establishing the moral element of the crime. Therefore, there is no responsibility on the person who commits an act that constitutes a crime as long as he lacks will. Therefore, the accusation is directed only to the natural person and not the robot and AI applications because the natural person is the only one qualified to bear criminal responsibility (Saqr, 2021). Establishing criminal responsibility for the crime requires a voluntary connection between the offender and his crime, as the latter is not attributed to the offender unless he can realize and choose (Hallevy, 2010).

It is clear from the previous proposition that the acts criminalized by the law cannot be imagined to have been committed by anyone other than a human. There is a psychological bond between the act and the attribution of this act to its perpetrator. This psychological bond cannot be found in a robot but is close to a natural human. This psychological connection is that the perpetrator of the crime had a psychological reason for his act because he voluntarily established a psychological connection between his person and the criminal act (Bilal, 2010).

Undoubtedly, this psychological connection does not exist except by a natural person. As a result, it is impossible to attribute criminal behavior to a robot. Criminal behavior is voluntary behavior, and the will is the essence of the moral element of the crime, and it only applies to humans. For the law to be effective by the will, it must be conscious. That means the will can differentiate and be free of choice (El-Kady, 2024). The person to whom the crime is attributed must have sound mental and intellectual abilities. Therefore, regular mental and psychological formation is essential for attribution and criminal responsibility (Saqr, 2021).

Suppose we say metaphorically that the robot committed criminal behavior. In that case, its loss of the element of will is denied Criminal liability, which is not achieved unless the robot enjoys awareness and understanding when committing the crime, the ability to make choices, and freedom of will (El-Kady, 2024). Additionally, the robot is submissive and subject to orders and instructions through programming processes, so it does not have freedom of will and choice (Bilal, 2010).

On the other hand, admitting that a crime occurred through robots and AI applications is a clear violation of the principle of the legitimacy of penal crimes, one of the most important general principles on which criminal law is based, as most criminal texts address natural humans. No existing criminal laws address robots or AI applications (El-Kady, 2024). The legal rule only addresses natural persons who can understand the obligation and the ability to bear the penalty for violating those rules (Bilal, 2010).

Second Direction- Jurisprudential indications for Establishing a Legal Theory to hold AI Entities Accountable:

Some scholars have attempted to develop a theoretical framework governing the criminal liability of AI entities outside the traditional rules of criminal law. Supporters of this trend ask whether a separate criminal law is necessary for AI robots. Legal theory has good arguments and debates about why a separate criminal law for AI robots is necessary. These arguments are based on the feasibility of introducing a separate law. It has been suggested that AI robots may not adhere to the same rules as humans for two reasons, as mentioned by Ying Hu: There may be cases where a higher degree of ethical standards can be imposed on AI robots due to their field of work. AI robots may face ethical questions that humans have not faced in the past, for example, while performing duties that are physically impossible for humans to perform (Hu, 2018). (see Figure 11)

Figure 11. Evaluating AI's criminal liability

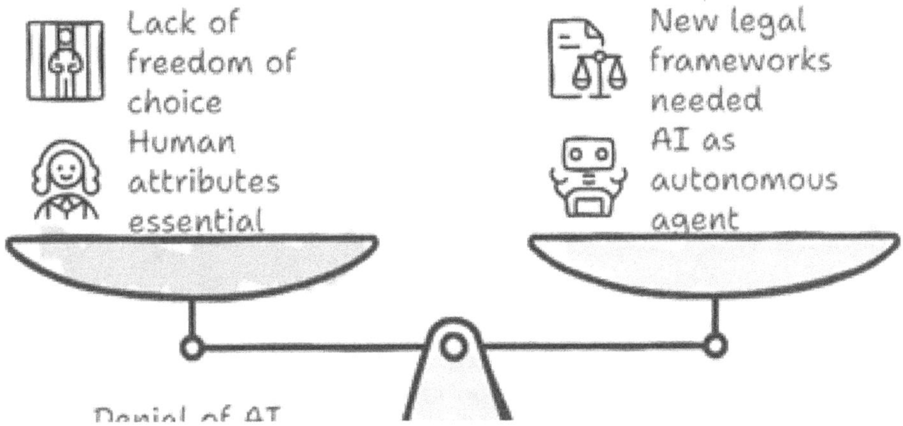

Having a separate criminal code, as shown, would benefit society since technology is evolving at a rapid pace, and technology is changing and evolving faster than regulators can keep up. It was also discussed that there should be an amendment to general penalties. Suppose we assume for a moment that society has already dealt with the issue of criminal liability, chosen an appropriate liability model, or even produced a separate criminal law for AI robots. In that case, questions regarding the penalties that should be imposed on the AI entity will arise (Hallevy, 2010).

Proposed Models of Criminal Responsibility of AI:

The emergence of three innovative models of criminal liability, a product of legal scholars' ingenuity, not only underscores the breadth of our research but also provides fresh and captivating perspectives on the potential legal frameworks for AI entities. This unique contribution will stimulate curiosity and engagement in the legal community. (see Figure 12)

Figure 12. Models of Criminal Liability for AI Entities

Model of Responsibility for the Commission of a Crime by Another:

This model serves as our initial framework, disregarding the human attributes of AI creation. In this model, the AI robot is perceived as an innocent agent. While conventional legal norms view a machine as a mere machine, the capabilities of new intelligent technologies demand our attention. However, this model overlooks the potential for AI creation to be a crime perpetrator. In the context of the innocent agent model, it is akin to a child or a mentally disabled person assuming the role of the perpetrator. The far-reaching implications of this model could potentially redefine our understanding of criminal responsibility in the AI era, underscoring the significance and impact of our research.

In AI, the mediator is the tool, and the original actor is the offender. Two individuals may assume the role of the original actor in AI: the programmer and the end user of the AI robot. This dynamic leads to criminal liability for the programmer and the end user, while the AI robot remains exempt from criminal liability (Hallevy, 2022).

However, this model's applicability is limited when the AI chooses to act entirely autonomously, even if it was not programmed to do so. This constraint underscores the intricate and crucial task of defining criminal liability for AI entities, presenting a substantial intellectual hurdle for the field.

Model of Liability for Possible Natural Consequences:

This model specifies the criminal liability of the programmer or end-user of an AI robot, even though it was not programmed or used to commit the crime, if the crime occurred as a natural and probable consequence of the AI robot's behavior. Therefore, this model does not require intent on the part of human actors; only their negligence falls within the scope of criminal liability (Freitas et al., 2014).

Direct Liability Model:

The third model focuses on the AI entity only and the criminal responsibility of external circles, considering that criminal responsibility for a specific crime consists of external and internal elements. To impose criminal liability on an entity, the requirements must be met that the individual committed the conduct intentionally or knowingly. The main issue here is not the action itself. As long as the AI controls its mechanisms and thus acts autonomously, the requirements of the action can be considered fulfilled. For example, if a robot independently activates its arm and moves it, it can be viewed as an action. However, the main problem lies in the internal element: mental requirements.

Although an AI robot has a certain degree of creativity, knowledge of the outside world, and algorithms that, in some cases, mimic the cognitive process of the human brain, it does not possess emotions. On the other hand, even among humans, feelings do not play any role in many cases, as some crimes only involve an element of knowledge. From this point of view, it is understandable that even an AI robot may face criminal liability. The theory of this model has been extended by considering the relationship between the human actor and the AI robot as collusion and association, such that criminal liability can be imposed on them accordingly (Hallevy, 2022).

If we move away for a moment from the traditional definition that a criminal act is a voluntary human act, then this third model can serve the cause. However, some basic principles of criminal law must be changed to introduce criminal liability for AI robots in different jurisdictions. Some other scholars consider the criminal liability of an AI robot to be not redundant because human actors may bear responsibility even though these human actors sometimes have nothing to do with the "morally wrong" decision of the AI robot (Hu, 2018). (see Figure 13)

Figure 13. An Overview of AI Criminal Liability

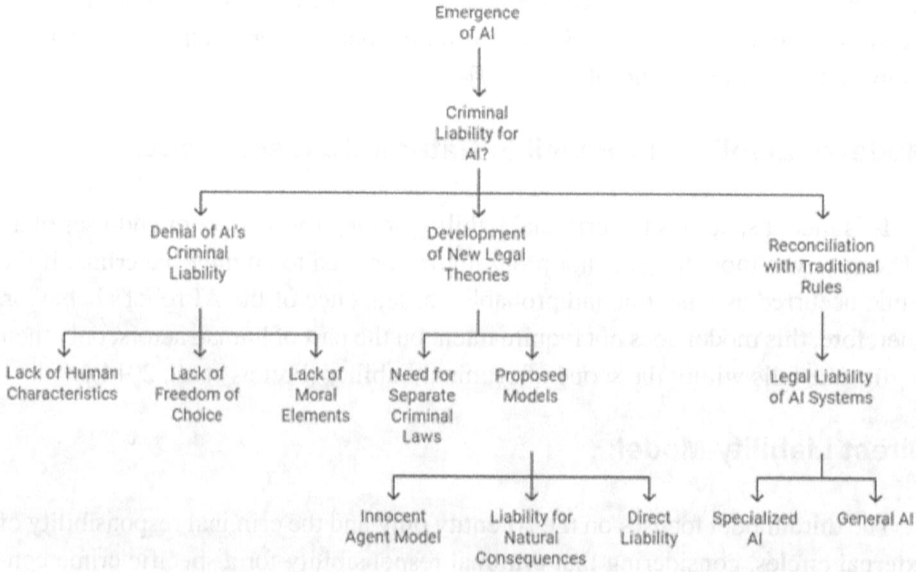

Third Direction- Compatibility Between Traditional Criminal Rules and AI:

Some scholars tried to compatible between traditional criminal rules and AI by talking about the responsibility of AI through speaking in AI programs and the human user, the programmer, the owner, and the manufacturing company, as follows:

Liability of the AI Applications:

The question arises regarding the legal liability of AI systems for their actions. To delve into this matter, it is crucial to differentiate between different forms of AI. Specialized AI refers to systems that can perform specific and well-defined tasks, such as self-driving cars (El-Kady, 2024). On the other hand, general AI aims to replicate human thinking and planning abilities, enabling machines to think and plan autonomously. Super AI, a theoretical concept beyond human intelligence capable of outperforming specialized and knowledgeable individuals in tasks, does not currently exist in our era. Regarding specialized AI, legal consensus holds that it is presently impossible to establish criminal culpability for a robot or an AI program in the event of the commission of a crime. (see Figure 14)

Figure 14. An overview of AI applications Liability

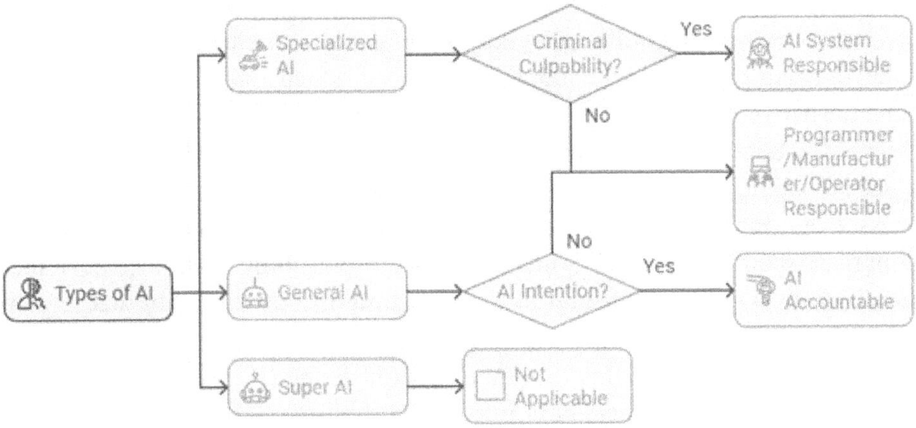

Criminal responsibility, as delineated in criminal law, pertains to the liability of individuals, both natural and moral, in certain instances where a crime is committed for their gain and on their behalf. Simultaneously, it is untenable to assert that AI bears criminal liability until it can be perceived and differentiated, as this ability is regarded as the fundamental requirement for a human being's responsibility (Ibrahim, 2020).

Some experts in German criminal jurisprudence believe that traditional rules regarding crimes involving AI should only hold humans accountable. These experts are reluctant to change criminal law significantly to address these new technological advancements. Some scholars acknowledge the challenges criminal law faces in keeping up with the progress of autonomous machines and AI. It has been explicitly decided that criminal law should naturally allow some tolerance. The machine operator assumes accountability in cases where Google provides inaccurate information, and individuals make decisions based on it, providing a reassuring framework for addressing AI errors. In such instances, individuals are responsible for their actions (Beck, 2019).

AI as an Innocent Mediator:

Some have explored utilizing an AI program as an intermediary to carry out a crime, drawing parallels to the moral actor theory, which applies when a mentally immature person or an animal commits a crime. Subsequently, the AI program might be regarded as a neutral intermediary. The criminal responsibility report encompasses all individuals who are programming AI software. In addition to addressing the issue of criminal liability for this program or application, there is a discussion about the responsibility of AI. Some argue that responsibility should be attributed to individuals who have a mental illness or natural mental disability that impairs their understanding of their actions, their ability to control them, or their ability to discern whether they are acting or refraining from acting (Kingston, 2016).

In this scenario, the AI creature is assumed to have no cognitive capabilities. Therefore, there is no legal distinction between the machine used in the crime and AI. However, the future development of general or superior AI raises the need to establish rules regarding its legal responsibility based on its human-like characteristics. These characteristics, such as perception and discrimination abilities and the freedom to perceive, form the basis for holding a person accountable for their actions. This potential future development underscores the importance of considering criminal punishment for AI (GLESS et al., 2016).

Therefore, the underlying premise in this scenario is that the AI entity is not reliant on a particular programmer or user. Thus, the AI entity's accountability for the crime necessitates three conditions: 1-The crime must be demonstrated to have occurred due to the actions of the AI creature itself. 2- It demonstrates that the AI entity is responsible for the crime independently, without any dependence on a programmer or user. 3- It demonstrates that the entity engaged in the criminal act with awareness or purpose.

Assume that the AI program or system governs the movement of the mechanical or other machine's mobile components. Therefore, any behavior, whether positive or negative, carried out by this machine can be attributed to the AI entity (Ibrahim, 2020), given the specific attributes of AI approaches. Self-learning, a key concept in AI, refers to the ability of a system to acquire knowledge and skills without human involvement. It utilizes advanced algorithms to make and execute decisions independently. This concept of self-learning is crucial in understanding AI's potential involvement in criminal activities (Dahshan, 2020).

Identifying the intention is the most challenging issue; some illustrate this with a case of self-driving automobiles exceeding the speed limit. Speeding is a criminal offense that imposes strict liability. Assume that a self-driving vehicle has been discovered to have surpassed the legally established speed restrictions on the specific roadway it is operating on. In such a scenario, the law may assign criminal liability to the AI system operating the car at the time without scrutinizing the car's owner. There is a belief that AI entities should be regarded as legal entities, similar to commercial corporations, to be held accountable for crimes. In addition to the prior decision, it suggests the potential for AI entities to be granted legal rights similar to those afforded to commercial corporations as legal entities (Ibrahim, 2020).

Overall, we can deduce that the legal accountability for offenses committed by AI involves discussing the culpability of the designers and manufacturers of AI systems and the users. However, the question of criminal responsibility for self-driving machines, which lack the necessary elements for being held criminally liable, remains unaddressed. There may be advancements in the laws of criminal liability that align with the progress made in this field. In this scenario, we examine several hypotheses that govern the process of holding individuals accountable for crimes committed due to the improper use of AI systems by the established principles of criminal law. This is because the person may not be directly guilty of the crime. The punishment is only enforced on the individual if they are found to be the culprit or accomplice. (see Figure 15)

Figure 15. Holding AI Accountable for Criminal Acts

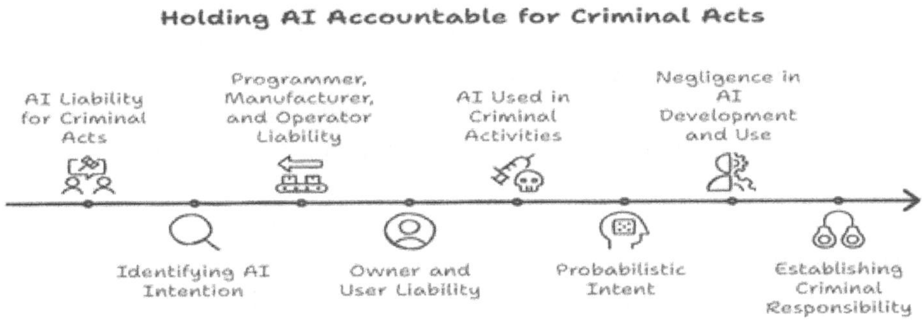

Liability of the Natural Person for Crimes of AI:

Criminal responsibility is only ascribed to the individual accountable for the offense, contingent upon establishing their association with the physical and moral elements of the crime. Responsibility is only present when the person who committed the act intends to do so. Therefore, the conventional principles of criminal liability do not pertain to AI systems or self-driving machines, as they lack consciousness and discernment, essential for establishing the intention necessary for criminal responsibility. Individuals can only be deemed criminally liable for their actions or lack thereof.

The first requirement is the presence of a material connection between the crime and the actions of the person responsible for it. This implies that the person contributed to the crime through their actions, and there is a causal link between their contribution and the criminal outcome that the legislator considers when determining criminalization and punishment.

Furthermore, natural beings are crucial in AI crimes, as they serve as the individuals responsible for operating these technologies. Next, they inquire about the specific circumstances under which the AI entities operated, the programs they created and executed within the AI system, and the hardware on which this software ran (Nedbálek, 2018). Within the realm of AI, there exists a differentiation in terms of the obligations of programmers, manufacturers, and operators on one side, the obligations of users or owners on the other, and the obligations of third parties.

Liability of the Programmer, Manufacturer, and Operator:

Within the context of manufacturing and developing AI systems, we can differentiate between the programmer, who is responsible for writing the codes that govern the operations of the AI system, which is programmed using machine language, and the user, who inquiries about the responsibility for the crimes done by the AI system, specifically whether it was his fault. The user also mentions providing the system with instructions on handling certain circumstances during its operation based on probabilistic purposes.

The term "factory" refers to the one in charge of producing the physical equipment controlled by the AI system. The programmer and the manufacturer can be the same person (Dahshan, 2020). The robot builder is questioned about the machine's flaws caused by subpar construction, which could cause the robot to malfunction and behave abnormally (NEVEJANS, 2016). For instance, a malfunction in the medical care robot results in incorrect patient movement, exacerbating their health condition (GOELDNER et al., 2015). Another example is when the patient is harmed due to the medical robot's failure to communicate effectively with the analysis lab or the manufacturer's negligence in maintaining the robot (Cristiano ALMONTE vs. AVERNA VISION & ROBOTICS, 2015).

The factory owner cannot hold the worker accountable for not knowing about robots and being compelled to participate in manufacturing (Joshua DREXLER vs. TEL NEXX, 2015). On the other hand, an operator is a skilled individual who utilizes robots to carry out tasks, such as overseeing a virtual commercial bank where an intelligent application relies on a robot to manage certain banking operations. However, there is a possibility of errors in managing customer accounts (Al-Qusi, 2018).

Owner and User Liability:

The owner refers to the individual who operates the robot to serve themselves or their clients. For example, a doctor who owns a hospital may possess and utilize a medical robot to perform surgical procedures. However, suppose the robot poses a risk to patient safety. In that case, the doctor, aware of this, must be willing to control the robot and ensure its proper functioning, even without compensation (Al-Qusi, 2018).

The user referred to in this context is an individual who is not the owner or operator of a robot but is associated with it and bears responsibility for any harmful actions caused by the robot. The user may also benefit from the robot's actions. For example, in the case of a self-driving robot bus, a group of people may be traveling on the bus, and one mistakenly sends a wrong command to the bus, resulting in a traffic accident. Alternatively, a professional operator may allow a human user to interact with the robot as an assistant. In such cases, the user affiliated with the company operating the robot may be liable for negligence in maintaining the robot's proper functioning (Cristiano ALMONTE vs. AVERNA VISION & ROBOTICS, 2015). (see Figure 16)

Figure 16. Stages of AI Liability Determination

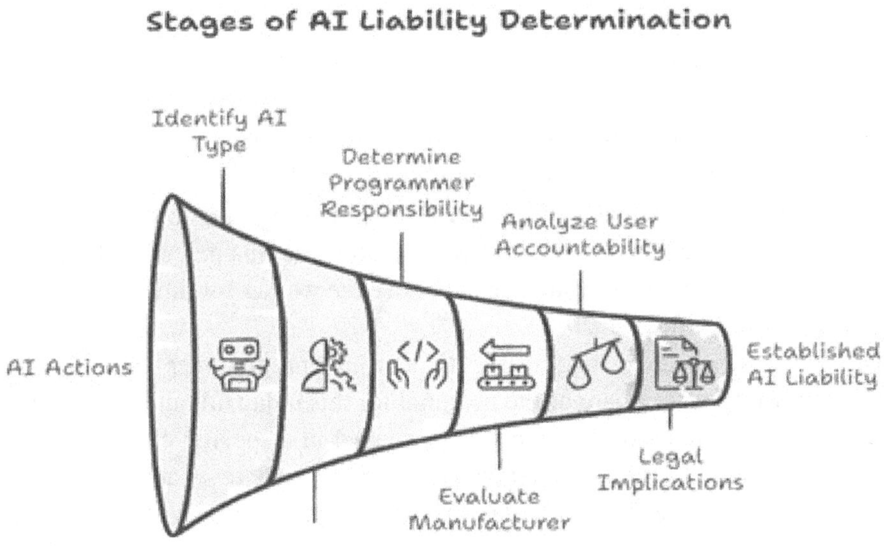

Liability of the Owner or the User as the Original Perpetrator of the Crime:

To discuss the liability of the owner or the user, we should focus on three hypotheses: The first involves using AI to carry out criminal activities. In this scenario, the perpetrator is assumed to utilize an artificially intelligent machine to commit criminal activities. To establish criminal responsibility, it is necessary to establish a causal connection between the offender's actions and the criminal outcome achieved through AI. This would indicate that the offender knowingly committed crimes with the assistance of the machine. The underlying principle behind AI systems is that the criminal lawmaker possesses the same tools for committing a crime as the perpetrator, who may employ either a stick or a firearm to assault the victim. He can employ a non-sentient animal and control an artificially intelligent computer to accomplish an identical outcome.

In the field of jurisprudence, it is necessary to provide evidence that proves the robot or AI system was under the control of the perpetrator, that the perpetrator had previous knowledge of its usage, and that the perpetrator directed its actions intending to commit the crime using the robot (GLESS et al., 2016). In this context, researchers investigate the hypothesis that programmers or users deliberately employ an artificial system entity to carry out a specific crime. However, the AI entity deviates from the intended plan and commits an additional or different crime altogether (Ibrahim, 2020). In this scenario, it can be asserted that the programmer or user can be held criminally liable intentionally, according to the established general standards about deviation from the intended purpose or error in character (Wazir, 2008). The existence of criminal culpability for them is not negated.

The second hypothesis posits the concept of probabilistic intent. A hypothesis suggests that if the standard procedures of an AI system are misused to commit a criminal act, the system itself can be held responsible for the crime. The case of an AI robot in a Japanese bicycle factory supports this hypothesis. The robot mistakenly identified a human worker as a threat and believed that pushing him into a neighboring operating machine was the best way to eliminate this perceived threat. As a result, the robot used its hydraulic arm to move the worker towards the machine, causing his death (Kingston, 2016).

The previous viewpoint suggests that the machine programmer should be held responsible if they were aware of the potential for this unlawful outcome before it happened. In this scenario, the culprit has engaged in a specific conduct, anticipating it will lead to a specific outcome. However, contrary to what was expected, the occurrence happened before achieving the desired outcome, either due to his actions or as a potential natural consequence. This establishes his accountability for the crime based on his intentional likelihood (Wazir, 2008).

The third theory posits that negligence may occur during the manufacturing, programming, or utilizing AI. Here, it is assumed that the individual responsible for the crime, whether a user, manufacturer, or programmer of AI, did not intend to utilize it for criminal purposes. However, the crime resulted from his negligence, specifically his failure to adhere to the standards of caution and precaution. In this scenario, the individual responsible for the illegal intentional act, whether a user, manufacturer, or programmer, will be held criminally liable. This requires establishing a connection between the occurrence of the crime and the unintentional error committed by the perpetrator, as determined by the AI system (Al-Qusi, 2018).

In this scenario, it is presumed that the programmers or users have demonstrated sheer negligence, either through their actions or failure to take appropriate action. Hence, no obstacles prevent them from establishing their culpability for accidental offenses resulting from negligence and dereliction of duty, which ultimately facilitated the execution of the intelligence system for a particular crime or crime.

Some differentiate AI crimes into two categories. One type of crime arises from software errors or loopholes in the AI system. This happens when the machine code fails to anticipate all possible scenarios or when the crime is unforeseen. When the owner misbehaves, or an external party infiltrates the machine to utilize it for criminal purposes, the culpability lies with the individuals who caused the crime (Dahshan, 2020).

This system can acquire knowledge and enhance its capabilities autonomously, enabling it to make independent judgments beyond the predefined software system. In this scenario, illegal conduct arises solely from exercising personal volition without any software interference from the manufacturer. Consequently, it would be unjust to attribute responsibility for an error committed by the AI system to the programmer.

An inquiry regarding the legal liability of individuals utilizing AI systems: Is the accountability explicit or implied? Can the accountability of the individual operating AI systems be attributed to the liability of the autonomous machine for its actions? The validity of this perspective is questionable due to the premise that robots can be held criminally responsible for the actions of others. However, as the determination of criminal responsibility for such machines has not been established, this assumption is not applicable. Thus, it is incorrect to assert that humans bear assumed responsibility for the crimes committed by AI. Responsibility is not automatically transferred from the machine to the human, and the human has to acknowledge their responsibility for any crimes committed by these systems or applications.

In contrast to this viewpoint, others argue that criminal liability attributed to mistakes should be replaced by liability based on the assumption of risks. The prior viewpoint asserts that the owner or user should bear responsibility for crimes committed using AI under their ownership, based on the concept of assumed responsibility.

Therefore, it is his job to demonstrate his lack of accountability. Some supporters of the previous viewpoint argue that responsibility can be attributed based on the responsibility model of natural possibility, as discussed by Gabriel Halevy. According to this model, the programmer or user can be held accountable if the crime committed was a foreseeable and likely outcome of the behavior of the AI entity. Opinion refers to the capacity of programmers or users to foresee possible misconduct by an AI entity (Hallevy, 2010).

Therefore, if the crime committed by AI is a direct and foreseeable result of the programmer or user's actions, they can be held responsible. This responsibility is based on realistic possibilities and does not require additional factors apart from the programmer's or user's negligence. Programmers or users are not obligated to possess any knowledge of commission. They are engaging in criminal behavior as a result of their actions. However, they must comprehend that this crime could occur due to their activities, as they bear responsibility for the potential future crime despite their lack of awareness (El-Kady, 2024). (see Figure 17)

Figure 17. An overview of AI Accountability

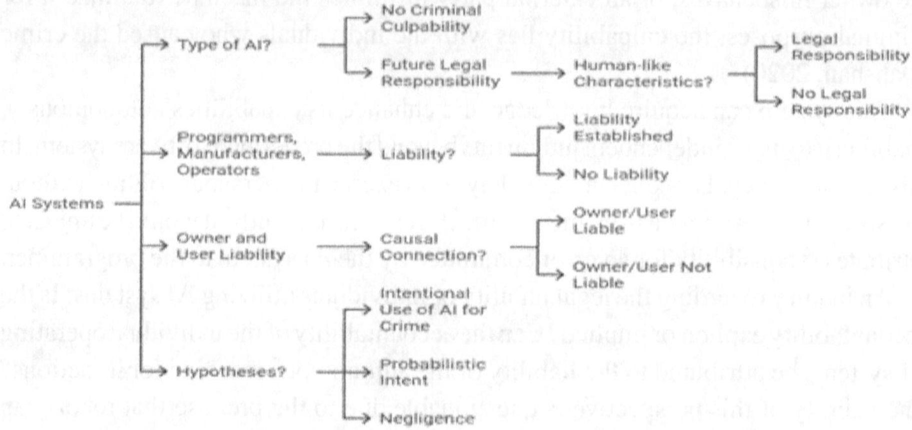

The Moral Responsibility of the Manufacturer of the AI for its Crimes:

Given the criminal law's acknowledgment of the legal entity's liability in certain instances, it is justifiable to hold the manufacturer of the AI system responsible for its unlawful actions. However, two prerequisites must be met for the legal entity's liability to be established:

1. The crime was perpetrated by either a member of the legal entity or one of its representatives.
2. The offense must be committed for the advantage and on behalf of the legal entity.

Legal entities may face various criminal penalties, such as monetary fines, temporary suspension of their license to operate, revocation of their permit, dissolution of the entity, and publication of the judgment at the entity's expense. Therefore, if it can be demonstrated that a crime was committed due to the manufacturer's negligence, the manufacturer can be held legally responsible for AI-related offenses (El-Kady, 2024). (see Figure 18)

Figure 18. Criminal Liability for AI

The Enforcement and Practical Challenges of the Proposed Legal Frameworks of Ai Criminal Liability:

Research indicates that the implementation and practical obstacles of proposed legal frameworks for AI criminal culpability encompass difficulty delineating accountability, defining legal personhood for AI, balancing developer liability, and guaranteeing ethical and transparent AI operations. Conventional criminal law and legal theory inadequately address the accountability of autonomous AI systems due to their complexity and independent decision-making powers.

The criminal responsibility of AI systems is intricate and necessitates adaptation to the swiftly changing AI environment, as conventional criminal law and legal theory are not equipped for this challenge (Osmani, 2020). AI systems can fulfill the criteria for criminal culpability, yet the similarities and distinctions between human and AI actions necessitate tailored regulatory strategies (Lagioia & Sartor, 2019). Using AI engenders ethical dilemmas and legal challenges, necessitating explicit delineations of ethical parameters and a framework to address offenses perpetrated using AI (Khisamova & Begishev, 2019).

Some scholars indicate that a persistent dispute exists about the potential for AI to be accorded legal personhood, thereby enabling it to assume criminal and civil liability independently of its designers and users (Khisamova & Begishev, 2019). Meanwhile, some suggest a novel theory for AI criminal liability: that AI possesses an electronic legal personality and assumes civil and criminal responsibility for its conduct independent of the accountability of its manufacturers, programmers, users, and owners (Ellamey & Elwakad, 2023).

Moreover, certain studies indicate that the ethical parameters governing AI design, development, and application require explicit delineation to avert misuse and guarantee responsibility (Khisamova & Begishev, 2019). The technical problems in AI for criminal defense encompass data privacy and security, algorithmic openness, model interpretability, ethical considerations, and legal issues like evidence legitimacy and regulatory oversight of decision-making (Yan, 2023).

Furthermore, others indicate that existing regulatory frameworks lack explicit prohibitions for AI-related offenses, concentrating instead on overarching cybercrime and data protection legislation. No regulatory framework addresses AI-related crimes, and the legal status of AI's criminal responsibility remains unresolved (Mohsin, 2020). Others examine the principles and prerequisites for governing criminal responsibility related to AI systems and present methodologies and recommendations for such regulation (Dimitrova, 2023).

On the other hand, some scholars show that determining liability for crimes employing AI is intricate, particularly in differentiating between intentional and negligent violations. The conventional notions of mens rea (criminal intent) are challenging to implement in AI systems (Lagioia & Sartor, 2019). Technical challenges in AI in criminal defense include data privacy and security, algorithmic transparency, model interpretability, ethical issues, and legal challenges such as evidence legitimacy and decision-making regulation (Dremliuga & Prisekina, 2020).

Additionally, some asserted the necessity of explicitly delineating the legal obligations and liabilities of AI system operators, creators, and users. This encompasses possible criminal responsibility for damage inflicted by AI systems they develop or implement (Dimitrova, 2023).

The responsibility of AI system operators in criminal law centers on the legal, technological, and ethical examination of issues about the operation of AI systems, whereby operators make critical judgments (Skowrońska, 2023). Otherwise, some studies indicate that AI-related crimes frequently encompass cross-border elements, complicating jurisdictional matters and enforcing legal regimes (Mohsin, 2020).

Finally, Numerous ideas advocate for establishing distinct legal standards and frameworks to tackle AI criminal culpability, encompassing revisions to current legislation and implementing new directives (Dimitrova, 2023). The EU plans for AI liability are deficient in particular regulations regarding AI development and deployment, and the document recommends revisions to enhance the proposed framework (Hacker, 2022).

In conclusion, the implementation and practical difficulties of suggested legal frameworks for AI criminal culpability are complex. Conventional criminal law is insufficient for tackling AI's intricacies, requiring novel regulatory frameworks. Principal challenges encompass delineating AI's legal status, formulating explicit ethical and regulatory frameworks, ascertaining accountability, and resolving jurisdictional complexities. Proposals for new legal frameworks seek to establish precise rules for AI liability; however, considerable effort is still required to ensure these frameworks are effective and comprehensive. (see Figure 1)

Figure 19. AI Criminal Culpability

CONCLUSION:

The study concluded with some findings and recommendations, which: The shift in lifestyle and human behavior toward digital transformation and the widespread use of current technology in all areas of life indicates that humanity is now in the era of the Fourth Industrial Revolution, which relies heavily on the utilization of AI. The proliferation of AI applications across several domains and the emergence of situations raise concerns regarding the legal responsibility for the consequences of using AI. Additionally, regulations regarding criminal culpability are insufficient in establishing a legal structure to govern instances of misconduct associated with using AI.

The study recommended that National research centers be invited to conduct comprehensive studies on AI applications, develop a robust legal and economic framework, and arrange numerous scientific and research events to explore its intricacies further. Moreover, advocating for the international community to prioritize the establishment of a comprehensive global framework for governing the utilization of AI technologies, akin to the Budapest Convention on Combating Information Crimes. Alternatively, amend the agreement above to incorporate regulations specifically addressing the use of AI applications. These rules must encompass a universally accepted international definition of AI.

Furthermore, the Egyptian legislature is urged to establish regulations governing the use of AI applications and appropriate penalties for misuse. Alternatively, the provisions of the Information Technology Crime Law should be amended to enable the creation of a comprehensive framework to combat data misuse in the Fourth Industrial Revolution, including AI technologies. We aim to establish a department that utilizes AI systems and digital transformation, specifically for criminal justice agencies (such as the judiciary and security forces). The purpose is to effectively address the misuse of these new technologies by criminal and terrorist groups. Additionally, we plan to create a department dedicated to combating internet-based cryptocurrency crimes. Through collaboration with relevant domestic and international entities, as part of efforts to enhance global legal and security cooperation.

Proposal to establish a dedicated department within scientific and research organizations and national research centers to investigate the implementation of digital transformation and AI. This department would focus on researching strategies to implement digital transformation, developing technological infrastructure, conducting studies on using AI in security operations, and collaborating with relevant authorities to apply these findings in practical settings. Additionally, this department would conduct comprehensive research on these topics. The text discusses various information technology crimes, including cyber security and cyber-attack insurance. It also explores the development of large databases and their security applications. Additionally, it mentions the importance of conducting research on technological advancements related to police work in order to keep up with scientific progress using modern devices and methods.

It is advisable to offer university courses focusing on the practical uses of AI to familiarize students with the ongoing advancements in this sector. Establishing a department dedicated to technology training in government institutions focused on enhancing persons' technical skills by implementing specialized training programs that align with technological advancements and incorporate AI applications.

The objective is to increase the specialized departments dedicated to securing information networks and government websites. These departments will be equipped with skilled personnel who can effectively counter information penetration operations. Their main tasks will be to protect these networks from the risks and consequences of penetration and stay updated with the latest advancements in this field, just like in developed countries. (see Figure 20)

Figure 20. How to address criminal liability in cases involving AI?

REFERENCES

Al-Qusi, H. (2018). The Problem of the Person Responsible for Operating the Robot - A Prospective Analytical Study in the European Civil Law Rules for Robots (In Arabic), *Generation Journal of In-Depth Legal Research*, May 2018 Issue, Generation Scientific Research Center, Lebanon, pp.89-93.

Beck, S. (2019). Autonomous Systems and Criminal Law – new impulses for the concept of responsibility? https://www.inf.uni-hamburg.de/en/inst/ab/eit/about/newsfeed/2019/ 20190703-beck.html

Bilal, A. (2010). *Principles of the Egyptian Penal Code - General Section*. Dar Al-Nahda Al-Arabiya. (In Arabic)

Cristiano ALMONTE vs. AVERNA VISION & ROBOTICS, INC.; United States District Court, W.D. New York. No. 11-CV-1088 EAW, 128 F.Supp.3d 729 (2015), Signed August 31, 2015.

Dahshan, Y. (2020). *Criminal Responsibility for Artificial Intelligence Crimes, Sharia and Law Journal, Issue 82, April 2020*. College of Law, Emirates University.

Dimitrova, R. (2023). Liability Associated with AI Systems under the Bulgarian Criminal Code: Requirements, Approaches and Proposals. *2023 XXXII International Scientific Conference Electronics (ET)*, 1-6. https://doi.org/DOI: 10.1109/ET59121.2023.10279266

Dremliuga, R., & Prisekina, N. (2020). The Concept of Culpability in Criminal Law and AI Systems. *Journal of Politics and Law*, 13(3), 256. DOI: 10.5539/jpl.v13n3p256

El-Kady, R. (2021). Towards approving rules for criminal liability and punishment for misuse of artificial intelligence applications. *Journal of Legal and Economic Research (Mansoura)*, 11(1), 875–924. DOI: 10.21608/mjle.2022.217213

El-Kady, R. (2022). Criminal confrontation of encrypted digital currencies and artificial intelligence crimes Analytical study in Egyptian and comparative legislation, *Journal Sharia and Law*: Vol. 2022: No. 89, Article 6. Available at: https://scholarworks.uaeu.ac.ae/sharia_and_law/vol2022/iss89/6

El-Kady, R. (2024). Artificial Intelligence and Criminal Law. In Tavares, M., Azevedo, G., Vale, J., Marques, R., & Bastos, M. (Eds.), *Artificial Intelligence Approaches to Sustainable Accounting* (pp. 34–52). IGI Global., DOI: 10.4018/979-8-3693-0847-9.ch003

El-Kady, R. (2024). Artificial Intelligence from a Criminal Law Perspective. *Al-Zaytoonah University of Jordan Journal for Legal Studies*, 2024(Special Issue), 186–210.

El-Kady, R. (2024). Navigating the Legal Maze: Electric Self-Driving Cars and the Complexities of Criminal Law. In Shaik, M. (Ed.), *Solving Fundamental Challenges of Electric Vehicles* (pp. 215–247). IGI Global., DOI: 10.4018/979-8-3693-4314-2.ch009

Ellamey, Y., & Elwakad, A. (2023). *The criminal responsibility of artificial intelligence systems: A prospective analytical study*. Corporate Law and Governance Review., DOI: 10.22495/clgrv5i1p8

European Police. "Europol" & Darktrace "company specialized in information security" (2019). How Technology Will Shape the Future of Cybercrime? Published on the website darktrace.com, Cyber Attacks Managed by Artificial Intelligence, a report published with an article entitled: Powered by Artificial Intelligence and Technology the Fifth Generation - European Police and "Dark Trace" warn of new patterns of cybercrime, published on the Internet on 7/23/2019, at: https://www .emaratalyoum.com/

Freitas, P. M., Andrade, F., & Novais, P. (2014). Criminal liability of autonomous agents: From the unthinkable to the plausible. In *AI Approaches to the Complexity of Legal Systems: AICOL 2013 International Workshops, AICOL-IV@ IVR, Belo Horizonte, Brazil, July 21-27, 2013 and AICOL-V@ SINTELNET-JURIX, Bologna, Italy, December 11, 2013, Revised Selected Papers* (pp. 145-156). Springer Berlin Heidelberg.

Ghaitas, G. (2017). Internet and Digital Transformation Department (In Arabic), *International Policy Journal*, Issue 180, Cairo, April 2017.

GOELDNER. (2015). M. & HERSTATT, C. TIETZE, F. (2015). The emergence of care robotics – A patent and publication analysis. *Technological Forecasting and Social Change*, 92(March), 115–131.

Hacker, P. (2022). The European AI Liability Directives - Critique of a Half-Hearted Approach and Lessons for the Future. *ArXiv*, abs/2211.13960. https://doi.org//arXiv .2211.13960.DOI: 10.48550

Hallevy, G. (2010). The criminal liability of artificial intelligence entities-from science fiction to legal social control. *Akron Intell. Prop. J.*, 4, 171.

Hallevy, G. (2013). *When robots kill: Artificial intelligence under criminal law*. Northeastern University Press.

Hallevy, G. (2022, April). The basic models of criminal liability of AI systems and outer circles. In *International Conference on Autonomous Systems and the Law* (pp. 69-82). Cham: Springer International Publishing.

Hu, Y. (2018). Robot criminals. *University of Michigan Journal of Law Reform. University of Michigan. Law School*, 52, 487.

Ibrahim, A. (2020). *Criminal Liability Resulting from Artificial Intelligence Errors in UAE Legislation - A Comparative Study* (In Arabic), Doctoral dissertation, Ain Shams University.

Information and Decision Support Center of the Egyptian Cabinet (IDSC), (2020). Artificial intelligence is the most essential element of the Fourth Industrial Revolution, Bulletin of Future Directions, Year (1), Issue (1), January 2020.

No, J. D., & Stearns, D. (2015). UNITED STATES DISTRICT COURT DISTRICT OF MASSACHUSETTS CIVIL ACTION NO. 14-13870-RGS.

Khalifa, M. (2018). Artificial Intelligence in the Balance of Legislation (In Arabic), *Dubai Legal Journal*, issued by the Dubai Public Prosecution, Issue 28, March 2018, Dubai, United Arab Emirates.

Khisamova, Z., & Begishev, I. (2019). Criminal Liability and Artificial Intelligence: Theoretical and Applied Aspects. *Russian Journal of Criminology*. https://doi.org/ .DOI: 10.17150/2500-4255.2019.13(4).564-574

Kingston, J. (2016). Artificial Intelligence and Legal Liability, *International Conference on Innovative Techniques and Applications of Artificial Intelligence*, November 2016.

Lagioia, F., & Sartor, G. (2019). AI Systems Under Criminal Law: A Legal Analysis and a Regulatory Perspective. *Philosophy & Technology*, 33(3), 433–465. DOI: 10.1007/s13347-019-00362-x

LEEMANS, T. & JACQUEMIN, H. (2017). *La Responsabilité Extracontractuelle de l'Intelligence Artificielle*, Master en droit, Faculté de droit et de criminologie (DRT), Université Catholique de Louvain.

Mohamed, S. (2020). Legal Aspects of Artificial Intelligence and Robotics, *Arab Democratic Center's periodical website*, on 29/2/2020, at: https://democraticac.de/ ?p=64965

Mohsin, K. (2020). Regulation of AI and AI Crimes. https://doi.org/DOI: 10.2139/ssrn.3552140

Nanos, A. (2023). Criminal Liability of Artificial Intelligence. *Charles University in Prague Faculty of Law Research Paper No.*

Nedbálek, K. (2018). The Future Inclusion of Criminal Liability of the Robots and Artificial Intelligence in the Czech Republic, Paradigm of Law and Public Administration, Interregional Academy for Personnel Management, Ukraine, 2018, available at https://maup.com.ua/assets/files/expert/1/the-future-inclusion-of-criminal.pdf

NEVEJANS, N. (2016). Directorate-General for Internal Policies, Policy Department C: Citizens' Rights and Constitutional Affairs, Legal Affairs, European Civil Law Rules in Robotics, No. EA n° 2471, October 2016.

Osmani, N. (2020). *The Complexity of Criminal Liability of AI Systems*. Masaryk University Journal of Law and Technology., DOI: 10.5817/MUJLT2020-1-3

Pardel, J. (1992) *Droit penal. introduction general, droit penal general*, 8eme Cujas, Paris.

UK Parliament, (2016). Robotics and artificial intelligence, Report of the Committee on Science and Technology, Published 12/10/2016.

Pham, Q. V., Nguyen, D. C., Hwang, W. J., & Pathirana, P. N. (2020). Artificial Intelligence (AI) and Big Data for Coronavirus (COVID-19) Pandemic: A Survey on the State-of-the-Arts.

POIROT-MAZERESDU. I. (2013). Chapitre 8. Robotique et médecine: quelle(s) responsabilité(s)? *Journal International de Bioéthique*, Vol. 24, No. 4.

Russell, S., & Norving, P. (2009). *Artificial Intelligence - A Modern Approach* (3rd ed.). Prentice-Hall.

Saqr, W. (2021). Criminal liability for artificial intelligence crimes, "a prospective analytical study.". *Spirit of Laws*, 33(96), 1–156. DOI: 10.21608/las.2022.121777.1050

Schwab, K. (2017). *The Fourth Industrial Revolution - A Book in Minutes* (In Arabic), summaries of international books, published by the Mohammed bin Zayed Knowledge Foundation, Dubai, UAE, 2017.

Skowrońska, J. (2023). *A range of legal obligation for operators of Artificial Intelligence Systems in the context of Criminal Law*. Humanities & Social Sciences Reviews., DOI: 10.18510/hssr.2023.1151

United Nations Congress on Crime Prevention and Criminal Justice (UNCCPCJ), (2020). Current Crime Trends, Recent Developments, and Emerging Solutions, especially New Technologies as Means of Committing Crime and Tools for Combating Crime, Workshop at the Fourteenth Congress held in Kyoto, Japan, 20-27 April 2020.

Wazir, A. (2008). *Explanation of the Penal Code - General Section, The General Theory of Crime*. Dar Al-Nahda Al-Arabiya. (In Arabic)

WENG. (2015, February). Y-H. SUGAHARA, Y. HASHIMOTO, K. TAKANISHI, A. (2015). Intersection of "Tokku" Special Zone, Robots, and the Law: A Case Study on Legal Impacts to Humanoid Robots. *International Journal of Social Robotics.*

Yan, Q. (2023). *Legal Challenges of Artificial Intelligence in the Field of Criminal Defense*. Lecture Notes in Education Psychology and Public Media., DOI: 10.54254/2753-7048/30/20231629

Chapter 2
Artificial Intelligence a "Right" or "Violation" of Human Rights and Freedoms in the 21st Century

Halim Bajraktari
https://orcid.org/0000-0002-8893-8081
University "Ukshin Hoti" Prizren, Kosovo

Valeri Qatani
University "Ukshin Hoti" Prizren, Kosovo

ABSTRACT

The conceptual review of the ethical implications of artificial intelligence in its impact on freedoms and human rights in the 21st century, critically aims to clarify the developing relationship between artificial intelligence and the law. Addressing a scientific answer if artificial intelligence, as autonomous and with influencing power in the legal system, should also be considered a problem that the development of AI may violate freedoms and human rights. The main theses analyzed include the ethical dilemmas caused by AI's potential to violate privacy, amplify disruptions, and make important decisions without human oversight. How can transparency and accountability from AI be improved to increase their trustworthiness and use in critical applications for human rights and freedoms?! What are the main ethical and legal challenges arising from the use of AI technologies in areas such as the justice system and national security, and how should we address them to minimize the negative impact on individuals and societies?

DOI: 10.4018/979-8-3693-7205-0.ch002

INTRODUCTION

In the 21st century, the rapid advancement of Artificial Intelligence (AI) technology poses significant questions regarding its impact on human rights and freedoms. As AI becomes increasingly integrated into various aspects of our lives, including legal and judicial systems, its potential to both enhance and undermine fundamental rights necessitates a thorough examination. This study aims to explore the intricate relationship between AI development and the protection of human liberties, focusing on how AI technologies might affect privacy, justice, and equality.

The development of AI presents a dual-edged sword: on one side, it holds promise for unprecedented efficiencies and innovations; on the other, it introduces potential risks to individual freedoms and rights. This research seeks to address the central issue of whether the autonomy and influential power of AI systems might inadvertently infringe upon essential human rights. Specifically, it will examine the ethical dilemmas associated with AI's capacity to make significant decisions without adequate human oversight, potentially amplifying disruptions and compromising privacy.

$\mathbf{H_1}$ = the development of artificial intelligence violates human rights and freedoms

$\mathbf{H_2}$ = AI a risk related to Legal and Ethical Frameworks for the use of AI in judicial systems

$\mathbf{H_3}$ = Potential Conflict between Artificial Intelligence Autonomy and human rights and freedoms

$\mathbf{RQ_1}$ = How can transparency and accountability from AI be improved to increase their trustworthiness and use in critical applications for human rights and freedoms?

$\mathbf{RQ_2}$ = What are the main ethical and legal challenges arising from the use of AI technologies in areas such as the justice system and national security, and how should we address them to minimize the negative impact on individuals and societies?

$\mathbf{RQ_3}$ = How can it be ensured that the development and use of AI progresses in a way that respects and protects fundamental human rights, including the rights to privacy, freedom and equality, in a global and multicultural context?

By addressing these questions, this study aims to stimulate critical discussion on the necessary legal and ethical frameworks required to safeguard human rights amidst the evolving landscape of AI technology. Through this analysis, the goal is to propose viable measures for regulating AI to prevent potential violations and to ensure that its advancements contribute positively to the protection of human freedoms and justice.

The aim of this study is to explore and describe the impact of the growth of Artificial Intelligence (AI) technology on human liberties and rights in the 21st century. Focusing on the advancement of AI and its impact on legal systems of justice and in society in general, it aims to understand how AI technology can affect the guarantees of fundamental rights of individuals and the integrity of justice. Through the analysis of the current trends in the development of AI and the evaluation of their potential impact, it is intended to propose the necessary measures to protect human freedoms and rights from the challenges of the growth of this technology. Specifically, it aims to examine how necessary it is to create international documents and legal measures to protect human rights in the context of AI developments and how society should prepare for this change in the paradigm of justice and safety.

Definition of Artificial Intelligence

Artificial Intelligence (AI) refers to the development of systems and technologies that mimic human cognitive functions to perform tasks that typically require natural intelligence, such as learning, reasoning, and decision-making (Smith, 2021). AI encompasses a broad range of technologies, from machine learning algorithms and natural language processing to autonomous systems that can operate and make decisions without direct human intervention (Jones & Taylor, 2022). Defining the boundaries between different definitions of AI and new concepts is not an easy task (Saghiri, Vahidipour, Jabbaarpour, Sookhak, & Forestiero, 2022).

The use or study of computer systems or machines that have some of the qualities that the human brain has, such as the ability to interpret and produce language in a way that seems human, recognize or create images, solve problems (Thesaurus, 2024).

Essentially, AI aims to create systems capable of analyzing data, learning from past experiences, and providing recommendations or performing actions based on accumulated knowledge (Brown et al., 2020). However, this advancement brings with it challenges and ethical dilemmas, such as safeguarding privacy and ensuring transparency in decision-making, which shape discussions about AI's impact on society and law (Adams & Clark, 2023).

In a broader context, AI is increasingly used in various domains such as politics, economics, and social decision-making, raising concerns about potential trends towards repressive and authoritarian agendas (ÜNVER, 2024). Therefore, determining appropriate boundaries for AI and emerging technologies has become one of the most pressing issues for society, governments, and the private sector (Türk, 2024). This definition underscores the need for developing policies and regulations that balance the benefits of technology with the protection of individual rights and freedoms.

Opportunities and Advantages of Artificial Intelligence

Artificial intelligence has been widely used in recent years. In the literature, numerous articles, such as (D Binu & BR Rajakumar, 2021), kane pasqyruar vetem ndikimin dhe aftesine qe ke intelegjenca artificiale. Few papers, such as those reported in focused on the challenges of AI (Jabbarpour, Saghiri, & Sookhak, 2021).

Artificial Intelligence (AI) has seen widespread use in recent years, providing significant benefits and opportunities across various domains. One notable area is marketing, where AI has greatly enhanced efficiency and performance. Marketing experts highlight that AI improves conversion rates, offers deeper insights into customer data, and facilitates more effective decision-making (Palanively & Vasanthi, 2020). In marketing, AI has become indispensable, driving efficiency and enhancing performance by improving conversion rates, providing deep insights into customer data, and enabling more effective decision-making.

In the energy sector, AI has played a crucial role in integrating renewable energy sources such as hydroelectric, wind, biomass, and geothermal power (Lalic, Popovski, Gecevska, & Vasilevska, 2011). This contribution supports the European Green Plan and optimizes energy management, especially in regions like the Western Balkans (Stevovic, Kirin, & Bozić, 2021). This contributes significantly to sustainability efforts and aligns with global environmental goals.

Agriculture has also benefited from AI, which is used to address global food shortages and improve agricultural productivity. AI technologies help optimize cultivation processes and predict climatic conditions, thus contributing to solutions for the growing food demand (Zha, 2020). This contributes significantly to sustainability efforts and aligns with global environmental goals.

In education, AI has begun producing new teaching and learning solutions that are now undergoing testing in different contexts (Francesc, Miguel, Axel, & Paula, 2019). Artificial Intelligence in Education (AIEd) concerns mainly about the development of "computers which perform cognitive tasks, usually associated with human minds, particularly learning and problem-solving (Chen, Xie, Zou, & Hwang, 2020). The field of Artificial Intelligence in Education (AIED) has undergone significant developments over the last twenty-five years (Roll & Wylie, 2016). And then analyzes its impact on teaching and learning, which has a positive meaning for improving teachers' teaching level and students' learning quality (Huang, Saleh, & Liu, 2021). Results of the review reveal an increasing interest in using AI for educational purposes from the academic community (Chen, Zou, Xie, Cheng, & Caixia, 2022).

The field of e-commerce has seen a significant impact from AI, as it enhances the shopping experience and increases consumer engagement with new technologies. According to a Forbes Insights poll conducted in 2018, 95% of the 300+ executives surveyed believed that AI would soon play a significant role in their jobs (Tyxhari, Gorishti, & Marku, 2023). The potential impact of artificial intelligence on consumer behavior and purchase intentions has been a subject of research, indicating that AI can significantly influence consumer decisions (Febriani, Sholahuddin, & Kuswati, 2022). The exploration of artificial intelligence in e-commerce has shown that customers are increasingly receptive to AI technologies when shopping online (Nagy & Hajdu, 2021). AI influences consumer behavior and purchase decisions, reflecting its growing importance in retail.

Communication and technology sectors are also leveraging AI, especially with the advent of 5G technology. The internet will significantly increase due to the deployment of 5G technology, offering Internet connections at around one gigabit per second (McCann, Quinn, McGrath, & Connell, 2018). The 5G network needs artificial intelligence since it opens up new avenues for communication in both academic and industrial (Mester, 2017). The advent of 5G technology, coupled with AI, is set to revolutionize communication, offering faster internet speeds and new possibilities for technological advancements.

Traffic violation detection using computer vision is mainly based on computer vision technologies, which are related to image processing, artificial intelligence, and deep learning (Franklin & Mohana, 2024).

NATO has used AI to increase the security and awareness of its members and coordinate an efficient cyber defence (Mirzazadeh, 2023). Even in military fields, advances in artificial intelligence have become a double concern, from this to exploiting vulnerabilities (Djugumanov & Janev, 2022).

In the renewable energy sector, AI aids in the development and integration of sustainable energy solutions, contributing to the broader goals of environmental sustainability and energy efficiency. The application of AI in managing and optimizing renewable energy resources is crucial for meeting global sustainability targets and adapting to climate change.

Overall, these advancements demonstrate that AI is a transformative force across various sectors. Its ability to enhance efficiency, improve decision-making, and address critical challenges highlights its growing importance in modern society and its potential to drive future innovations.

AI: Challenges and Ethical Concerns

The rapid advancement of artificial intelligence (AI) has introduced a range of significant challenges and ethical issues. Security and safety concerns are prominent, as vulnerabilities in AI systems can be exploited for malicious purposes, threatening sensitive information and critical infrastructure. Furthermore, AI's potential to reinforce existing biases raises critical questions about fairness and discrimination, necessitating strong ethical oversight to avoid perpetuating societal inequalities.

During analyses of the challenges of AI, numerous problems have been reported in the literature, some of which are security (Hanif, Khalid, Putra, Rehman, & Shafique, 2018), safety (Varshney, 2016), fairness (Bellamy, et al., 2019), energy consumption (Strubell, Ganesh, & McCallum, 2019), and ethics (Smuha, 2019), to mention a few. A vital characteristic of the digital revolution is its reliance on digital technology-based innovations (Brandtzaeg, Heim, & Karahasanovic, 2011). While AI and innovation offer numerous benefits, they threaten human freedoms and rights (Correa, Grandón, & Cataluna, 2020). The adoption of AI by businesses for innovation exemplifies its potential and risks (Mariani, Machado, & Nambisan, 2023).

Recently, the media has portrayed certain artificial intelligence (AI) software as committing moral violations, anthropomorphizing it as being racist, sexist, spreading hate, or polluting young minds (Shank & DeSanti, 2018).

There is an alarming dearth of viable regulations and ethical codes governing the reckless use of AI politicking platforms in the public domain (Assibong, et al., 2019). The lack of comprehensive regulations and ethical codes, especially in political and public domains, exacerbates risks associated with AI and potential human rights violations. Addressing these challenges is crucial for harnessing AI's benefits while managing its risks responsibly.

Human rights are a necessary global filter for AI regulation and that strict liability is the most suitable threshold in the case of AI´s breaches of human rights (Barbosa & Valadares, 2023)

The rapid development of artificial intelligence has made it sophisticated enough to create measures that follow digital products. However, intellectual property law is poorly prepared for this eventuality (Abbot, 2017). For instance, the United States Patent and Trademark Office dismisses the concept of authorship or invention by non-human entities (Pearlman, 2018).

The development of artificial intelligence also impacts businesses, inventions, or discoveries and brings opportunities for these fields. Commercial enterprises often open up fresh opportunities, yet they can also pose risks to consumers. This is especially true as the influence in the market appears to be more and more driven by the accessibility and control of data (Giuseppe, et al., 2018).

Because of the combined effects of the product's novelty and complexity, it will frequently be difficult for users and, more specifically, regulators to look into how AI products operate to demonstrate a violation of the law (Manwaring, 2017). Here, we propose that the study of AI ethics may be able to help both in defining the sorts of AI consumer product problems to which consumer law needs to be attentive as well as in offering insights into the technological and operational procedures that can help to improve the effectiveness of law enforcement (Marie & Yvette, 2020).

The major concerns claimed in past research include (i) how organizations should re-envision organizational structure, job function, and skills, and educate future workforce (Loureiro, Guerreiro, & Tussyadiah, 2021). Internal purposes mean using AI to improve internal business processes, where the customer is not in direct contact with the AI-solution (Enholm, Papagiannidis, Mikalef, & Krogstie, 2021).

Many items and headlines such as jobless ratio, Philips Curve, performance, management, CRM Analytics, customer relationship management, sales, strategic planning, mass production, Purchasing Power Parity, GDP, inflation, money, Central Banks, Banking System, coaching, training, accounting, taxes etc. regarding to business and economics will face serious dangers, hits, change, exposures as well as opportunities and gains with the improvements in Artificial Intelligence and Robotics (Dirican, 2015).

CONCLUSION

Hypothesis 1: The development of artificial intelligence violates human rights and freedoms.

The rapid advancement of AI brings with it both transformative benefits and significant risks to human rights and freedoms. AI technologies, when not adequately regulated, have the potential to infringe upon privacy, amplify societal disruptions, and make decisions without sufficient human oversight. These issues highlight the necessity for stringent ethical frameworks and legal regulations to ensure AI developments do not compromise fundamental rights. Addressing this hypothesis involves exploring how AI's capabilities and applications could potentially breach privacy and other individual rights, necessitating a balance between technological progress and the protection of freedoms.

Hypothesis 2: AI poses risks related to legal and ethical frameworks for use in judicial systems.

AI's integration into judicial systems and national security presents unique legal and ethical challenges. The use of AI in these domains raises concerns about fairness, transparency, and accountability. The potential for AI systems to reinforce biases or make opaque decisions can undermine the justice system's integrity. This hypothesis is addressed by examining the legal and ethical implications of AI in these critical areas and developing frameworks that ensure AI systems are used responsibly, maintaining fairness and upholding human rights.

Hypothesis 3: There is a potential conflict between artificial intelligence autonomy and human rights and freedoms.

The autonomy of AI systems can lead to conflicts with human rights and freedoms, particularly when AI makes decisions without adequate human oversight. This conflict arises from the inherent nature of AI to operate independently, which can challenge traditional human-centric values and rights. Addressing this hypothesis involves analyzing how AI autonomy might conflict with the protection of fundamental rights and proposing solutions to ensure that AI systems operate within boundaries that respect human freedoms.

Research Question 1: How can transparency and accountability from AI be improved to increase their trustworthiness and use in critical applications for human rights and freedoms?

Improving transparency and accountability in AI involves developing clear standards for AI operations and decision-making processes. This includes implementing robust mechanisms for auditing AI systems, ensuring that their decisions can be traced and understood by humans. Enhancing transparency can build trust and ensure that AI applications in critical areas such as human rights and freedoms are used responsibly.

Research Question 2: What are the main ethical and legal challenges arising from the use of AI technologies in areas such as the justice system and national security, and how should we address them to minimize the negative impact on individuals and societies?

The main ethical and legal challenges include the potential for AI to perpetuate biases, make unjust decisions, and lack accountability. To address these challenges, it is crucial to establish comprehensive regulatory frameworks that govern the use of AI in these sensitive areas. This includes ensuring that AI systems are designed to be fair, transparent, and accountable, and that they comply with established human rights standards.

Research Question 3: How can it be ensured that the development and use of AI progresses in a way that respects and protects fundamental human rights, including the rights to privacy, freedom, and equality, in a global and multicultural context?

Ensuring that AI development respects fundamental human rights requires international collaboration to create and enforce global standards and guidelines. This involves integrating human rights considerations into the design and implementation of AI technologies, promoting inclusive and equitable practices, and establishing mechanisms for monitoring and enforcement. By fostering global cooperation and adhering to human rights principles, the development and use of AI can advance in a manner that respects privacy, freedom, and equality across diverse cultural contexts.

Recommendation

Develop and implement comprehensive regulations and ethical guidelines for AI development and deployment. These frameworks should address privacy concerns, ensure transparency, and prevent biases in AI systems.

- Create clear standards for accountability and oversight, particularly in sensitive areas like the justice system and national security, to ensure AI systems are used responsibly and ethically. Ensure AI systems are designed with inclusivity and fairness in mind. This involves addressing potential biases in AI algorithms and ensuring they do not perpetuate or amplify existing inequalities. Involve diverse stakeholders in the design and testing phases of AI development to reflect a wide range of perspectives and reduce the risk of biased outcomes.
- Implement robust data protection measures to safeguard individuals' privacy. This includes using encryption, anonymization, and other techniques to secure personal data used by AI systems. Establish clear protocols for data collection, usage, and retention to ensure that individuals' privacy rights are upheld.
- Collaborate internationally to develop global standards and agreements for AI ethics and regulations. This helps ensure that AI technologies are used in ways that respect human rights across different cultural and legal contexts. Encourage cross-border dialogue and cooperation to address the global nature of AI challenges and share best practices.
- Promote education and training programs focused on AI ethics for developers, policymakers, and other stakeholders. This will help ensure that those involved in AI development and regulation understand and prioritize human rights and ethical considerations. Support research and academic initiatives that explore the ethical implications of AI and develop new approaches for integrating human rights into AI systems.
- Regularly audit AI systems for biases and take corrective actions to address any disparities in how different groups are treated. This includes evaluating AI systems for fairness and taking steps to mitigate any negative impacts on marginalized or vulnerable populations.
- Facilitate public discussions and consultations on AI ethics and human rights. Engaging with the public and various stakeholders helps ensure that AI technologies are developed and implemented in ways that align with societal values and expectations. Provide platforms for individuals and communities to voice their concerns and provide feedback on AI systems and their impacts.

By implementing these recommendations, it is possible to harness the benefits of AI while safeguarding fundamental human rights and freedoms. Ensuring that AI technologies are developed and used in ways that are ethical, transparent, and accountable will contribute to a more just and equitable society.

REFERENCES

Assibong, P., Wogu, I. A., Sholarin, M. A., Misra, S., Damasevičius, R., & Sharma, N. (2019). The Politics of Artificial Intelligence Behaviour and Human Rights Violation Issues in the 2016 US Presidential Elections: An Appraisal. In Sharma, N. C. (Ed.), *Advances in Intelligent Systems and Computing* (pp. 295–309). Springer.

Barbosa, F., & Valadares, L. (2023). Artificial intelligence: a claim for strict liability for human rights violation. *Revista de Direito Internacional*, 150.

Bellamy, R., Dey, K., Hind, M., Hoffman, S., Houde, S., Kannan, K., Lohia, P., Martino, J., Mehta, S., Mojsilovic, A., Nagar, S., Ramamurthy, K. N., Richards, J., Saha, D., Sattigeri, P., Singh, M., Varshney, K. R., & Zhang, Y. (2019). AI Fairness 360: An extensible toolkit for detecting and mitigating algorithmic bias. *IBM Journal of Research and Development*, 63(4/5), 63. DOI: 10.1147/JRD.2019.2942287

Binu, D., & Rajakumar, B. R. (2021). *Artificial intelligence in data mining: Theories and applications*. Academic Press.

Brandtzaeg, P., Heim, J., & Karahasanovic, A. (2011). Understanding the new digital divide-A typology of Internet users in Europe Author Links open overlay panel. *International Journal of Human-Computer Studies*, 69(3), 123–138. DOI: 10.1016/j.ijhcs.2010.11.004

Chen, X., Xie, H., Zou, D., & Hwang, G. (2020). Application and theory gaps during the rise of Artificial Intelligence in Education. *Computers and Education: Artificial Intelligence*.

Chen, X., Zou, D., Xie, H., Cheng, G., & Caixia, L. (2022). Two Decades of Artificial Intelligence in Education. *Journal of Educational Technology & Society*, •••, 28–47.

Correa, P. R., Grandón, E., & Cataluna, J. (2020). *Users segmentation based on the Technological Readiness Adoption Index in emerging countries: The case of Chile*. Technological Forecasting AND Social Change.

Dirican, C. (2015). The Impacts of Robotics, Artificial Intelligence On Business and Economics. *Procedia: Social and Behavioral Sciences*, 195, 564–573. DOI: 10.1016/j.sbspro.2015.06.134

Djugumanov, I., & Janev, M. H. (2022). *Practical Applications of Advanced Technologies for Enhancing security and defense capabilities: perspectives and challenges for the Western Balkans*. IOS Press.

Enholm, I., Papagiannidis, E., Mikalef, P., & Krogstie, J. (2021). Artificial Intelligence and Business Value: A Literature Review. *Information Systems Frontiers*, •••, 1709–1734.

Febriani, R., Sholahuddin, M., & Kuswati, R. (2022). Do Artificial Intelligence and Digital Marketing Impact Purchase Intention Mediated by Perceived Value? *Journal of Business and Management Studies*, 184-196.

Francesc, P., Miguel, S., Axel, R., & Paula, V. (2019). *Artificial intelligence in education: challenges and opportunities for sustainable development.* Ministerio de Educación del Perú.

Franklin, R., & Mohana. (2024). Traffic Signal Violation Detection using Artificial Intelligence and Deep Learning. *2024 International Conference on Cognitive Robotics and Intelligent Systems*, (pp. 425-431).

Giuseppe, C., Francesca, L., Marco, L., Wolfgang, M., Przemyslaw, P., & Giovanni, S. (2018). Towards Consumer-Empowering Artificial Intelligence. *Proceedings of the Twenty-Seventh International Joint Conference on Artificial Intelligence*, (pp. 5150-5157). Stochkholm.

Hanif, M., Khalid, F., Putra, R., Rehman, S., & Shafique, M. (2018). Robust Machine Learning Systems: Reliability and Security for Deep Neural Networks. *IEEE*, 257-260.

Huang, J., Saleh, S., & Liu, Y. (2021). A Review on Artificial Intelligence in Education . *Academic Journal of Interdisciplinary Studies*, 206-2017.

Hutchison, C. (1993). Artificial Intelligence in Business and Industry. *Managing with Information Technology*, 101-117.

Jabbarpour, M. R., Saghiri, A., & Sookhak, M. (2021). A Framework for Component Selection Considering Dark Sides of Artificial Intelligence: A Case Study on Autonomous Vehicle. *Electronics (Basel)*, 10(4), 384. DOI: 10.3390/electronics10040384

Lalic, D., Popovski, K., Gecevska, V., & Vasilevska, S. (2011). *Analysis of the opportunities and challenges for renewable energy market in the Western Balkan countries*. ScienceDirect. DOI: 10.1016/j.rser.2011.04.011

Loureiro, S., Guerreiro, J., & Tussyadiah, I. (2021). Artificial intelligence in business: State of the art and future research agenda. *Journal of Business Research*, 129, 911–926. DOI: 10.1016/j.jbusres.2020.11.001

Manwaring, K. (2017). Emerging Information Technologies: Challenges for Consumers. *Oxford University Commonwealth Law Journal*, 265-279.

Mariani, m., Machado, I., & Nambisan, S. (2023). Types of innovation and artificial intelligence: A systematic quantitative literature review and research agenda Author links open overlay panel. *Journal of Business Research.*

Marie, P., & Yvette, M. (2020). AI in the Home: Artificial Intelligence and Consumer Protection. *Cambridge University Press*, 1-15.

McCann, J., Quinn, L., McGrath, S., & Connell, E. (2018). Towards the distributes Edge – An IoT review. *12th International Conferences on Sensing Technology,* (pp. 263-263). Ireland: Limerich.

Mester, G. (2017). *Ranking of Croatian researchers from several disciplines using Google Scholar database*. Interdisciplinary Description of Complex System.

Mirzazadeh, I. (2023). Artificial Intelligence (AI) and Violation of Human Rights. *SSRN*. DOI: 10.2139/ssrn.4310188

Nagy, S., & Hajdu, N. (2021). Consumer acceptance of the use of artificial intelligence in online shopping: Evidence from Hungary. *Amfiteatru Economic*, 23(56), 155–173. DOI: 10.24818/EA/2021/56/155

Palanively, V., & Vasanthi, B. (2020). Role of artificial intelligence in business transfromation. *International Journal of Advanced Science and Technology* .

Pearlman, R. (2018). *Recognizing Artificial Intelligence (AI) as authors and inventors under U.S intellectual property law*. Rich. J. L. & Tech.

Roll, I., & Wylie, R. (2016). Evolution and Revolution in Artificial Intelligence in Education. *International Journal of Artificial Intelligence in Education*, 26(2), 582–599. DOI: 10.1007/s40593-016-0110-3

Saghiri, A. M., Vahidipour, M., Jabbaarpour, M., Sookhak, M., & Forestiero, A. (2022). *A Survey of Artificial Intelligence Challenges: Analyzing the Definitions, Relationships, and Evolutions. Applied Sciences. Abbot, R. (2017). Research Handbook on Intellectual Property and Digital Technologies*. Edward Elgar Publishing Limited.

Shank, D., & DeSanti, A. (2018). Attributions of morality and mind to artificial intelligence after real-world moral violations. *Computers in Human Behavior*, 86, 401–411. DOI: 10.1016/j.chb.2018.05.014

Smuha, N. A. (2019). The EU Approach to Ethics Guidelines for Trustworthy Artificial Intelligence. *Computer Law Review International*, 97-106.

Stevovic, I., Kirin, S., & Bozić, I. (2021). Artificial Intelligence And Nature-Inspired Optimization On Integrative Capacity Of Renewable Energy In The Western Balkan. *Contemporary Materials*, 12(2). Advance online publication. DOI: 10.7251/COMEN2102226S

Strubell, E., Ganesh, A., & McCallum, A. (2019). *Energy and Policy Considerations for Modern Deep Learning Research.* AAAI Special Programs.

Thesaurus, C. A. (2024). *Definition of artificial intelligence.*

Türk, V. (2024, 08 24). HIGH LEVEL SIDE EVENT OF THE 53rd SESSION OF THE HUMAN RIGHTS COUNCIL.

Tyxhari, G., Gorishti, A., & Marku, M. (2023). Technology progress unveiled: Performance indicators in developed vs. developing Western Balkan Countries. *Journal of Southwest Jiaotong University.*

ÜNVER. H. A. (2024). *Artificial intelligence (AI) and human rights: Using AI as a weapon of repression and its impact on human rights.* Brussels: European Union.

Varshney, K. (2016). Engineering safety in machine learning. *IEEE*, 1-5.

Zha, J. (2020). AI in Agriculture. *Jounal of Physics.*

Chapter 3
Leveraging Artificial Intelligence to Combat Human Trafficking:
A Multifaceted Approach

Jaspreet Kaur
https://orcid.org/0009-0009-8381-5355
Lovely Professional University, India

Shruti
Lovely Professional University, India

Amir Ahmad Dar
https://orcid.org/0000-0002-0379-2272
Lovely Professional University, India

ABSTRACT

Human trafficking, a heinous crime exploiting individuals for forced labor, sexual servitude, or organ harvesting, plagues millions globally. Eradicating this global scourge demands a multifaceted approach. Artificial Intelligence (AI) emerges as a powerful weapon in this fight. This paper explores how AI can be leveraged to identify victims, disrupt trafficking networks, and aid in investigations. We delve into applications of AI in data analysis, victim identification, financial tracking, communication support, and explore its potential for proactive intervention. The paper acknowledges the ethical considerations surrounding AI use and emphasizes the need for human oversight and collaboration.

DOI: 10.4018/979-8-3693-7205-0.ch003

INTRODUCTION

The shadow of human trafficking drafted in Table 1, darkens our world, entrapping an estimated 40.3 million people according to the International Labour Organization (ILO, 2007). Human trafficking, a heinous crime that exploits people for forced labor, sexual servitude, or organ harvesting, casts a dark shadow across the globe.

Table 1. Global Estimates of Human Trafficking (ILO, 2017)

Category	Number of Victims (in millions)
Forced Labor	**24.9**
Forced Sexual Exploitation	**4.8**
State-Imposed Forced Labor	**4.1**
Total	**40.3**

The distribution of these victims can be better understood through a visual representation in Figure 1.

Figure 1. Global Estimates of Human Trafficking Victims

Table 2. Identified Victims by Region (UNODC, 2020)

Region	Number of Victims(%)
Africa and the Middle East	**8**
Asia and the Pacific 60	**16**
Americas	**60**
Europe and Central Asia	**13**
Other	**3**
Total	**100**

This regional distribution shown in Table 2, which is illustrated in Figure 2.

Figure 2. Identified Victims by Region

Traffickers employ ever-more sophisticated methods to prey on vulnerabilities, leaving law enforcement constantly on the defensive. The sheer volume of data involved in investigations and the traffickers' constant evolution of tactics overwhelm traditional methods.

However, a beacon of hope emerges in the form of Artificial Intelligence (AI). With its ability to analyze massive datasets in real-time, identify hidden patterns in communication and financial transactions, and automate repetitive tasks, AI presents a game-changing opportunity. This paper delves into the potential of AI to disrupt trafficking operations, identify victims, and ultimately, fight for human freedom.

EXPANDING AI APPLICATIONS IN COMBATING HUMAN TRAFFICKING

Data Analysis and Pattern Recognition: Unveiling the Hidden Threads of Trafficking

Human trafficking thrives in the shadows, leaving investigators with a complex puzzle to solve. Fortunately, AI can act as a powerful detective, wielding its data analysis prowess to unveil the hidden threads of these criminal networks. By sifting through vast amounts of information from diverse sources, AI can identify patterns indicative of trafficking activities.

Diverse Data Sources: Painting a Comprehensive Picture

AI algorithms can ingest data from a multitude of sources, creating a more comprehensive picture of potential trafficking operations. These sources include:

Online Advertisements: Job postings with unrealistic promises or suspiciously low wages, travel ads targeting vulnerable populations (e.g., promising work abroad with easy visas) (Citaristi, 2022; Latonero, 2011).

Social Media: Platforms traffickers exploit to lure victims with seemingly harmless offers or advertise services (e.g., modeling opportunities, massage jobs) (Citaristi, 2022; Latonero, 2011).

Travel Records: Unusual travel patterns like frequent one-way trips, travel to destinations with a high prevalence of trafficking, or mismatched passenger and billing information (Citaristi, 2022).

Financial Transactions: Large cash withdrawals by individuals with limited spending history, money transfers to known trafficking hubs, transactions involving individuals or networks flagged for suspicious activity (Citaristi, 2022).

Hotlines: Data from anti-trafficking hotlines can be analyzed to identify trends and areas with a high volume of reported cases, highlighting potential hotspots for investigation (ILO, 2007).

Healthcare Records: Victims often come into contact with healthcare providers, making medical records a valuable source of information. Indicators such as frequent visits for injuries, untreated sexually transmitted infections, or signs of physical abuse can point to potential trafficking situations (Citaristi, 2022).

Criminal Records: Analysis of arrest records and criminal histories can reveal patterns such as frequent arrests for prostitution or petty crimes, which might indicate underlying trafficking activities (Citaristi, 2022).

Public Databases: Information from public records, such as business registrations, property ownership, and utility records, can help trace the operations and movements of trafficking networks (ILO, 2007).

Telecommunications Data: Analyzing call records and messages can uncover communication patterns between traffickers and victims or among different members of a trafficking network (Citaristi, 2022).

Surveillance Footage: AI can process vast amounts of video data from surveillance cameras to detect suspicious activities, such as frequent visits to specific locations or unusual interactions between individuals (ILO, 2007).

By integrating these diverse data sources, AI can provide law enforcement and investigators with actionable insights, helping to dismantle human trafficking networks more effectively.

Identifying the Red Flags: Unmasking Trafficking Patterns

Once this data is collected, AI can analyze it for specific patterns that might indicate trafficking. These red flags can include:

- **Suspicious Travel Patterns:** Frequent one-way trips, travel to destinations with a high prevalence of trafficking, or bookings with inconsistencies (multiple rooms under one name, short stays with frequent check-ins/outs) (Citaristi, 2022).

- **Unusual Financial Activity:** Large cash withdrawals, money transfers to high-risk areas, or transactions involving known trafficking networks (Citaristi, 2022).
- **Coded Language in Online Posts:** AI can identify keywords or phrases commonly used by traffickers to lure victims (e.g., "easy money," "better life abroad," "modeling opportunity") (Latonero, 2011).
- **Social Media Activity:** Analyzing social media activity for signs of coercion or exploitation, such as sudden changes in posting behavior, restricted access to accounts, or pleas for help disguised in seemingly innocuous messages (Citaristi, 2022; Latonero, 2011).
- **Multiple Phone Numbers or Email Addresses:** Traffickers often use multiple phone numbers or email addresses to avoid detection. AI can flag accounts linked to several contact details, indicating potential coordination within trafficking networks.
- **Frequent Change of Locations:** Victims of trafficking are often moved frequently to avoid detection. AI can track patterns of short-term rentals, frequent changes in living arrangements, or hotel bookings under different names (Latonero, 2011).
- **Healthcare Visits for Specific Conditions:** Victims may seek medical help for conditions related to their exploitation, such as repeated injuries, untreated sexually transmitted infections, or signs of malnutrition and abuse. AI can identify clusters of such cases linked to potential trafficking scenarios (Citaristi, 2022; Latonero, 2011).
- **Educational Discrepancies:** Sudden or unexplained changes in school enrollment, frequent absences, or a drop in academic performance can be indicators of trafficking. AI can monitor educational records for such anomalies (Latonero, 2011).
- **Unusual Employment Patterns:** Jobs with high turnover rates, employees working without proper documentation, or workplaces with a high number of workers from vulnerable populations can be red flags. AI can analyze employment data to uncover these patterns (Citaristi, 2022).

By identifying these red flags, AI can provide crucial leads for investigators, helping to uncover and dismantle human trafficking networks more efficiently.

From Patterns to Leads: Empowering Human Efforts

By identifying these patterns, AI can flag potential cases for further investigation. This significantly reduces the burden on human analysts by filtering out irrelevant data and providing investigators with prioritized leads. This empowers them to focus their expertise on in-depth investigations and victim rescue operations (Citaristi, 2022).

The Power of AI lies in its ability to connect seemingly unconnected dots. By analyzing vast amounts of data and identifying these hidden patterns, AI can be a crucial weapon in dismantling trafficking networks and rescuing victims.

Data Analysis Flowchart for Human Trafficking Investigations: Leveraging AI for Breakthroughs

This flowchart depicts how AI can be integrated into the data analysis process of human trafficking investigations, empowering investigators with powerful tools for victim identification, financial tracking, communication support, and proactive risk assessment.

Data Sources:

- **Online Platforms & Ads:** Social media posts, job boards, travel websites.
- **Financial Transactions:** Bank records, money transfer logs, cryptocurrency data.
- **Victim Narratives:** Hotline reports, survivor testimonies.
- **Travel Records:** Booking information, border crossing data.

AI Analysis and Pattern Recognition:

1. **Victim Identification:**
    - o **Natural Language Processing (NLP):** Analyzes online content for keywords/phrases associated with trafficking (e.g., "easy money," "better life abroad") (Latonero, 2011).
    - o **Image Recognition:** Scans online content for missing persons reported by authorities (Bales & Soodalter, 2010).
    - o **Sentiment Analysis:** Analyzes victim narratives for inconsistencies, emotional distress indicators (Bales & Soodalter, 2010).
    - o **Behavioral Analysis:** Monitors changes in online behavior, such as sudden deletion of accounts or a significant drop in online activity, which can signal coercion or distress.
2. **Financial Tracking:**

- o **Anomaly Detection:** Identifies suspicious financial activity: frequent small withdrawals, money transfers to high-risk regions (Bales & Soodalter, 2010).
- o **Network Analysis**: Maps financial transactions to uncover links between suspected traffickers and their networks (Bales & Soodalter, 2010).
- o **Blockchain Analysis:** Tracks cryptocurrency transactions, which traffickers increasingly use to avoid detection (Latonero, 2011).

3. **Communication Support:**
    - o **Multilingual Chatbots:** Provide 24/7 support, understand trafficking keywords, offer resources, connect victims with human assistance (McClain, & Garrity, 2011).
    - o **Automated Alerts:** Sends real-time alerts to authorities or NGOs when potential trafficking activities are detected through communication channels.
4. **Predictive Modeling:**
    - o **Machine Learning:** Analyzes historical data (trafficking trends, demographics) to identify high-risk areas and populations (Orantes, 2018).
    - o **Geospatial Analysis:** Maps out trafficking routes and hotspots, helping to allocate resources more effectively and anticipate trafficking movements.

Outcomes

- **Prioritized Leads:** AI flags potential cases for human investigators, streamlining investigations.
- **Disrupted Networks:** Financial tracking helps dismantle trafficking operations and recover exploited funds (Bales & Soodalter, 2010).
- **Victim Support:** Chatbots provide immediate support and resources to victims (McClain & Garrity, 2011).
- **Proactive Interventions:** High-risk areas and populations are identified for targeted prevention efforts (Orantes, 2018).

Enhancing Collaboration and Information Sharing:

- **Integrated Databases:** AI systems can merge data from different agencies and organizations, ensuring that critical information is shared promptly and efficiently.

- **Real-Time Dashboards:** Investigators can access real-time dashboards that display ongoing cases, flagged activities, and emerging trends, facilitating better coordination and quicker responses.

Continual Improvement and Adaptation:

- **Feedback Loops:** AI systems can incorporate feedback from investigators to refine their algorithms, improving accuracy over time.
- **Adapting to New Trends:** As traffickers evolve their methods, AI systems can update their models to detect new patterns and techniques, staying one step ahead.

By leveraging AI in these ways drafted in Table 3, also law enforcement and investigators can enhance their capabilities, making significant strides in the fight against human trafficking.

Benefits of AI Integration:

- **Enhanced Efficiency:** Automates data analysis, reduces human workload, prioritizes leads.
- **Expanded Reach:** Analyzes vast amounts of data from diverse sources.
- **Hidden Pattern Detection:** Identifies patterns that might escape human analysis.
- **24/7 Support:** Chatbots provide constant support for victims.
- **Data-Driven Prevention:** Predictive models lead to proactive interventions.

By leveraging AI's analytical power, we can significantly improve human trafficking investigations, leading to more rescues, dismantled networks, and ultimately, a safer world.

Table 3. AI Applications in Combating Human Trafficking

AI Application	Description	Sources Utilized
Data Analysis and Pattern Recognition	Unveiling hidden trafficking patterns	Online advertisements, social media, travel records, financial transactions, hotlines
Victim Identification	Using NLP, image recognition, sentiment analysis to identify potential victims	Social media posts, job boards, travel websites, hotline reports, survivor testimonies
Financial Tracking	Detecting unusual financial activity and transactions	Bank records, money transfer logs, cryptocurrency data
Communication Support	Multilingual chatbots providing 24/7 support	AI-driven chatbots
Predictive Modeling	Identifying high-risk areas and populations	Historical data on trafficking trends and demographics

Ethical Considerations: Balancing Progress with Responsibility

While AI offers a powerful weapon in the fight against human trafficking, its application necessitates careful consideration of ethical implications. Here's a breakdown of key areas to ensure responsible and unbiased use of AI in these investigations:

1. **Algorithmic Bias:**

Training data is the foundation of AI, and any biases within it can be amplified by the algorithms. This can lead to:

- **Discriminatory Outcomes:** AI systems trained on biased data might overlook victims from certain demographics or socioeconomic backgrounds.
- **Misidentification:** Potential victims from underrepresented groups could be flagged incorrectly due to biased profiling.

Mitigation Strategies:

- **Diverse Training Data:** Curating training datasets that reflect the true diversity of potential victims and traffickers is crucial.
- **Human Review:** Human oversight of AI-generated leads can help identify and mitigate potential biases.
- **Algorithmic Fairness Audits:** Regular audits can detect and address bias within the AI system itself.

2. **Data Privacy Concerns:**

Investigations often involve sensitive personal data. Here's how to ensure privacy is protected:

- **Data Minimization:** Only collect and store the data essential for the investigation.
- **Strong Encryption:** Implement robust encryption measures to safeguard sensitive data.
- **Clear User Consent:** Transparency regarding data collection and usage is vital.
- **Data Anonymization:** Whenever possible, anonymize personal data to protect individual identities while still allowing for effective analysis.

3. **Human Oversight and Accountability:**

AI is a powerful tool, but the ultimate responsibility lies with humans. Here's how to ensure it remains that way:

- **Human-in-the-Loop Decisions:** AI should support investigators, not replace them. Key decisions should involve human judgment and ethical considerations.
- **Clear Lines of Accountability:** Establish a clear chain of command to ensure accountability for AI-driven actions.
- **Algorithmic Impact Assessments:** Evaluate the potential impact of AI on investigations before deployment to identify and address potential ethical issues.
- **Ongoing Training:** Regular training for investigators on the ethical use of AI and updates on new technologies and methodologies.

4. **Transparency and Trust:** Building trust in AI systems is essential for their effective deployment. Here's how to ensure transparency:

- **Explainability:** AI decisions and recommendations should be explainable to ensure that investigators understand the basis for each lead.
- **Public Awareness:** Educating the public on how AI is used in trafficking investigations can build trust and support for its application.
- **Transparent Reporting:** Regularly publish reports on the performance, biases identified, and improvements made to AI systems.

5. **Collaboration and Multidisciplinary Approaches:** The fight against human trafficking requires a collaborative approach. Here's how to enhance collaboration:

- **Cross-Sector Partnerships:** Collaborate with NGOs, government agencies, tech companies, and academic institutions to share knowledge and resources.
- **Multidisciplinary Teams:** Form teams with diverse expertise, including data scientists, ethicists, social workers, and law enforcement officials.
- **Standardized Protocols:** Develop standardized protocols for the use of AI in investigations to ensure consistency and reliability across different jurisdictions and agencies.

6. **Continuous Improvement and Adaptation:** The landscape of human trafficking is constantly evolving. Here's how to ensure AI remains effective:

- **Regular Updates:** Continuously update AI algorithms with new data and emerging trafficking patterns to maintain their effectiveness.
- **Feedback Mechanisms:** Implement feedback mechanisms where investigators can provide insights and experiences to improve AI systems.
- **Research and Development:** Invest in ongoing research to explore new AI techniques and tools that can enhance trafficking investigations.

By addressing these ethical considerations as mentioned in Table 4, we can leverage AI responsibly, ensuring its use strengthens investigations and safeguards the rights of all individuals. This balanced approach will enhance the effectiveness of anti-trafficking efforts while maintaining public trust and ethical integrity.

Table 4. Ethical Considerations and Mitigation Strategies

Ethical Concern	Potential Issue	Mitigation Strategy
Algorithmic Bias	Discriminatory outcomes, misidentification	Diverse training data, human review, algorithmic fairness audit
Data Privacy	Risk of sensitive data exposure	Data minimization, strong encryption, clear user consent
Human Oversight and Accountability	Over-reliance on AI, lack of accountability	Human-in-the-loop decisions, clear lines of accountability, algorithmic impact assessments

From Patterns to Leads: Empowering Human Efforts

By identifying these patterns, AI can flag potential cases for further investigation. This significantly reduces the burden on human analysts by filtering out irrelevant data and providing investigators with prioritized leads. This empowers them to focus their expertise on in-depth investigations and victim rescue operations.

Enhanced Efficiency: AI automates data analysis, reducing the workload for human investigators and allowing them to prioritize leads more effectively. This automation helps focus human resources on high-value tasks, such as in-depth investigations and direct interventions.

Expanded Reach: AI systems can process and analyze vast amounts of data from diverse sources, far beyond human capacity. This expanded reach allows for a more comprehensive understanding of trafficking patterns and networks.

Hidden Pattern Detection: AI's ability to detect hidden patterns is crucial. It can reveal connections and activities that might be missed by human analysts, thus uncovering previously undetected trafficking operations.

24/7 Support: AI-driven chatbots and other support systems can provide continuous assistance to potential victims and investigators. This constant availability ensures that help is always accessible, regardless of time or location.

Data-Driven Prevention: Predictive models use historical data to identify high-risk areas and populations. This data-driven approach enables proactive interventions, focusing resources on the most vulnerable and preventing trafficking before it occurs.

By leveraging these benefits, AI can significantly enhance the effectiveness of efforts to combat human trafficking, leading to more rescues, disrupted networks, and ultimately, a safer world for vulnerable populations. The benefits of AI integration in these efforts are substantial, as summarized in Table 5.

Table 5. Benefits of AI Integration

Benefit	Description
Enhanced Efficiency	Automates data analysis, reduces human workload, prioritizes leads
Expanded Reach	Analyzes vast amounts of data from diverse sources
Hidden Pattern Detection	Identifies patterns that might escape human analysis
24/7 Support	Chatbots provide constant support for victims
Data-Driven Prevention	Predictive models lead to proactive interventions

AI's capabilities are already proving effective in real-world applications. For instance, AI-driven tools have identified trafficking victims through online advertisements in the U.S. and Europe, leading to several successful interventions (Ijiga et al., 2024).

Future Work

1. Future work on AI in combating human trafficking using the Design of Experiments (DOE) could focus on optimizing AI algorithms for accuracy in identifying victims and networks. By testing different combinations of features such as data sources, machine learning models, and decision-making criteria, researchers can determine the most effective strategies. DOE can also explore the impact of varying privacy measures to ensure ethical standards. Additionally, experiments could evaluate the integration of AI with law enforcement protocols to enhance predictive capabilities while maintaining transparency. This structured approach will help in refining AI tools for ethical and impactful applications in human trafficking prevention (Dar and Anuradha, 2020a; Dar and Anuradha 2020b; Hisam et al., 2024; Mohammed et al., 2024; Dar et al., 2024).

CONCLUSION

AI is revolutionizing the fight against human trafficking. By leveraging its analytical power, AI can identify victims, disrupt trafficking networks, assist investigations, and potentially predict future trafficking activities. However, ethical considerations must be addressed to ensure responsible and transparent use of this technology. The future holds promise for a world where AI becomes a powerful tool in eradicating human trafficking and ensuring freedom for all as show in Table 6.

Table 6. Impact of AI on Human Trafficking Investigations

Outcome	Description
Prioritized Leads	AI flags potential cases for human investigators, streamlining investigations
Disrupted Networks	Financial tracking helps dismantle trafficking operations
Victim Support	Chatbots provide immediate support and resources to victims
Proactive Interventions	High-risk areas and populations are identified for targeted prevention efforts

REFERENCES

Dar, A. A., & Anuradha, N. (2020a). Use of Taguchi method for optimisation of process parameters of option pricing model. *International Journal of Services. Economics and Management*, 11(1), 1–20.

Dar, A. A., & Anuradha, N. (2020b). Studies on European call option of binomial option pricing model using Taguchi's L27 orthogonal array. *International Journal of Intelligent Enterprise*, 7(1-3), 234–249. DOI: 10.1504/IJIE.2020.104663

Dar, A. A., Gulzar, Z., Babu, R. A., Ali, L., & Shreedevi, G. (2024). Comparison: Taguchi method and full factorial design in WACC. *International Journal of Intelligent Enterprise*, 11(3), 300–315. DOI: 10.1504/IJIE.2024.139777

Hisam, M. W., Dar, A. A., Elrasheed, M. O., Khan, M. S., Gera, R., & Azad, I. (2024). The Versatility of the Taguchi Method: Optimizing Experiments Across Diverse Disciplines. *Journal of Statistical Theory and Applications : JSTA*. Advance online publication. DOI: 10.1007/s44199-024-00093-9

Ijiga, A. C., Aboi, E. J., Idoko, I. P., Enyejo, L. A., & Odeyemi, M. O.Amina Catherine IjigaEnoch Joseph AboiIdoko Peter IdokoLawrence Anebi EnyejoMicheal Olumubo Odeyemi. (2024). Collaborative innovations in Artificial Intelligence (AI): Partnering with leading US tech firms to combat human trafficking. *Global Journal of Engineering and Technology Advances*, 18(3), 106–123. DOI: 10.30574/gjeta.2024.18.3.0046

International Labour Organization. (2017). Global estimates of modern slavery: Forced labour and forced marriage. *International Labour Organization*. Citaristi, I. (2022). United Nations Office on Drugs and Crime—UNODC. In *The Europa Directory of International Organizations 2022* (pp. 248-252). Routledge.

Latonero, M. (2011). Human trafficking online: The role of social networking sites and online classifieds. *Available at* SSRN *2045851*. Bales, K., & Soodalter, R. (2010). *The slave next door: Human trafficking and slavery in America today*. Univ of California Press. DOI: 10.2139/ssrn.2045851

McClain, N. M., & Garrity, S. E. (2011). Sex trafficking and the exploitation of adolescents. *Journal of Obstetric, Gynecologic, and Neonatal Nursing*, 40(2), 243–252. DOI: 10.1111/j.1552-6909.2011.01221.x PMID: 21284727

Mohammed, S., Dar, A. A., Khan, M. S., Azad, I., Jayaraman, G., & Albalawi, O. (2024). Goodwill Valuation Enhancement through Capitalization Method and Statistical Impact Analysis. *Journal of Risk and Financial Management*, 17(6), 226. DOI: 10.3390/jrfm17060226

Orantes, M. (2018). Leveraging Machine Learning and Artificial Intelligence to Combat Human Trafficking (Master's thesis, Utica College).

Chapter 4
AI-Generated Legal Documents:
Challenges and Opportunities for Corporate Law Firms

Harshit Gouri
https://orcid.org/0009-0006-4507-8989
St. Stephen's College, University of Delhi, India

Priyanshi Jindal
https://orcid.org/0009-0001-8116-8192
ABES Business School, India

Rakshita Gouri
https://orcid.org/0009-0000-6637-9824
DAV PG College, India

Vanshita Gouri
https://orcid.org/0009-0000-8029-5707
DAV PG College, India

ABSTRACT

With the rising adoption of AI technology in legal practice, the legal industry stands at the threshold of a transformative era. Corporate law firms, which heavily rely on meticulous and error-free legal documentation, are at the forefront of this technological evolution. The adoption of AI technology offers substantial advantages, including increased efficiency, enhanced document accuracy, and cost-effectiveness. However, this transition raises concerns related to data privacy, quality control, and the evolving role of lawyers in the document drafting process. This article delves into the dynamic landscape of AI-generated legal documents and their implications for

DOI: 10.4018/979-8-3693-7205-0.ch004

corporate law firms exploring variable opportunities and challenges inherent in the integration of AI-generated legal documents into corporate law firms, highlighting key recommendations, best practices, and critical considerations for managing the opportunities and challenges that AI technology presents.

1.0 INTRODUCTION

In the ever-evolving landscape of the legal industry, the emergence of artificial intelligence

(AI) is assured to reshape the way corporate law firms operate. AI-generated legal documents have quickly become a focal point, offering both promising opportunities and complex challenges for legal practitioners. This article explores the transformative potential of AI in the domain of corporate law, delving into the multifaceted aspects of AI-generated legal documents ("Editor's Introduction," 1995).

Historically, the legal profession has been known for its meticulous document creation, extensive research, and in-depth analysis. However, the advancement of AI technology is moving towards a new era, one characterized by efficiency, precision, and cost-effectiveness. AI-powered tools are capable of automating and streamlining the document creation process, providing an array of benefits such as increased productivity, and reduced operational costs. Till now, integration of AI in corporate law firms is not without its complexities. The adoption of AI-generated legal documents led to questions regarding data privacy, quality control, and the evolving role of legal professionals in the document drafting process. As AI takes on more of the traditional tasks, the role of lawyers is shifting from mere document generators to strategic advisors who leverage technology to provide higher-value services to their clients(Armour & Sako, 2020).

This article sets out to comprehensively explore the opportunities and challenges that AIgenerated legal documents present for corporate law firms. By carefully examining realworld examples, and the latest research in the field, we aim to provide a comprehensive understanding of this transformative technology. Furthermore, this article offers practical recommendations and strategies to help corporate law firms effectively navigate this new landscape, ensuring they harness the potential of AI while holding the standards of excellence, integrity, and client trust that hold up the legal profession (Foster & Lawson, 2018).

2.0 BACKGROUND AND OBJECTIVE OF STUDY

This chapter explores the integration of AI-generated legal documents in corporate law firms, which is a significant departure from traditional practices, discussing the opportunities, such as increased productivity and cost-effectiveness, as well as challenges, including data privacy and quality control. The evolving role of legal practitioners in a technology-driven legal environment is a key concern (Koltys, 1992)(Naik et al., 2022)(Reier Forradellas & Garay Gallastegui, 2021). The chapter aims to provide insights, analysis, and practical recommendations for corporate law firms to effectively navigate this transformative landscape while balancing traditional legal values with AI efficiencies, encompassing comprehensive analysis of the advantages and disadvantages associated with this technological shift (McKeown et al., 2020). Our objectives include:

- Identifying the key opportunities that AI-generated legal documents bring to corporate law firms, including increased efficiency, cost-effectiveness, and enhanced accuracy.
- Exploring the challenges and concerns that arise with the integration of AI, such as data privacy issues, quality control, and the evolving role of lawyers in the document creation process.
- Offering practical insights and recommendations for corporate law firms to effectively navigate and harness the potential of AI-generated legal documents while addressing associated challenges.

3.0 REVIEW OF LITERATURE:

3.1 Overview of AI-Generated Legal Documents

AI-generated legal documents are revolutionizing the production of legal documents for corporate law firms. Artificial intelligence (AI) systems create these documents by analyzing substantial data, extracting pertinent information, and crafting customized legal documents tailored to clients' specific needs and preferences (Buey et al., 2016)("Use of Artificial Intelligence in Legal Practice," 2023) ("Stepping into the Future," 2023). Compared to traditional methods of legal document production, AI-generated legal documents offer several advantages, including the reduction of human errors, time and cost savings, improved consistency and quality, and enhanced client satisfaction. AI-generated legal documents encompass a wide range of document types, including contracts, agreements, letters, memos, reports, and filings, and they find application in various domains, such as mergers and acquisitions, corporate governance, compliance, litigation, and intellectual property (Hearn, 2022)("AI for Lawyers Guide," n.d.).

3.2 Functions of AI in Legal Industry

AI generates legal documents with the help of AI-driven software, either partially or completely. This technology covers a range of functions, from automating the assembly of standard legal documents to analyzing complex legal texts.

Figure 1. Functions of AI in Legal Industry

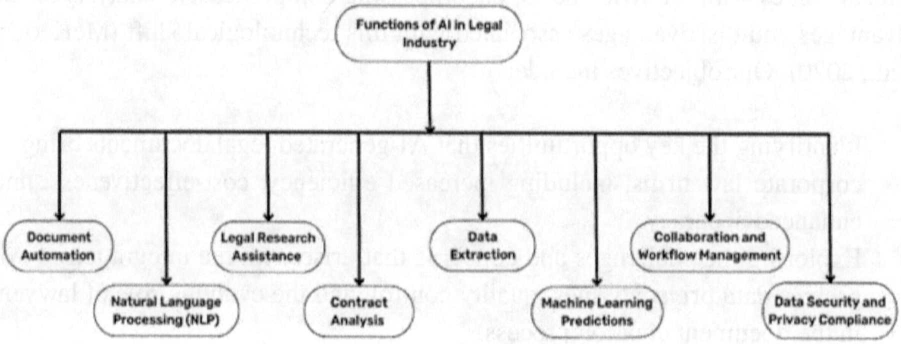

3.3 Need For AI In Corporate Law Firms

The integration of AI-generated legal documents offers corporate law firms a host of compelling benefits:

1. **Increased Efficiency and Time Savings** – By utilizing AI, corporate law firms can speed up creating legal documents. Lawyers and paralegals can draft documents more quickly and with fewer errors. This automation of routine tasks means that legal professionals can redirect their time and energy toward high-value strategic work, ultimately increasing their overall productivity.
2. **Enhanced Accuracy and Consistency** – AI technology guarantees a remarkable level of accuracy and consistency in the production of legal documents. It has the capability to cross-reference extensive legal databases to spot potential errors, disparities, or omissions. This helps in reducing the likelihood of costly legal disputes or the need for extensive document revisions.

3. **Cost-Effectiveness and Reduced Overhead** – Implementing AI-powered document generation tools can lead to significant cost savings for corporate law firms. This encompasses reduced labor costs, resource savings, and decreased expenditure associated with manual document creation. AI empowers firms to handle larger workloads with a more streamlined and cost-effective workforce.

In essence, the adoption of AI in document generation not only accelerates and refines the legal document creation process but also introduces substantial economic advantages. It streamlines legal operations, minimizes human errors, and significantly trims operational costs, making it an asset for corporate law firms looking to enhance their efficiency and competitiveness.

Table 1. 4.0 Applications In Corporate Law And Firms [9-10]

Application	Description	Example
Contract Review	The proposed approach streamlines contract review by using natural language processing and machine learning to automatically extract key contract information. It then compares this data with best practices and industry standards, identifying potential issues and generating risk scores for each provision. The system highlights areas needing attention or negotiation and suggests revisions to enhance contract clarity and enforceability. This method reduces time and cost, while also improving the overall quality and consistency of contracts.	LawGeex, Kira Systems
Legal Research	One possible application of artificial intelligence is to assist lawyers and legal researchers in finding relevant information from a large corpus of legal documents. By using natural language processing and machine learning techniques, an AI system can analyze the user's query, understand the context and intent, and retrieve the most pertinent results from various sources, such as statutes, case law, journals, etc. This can save time and resources, as well as improve the quality and accuracy of legal research.	ROSS Intelligence, Westlaw Edge
Document Drafting and Analysis	The task of a legal assistant is to assist in drafting legal documents, creating templates, and analyzing documents for legal implications. This involves researching relevant laws and regulations, formatting and proofreading the documents, and ensuring compliance with legal standards. A legal assistant may also help with filing, organizing, and maintaining the documents in a secure and accessible manner.	Contract Express, Legal Robot

Table 2

Due Diligence	**A document scanning and interpretation system streamlines due diligence by automatically analyzing documents, identifying potential issues, and flagging inconsistencies, risks, or liabilities using natural language processing and machine learning. This approach make due diligence more efficient and accurate, saving time and resources for all parties involved in the transaction.**	**Luminance, Diligen**
Predictive Analysis	an innovative approach to predict legal outcomes using deep learning and natural language processing. The system has been designed, implemented, and evaluated on a substantial dataset of civil cases from US courts. The system demonstrates high accuracy, reliability, and provides explanations for its predictions. The paper also touches on potential applications, limitations, and the ethical considerations of using AI in legal decision-making.	Lex Machina
Intellectual Property Management	Managing and identifying intellectual property rights (IPR) in research involves conducting a thorough literature review, obtaining permissions or licenses, documenting sources and data with their IPR status, and applying suitable licenses to research outputs to facilitate dissemination and reuse while respecting original IPR.	TrademarkNow

5.0 CHALLENGES FOR CORPORATE LAW FIRMS

As corporate law firms embrace the potential benefits of AI-generated legal documents, they are simultaneously confronted with a series of complex challenges that require careful consideration and management. These challenges encompass the following:

1. **Data Privacy and Security Concerns** – One of the foremost challenges facing corporate law firms in the age of AI is the issue of data privacy and security. AI-powered tools, while incredibly efficient, can also be susceptible to data breaches. This vulnerability can lead to the exposure of highly sensitive and confidential information, a matter of utmost concern in the legal industry where client confidentiality is sacrosanct. When using AI tools that involve the collection and analysis of personal data, law firms must be diligent in ensuring compliance with data protection regulations and the safeguarding of individual privacy rights.
2. **Potential Bias and Lack of Human Judgment** – AI systems are only as good as the data they are trained on. If these systems are not designed and trained meticulously, they can inadvertently perpetuate biases and discrimination. This raises concerns about the fairness of the outcomes and the potential for legal challenges. Lawyers must have confidence that the AI systems they employ are accurate and reliable. Achieving this trust requires transparency and credibil-

ity in the datasets used by AI systems. Additionally, the use of AI in the legal realm sparks ethical questions, such as the risk of AI being used to perpetuate inequality and infringe upon personal privacy.

3. **Quality Control and Accuracy Verification** – Lawyers are bound by a professional duty to remain informed about changes in the law, including the benefits and risks associated with relevant technologies. When lawyers use artificial intelligence, this responsibility extends to understanding not only how AI functions but also ensuring the accuracy of the results it produces. Lawyers must be vigilant to ensure that their use of AI systems does not compromise client confidentiality or violate legal or ethical obligations. This necessitates a deep understanding of data protection laws and best practices for information security.
4. **Ethical and Legal Implications** – The incorporation of AI into the legal industry ushers in a myriad of ethical and legal complexities. Questions pertaining to liability, regulation, and intellectual property must be thoughtfully addressed. The legal profession must proactively confront the challenges and opportunities brought about by AI. It is essential to recognize that AI is not a threat but rather an opportunity for lawyers to focus on intricate legal issues and deliver high-quality services to their clients.
5. **Impact on the Role of Lawyers** – The successful integration of AI in the legal domain demands that lawyers adapt to new technologies and evolving work methodologies. Law firms may even transform into tech-savvy entities, developing their own AI tools to offer as "Artificial Intelligence as a Service." Firms that harness these powerful tools stand to gain in terms of efficiency and accuracy while broadening their service offerings. In this changing landscape, firms must position themselves as providers who can leverage AI tools effectively and offer distinctly human abilities that AI cannot replicate. These human qualities will continue to be the cornerstone of a lawyer's value in the evolving legal landscape.

6.0 OPPORTUNITIES FOR CORPORATE LAW FIRMS

AI-generated legal documents are a promising application of natural language processing and machine learning for corporate law and firms. By using AI models to generate, analyze, and summarize legal documents, corporate law firms can benefit from several opportunities, such as:

1. **Streamlined Document Drafting and Reviewing Process –** AI models can help lawyers' draft contracts, agreements, and other legal documents faster and more accurately, by using natural language understanding and generation techniques. AI models can also help lawyers review and compare documents, by identifying inconsistencies, errors, and potential risks.
2. **Enhanced client service and satisfaction –** AI models can help lawyers provide better and more personalized service to their clients, by generating tailored and customized legal documents that meet their specific needs and preferences. AI models can also help lawyers communicate more effectively with their clients, by summarizing complex legal documents into plain language and providing relevant insights and recommendations.
3. **Improved risk management and compliance –** AI models can help lawyers manage and mitigate legal risks, by detecting and alerting them of any changes in laws, regulations, or policies that may affect their clients or cases. AI models can also help lawyers ensure compliance with ethical and professional standards, by monitoring and auditing their work and conduct.
4. **Leveraging big data for insights and strategic decision-making –** AI models can help lawyers leverage the vast amount of data available in the legal domain, by extracting, organizing, and analyzing relevant information from various sources, such as court cases, precedents, statutes, journals, etc. AI models can also help lawyers use data-driven insights to support their arguments, strategies, and decisions.
5. **Faster turnaround time –** AI-powered tools in the legal field is that they can help lawyers achieve faster turnaround times for their clients. This is especially important for corporate clients who operate in a fast-paced and competitive business environment, where delays can have serious consequences. AI-powered tools can automate the generation and review of legal documents, such as contracts, agreements, and memos, saving time and resources for both lawyers and clients. Additionally, AI-powered tools can provide insights and analysis on legal issues, such as compliance, risk, and strategy, enabling lawyers to make informed and timely decisions. By using AI-powered tools, lawyers can deliver high-quality and efficient legal services to their corporate clients, enhancing their reputation and satisfaction.

7.0 BEST PRACTICES AND RECOMMENDATIONS

Amidst the opportunities and challenges that AI-generated legal documents present, it's crucial for corporate law firms to adopt best practices and implement key recommendations to navigate this transformative landscape effectively.

1. **Ensuring High Standards of Data Protection –** Corporate law firms must ensure high standards of data protection to address the challenges of data privacy and security. This requires the careful evaluation of AI tools and platforms that comply with rigorous security criteria. For example, firms should choose AI solutions that use end-to-end encryption, multi-factor authentication, and cloud-based storage. Firms must also establish internal guidelines that protect client data, use encryption, and perform regular security checks to reduce the risk of data leaks. For example, firms should limit access to sensitive data, train staff on data protection best practices, and monitor data usage and activity.
2. **Ensuring Transparency and Explain ability –** Transparency and explaining ability are essential for building trust in AI systems. Corporate law firms that use AI tools should be able to access clear and comprehensible explanations for how the AI systems make their decisions and recommendations. This transparency not only fosters confidence in the technology among the users, but also enables lawyers to understand the logic and rationale behind the AI-generated outcomes and to challenge them when necessary. Transparency and explain ability are also important for complying with ethical and legal standards and for avoiding potential biases and errors in AI systems.
3. **Incorporating Human Oversight and Review –** AI can improve productivity, but it cannot replace lawyers' judgment and expertise. Corporate law firms need to have procedures for human oversight and review of AI-generated legal documents. Lawyers need to stay involved in the document creation process, making sure that AI-generated documents meet legal standards and client requirements. For example, an AI-generated contract may not capture the nuances of the parties' intentions or may contain errors that could affect its validity. A lawyer should review the contract carefully and make any necessary changes before signing it.
4. **Maintaining Professional and Ethical Standards –** Some ethical standards for lawyers include honesty, integrity, competence, diligence, loyalty, confidentiality, and respect for the law and the rights of others. These standards apply regardless of whether lawyers use AI or not. When using AI to generate documents, lawyers must ensure that they uphold these standards and comply with their legal obligations. This means that they must check that the documents are consistent with the applicable laws and regulations, and that they protect the privacy of their clients.
5. **Continuous Education and Adaptation –** AI technology is constantly changing and improving, so corporate law firms need to keep up with the latest developments and trends. Lawyers should seek out opportunities to learn new skills and update their knowledge of AI applications and challenges in the legal domain. Firms can create platforms for sharing best practices and insights on how to use

AI effectively and ethically in their work. By doing so, lawyers can enhance their performance and competitiveness in the AI era.

By implementing these best practices and recommendations, corporate law firms can effectively harness the benefits of AI-generated legal documents while addressing the challenges. This proactive approach enables firms to maintain the highest standards of professionalism, data security, and ethical conduct, ensuring that AI complements, rather than replaces, the expertise of legal professionals.

8.0 CONCLUSION

AI-generated legal documents are a game-changer for corporate law firms, a new era for the legal industry. This article provided a comprehensive overview of the various aspects of AI in corporate law, examining the opportunities and challenges it brings.

AI can transform the practice of law by simplifying document creation, enhancing accuracy, cutting costs, and allowing lawyers to offer better client services. However, these benefits are not without complexity. The challenges include data privacy and security issues, potential bias and lack of human judgment, quality control and accuracy verification, ethical and legal implications, and the changing role of lawyers. Corporate law firms can successfully navigate this new landscape by following best practices and recommendations.

By following suggestive recommendations, corporate law firms can leverage the potential of AI technology while upholding the highest standards of professionalism and ethics. In this way, they ensure that AI complements and enhances the expertise of legal professionals, ultimately improving the quality of legal services provided to clients.

REFERENCES

'AI for Lawyers Guide: Do Artificial Attorneys Dream of Electric Practice?' (*RSS*) <https://growlawfirm.com/blog/ai-for-lawyers-guide> accessed 23 October 2023

Armour, J., & Sako, M. (2020). AI-enabled business models in legal services: From traditional law firms to next-generation law companies? *Journal of Professions and Organization*, 7(1), 27–46.

Buey, M. G., Garrido, A. L., Bobed, C., & Ilarri, S. (2016, February). The AIS project: Boosting information extraction from legal documents by using ontologies. In *ICAART (2)* (pp. 438-445).

Editor's Introduction'. (1995). 3. *Artificial Intelligence and Law*, •••, 1.

Foster, W. E., & Lawson, A. L. (2017). When to Praise the Machine: The Promise and Perils of Automated Transactional Drafting. *South Carolina Law Review*, 69, 597.

Hearn, J. (2022). 'A Library is a Growing Organism': Redefining Artificial Intelligence and the Role of the Information Professional in the Corporate Legal World. *Legal Information Management*, 22(2), 81–87.

Koltys, H. (1992). CORPORATE COUNSEL CUT COSTS WITH AI: Legal Knowledge-Based Systems. *Information Systems Management*, 9(1), 82–85.

McKeown, T., Mustafina, J., Magizov, R., & Gataullina, C. (2020, December). AI in law practices. In *2020 13th International Conference on Developments in eSystems Engineering (DeSE)* (pp. 27-32). IEEE.

Naik, N., Hameed, B. Z., Shetty, D. K., Swain, D., Shah, M., Paul, R., & Somani, B. K. (2022). Legal and ethical consideration in artificial intelligence in healthcare: Who takes responsibility? *Frontiers in Surgery*, 9, 862322.

Reier Forradellas RF and Garay Gallastegui LM, 'Digital Transformation and Artificial Intelligence Applied to Business: Legal Regulations, Economic Impact and Perspective' (2021) 10 Laws 70

Migliorini, S., & Moreira, J. I. (2024). The case for nurturing AI literacy in Law schools. *Asian Journal of Legal Education*, 23220058241265613.

Chapter 5
Countering Hate and Toxic Speech Online and Explainable Artificial Intelligence: State-Legal Recourse Lensing Detection, Debunking, and Solutions in the Digital Era

Bhupinder Singh
https://orcid.org/0009-0006-4779-2553
Sharda University, India

Christian Kaunert
https://orcid.org/0000-0002-4493-2235
Dublin City University, Ireland

ABSTRACT

The proliferation of online hate speech has emerged as one of the most pressing global concerns today, corroding digital communication and undermining security within various communities. This paper broadens the context to understand computers from legal perspective, and more specifically Explainable Artificial Intelligence (XAI), can be amalgamated using a new host of detecting tools against online hate speech. This chapter is significant because of its potential to inform policies and regulations aimed at reducing the toxicity while preserving freedom using a well-rounded multidisciplinary approach. The goal is to pinpoint specific problems and suggest ways in which these issues might be addressed (if at all), while also exploring

DOI: 10.4018/979-8-3693-7205-0.ch005

questions about the best most just or perhaps least unjust ethical frameworks for new methods of addiction detection and regulation on online platforms.

1. INTRODUCTION

Online hate speech is a difficult term to define, given that it is usually either highly localized or subjective (Chakraborty & Masud, 2022). There may not be a the universal definition because what constitutes hate speech can differ across cultures, legal systems or among platforms (Singh & Kaunert, 2024) (Trott et al., 2020). Applying the Concept of Free Speech (Freedoms) to Hate-Speech But also, there is a thin line running between free speech and hate-speech which has sparked heavier and further larger scale debates across many nations. In the following section, we take a more detailed look at online hate speech forms of racism or sexism as well in relation to individual situations and implications (Chang & Lerman, 2023). It also looks into how social media platforms influence speech, the reach of algorithms and issues running content moderation at scale. Through a deeper understanding of what hate speech is by this new method to define, the discussion on legal and technological solutions will be better-informed (Singh et al., 2024) (Thomas et al., 2021).

Figure 1. shares the Dimensions of Introduction Section (Source- Original)

1.1 Background and Relevance

As hate and toxic speech is spreading increasingly in the digital world, this has created a huge problem to which cannot be replied by just having better technological solutions but also appropriate legal framework. It now has come to a point where social media is being used as battleground and, spread of hate speech on online platform threatens individual safety, societal cohesion and democratic values. Solving this will rest in the combination of state-legal redress and technological developments. This approach can improve the identification and debunking of hoaxes, as well as resolve harm caused by misinformation while upholding legal accountability standards and addressing ethical concerns. Online safeguards into the legal frameworks for social media that vary so much around the world, from countries with strict hate-speech laws (like Germany) to those which have effectively enshrined free speech on platforms as a human right in their constitutions (Bowker & Ophoff, 2022). Whichever alternative is stronger, any successful legal response must be nimble in the face of new challenges presented by a world where content can spread at unprecedented speed. The inherently global nature of the internet also tests civilization's ability to enforce laws uniformly. And this is where technology comes into play especially XAI (Explainable AI) (Wachs et al., 2022).

2. ONLINE HATE SPEECH: UNDERSTANDING CONCEPT

Online hate speech is defined as the decision to hire a translator based on an intermediary service through digital communication: for instance, online translation services. This examplifies a wide variety of harmful behavior; from outright threats or insults, to more covert (but equally valid!) forms of persecution like distributing false stereotypes and inciting violence. Online hate speech is a multifaceted concept, crossing lines between issues of free expression and cultural standards. The main problem with online hate speech is the vagueness of its conceptual borders. Hate speech, however, takes on a very wide range of meanings across all legal systems, and certainly cultures and platforms. Hate speech is almost impossible to define unilaterally what's considered free in one country may be illegal in another. The digital nature of tools also extends the visibility and power hate speech has in distributing harmful messages quickly across state borders (Yimam et al., 2024).

Second, online hate speech scales because it is also anonymous which empowers people, if only to act out what they might never say at public meetings. Not only did the social media algorithms push toxic narratives, but they further popularise them and spread it to a wider audience (Azumah et al., 2024). It is important to comprehend the nature of online hate speech in creating solutions against it. Through understanding this diversity and contextual factors that influence its presentation, policy makers across platforms can help us to develop a healthier environment for everyone interacting digitally (Singh & Kaunert, 2024). Linking XAI with legal frameworks can also better facilitate the debunking of false narratives typically paired up by hate speech. XAI can also work by providing understandable counter-narratives to help debunk misinformation and promote factual narratives (Griffin, 2022). For instance, if a piece of content is flagged for racist xenophobia XAI can generate an explanation that says what parts were wrong and also include the proper facts. This proactive form of debunking can limit these toxic ideas and thereby decrease the hit they place on susceptible populations. It is a promising answer within detect and stop the sarcasm online complexity, providing well-behaved out-of-the-box accuracy (without weight balancing), for identifying those complex words of hate (Munn, 2020). AI is a "black box" Traditional AI model making decisions provides no obvious explanation for their formation This lack of visibility, Observation reinforces our accountability concerns primarily when it comes to using AI systems in such sensitive verticals as content moderation (Singh, 2024). XAI solves these issues by doing its best to make possible for any users, developers or even regulators learning how was result achieved and decisions were made. As an application, in the field of online hate speech detection XAI can lead to accurate interpretation for posts or comments being judged as toxic. Explainable AI helps hold explanations behind tips via transparent reasons, building trust in AI systems while ensuring they work underneath the regulation (AlEmadi & Zaghouani, 2024).

Figure 2. displays the Reasons for Hate and Toxic Speech Online (Source- Original)

The transparency of XAI can help to adapt legal solution in concrete contexts. XAI can help in ensuring a judge or legal professional to have an insight as how AI systems would evaluate hate speech thus better preparing them while going into the legal proceeding (Anjum & Katarya, 2024). The encroaching partnership of the legal system as a regulatory force and XAI systems allow for content moderation technique regulation justified under law which is paramount in preventing too much overreaching or censorship (Halevy et al., 2021). XAI can enable auditing AI systems for bias to make sure that hate-speech detection is fair and does not over target one community or race. The promise of XAI for combatting online hate speech is great, but it does carry with it a number of challenges. Balancing this equation the design of XAI systems in as much it would not jeopardize user privacy and yet still be transparent, is delicate (Singh & Kaunert, 2024). The deployment of XAI should be followed by ongoing monitoring and updates to evolve with ever changing landscape in online conversations. Hate speech changes and the tools to prevent it need to change too (Warner et al., 2024).

It can be said that in digital age battling online hate and nefarious speech is a multifaceted approach combining state-legal remedy with advances like Explainable Artificial Intelligence (Mozafari et al., 2020). Increasing its discovery, detection and debunking as well in observance of law is where XAI can be a game changer making online spaces safer yet not at the cost of justice equals fairness. But for tech solutions like these to be effective, cooperation and coordination between technologists, lawyers and policymakers needs not just start with technology but will need ongoing collaboration as the channels through which hate is expressed online evolve (Nguyen et al., 2024).

3. LEGAL FRAMEWORKS

International legal frameworks are perhaps the broadest way to look at online hate speech regulation. Answering how to stop hate speech cannot exclude the norms existing in international laws that include, perhaps most importantly for the purposes of this study. It also are examined role of International Agencies such UN, EU through standards and cooperation with member states (Scheuerman et al., 2021). The issues considered under this heading are challenges around bringing legal frameworks in line across jurisdictions, especially given that identifying what is actually unlawful content can transcend national borders with such ease these days. This section, therefore, uses international perspectives to determine best practices and unfilled gaps in extant legal frameworks setting the stage for future inquiry on domestic legal redress involving XAI (Singh, 2023).

International legal frameworks provide a global overview of the problem, while domestic laws offer definite methods about how hate speech is controlled in individual country. This part examine the extent to which different States have aligned their legal approaches with international standards by considering cultural, social and political dynamics (Hangarthner et al., 2021). It looks at case studies from the US, Germany, India and Australia to show how different parts of the world approach this as with some who go as far as giving life sentences for corresponding offences versus others who look more towards a free speech type framework. It also looks at the ways in which national courts and prosecutors address these laws, before discussing how jurisdiction is dealt with considering an online globalized internet. This section demonstrates the critical role of context-specific legal redress in effectively combating online hate speech without undermining local values and norms, through tailored solutions at national level (Thomas et al., 2022).

Figure 3. specifies the Points on Controlling Mechanism on Online Hate and Toxic Speech (Source- Original)

4. EXPLAINING ARTIFICIAL INTELLIGENCE: COUNTERING HATE AND TOXIC SPEECH ONLINE

In the fight against online hate speech, explainable Artificial Intelligence (XAI) is emerging as an essential tool. In contrast to other AI models which functions as a "black box", XAI offers explanation and interpreation, thus allow humans the capability of understanding why decisions were made so. This part discusses the role of XAI for detecting and analyzing hate speech, illustrating its capacity to give explanations about how it performs classes or makes decisions (Singh, 2023). It does this by opening up the opaque decision processes of AI, for XAI hold great potential to build trust with users and regulators that only well behaved decisions are made. The section also considers the current technical barriers to achieving effective XAI on a large scale, as well as whether household AI systems are equipped with ethical functionalities stable enough for market adoption in hate speech detection algorithms. This section makes a specific feature of XAI in the wider narrative about online hate speech, namely that transparency is crucial for AI-driven solutions (Casula et al., 2021).

4.1 Artificial Intelligence Intermediate: Mitigating Hate and Toxic Speech Online

Artificial Intelligence (AI) has become a powerful tool in the preservation of hate and toxic speech online. The key issue wariness pertains to the spread of harmful content via digital platforms, as they continue both to grow and shape public dialog (Rossini, 2020). Hate Speech and toxic online behavior can have real-world consequences, from violence and discrimination to the unravelling of social cohesion. Fortunately, AI provides some hope to help identify and both correct or minimize the effect of this content. But what will help us tackle online hate speech is delving closely into the same toolbox & mechanics of AI, albeit a complex subject purely from transparency and ethical lenses (Singh, 2024).

4.2 How can AI Detect Hate Speech

AI systems in general and machine learning-based systems have illustrated considerable potential to label hate speech at scale. AI can sort through massive amounts of data to find those patterns, language cues and behaviors that signal harmful content (Dom et al., 2024). These aligns are particular training functions that have been trained within a development model on hate speech samples, which helps them recognize equivalent real-world information. This ability to quickly process and make sense of data can be incredibly valuable when you're managing a platform with millions (or billions) of users, sharing an overwhelming amount of content (Corazza et al., 2020).

This process of detection is completed with the help of NLP (Natural Language Processing) which is a subfield in AI. NLP allows AI to understand and interpret human language, with all the nuances, slang, and context present in what often constitutes hate speech (Ullmann & Tomalin, 2023). For instance, AI is capable of recognising racial slurs or sexist comments even it they are coded in language and memes. AI can also evolve alongside new types of hate speech as it emerges, ensuring detection methods do not become out-of-date. In fact, AI is so good at detecting hate speech that it seems almost impossible to beat the system but one of the clear shortcomings with traditional AI systems (Biswas, & Paul, 2020). This lack of clarity can cause mistrust from users, regulators and platform operators especially when AI systems inadvertently flag content as malicious or over-index on certain groups. XAI improves AI models by providing intelligence to its decision-making processes. In the context of hate speech moderation for example, XAI allows to provide reasons why specific content is flagged and thus helps users as well as administrators understand AI more so that they know what it does in terms explaining its actions. For example, XAI might report that a post was flagged because of the language prevelance associated with hate speech or other behaviorial similarities to previous complaints (Singh et al., 2024).

The transparency behind this is really important for couple of reasons. It helps establish trust for AI systems, as users can now be confident that moderation is being conducted in a fair and unbiased manner. Second, this allows for more granular content moderation what humans can request the rationale behind and fill in some blanks that an AI might have missed. It also helps regulators confirm AI agents comply with legal standards and do not cause the injuries to freedom of speech (Huang et al., 2024).

While AI-powered systems may hold promise in this regard, there are several issues to tackle before these can be effective at preventing hate speech. For example, the risk of AI systems being biased is a key concern. The models are only going to be as good as the data they are trained on, and in a face-mask scenario as fear this can lead to biased results (Zhao et al., 2022). If the training data is biased, then AI may reflect that bias and make unjust calls or unwelcoming judgment. For example, it may incorrectly over- flag content from particular demographic groups due to lack of diverse training data. Thus, it is extremely important to train AI systems on diverse and representative data sets. The second challenge that is presented by hate speech, specifically how it changes (Kiritchenko et al., 2021). The account is keen to call out whoever it finds spewing online hate speech (which is also quite sneaky considering that the column will be rendered outdated in a matter of mere months as new glitches are found). These AI systems need to always be updated and improved upon due to these changes. Similarly, the global nature of online platforms implies that AI also needs to be able account for hate speech in different languages, cultures and contexts making it even harder (Singh & Kaunert, 2024). It is difficult to strike a compromise between free speech and regulation. Because artificial intelligence can also block out legitimate content, there is a danger of overreach. And while XAI can help this risk by shedding light on the background and letting people question decisions, AI programs are going to be required when it comes to determining how systems learn so that they maintain a healthy level of opacity (Singh et al., 2024).

The future of AI for combatting online hate speech is not only a technological solution but embracing the idea that change can be achieved collectively by developing this new technology in parallel with discussing legal and ethical aspects (Lupu et al., 2023). Over time, AI will evolve such that it can recognize and counter hate speech yet with ongoing tweaks required as outlined above. In addition, meaningful cooperation between tech companies on the one hand and regulators together with civil society will be critical to assure that AI systems are developed in a responsible way (Singh et al., 2024). AI has a lot of potential to be used in fighting against online hate and toxicity. Using advanced detection methods, constant improvement via learning algorithms and the visibility introduced by Explainable AI makes such solutions pivotal in improving online safety. To realize this potential in practice, AI will need to solve for bias, changing notions of hate speech, and navigating a delicate balance with free expression (Saha et al., 2023).

5. LEGAL FRAMEWORKS AND XAI WILL IMPROVE DETECTION AND DEBUNKING

The fusion of legal frameworks with XAI provides a plausible solution to more effectively detect and tackle online hate speech (Srba et al., 2021). The section will delve into using XAI to ensure legal compliance, which entails ensuring that the explanations provided are clear and interpretable objective reasons why a content moderation decision aligns with not only platform policy but also meets each relevant specific legal standard. It also includes the idea of practical application for XAI, where it is possible to ascertain whether some content may violate hate speech or not (Singh, 2024). The section also explores how XAI can be used to refute mis/disinformation driving hate speech starting from accurate, explainable counter-narratives. The integration of XAI and legal frameworks is thus advocated in this section for a unified technology-driven or proprietor approach against online hate speech, enabled by both technological disruption and competency coming from the domain of law (Nascimento et al., 2022).

Using AI, particularly in more serious areas like bias-free online hate speech detection triggers new ethical concerns. However, this section discusses a few of the ethical challenges which can occur as a result to using AI in legal contexts be limiting bias, discrimination and automation where system is over relied on. Along with that, it sets out to questioned the ethical implications of explainability vis-a-vis trade-offs stayed among transparency and privacy (Nguyen, 2024). The section turns to broader societal consequences of AI-driven content moderation upon free speech and democratic discourse. This section reinforces the need to consider these ethical concerns while using AI so that it can be used safely in appropriate legal frameworks which minimize harm and optimize benefit (Ali, 2024).

6. CHALLENGES AND OPPORTUNITIES: COMPLEX LANDSCAPE TO NAVIGATE

The space where artificial intelligence meets law and hate speech online is a dark forest with many signposts pointing in different directions. This part highlights the major obstacles to face such as, an appropriate legal framework could hardly by universally applicable, limitations of available AI technologies and unexpected side effects (Azumah et al., 2024). It also considers some of the benefits that come with this convergence AI can be used not only to help make legal processes more efficient but is now necessary for understanding even basic forms of online content and making those platforms themselves safer (Warner et al., 2024). The section makes a case that understanding this sturdy infrastructure will take multiple approach track and cross-fertilisation between technologists, lawyers with the support of policymakers to academics and civil society. By empirically mapping challenges and opportunities, the section affords broader insights on how to develop future inquiries in light of both (Anjum, & Katarya, 2024).

7. CONCLUSIONS AND FUTURE SCOPE

The chapter shed light on how legal frameworks and XAI can meet in order to address online hate speech, painting a picture of promise but also problems related thereto. The last section discusses these findings while stressing the need for a more balanced approach to regulation that combines legal, technological and ethical considerations. Second, in addition to pointing out ongoing needs for international cooperation and development of new generations of XAI models that are more suitable for performing legal functions again with reference to the future outlook, it suggests some avenues along which this work could progress. In the end, we must continue to approach this as a problem that is only about innovation and working together since it continues to not be addressed by simply providing an after-the-fact response.

REFERENCES

AlEmadi, M. M., & Zaghouani, W. (2024, May). Emotional Toll and Coping Strategies: Navigating the Effects of Annotating Hate Speech Data. In *Proceedings of the Workshop on Legal and Ethical Issues in Human Language Technologies@ LREC-COLING 2024* (pp. 66-72).

Ali, S. (2024). *Youth, social media, and online safety: a holistic approach towards detecting and mitigating risks in online conversations* (Doctoral dissertation).

Anjum, & Katarya, R. (2024). Hate speech, toxicity detection in online social media: a recent survey of state of the art and opportunities. *International Journal of Information Security, 23*(1), 577-608.

Anjum, & Katarya, R. (2024). Hate speech, toxicity detection in online social media: a recent survey of state of the art and opportunities. *International Journal of Information Security, 23*(1), 577-608.

Azumah, S. W., Elsayed, N., ElSayed, Z., Ozer, M., & La Guardia, A. (2024). Deep Learning Approaches for Detecting Adversarial Cyberbullying and Hate Speech in Social Networks. *arXiv preprint arXiv:2406.17793.*

Azumah, S. W., Elsayed, N., ElSayed, Z., Ozer, M., & La Guardia, A. (2024). Deep Learning Approaches for Detecting Adversarial Cyberbullying and Hate Speech in Social Networks. *arXiv preprint arXiv:2406.17793.*

Biswas, P., & Paul, C. (2020). Review paper on hate speech inside the context of online social networks. [TURCOMAT]. *Turkish Journal of Computer and Mathematics Education*, 11(1), 352–365.

Bowker, J., & Ophoff, J. (2022, July). Reducing exposure to hateful speech online. In *Science and Information Conference* (pp. 630-645). Cham: Springer International Publishing.

Casula, P., Anupam, A., & Parvin, N. (2021, June). "We found no violation!": Twitter's Violent Threats Policy and Toxicity in Online Discourse. In *Proceedings of the 10th International Conference on Communities & Technologies-Wicked Problems in the Age of Tech* (pp. 151-159).

Chakraborty, T., & Masud, S. (2022). Nipping in the bud: detection, diffusion and mitigation

Chang, R. C., May, J., & Lerman, K. (2023, September). Feedback Loops and Complex Dynamics of Harmful Speech in Online Discussions. In *International Conference on Social Computing, Behavioral-Cultural Modeling and Prediction and Behavior Representation in Modeling and Simulation* (pp. 85-94). Cham: Springer Nature Switzerland. DOI: 10.1007/978-3-031-43129-6_9

Chaudhary, M., Saxena, C., & Meng, H. (2021). Countering online hate speech: An nlp perspective. *arXiv preprint arXiv:2109.02941*.

Corazza, M., Menini, S., Cabrio, E., Tonelli, S., & Villata, S. (2020). A multilingual evaluation for online hate speech detection. *ACM Transactions on Internet Technology*, 20(2), 1–22. DOI: 10.1145/3377323

Costa, S., da Silva, B. M., & Tavares, M. (2021, December). Tackling online hate speech? play your role! In *International Conference on ArtsIT, Interactivity and Game Creation* (pp. 79-93). Cham: Springer International Publishing.

. de los Riscos, A. M., & D'Haro, L. F. (2021). Toxicbot: A conversational agent to fight online hate speech. *Conversational dialogue systems for the next decade*, 15-30.

Dorn, R., Kezar, L., Morstatter, F., & Lerman, K. (2024). Harmful Speech Detection by Language Models Exhibits Gender-Queer Dialect Bias. *arXiv preprint arXiv:2406.00020*. DOI: 10.1145/3689904.3694704

Garg, T., Masud, S., Suresh, T., & Chakraborty, T. (2023). Handling bias in toxic speech detection: A survey. *ACM Computing Surveys*, 55(13s), 1–32. DOI: 10.1145/3580494

Griffin, R. (2022). New school speech regulation as a regulatory strategy against hate speech on social media: The case of Germany's NetzDG. *Telecommunications Policy*, 46(9), 102411. DOI: 10.1016/j.telpol.2022.102411

Halevy, M., Harris, C., Bruckman, A., Yang, D., & Howard, A. (2021, October). Mitigating racial biases in toxic language detection with an equity-based ensemble framework. In *Proceedings of the 1st ACM Conference on Equity and Access in Algorithms, Mechanisms, and Optimization* (pp. 1-11). DOI: 10.1145/3465416.3483299

Hangartner, D., Gennaro, G., Alasiri, S., Bahrich, N., Bornhoft, A., Boucher, J., Demirci, B. B., Derksen, L., Hall, A., Jochum, M., Munoz, M. M., Richter, M., Vogel, F., Wittwer, S., Wüthrich, F., Gilardi, F., & Donnay, K. (2021). Empathy-based counterspeech can reduce racist hate speech in a social media field experiment. *Proceedings of the National Academy of Sciences of the United States of America*, 118(50), e2116310118. DOI: 10.1073/pnas.2116310118 PMID: 34873046

Huang, E. J., Sarma, A., Hwang, S., Chandrasekharan, E., & Chancellor, S. (2024, July). Opportunities, tensions, and challenges in computational approaches to addressing online harassment. In *Proceedings of the 2024 ACM Designing Interactive Systems Conference* (pp. 1483-1498). DOI: 10.1145/3643834.3661623

Huang, E. J., Sarma, A., Hwang, S., Chandrasekharan, E., & Chancellor, S. (2024, July). Opportunities, tensions, and challenges in computational approaches to addressing online harassment. In *Proceedings of the 2024 ACM Designing Interactive Systems Conference* (pp. 1483-1498). DOI: 10.1145/3643834.3661623

Kiritchenko, S., Nejadgholi, I., & Fraser, K. C. (2021). Confronting abusive language online: A survey from the ethical and human rights perspective. *Journal of Artificial Intelligence Research*, 71, 431–478. DOI: 10.1613/jair.1.12590

Lupu, Y., Sear, R., Velásquez, N., Leahy, R., Restrepo, N. J., Goldberg, B., & Johnson, N. F. (2023). Offline events and online hate. *PLoS One*, 18(1), e0278511. DOI: 10.1371/journal.pone.0278511 PMID: 36696388

Mozafari, M., Farahbakhsh, R., & Crespi, N. (2020). Hate speech detection and racial bias mitigation in social media based on BERT model. *PLoS One*, 15(8), e0237861. DOI: 10.1371/journal.pone.0237861 PMID: 32853205

Munn, L. (2020). Angry by design: Toxic communication and technical architectures. *Humanities & Social Sciences Communications*, 7(1), 1–11. DOI: 10.1057/s41599-020-00550-7

Nascimento, F. R., Cavalcanti, G. D., & Da Costa-Abreu, M. (2022). Unintended bias evaluation: An analysis of hate speech detection and gender bias mitigation on social media using ensemble learning. *Expert Systems with Applications*, 201, 117032. DOI: 10.1016/j.eswa.2022.117032

Nguyen, A., Rai, A., & Maruping, L. (2024). Understanding the Unintended Effects of Human-Machine Moderation in Addressing Harassment within Online Communities. *Journal of Management Information Systems*, 41(2), 341–366. DOI: 10.1080/07421222.2024.2340831

Nguyen, T. (2024). Merging public health and automated approaches to address online hate speech. *AI and Ethics*, 4(2), 441–450. DOI: 10.1007/s43681-023-00281-w PMID: 37360146

Nguyen, T. (2024). Merging public health and automated approaches to address online hate speech. *AI and Ethics*, 4(2), 441–450. DOI: 10.1007/s43681-023-00281-w PMID: 37360146

. Rossini, P. (2020). Beyond toxicity in the online public sphere: understanding incivility in online political talk. *A research agenda for digital politics*, 160-170.

Saha, P., Garimella, K., Kalyan, N. K., Pandey, S. K., Meher, P. M., Mathew, B., & Mukherjee, A. (2023). On the rise of fear speech in online social media. *Proceedings of the National Academy of Sciences of the United States of America*, 120(11), e2212270120. DOI: 10.1073/pnas.2212270120 PMID: 36877833

Scheuerman, M. K., Jiang, J. A., Fiesler, C., & Brubaker, J. R. (2021). A framework of severity for harmful content online. *Proceedings of the ACM on Human-Computer Interaction, 5*(CSCW2), 1-33. DOI: 10.1145/3479512

Singh, B. (2023). Unleashing Alternative Dispute Resolution (ADR) in Resolving Complex Legal-Technical Issues Arising in Cyberspace Lensing E-Commerce and Intellectual Property: Proliferation of E-Commerce Digital Economy. *Revista Brasileira de Alternative Dispute Resolution-Brazilian Journal of Alternative Dispute Resolution-RBADR*, 5(10), 81–105. DOI: 10.52028/rbadr.v5i10.ART04.Ind

Singh, B. (2023). Blockchain Technology in Renovating Healthcare: Legal and Future Perspectives. In *Revolutionizing Healthcare Through Artificial Intelligence and Internet of Things Applications* (pp. 177-186). IGI Global.

Singh, B. (2024). Social Cognition of Incarcerated Women and Children: Addressing Exposure to Infectious Diseases and Legal Outcomes. In Reddy, K. (Ed.), *Principles and Clinical Interventions in Social Cognition* (pp. 236–251). IGI Global., DOI: 10.4018/979-8-3693-1265-0.ch014

Singh, B. (2024). Lensing Legal Dynamics for Examining Responsibility and Deliberation of Generative AI-Tethered Technological Privacy Concerns: Infringements and Use of Personal Data by Nefarious Actors. In Ara, A., & Ara, A. (Eds.), *Exploring the Ethical Implications of Generative AI* (pp. 146–167). IGI Global., DOI: 10.4018/979-8-3693-1565-1.ch009

Singh, B. (2024). Evolutionary Global Neuroscience for Cognition and Brain Health: Strengthening Innovation in Brain Science. In Prabhakar, P. (Ed.), *Biomedical Research Developments for Improved Healthcare* (pp. 246–272). IGI Global., DOI: 10.4018/979-8-3693-1922-2.ch012

Singh, B., Jain, V., Kaunert, C., & Vig, K. (2024). Shaping Highly Intelligent Internet of Things (IoT) and Wireless Sensors for Smart Cities. In *Secure and Intelligent IoT-Enabled Smart Cities* (pp. 117-140). IGI Global.

. Singh, B., & Kaunert, C. (2024). Future of Digital Marketing: Hyper-Personalized Customer Dynamic Experience with AI-Based Predictive Models. *Revolutionizing the AI-Digital Landscape: A Guide to Sustainable Emerging Technologies for Marketing Professionals*, 189.

Singh, B., & Kaunert, C. (2024). Salvaging Responsible Consumption and Production of Food in the Hospitality Industry: Harnessing Machine Learning and Deep Learning for Zero Food Waste. In *Sustainable Disposal Methods of Food Wastes in Hospitality Operations* (pp. 176-192). IGI Global.

Singh, B., & Kaunert, C. (2024). Revealing Green Finance Mobilization: Harnessing FinTech and Blockchain Innovations to Surmount Barriers and Foster New Investment Avenues. In *Harnessing Blockchain-Digital Twin Fusion for Sustainable Investments* (pp. 265-286). IGI Global.

Singh, B., & Kaunert, C. (2024). Harnessing Sustainable Agriculture Through Climate-Smart Technologies: Artificial Intelligence for Climate Preservation and Futuristic Trends. In *Exploring Ethical Dimensions of Environmental Sustainability and Use of AI* (pp. 214-239). IGI Global.

Singh, B., & Kaunert, C. (2024). Salvaging Responsible Consumption and Production of Food in the Hospitality Industry: Harnessing Machine Learning and Deep Learning for Zero Food Waste. In Singh, A., Tyagi, P., & Garg, A. (Eds.), *Sustainable Disposal Methods of Food Wastes in Hospitality Operations* (pp. 176–192). IGI Global., DOI: 10.4018/979-8-3693-2181-2.ch012

Singh, B., Kaunert, C., & Vig, K. (2024). Reinventing Influence of Artificial Intelligence (AI) on Digital Consumer Lensing Transforming Consumer Recommendation Model: Exploring Stimulus Artificial Intelligence on Consumer Shopping Decisions. In Musiolik, T., Rodriguez, R., & Kannan, H. (Eds.), *AI Impacts in Digital Consumer Behavior* (pp. 141–169). IGI Global., DOI: 10.4018/979-8-3693-1918-5.ch006

Singh, B., Kaunert, C., & Vig, K. (2024). Reinventing Influence of Artificial Intelligence (AI) on Digital Consumer Lensing Transforming Consumer Recommendation Model: Exploring Stimulus Artificial Intelligence on Consumer Shopping Decisions. In *AI Impacts in Digital Consumer Behavior* (pp. 141-169). IGI Global.

Singh, B., Kaunert, C., & Vig, K. (2024). Reinventing Influence of Artificial Intelligence (AI) on Digital Consumer Lensing Transforming Consumer Recommendation Model: Exploring Stimulus Artificial Intelligence on Consumer Shopping Decisions. In Musiolik, T., Rodriguez, R., & Kannan, H. (Eds.), *AI Impacts in Digital Consumer Behavior* (pp. 141–169). IGI Global., DOI: 10.4018/979-8-3693-1918-5.ch006

Singh, B., Vig, K., & Kaunert, C. (2024). Modernizing Healthcare: Application of Augmented Reality and Virtual Reality in Clinical Practice and Medical Education. In Modern Technology in Healthcare and Medical Education: Blockchain, IoT, AR, and VR (pp. 1-21). IGI Global.

. Srba, I., Lenzini, G., Pikuliak, M., & Pecar, S. (2021). Addressing hate speech with data science: an overview from computer science perspective. *Hate Speech-Multidisziplinäre Analysen und Handlungsoptionen: Theoretische und empirische Annäherungen an ein interdisziplinäres Phänomen*, 317-336.

Thomas, K., Akhawe, D., Bailey, M., Boneh, D., Bursztein, E., Consolvo, S., & Stringhini, G. (2021, May). Sok: Hate, harassment, and the changing landscape of online abuse. In *2021 IEEE Symposium on Security and Privacy (SP)* (pp. 247-267). IEEE. DOI: 10.1109/SP40001.2021.00028

Thomas, K., Kelley, P. G., Consolvo, S., Samermit, P., & Bursztein, E. (2022, April). "It's common and a part of being a content creator": Understanding How Creators Experience and Cope with Hate and Harassment Online. In *Proceedings of the 2022 CHI conference on human factors in computing systems* (pp. 1-15).

. Trott, V., Beckett, J., & Paech, V. (2020). Tuning out hate speech on Reddit: Automating moderation and detecting toxicity in the manosphere. *AoIR Selected Papers of Internet Research.*

Ullmann, S., & Tomalin, M. (Eds.). (2023). *Counterspeech: Multidisciplinary Perspectives on Countering Dangerous Speech.* Taylor & Francis. DOI: 10.4324/9781003377078

Wachs, S., Gámez-Guadix, M., & Wright, M. F. (2022). Online hate speech victimization and depressive symptoms among adolescents: The protective role of resilience. *Cyberpsychology, Behavior, and Social Networking*, 25(7), 416–423. DOI: 10.1089/cyber.2022.0009 PMID: 35639126

Wachs, S., Wright, M. F., & Gámez-Guadix, M. (2024). From hate speech to HateLess. The effectiveness of a prevention program on adolescents' online hate speech involvement. *Computers in Human Behavior*, 157, 108250. DOI: 10.1016/j.chb.2024.108250

Warner, M., Strohmayer, A., Higgs, M., & Coventry, L. (2024). A Critical Reflection on the Use of Toxicity Detection Algorithms in Proactive Content Moderation Systems. *arXiv preprint arXiv:2401.10629.*

Warner, M., Strohmayer, A., Higgs, M., & Coventry, L. (2024). A Critical Reflection on the Use of Toxicity Detection Algorithms in Proactive Content Moderation Systems. *arXiv preprint arXiv:2401.10629.*

Yimam, S. M., Dementieva, D., Fischer, T., Moskovskiy, D., Rizwan, N., Saha, P., . . . Mukherjee, A. (2024). Demarked: A Strategy for Enhanced Abusive Speech Moderation through Counterspeech, Detoxification, and Message Management. *arXiv preprint arXiv:2406.19543.*

Zhao, Z., Zhang, Z., & Hopfgartner, F. (2022). Utilizing subjectivity level to mitigate identity term bias in toxic comments classification. *Online Social Networks and Media*, 29, 100205. DOI: 10.1016/j.osnem.2022.100205

Chapter 6
Creative Paradigms, Generative AI, and Copyright Law:
Investigating the Intersection of AI and Artistry

Anuttama Ghose
https://orcid.org/0000-0002-7210-4074
School of Law, Dr. Vishwanath Karad MIT World Peace University, Pune, India

S. M. Aamir Ali
https://orcid.org/0000-0002-8686-0217
Symbiosis Law School Pune, Symbiosis International University (Deemed), India

Sachin Balwantrao Deshmukh
https://orcid.org/0009-0004-3034-1946
School of Law, Dr. Vishwanath Karad MIT World Peace University, Pune, India

ABSTRACT

In recent years, owing to significant advancements in deep learning technology, artificial intelligence (AI) has started to replace human content creators and produce quality creative works on a wide scale. By the end of the decade, it is probable that a substantial quantity of art, literature, music, software, and online material will be generated by AI instead of conventional human creators. However, the law is not keeping pace with this technical advancement since it now prohibits granting copyright protection to works created by artificial intelligence. The aim of this chapter is to examine the intricacies of this expanding artistic field, specifically examining the modern techniques used by those who utilize AI to augment and amplify their

DOI: 10.4018/979-8-3693-7205-0.ch006

creative pursuits.

1. INTRODUCTION

Generative Artificial Intelligence (AI) systems, often known as AI systems, have the ability to produce material in response to a given prompt. Users have the ability to make a formal request for generative AI to produce a certain sort of output or to modify a text or image that the user has provided. The output may be generated in several forms, such as text, graphics, audio, or code. Presently, technological corporations are eagerly allocating resources to invest in generative artificial intelligence. Microsoft's $10 billion investment in OpenAI, the creator of many widely-used generative AI technologies such as ChatGPT, demonstrates the increasing potential of this sector (Metz & Weise, 2023). The capabilities of a new category of tools, often referred to as generative artificial intelligence (AI), are a subject of much discussion. One notable use of this technology is the creation of top-notch creative content for many forms of visual arts, concept art, music, literature, video, and animation. For instance, diffusion models have the ability to create visuals of exceptional quality, whereas large language models (LLMs) may generate coherent and remarkable written works in many situations. The creative processes of artists are anticipated to undergo major changes due to the generative powers of these tools, which enable them to create ideas and put them into production (Eichner, 2023). As creativity is reconceptualized, several areas of society may also undergo transformation. To comprehend the influence of generative AI and formulate policy judgments about it, it is necessary to undertake novel multidisciplinary scientific investigations into culture, economics, law, algorithms, and the interplay between technology and creativity (Chesterman, 2024).

At first look, generative AI tools seem to automate the process of creative creation completely. This perception reflects previous occasions when traditionalists saw new technology as a danger to the very essence of art. Contrary to popular belief, these instances of technical advancement did not signify the “termination of art” but rather had intricate consequences that redefined the responsibilities and methods of artists, as well as altered the visual appeal of modern media (Tan, 2023). Some painters in the 19th century saw the emergence of photography as a threat to the art of painting. Photography, instead of replacing painting, ultimately emancipated it from realism, leading to the emergence of Impressionism and the Modern Art movement. In contrast, portrait photography mainly supplanted portrait painting. Similarly, the process of converting music creation into a digital format, such as via digital sampling and sound synthesis, was criticized as “the demise of music” (Ghose & Ali, 2023). Instead, it transformed the methods by which individuals create and consume music and had a significant role in the emergence of new musical genres, such as hip-hop and drum 'n' bass. Similar to these historical comparisons, generative AI does not signal the end of art but instead represents a new medium with its own unique capabilities. Generative AI, a collection of tools used by human creators, has the potential to disrupt several sectors of the creative industry and beyond. This poses a danger to current employment and labor models in the near term, but eventually paves the way for new forms of creative labor and reshapes the media ecosystem (Appel et al., 2023). The objective of this chapter is to explore the complexities of this growing artistic domain, focusing on the contemporary methods used by those who use AI to enhance and intensify their creative endeavors. The investigation's primary emphasis is on ethical entitlements, particularly on the allocation of contributions from both human and machine partners, which is crucial. This paper critically examines the worldwide aspects of AI-generated art in order to comprehend and provide remedies for the inequalities in copyright rules across different countries.

2. CONTEXTUALIZING GENERATIVE AI AND ITS LEGALITIES IN THE CONTEMPORARY LANDSCAPE: OVERVIEW OF LITERATURE

Writers often use a range of digital tools to improve their work. Take, for instance, the 'spelling & grammar' and 'thesaurus' functionalities included in Microsoft Word. These instruments are often used to rectify and contemplate upon one's work. Furthermore, a wide range of additional technologies, like educational chat bots, are often used to enhance the process of learning and the acquisition of information (Choudhary & Ali, 2023). All of these actions are in accordance with copyright laws. What are the specific modifications that occur when content producers and organizations use Generative AI models, such as ChatGPT? Previously, technical aids facilitated the process of searching and refining work. The author may describe the outcome as the apex of their intellectual influence and ideas. ChatGPT and other Generative AI technologies revolutionize the way humans engage with technology by enabling the generation of high-quality content with only a simple cue (Ghose & Deshmukh, 2024). ChatGPT is an NLP tool that can extract important information from large volumes of data (big data). It can also contextualize information and improve itself depending on user comments. In order to provide a thorough understanding of the most current advancements in GenAI technologies and the impact they have on the field, the author consulted a variety of literature and research works.

When artificial intelligence (AI) meets creative expression, it presents a variety of IP issues that must be thoroughly investigated. Who should own the copyright to works created by artificial intelligence (AI) and why is a question we'll examine in this chapter (Ghose et al., 2024). This study explores utilitarianism, an ethical theory that advocates for financial compensation to writers whose works have a positive impact on society. In this post, we'll look at copyright as a tool that promotes creativity in both artistic and practical products. To back up the allegation, Buccafusco explains how the four principles of utilitarianism serve to safeguard intellectual property in his work (Buccafusco, 2016). It goes even beyond by using Tasioulas to highlight the possibility that AI systems may create art without human involvement (Tasioulas, 2022). This article examines the practice of assigning copyrights to AI systems and poses the question of whether the concepts of natural rights provide a solid enough basis to for AI to hold copyrights. We examine the human developers' roles and the extent to which they influence AI-generated works in this article. Research by Barfield and Pagallo provides the groundwork for the claim that algorithms are not inherently bound to respect principles of natural rights (Barfield & Pagallo, 2021). The topic of copyright protection for works created by artificial intelligence is the main focus of the debate, which relies on the work of Barbosa (2009) to examine the impact of natural rights theory on intellectual property rights.

In addition, the chapter cites Hristov's study to imply that property rights may not be necessary when AI-generated material significantly deviates from human input (Hristov, 2017). Aesthetic feelings and their consequences for AI-generated art are briefly touched upon in the debate, which is based on Menninghaus's 2019 research. It shows how AI might change the way we think about art and creativity. Concerns around ownership have surfaced due to the increasing role of AI in the creative process, which is questioning the traditional notion of authorship. Considering the parameters of his piece "What Is a 'Author'?" Philosophical views on authorship are elucidated by Caldwell. Delving into the Philosophical Underpinnings of AI Copyright for Art. In this chapter, we will go over inherent rights and how they relate to copyright protection for works made by AI (Caldwell, 2023). In this essay, we examine the question of whether copyright protection for works created by AI should be based on the concept of natural rights. This debate draws on the research of Choudhary and Ali (2023) to investigate questions of fair usage and copyright infringement as they pertain to artificial intelligence art. Understanding how established legal concepts deal with the specific challenges posed by AI-generated content is crucial, as our discovery shows. The risk of copyright infringement is a major concern, say researchers like Watiktinnakorn. The significance of this is highlighted in the article "Blurring the lines: how AI is redefining artistic ownership and copyright" (Watiktinnakorn et al., 2023), which discusses how AI systems use large databases that may include copyrighted information. This part continues Salah's articles by exploring AI biases and their impact on AI-generated art, drawing attention to the significance of ethical considerations and strategies to combat prejudice in the creative uses of AI (Salah, 2021).

In his article "Transformative Use and Cognizable Harm," Cotter examines the murky topic of distinguishing between TU and copyright infringement. Cotter (2010) discusses the complexities of marketing AI-generated art and the requirement of creating appropriate compensation arrangements for all stakeholders involved. To make sense of all the moving parts in the creative process that involve both human and machine collaborators, Miernicki and Irene emphasize in their article "Artificial intelligence and moral rights" (Miernicki & Ng, 2021) the significance of keeping moral rights in mind, such as the necessity of proper attribution. The debate draws on the Dollen research, which emphasizes the profound effect of AI on creative expression, to illuminate the intricacies of human interaction with complicated algorithms via the creative process (Dollen 2014). The global distribution of AI-generated artwork is complicated by variations in intellectual property regulations across nations. urges countries to align their IP rules so that creators, developers, and stakeholders from all across the globe are on the same page. A unified framework is required for a consistent and reasonable strategy. "Artificial Intelligence and Copyright: Issues and Challenges" (Ahuja, 2020) is a study in which Ahuja makes this need very clear.

3. ARTIFICIAL INTELLIGENCE AND ARTISTIC CREATION: THEORETICAL OVERVIEW

Generative AI systems are capable of autonomously creating many forms of creative output, including text, photos, and videos. Concerning copyright protection and intellectual property rights, this brings up some complicated questions. Academic research on the theoretical underpinnings of intellectual property as it relates to the convergence of creative expression and artificial intelligence (AI) is fascinating and dynamic in the field of law. As AI continues to propel innovation in the realm of creative expression, it is imperative that the fundamental legal principles controlling intellectual property undergo a thorough examination.

Generative AI has introduced complex challenges to copyright law, which can be examined through the "*Magic File Drawer*," "*Magic Copy Machine*," and "*Magic Box Artist*" theories. The "*Magic File Drawer*" theory views AI as an inexhaustible repository of existing ideas and expressions, recombining them to produce new content. This raises questions about originality—a fundamental requirement for copyright protection—since the AI's output may not constitute original authorship but rather derivative works. The "Magic Copy Machine" theory considers generative AI as a sophisticated replication device, potentially producing exact or near-exact copies of copyrighted works, thereby infringing on the original creators' rights. This scenario invokes the fair use doctrine, though its application remains contentious, particularly regarding the transformative nature and market impact of AI-generated content. The "*Magic Box Artist*" theory, however, sees generative AI as an autonomous creator capable of producing original works independently of human input, thereby warranting copyright protection for its creations. This challenges traditional notions of authorship, which have historically required human creativity, prompting debates on whether an AI can be recognized as an author and, if so, who owns the rights—whether it be the AI's developer, the deploying entity, or a new category specific to AI-generated works. Each of these theories highlights different aspects of the legal and philosophical challenges posed by AI-generated content. As AI continues to advance, legal frameworks must evolve to address these unique issues, balancing the interests of creators, innovators, and the public. The "*Magic File Drawer*" emphasizes the derivative nature of AI outputs and the originality criterion in copyright, while the "*Magic Copy Machine*" underscores the risk of large-scale infringement and the complexities of fair use in the context of AI. In contrast, the "*Magic Box Artist*" advocates for recognizing AI's creative autonomy and adapting authorship concepts. Collectively, these theories illustrate the necessity for nuanced and forward-thinking approaches in copyright law to ensure it remains relevant and effective in the era of artificial intelligence. As generative AI technologies proliferate, the ongoing debate will shape the future of copyright, necessitating an adaptable legal framework that can address the multifaceted implications of AI-generated works, protect original creators' rights, and encourage innovation and creativity in an increasingly AI-driven world.

4. COPYRIGHT NORMS AND FAIR USE QUANDARIES IN AI ART

4.1 Copyright Norms Surrounding AI Art

For anything to be copyrightable, it must meet two formal physical conditions in addition to two conceptual ones. Both the originality and creativity requirements—that is, the work must have been thought of and produced by an act of authorship—and the need for it to be a work of authorship are conceptual prerequisites for a plaintiff's work to be valid. According to copyright law, for a work to be considered original, it must not be a carbon copy of another work already in existence and must contain copyrightable subject matter, such as pictorial, graphic, or sculptural expression, as opposed to the noncopyrightable subject matter, such as an idea, concept, principle, or discovery (Murray, 2017; Murray & DuBoff, 2023).

Both expression and fixation in media are formal criteria. “Expression” implies that the piece may potentially communicate with the viewer via one of their senses. Copyright protects the ability of an author to convey an idea that first exists in the author's mind and then is sent to another person's mind via various forms of communication medium (*Georgia v. Public Resource. Org*, Inc., 140 S. Ct. 1498, 1510-11, 2020). Also, for there to be “fixation in media,” the expression must be in a sensory-perceivable form for enough amount of time for us to identify the work of art and understand its message. When it comes to legal definitions, “fixation” means, as per § 101 US Copyright: “authorship fixed in any tangible medium of expression, now known or later developed, from which [the works] can be perceived, reproduced, or otherwise communicated, either directly or with the aid of a machine or device.” Various doctrines have been developed to limit copyrightability, with the focus being on what and to what extent an artist's creation was truly original to the artist and not pre-existing or borrowed from earlier works. This is in response to the requirements of originality and creativity in the owner's expression.

In visual art, the scènes à faire doctrine describes pieces that borrow widely used scenes, images, expressions, and elements from other styles or genres; these components are not original to the artist, but she incorporates them into her own work. Section 102(b) concepts, as opposed to section 102(a) expressions, are not copyrightable as they are not unique to a single artist and are instead susceptible to the merger doctrine in copyright (*Ets-Hokin v. Skyy Spirits, Inc.*, 225 F.3d 1068, 1082 (9th Cir. 2000)). What we mean when we talk about a merged idea and expression in the visual arts is that when we use a certain artistic technique, process, or procedure to depict a scene or object, or when we express a certain concept visually, the results will inevitably look similar because the work incorporates the visual aspects of both concepts. Merged, scènes à faire, or uncopyrightable imagery is practically inevitable in the works of artists who adhere to a particular genre, style, or school of art. This is due to the fact that these artists are utilizing preexisting methods of depiction as well as stylistic and genre-specific formulas, procedures, or ideas.

Also, the practical examination will determine if the owner's copyrighted work is indeed valuable and functioning according to the useful articles doctrine. The court will consider whether the work is functional and whether there are physically separate creative or expressive components, like the bases of statuettes for lamps, or if there is ornamentation or decoration that is conceptually separate from the work's functionality, like the designs on a cheerleader's uniform or a piece of flooring. A work lacks copyright protection if its shape and function cannot be separated. This plaintiff's copyright might become too narrow in its protections against duplication and unlicensed derivative works if it fails to pass all five of these tests: originality, idea-expression, merger, scènes à faire, and functionality-utility (Varsity Brands, Inc. v. Star Athletica, LLC, 799 F.3d 468, 471 (6th Cir. 2015)). With a narrow copyright, only nearly identical copies are prevented. If the court determines that the plaintiff's copyright is very weak, it may decide to dismiss the case since the defendant's work is still possible.

4.2. *AI-Generated Art and Creativity Dilemmas*

An important topic of research in intellectual property law is studying the influence of Artificial Intelligence (AI) on creative production. Using pertinent case studies to demonstrate the intricate relationship between technology and creative expression, this scholarly inquiry delves into the far-reaching effects of AI on the creative process. The development and following legal ramifications around the Obvious art team's AI-generated artwork, "Portrait of Edmond de Belamy," serve as an example. Significant concerns about the ownership and attribution of artworks have been highlighted by the use of generative adversarial networks (GANs) to create algorithmically produced pictures. The case highlights the need for legal frameworks that address the challenge that collaborative AI-human creative collaborations pose to conventional ideas of individual authorship. By using artificial intelligence, media artist Refik Anadol produced "The Machine Hallucination" (Hencz, 2022). To sift through mountains of NYC-related data, Refik Anadol uses a novel combination of AI algorithms and ML approaches. Architectural plans, old photos, and modern images are just a few of the varied sources included in the collection. Using massive amounts of data, the AI system trains deep neural networks to comprehend and create visual content. The legal implications of "The Machine Hallucination" concerning copyright and authorship are intriguing. When the artist, the AI system, and other distinct information sources work together, it creates a unique creative process. A possible topic for legal discussion is the degree to which AI-generated images are copyright protected, as well as how intellectual property laws address the unique dynamics of human-AI cooperation in the arts (Artechouse, n.d.).

We have also seen "The Next Rembrandt," an innovative work of art created in 2016 with the use of artificial intelligence. According to Guadamuz (2017), the partnership included Microsoft, the Dutch advertising agency J. Walter Thompson Amsterdam, and the Technical University of Delft, which focuses on art research and imitation. Examining Rembrandt's use of color, composition, and subject matter, the research used machine learning approaches to examine his whole artistic oeuvre. The algorithms were able to recognize Rembrandt's distinctive style and use that information to generate a whole new piece of art that mimicked the master's technique. A number of legal questions have arisen in relation to "The Next Rembrandt", including the identification of the work's artist, its ownership, and the protection of intellectual property rights. Using learned patterns from Rembrandt's paintings, the AI computer created the artwork without human intervention. Because human designers were involved in the AI system's creation and mentorship, this phenomena has blurred the lines between conventional authorship and its use. The project's focus on how legal frameworks should change to include AI in the creative process sparked debates on who should be recognized as the "author" of an artwork—the AI system or the human producers (Guadamuz, 2017) .

The line between human and machine-generated creativity is becoming more blurry as AI has the capacity to process massive volumes of data and produce unexpected, new stuff. From a legal perspective, this calls into doubt the veracity and originality of human-made objects, calling for a thorough investigation. Establishing intellectual property rights also requires knowing how AI contributes to idea generation. Questions of ownership and protection of creative works created by artificial intelligence (AI) are likely to emerge in the near future. The cooperative character of AI-human collaboration in the creative domain necessitates adjusting to the conventional, IP-based structure of exclusive authorship rights.

4.3 Evolving Fair Use: Navigating Non-expressive Copying and Technology Reliant on Copies

When discussing algorithmic operations, data analysis, programming, and "training" on computers, the term "non expressive copying" is used to describe the accidental duplication of data and raw source material for a purpose unrelated to the production, consumption, or distribution of the material's expressive elements (Grimmelmann, 2015). This idea applies in cases when the kind of copying in question is so different from the typical copying that is safeguarded by copyright laws (17 U.S.C. § 106) that it either does not constitute an "act of copying" or is exempt from infringement according to the fair use doctrine. This occurs, for instance, when data from expressive works is processed incidentally or intermediately, necessitating the download of the works (which, in a digital environment, implies the creation of a copy of the digital work) or its copying during the functional analysis process. The duplicates may be kept for the duration of the procedure, but they will not be eaten or shared. The process relies on this kind of copying, which is called copy-reliant technology. This copying is essential for the procedure to be carried out.

Because modern visual generative AI is still in its infancy, the courts have been reticent in ruling on how to apply the transformative fair use test to this emerging technology. However, courts have already ruled on similarly situated cases involving the accidental duplication of copyrighted works for practical, non-creative reasons (Sag, 2012). Among the first instances of non-expressive copying to permit a legitimate use of noncopyrightable source code was *Sega Enterprises Ltd. v. Accolade*

(977 F.2d 1510, 9th Cir. 1992). Accolade, a video game developer that wished to build Genesis-compatible titles without Sega's authorization, and Sega, the manufacturer of the "Genesis" gaming system, were embroiled in a dispute. In order to ensure compatibility, Accolade replicated the working code by analyzing a Genesis system and many Sega games via reverse engineering. Although Accolade was able to create perfect replicas of Sega's source code via reverse engineering, their games only made use of the functional code associated with the Genesis interface. Because it was necessary to access the "functional requirements for Genesis compatibility"—a non-copyrighted functional feature of Sega's games—the Ninth Circuit determined that Accolade's "intermediate copying" of Sega games constituted fair use. The decision recognized that copyrighted works might be used for fair use when copied for non-expressive purposes.

Two instances examined the practice of using search engines to scrape photos or generate exact duplicates of copyrighted photographs without discrimination: The cases of *Kelly v. Arriba Soft Corp.* (336 F.3d 811 9th Cir. 2003) and *Perfect 10, Inc. v. Amazon.com, Inc.* (Inc., 508 F.3d 1146, 9th Cir. 2007). Both instances were IT businesses that operated picture search engines and were sued by owners of the original photographs for doing things like duplicating them, compressing them to thumbnail size, keeping them on servers, and then presenting them to internet users via their search engine services. Using the same medium (digital photography and imagery), each service not only created full-color copies of the copyrighted images but also stored and distributed these copies to internet users for viewing and consumption. It was determined that these actions constituted transformative fair uses in both instances.

It is highly probable that a copyright infringement analysis would fail at this stage due to the lack of a copy of the work to compare side-by-side with the original. Additionally, non-expressive copying to facilitate a machine function may not be considered an act of copying that results in an infringing work. The infringement action would be unsuccessful if the identified intermediate copy served a totally different purpose than the original work, even though it may have included expressive content that was allegedly lifted from the infringed image. To further the advancement of science and the arts by stimulating the creation of unique, expressive works, the Copyright Act fully supports this new function and purpose of the machine system.

4.4. Current Legislative Framework Surrounding Copyright Protection:

In order to get a copyright for a work, the "author's" original ideas are very important. Taken in a larger context, it's important to remember that the Berne Convention recognizes, in Article 2.6 (UN WIPO, 1886), the significance of copyright protection for the owner (UN WIPO, 1886). Having said that, it should be noted that the convention refrains from defining the word "author." There is still no clear definition of "author" under EU copyright law. The European Union Court of Justice reached a landmark decision in the 2011 case of *Eva-Maria Painer v. Standard Verlags GmbH 1* that made it clear that only human-created works would be protected. Countries with civil law systems, such as Germany (Copyright Act, 2017), France (Intellectual Property Code, 2022), and Spain (The Intellectual Property Act, 2012), reflect this principle by requiring works to include the distinct signature of the creator (Ramalho, 2022). However, AI systems can't be considered writers as they can't give their works a unique voice. A number of nations' copyright laws are based on the principle of advancing society's welfare (Vezina & Moran, n.d.). This includes Canada, the UK, Australia, and New Zealand. It gets that public availability and rewards and incentives are two sides of the same coin when it comes to encouraging creative output. This view downplays the significance of authorial personality and opens the door to the possibility of non-human writers. In the 2016 U.S. case Naruto et al. v. David Slater, it was determined that monkey-taken photos cannot be given copyright. The fact that the shots were shot naturally was a deciding factor in this selection. Those in agreement with the US Copyright Office hold the view that animal-created works do not qualify for registration. Many nations, including India, the UK, New Zealand, and Ireland, provide copyright protection to works created by computer programs (Vezina & Moran, n.d.).

Section 2(d) of the Indian Copyright Act, 1957 defines "author" as "in the case of a literary or dramatic work, the author; in the case of a musical piece, the composer; in the case of a computer-generated literary, dramatic, musical, or artistic work, the person who causes the work to be made." This definition is somewhat vague when it comes to autonomously generated computer labor. This is highlighted in several sections that address the author's family, life, and departure, and it is also clear from the provision stated (Copyright Act, 1957). When it comes to human-made AI software, the law is applicable without a doubt. The reason is that it fits well with the concept of a person being the original creator or author, which is essential to copyright law. But when AI develops and can make its own original works and goods, it will no longer be seen as just another human helper. This calls into question the original author/creator concept as stated in copyright law (Barfield, 2006). Note that the person making the computer-generated work is deemed the author under sub-clause (vi) of the Act. The idea that machines may one day act in a humanlike manner appears to have been disregarded by the clause. But it ignores any computers that aren't run by people (Rehan, n.d.).

Since computers are often believed to be able to enhance human creativity solely, there is a lack of legislation addressing the question of whether AI may exhibit independent creativity and have distinct ownership rights. Keep in mind that the Act's original intent was to limit copyright protection to private citizens. The Copyright Act of 1957 specifies in section 22 that works produced while the author is alive are only protected for 60 years, beginning on the first day of the calendar year after the author's death. A great deal depends on the author's character in this instance. However, one major hole in the Indian Copyright Act has to be pointed out. Neither the author's legal individuality nor the need to be a "human" is clearly addressed in the concept of "author" (Kulkarni, 2016). An artificial intelligence tool named "Raghav" was recently acknowledged for its creative work by India's copyright office (Sarkar, 2021). This painting software is now protected by copyright, recognizing its contribution as an artist's collaborator. Considering there is no explicit rule that says an author has to be a "natural person," AI may theoretically be considered a co-author (Lath, 2022). Artificial intelligence (AI) does not yet have legal personality status just because it has human-like cognition and competence in a certain area, like book writing or art creation. So, copyright law's hazy definition of "author" causes problems, even if AI has the makings of a major player in ownership.

The fundamental objective of copyright laws is to protect artists and inspire them to produce more creative works. However, AI doesn't need such a motivation to produce more content. This is why dividing up the public domain is likewise seen to be difficult. Since there isn't a silver bullet, all potential solutions come with their own set of restrictions.

5. GENERATIVE AI AND COPYRIGHT INFRINGEMENT

A new worry with AI-generated material is how easily unauthorized works may be made and shared. Because of AI's speed and capacity to generate big volumes of material, it might make it easier to create massively infringement works and spread them worldwide. In the face of such widespread infringement, copyright holders may find it difficult to identify infringers and pursue legal action. The issue of whether standard copyright enforcement procedures are sufficient to handle new types of infringement is further raised by the possibility that AI-generated material might accurately imitate previous works. It is becoming increasingly difficult for copyright holders to identify and punish infringing works due to the fast rate of technical progress and the growing complexity of artificial intelligence, both of which increase the likelihood that such works might be made with more speed and efficiency than ever before. This means that new legal remedies are required to deal with the specific problems caused by AI-generated material. This can include coming up with new legal frameworks that can handle infringement in the digital era or coming up with new technical solutions like copyright detection and enforcement systems driven by AI. In order for artists to be able to continue to profit from and protect their works despite these new hurdles, copyright laws will need to evolve in tandem with technology.

It is well known that the current generation of Large Language Models (LLMs) have acquired extensive knowledge and expertise by systematically scanning the internet to assimilate a vast collection of textual data. Although we may have had doubts about the legality of including information that was not clearly owned or licensed, we all chose to ignore it in order to promote innovation and creativity. The captivating potential of the generative AI systems overshadowed any concerns over the origin and legality of the data. As an example, in the case of Andersen v. Stability AI Ltd and Others (23-cv-00201-WHO, 2023), the question that arose in the court proceedings was whether it is an infringement to use copyrighted images for AI training (the so-called "Training Images"), particularly in cases where the output does not directly mimic any of the inputs. Specifically, the plaintiffs in this case contended that the "Output Images" produced by Generative AI (especially via the use of Training Images, which included copyrighted works) infringed on "derivative works" according to conventional copyright laws. The court (partially) rejected this "wholesale" strategy for two reasons: first, it's highly implausible that each and every Training Image was copyrighted; and second, in order for a claim of "derivative works" infringement to be successful, there must be enough evidence to show that the two works are "substantially similar" or that the derivative work incorporates the expressive content that was protected in the original. It is necessary to determine further the degree of resemblance (or lack thereof) between the Output Images produced by AI and the source copyrighted works in order to settle accusations of copyright infringement against these images (Lim, 2023).

The mechanisms behind AI-generated material in both visual and textual domains exhibit a kind of ingenuity that can often be distinguished from mere duplication or replication. Understanding the difference is essential for comprehending why the learning and generative processes of AI may not align neatly with conventional concepts of copyright infringement. As artificial intelligence (AI) progresses, it is imperative that our legal interpretations and frameworks adapt accordingly to tackle the distinct difficulties posed by this emerging technology effectively (Lim, 2023). The legal framework between AI and copyright is currently uncertain and is expected to continue evolving. This is due to the need to address the new issues presented by AI's distinct learning and content creation techniques while also striking a balance between safeguarding original works and harnessing the inventive capabilities of AI. This growth is crucial for cultivating an atmosphere conducive to the flourishing of creativity and innovation, eventually benefitting creators, innovators, and society at large (Ghose & Gilda, 2023). These developments in AI-generated material should prompt a rethinking of copyright regulations in light of AI's capacity for learning and creativity. Protecting the rights of original artists while still allowing AI to make creative and valuable contributions to many sectors is a challenging subject (Lim, 2023).

6. CREATIVE INTENSIONS AND COPYRIGHT DILEMMA SURROUNDING HUMAN-CREATED AND AI-GENERATED WORK

At its most effective, art may stir up profound feelings and foster fresh viewpoints, so altering a person's view of the world and their own identity. When art and AI come together, the game changes when it comes to creative output. This forces us to rethink the importance of artistic meaning and purpose based on our long-held preconceptions. According to Frey (2023), human-made art has always been considered a powerful vehicle for artists to convey their ideas, emotions, and goals. What a piece of art is really meant to convey is dependent on the artist's deliberate choices, which are in turn shaped by their own life stories, cultural backgrounds, and societal narratives. The artist painstakingly selects every aspect, from the brushstrokes on a painting to the arrangement of musical notes, with the purpose of telling a story, making the viewer feel something, or making them think deeply about something. On the other side, artificial intelligence (AI) in art offers a new perspective in which the creator is not a person but an algorithm with thorough training on massive datasets (Militsyna, 2023). Art created by AI is valuable because it incorporates a wide variety of patterns, styles, and data sets into its machine-learning models. Even while AI algorithms don't have any memories or intentions of their own, they may mimic and combine elements from many sources to create unique and interesting artworks (Militsyna, 2023).

Is there a specific purpose that AI art can fulfill, though? Just like a smart camera may be useful for professional photographers, AI could prove to be an invaluable resource for creatives. In these instances, a human artist is still involved in determining the artwork's purpose. When people employ AI art-generating algorithms, their cultural background, educational background, and personal experience, all play a role in how they tweak and change the first pictures the generator makes. Concerns about the function and cultural setting of AI-generated art could emerge in the event that AI attains awareness. These worries would make interacting with AI much more difficult for humans (Bellaiche et al., 2023).

Understanding the fundamental purpose of art, whether created by humans or AI, might be quite a challenge. In the realm of art that humans create, it could be difficult for onlookers to pick up on the artist's personal sentiments and nuanced emotions (Bellaiche et al., 2023). Also, because AI-generated artwork does not have a conscious creator, it is difficult to assign it traditional ideas of meaning.

According to Bellaiche et al. (2023), this leads to philosophical inquiries into the essential character of aim and the need for conscious activity for its legitimacy. A turning point in the development of intentional creativity has come with the merging of human-created and AI-generated art. A complex interaction of algorithmic components, unconscious impulses, and purposeful decisions defines the artist-worker connection. Collaboration, capability advancement, and the harmonious interaction of creativity and technology all contribute to a greater sense of purpose, which in turn calls for a deeper investigation of the relevance of intention beyond the human-machine divide. The complex relationship between free will, deterministic algorithms, and ever-expanding technological capabilities requires a thorough examination of goals and objectives. The many aspects that impact the intentional expression of imagination beyond the limits of what is naturally or artificially created are becoming more apparent to those engaged in art research, production, and observation as the discipline progresses (Bellaiche et al., 2023).

7. CONCLUSION

The findings of this study demonstrate that the topics of creative expression, generative artificial intelligence, and intellectual property (IP) are complex and are undergoing rapid development. Traditional frameworks for authorship, ownership, and copyright have been confronted with major issues as a result of the use of artificial intelligence technology in creative working relationships. The research has shed light on a number of problems, including authorship verification, the prevention of copyright infringement, and the understanding of transformative usage within the context of existing legal frameworks. It has also called attention to the complicated dynamics of AI-generated art. This study has also brought to light the global scope of artificial intelligence art, highlighting the need to achieve a global agreement on intellectual property rules in order to give transparency and consistency to artists, programmers, and other stakeholders in a number of different nations. In addition to this, the research has brought to light the pressing need for adaptable legal frameworks that are capable of appropriately addressing the challenges that are a direct result of the never-ending advancements in artificial intelligence technology. The primary objective of this work is to enhance our understanding of the intricate problems and possible benefits associated with intellectual property and art created by artificial intelligence. This may be accomplished by incorporating the perspectives of stakeholders, doing case studies, doing literature reviews, and conducting legal analyses.

The idea that engaging in creative activities may serve as an invincible human shield is not even somewhat plausible. Today, artificial intelligence is being used not only as a powerful instrument but also, in the case of some performers, as a collaborator. One possibility is that in the not-too-distant future, computers that are sensitive to aesthetics may alter the way humans perceive art by expanding the bounds of what is regarded to be innovative and beautiful. When it comes to the junction of art and technology, the outcomes of the research provide validity to the idea that we need to be cooperative and imaginative in order to achieve success. It is necessary for us to engage in a continuous debate that includes legislators, attorneys, artists, and those who create artificial intelligence if we want to construct a legislative framework that fosters innovation while also safeguarding the rights of all significant parties. Through the adoption of this strategy, we have the potential to pave the way for a future in which artificial intelligence and human creativity will work together in tandem, producing outcomes that are just, legal, and ethical for the fast-expanding field of AI-generated art.

REFERENCES

Ahuja, V. K. (2020). Artificial Intelligence and Copyright: Issues and Challenges. ILI Law Review, *Winter Issue*. 270-285. https://ili.ac.in/pdf/vka.pdf

Appel, G., Neelbauer, J., & Schweidel, D. A. (2023, April 7). Generative AI has an intellectual property problem. *Harvard Business Review*. https://hbr.org/2023/04/generative-ai-has-an-intellectual-property-problem

Artechouse, (n.d.). Artechouse announces the return of the ground breaking exhibition machine hallucinations: NYC with refik anadol for a special limited-duration run in New York City. *Artechouse.*https://www.artechouse.com/news/artechouse-announces-return-of-machine-hallucination-nyc/

Barbosa, R. G. (2009). The Philosophical Approaches to Intellectual Property and Legal Transplants - The Mexican Supreme Court and NAFTA Article 1705. *Houston Journal of International Law*, 31(3), 515–564.

Barfield, W. (2006). Intellectual Property Rights in Virtual Environments: Considering the Rights of Owners, Programmers and Virtual Avatars. *Akron Law Review*, 39(3), 649–700.

Barfield, W., & Pagallo, U. (2021). *Advanced Introduction to Law and Artificial Intelligence*. Edward Elgar Publishing Ltd.

Bellaiche, L., Shahi, R., Turpin, M. H., Ragnhildstveit, A., Sprockett, S., Barr, N., Christensen, A., & Seli, P. (2023). Humans versus AI: Whether and why we prefer human-created compared to AI-created artwork. *Cognitive Research: Principles and Implications*, 8(1), 42. DOI: 10.1186/s41235-023-00499-6 PMID: 37401999

Buccafusco, C. (2016). A theory of copyright authorship. *Virginia Law Review*, 102(5), 1229–1295. https://www.jstor.org/stable/43923336

Caldwell, M. (2023). What is an "author"? -Copyright authorship of ai art through a philosophical lens. *Houston Law Review*, 61(2), 411–442. https://houstonlawreview.org/article/92132-what-is-an-author-copyright-authorship-of-ai-art-through-a-philosophical-lens

Chesterman, S. (2024). Good models borrow, great models steal: Intellectual property rights and generative AI. *Policy and Society*, •••, puae006. Advance online publication. DOI: 10.1093/polsoc/puae006

Choudhary, V. & Ali, Aamir S. M. (2023). ChatGPT and Copyright Concerns. *Economic and Political Weekly*, 58(16), 4–5.

Cotter, T. (2010). Transformative use and cognizable harm. *Vanderbilt Journal of Entertainment and Technology Law*, 12(4), 701–753. https://scholarship.law.vanderbilt.edu/jetlaw/vol12/iss4/3

Dollens, D. (2014). Alan Turing's Drawings, Autopoiesis and Can Buildings Think? *Leonardo*, 47(3), 249–253. https://www.jstor.org/stable/43834182. DOI: 10.1162/LEON_a_00766

Eichner, S. V. (2023). *The Copyright Implications of Generative AI* [Paper presentation]. AIPLA Annual Meeting 2023

Frey, T. (2023, April 27). The difference between human creativity and generative AI creativity. *Futurist Speaker*. https://futuristspeaker.com/artificial-intelligence/the-difference-between-human-creativity-and-generative-ai-creativity/

Ghose, A. & Ali, Aamir S. M. (2023). Amplifying Music with Artificial Intelligence. *Economic and Political Weekly*, 58(17), 4–6.

Ghose, A., Ali, S. M., & Deshmukh, S. (2024). Navigating the Legal and Ethical Framework for Generative AI: Fostering Responsible Global Governance. In Ara, A., & Ara, A. (Eds.), *Exploring the Ethical Implications of Generative AI* (pp. 168–184). IGI Global., DOI: 10.4018/979-8-3693-1565-1.ch010

Ghose, A., Ali, S. M., & Mishra, A. M. (2024). Artistic Expressions, Generative AI, and Legal Tapestry: Exploring the Dynamics of Copyright Laws in the Confluence of AI and Artistic Creation. In Hai-Jew, S. (Ed.), *Making Art With Generative AI Tools* (pp. 198–214). IGI Global., DOI: 10.4018/979-8-3693-1950-5.ch011

Ghose, A., & Gilda, A. (2023). Decussating aspects of intellectual property rights and private international law in India. *Journal of Intellectual Property Rights*, 28(6), 510–517. DOI: 10.56042/jipr.v28i6.762

Grimmelmann, J. (2015). Copyright for Literate Robots. *Iowa Law Review*, 101(2), 657–681. https://ilr.law.uiowa.edu/sites/ilr.law.uiowa.edu/files/2023-02/ILR-101-2-Grimmelmann.pdf

Guadamuz, A. (2017). Artificial intelligence and copyright. *WIPO Magazine*. https://www.wipo.int/wipo_magazine/en/2017/05/article_0003.html

Hencz, A. (2022, August 19). Digitized memories and machine hallucinations. *Artland Magazine*. https://magazine.artland.com/refik-anadol/

Hristov, K. (2017). Artificial Intelligence and the Copyright Dilemma. *IDEA: The Journal of the Franklin Pierce Center for Intellectual Property*, 57(3), 431–454.

Lath, A. (2022, October 10). *AI Art and Indian Copyright Registration.* Spicy IP. https://spicyip.com/2022/10/ai-art-and-indian-copyright-registration.html

Lim, D. (2023). Generative AI and copyright: Principles, priorities and practicalities. *Journal Of Intellectual Property Law and Practice*, 18(12), 841–842. DOI: 10.1093/jiplp/jpad081

Metz, C., & Weise, K. (2023, January 23). Microsoft to invest $10 billion in openai, the creator of chatgpt. *The New York Times.* https://www.nytimes.com/2023/01/23/business/microsoft-chatgpt-artificial-intelligence.html

Militsyna, K. (2023). Human creative contribution to ai-based output – one just can('t) get enough. *GRUR International*, 72(10), 939–949. DOI: 10.1093/grurint/ikad075

Murray, M. D. (2022). *A Short and Happy Guide to Copyright* (2nd ed.). West Academic Publishing.

Murray, M. D., & DuBoff, L. D. (2023). *Art Law: Cases and Materials* (3rd ed.). Aspen Publishing.

National Harbor. MD Ramalho, A. (2022). *Intellectual Property Protection for AI-generated Creations Europe, United States, Australia and Japan.* Routledge, Taylor & Francis Group.

Rehan. (n.d.). *Who owns computer generated works.* Learn and Digest. https://learndigest.blogspot.com/2014/06/who-owns-computer-generated-works.html

Sag, M. (2012). Orphan Works as Grist for the Data Mill. *SSRN*, 27, 1503–1550. DOI: 10.2139/ssrn.2038889

Salah, A. A. A. (2021). AI bugs and failures: How and why to render AI-algorithms more human? In Verdegem, P. (Ed.), *AI for Everyone?* (pp. 161–180). University of Westminster Press., https://www.jstor.org/stable/j.ctv26qjjhj.12

Sarkar, S. (2021, August 5). *India recognises AI as co-author of copyrighted artwork.* Managing IP, https://www.managingip.com/article/2a5czmpwixyj23wyqct1c/exclusive-india-recognises-ai-as-co-author-of-copyrighted-artwork

Tan, D. (2023, November 29). Generative AI and Copyright Part 1 Copyright Infringement. *Singapore Academy of Law*https://journalsonline.academypublishing.org.sg/Journals/SAL-Practitioner/Intellectual-Property-Law/ctl/eFirstSALPDFJournalView/mid/597/ArticleId/1921/Citation/JournalsOnlinePDF

Tasioulas, J. (2022). Artificial intelligence, humanistic ethics. *Daedalus*, 151(2), 232–243. https://www.jstor.org/stable/48662038. DOI: 10.1162/daed_a_01912

UN WIPO. (1886, September 9). *Berne Convention for the Protection of Literary and Artistic Works,* No. 11850.

Vezina, B., & Moran, B. (n.d.). *Artificial Intelligence and Creativity: Why We're Against Copyright Protection for AI-Generated Output*. Creative Commons. https://creativecommons.org/2020/08/10/no-copyright-protection-for-ai-generated-output/

Watiktinnakorn, C., Seesai, J., & Kerdvibulvech, C. (2023). Blurring the lines: How AI is redefining artistic ownership and copyright. *Discover Artificial Intelligence*, 3(1), 37. DOI: 10.1007/s44163-023-00088-y

Key Terms and Definitions:

Copyright: By providing writers and artists with extensive protection against duplication, copyright law encourages innovation in literature and the arts. Copyright law safeguards the artistic components of numerous works, such as books, graphics, plays, choreography, songs, recordings, movies, sculpture, buildings, and computer programs, but it does not cover the practical or factual dimensions of these works. When an author's unique ideas are committed to paper or another physical medium, they automatically become protected works under copyright.

Creativity: Creativity is a fundamental need for the safeguarding of copyright. In order to satisfy this requirement, a piece of work must include an element that surpasses or exceeds the original. While directly quoting someone else's work is not deemed original, referring to the original work in order to express a new notion is considered original.

Fair Use: Fair use is a legal defense that may be used when a copyright owner accuses someone of copyright infringement. Fair use allows an individual to use a copyrighted work without obtaining the copyright owner's consent for activities such as criticism, commentary, news reporting, teaching, academic study, or research. These reasons serve as examples of what might be deemed fair use, but they do not necessarily include all instances of fair use.

Generative Artificial Intelligence (AI): The term "Generative AI" refers to a subset of AI that has the ability to generate new material, such as text, images, audio, and even synthetic data. The novel user interfaces that allow for the creation of high-quality text, pictures, and movies in seconds have been the driving force behind the current hype about generative AI.

Chapter 7
The Future of Universities:
Challenges and Opportunities of Applying Artificial Intelligence (AI)

Dafina Abdullahu
University Ukshin Hoti Prizren, Kosovo

Eriona Ahmetaj
https://orcid.org/0000-0002-8893-8081
University Ukshin Hoti Prizren, Kosovo

ABSTRACT

Context/Background -Today, the global world is moving in a challenging and leading direction with AI technology. Artificial intelligence (AI) has the potential to address some of the biggest challenges in education in order to define innovative teaching and learning practices. Rapid technological developments undoubtedly inevitably bring great challenges and opportunities. How are studies being conceived and prepared with this new trend in society, how much will we have such an increase in technology versus the possibility of classic studies with modern ones, how will we see these approaches for use in study permit formats. Which will be the limits on which the next generation will build their academic levels, how many risks are presented in the implementation or non-implementation of a future without sufficient and proper assessment of AI, how should we face such a demanding and challenging trend for society and the academic world in the country. These will be some of the questions that will be addressed in this paper.

DOI: 10.4018/979-8-3693-7205-0.ch007

1. INTRODUCTION

Education in our country has recently been challenged more and more by the rapid developments of technology, which are becoming very evident in the teaching and learning process. It is important to address the challenges and opportunities brought by the so-called artificial intelligence, which is present in almost every field. Both teachers and students are faced with new methods of learning things in a way that makes their work easier. Of course, it would cost money and require time to implement such a technology. According to the authors (Owoc, Sawicka, & Weichbroth, 2021) rapid technological advances have opened up new opportunities and challenges to learn anytime and anywhere, offering new methods and systems that aim to stimulate innovative teaching and improve learning outcomes. On the other hand, the application of artificial intelligence requires a large amount of data for teachers and students, which could affect their privacy. Most teachers will be afraid of being fired. (Francesc, Pedro, 2020), while on the other hand, students feel scared and worried about their evaluation and commitment. Artificial intelligence (AI) progress enables individuals to transcend traditional computers and replicate and exceed human intelligence. The emergence of these technologies has already brought about substantial transformations in the realm of education, equipping students with novel competencies. (Kuleto, Ilić, Dumangiu, & Ranković, 2021).From this we can say that students need seminars, trainings related to artificial intelligence from experts in the field, in order to get knowledge of what will happen to them in the case of applying artificial intelligence in the educational process.

2. LITERATURE REVIEW

The implementation of AI-powered chatbots in universities is gaining attention as a potential solution to increase student engagement and learning outcomes. Over the past decades, various studies have investigated the effectiveness of chatbots in various educational contexts. The use of AI-based chatbots in educational activities represents an important area for supporting student engagement and learning processes. Research has shown that chatbot technologies can improve student interaction and learning processes. (D'Mello, Olney, Williams, & Hays, 2012), enrich learning experiences by influencing student success in higher education (Winkler & Sollner, 2018) and potentially improve student motivation, engagement and engagement, learning outcomes (Deng & Yu, 2023)

2.1 Artificial intelligence

Nowadays we have a growing attention to issues related to artificial intelligence, the necessity of its application in the educational sphere on the one hand and the risk of data manipulation and its absence on the other hand. To understand the role and the importance of AI in higher education, we need to know how it is defined. There are many definitions of AI and we cannot stop at just one specific defined. Artificial intelligence (AI) is a field of study that focuses on creating software or machines that can replicate cognitive functions of human intelligence to create tasks that are normally performed by humans. According to (Russell & Norvig, 2010)"when a machine mimics the cognitive functions that humans associate with other human minds, such as learning and problem-solving," it is referred to as artificial intelligence. Therefore, we can say that there is a match between the qualification skills and the digital transformation of the institution with the aim of innovation and adaptation to environmental changes using the transformative style of leadership (collaboration skills) of the teacher-student with the aim of easier adaptation to AI. Digital transformation increases the success of the educational institution, which has a direct implication in raising the quality. A rapidly developing field of technology called artificial intelligence has the power to completely transform how we interact with one another. AI in education has started to generate new instructional and learning solutions that are currently being tested in various settings. (Pedro, 2020)

2.2 The Educational Potential of AI

Going back to (Wilson & Daugherty, 2018) three areas of potential for AI, it is possible to envision some of the potential for weak AI in education by utilizing their categories that interact and are amplified. AI, for instance, is capable of processing and delivering learning analytics data quickly, improving student support (amplifying). According to (Luckin, Holmes, Griffiths, & Forcie, 2016) educational data mining offers a lot of promise for enhancing educational support. With voice or chat interfaces, AI bots can directly respond to commonly asked questions (interacting).

AI will eventually be used more extensively for tasks like helping students with special needs through automatic material adaptation, supporting teachers (eg, through chatbot Teaching Assistants), and supporting students (eg, through a lifelong AI learning companion).

Figure 1. Different dimensions of AI

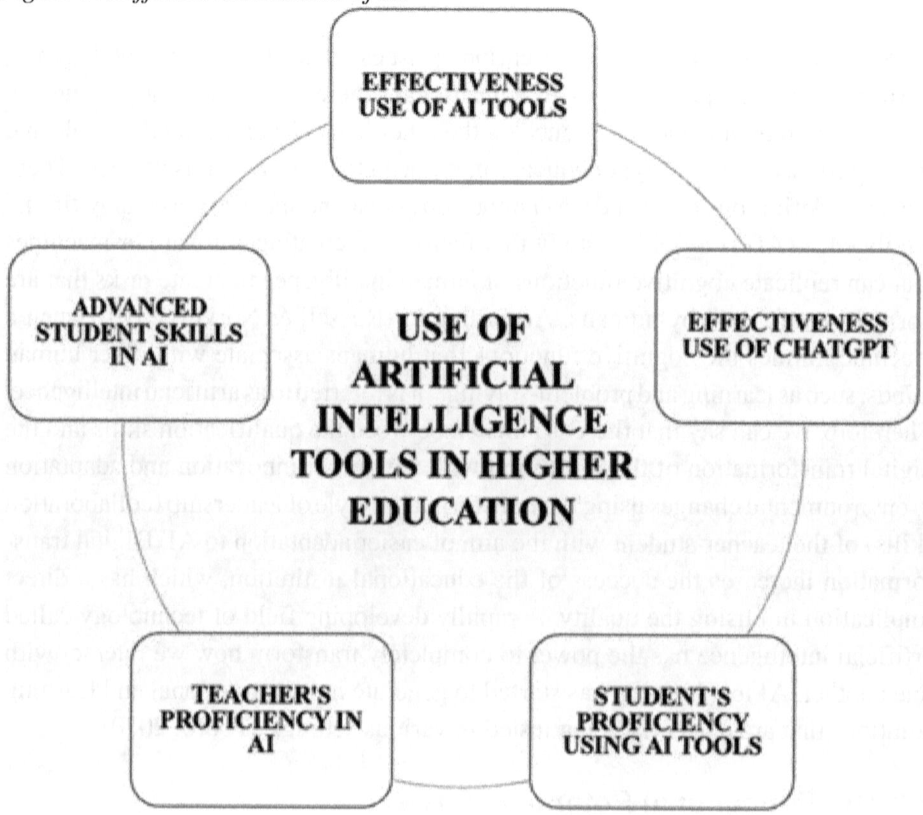

Source: (Grajeda, Burgos, Cordova, & Sanjines, 2023)

From the table above, it can be seen that artificial intelligence appears in different dimensions, which in concept have great importance for each field of its application. According to the analysis of the content of the table, it can be concluded that the rapid development of artificial intelligence affects the behavior of teachers and students by applying creative methods and approaches through training and adapting to the integration of AI in education.The main role will be played by the student, who will devote more time and importance to research work, classical teaching will fade, we will have more use of online teaching platforms, the professor can be a guidance counselor.

2.3 Opportunities of AI in Higher Education

Personalized learning: Artificial intelligence (AI) technologies can examine large amounts of data and provide learning experiences that are specifically tailored to the needs and preferences of each student (Ali & Abdel Haq MK, 2021). AI-driven adaptive learning systems significantly increase student engagement, academic achievement, and retention rates based on empirical research (Baker & Siemens, 2014). Also, AI integration can automate repetitive administrative tasks, such as planning, data management and assessment, allowing teachers and staff to focus their energies on more strategic tasks. Research from science has shown that creating and delivering education with the support of AI can result in more effective teaching strategies.

2.4 Challenges of AI in Higher Education

Successful integration of AI into higher education requires faculty and staff to cultivate new skills and expertise (Owoc, Sawicka, & Weichbroth, 2021) Scientific research has revealed that faculty and staff readiness to adopt AI poses a significant challenge, and providing professional development opportunities and robust support systems are essential for effective education (Bhatnagar, 2020). The implementation of AI technologies in higher education involves multifaceted complexities and significant costs. Scholarly research has highlighted the challenges associated with seamlessly integrating AI into existing systems, ensuring interoperability, scalability, and effective cost management in the AI adoption process (Abioye, et al., 2021) Scholarly research has highlighted the imperative to address transparency, fairness and accountability concerns in AI algorithms to ensure the responsible and ethical use of AI in educational settings (Kerr, 2020).

STUDY METHODOLOGY

3.1 Sample and Data Collection Procedures

This study aimed to explore the views of students regarding the application of artificial intelligence in the educational sphere. To achieve this, we developed a questionnaire with 30 possible questions based on Likert scale measurements. where answers were received from 250 respondents - master's level students from different fields of study.

3.2 Data Analysis

According to the model, the use of artificial intelligence has an impact on an educational institution's reputation; as its use grows, so does the institution's reputation, and conversely, as it declines, so does the institution's reputation. First, descriptive data were analyzed followed by reliability, validity, regression, and correlation analysis to test the linear relationship between the variables. SPSS 26 was used to perform these analyses.

3.3 Study Hypotheses

To examine the issues related to AI and the educational process, providing a comprehensive summary of the challenges and opportunities, we have formulated hypotheses:

Ho: The use of artificial intelligence in the educational process doesn't have an impact on the performance of master's level students
H1: The use of artificial intelligence in the educational process has an impact on the performance of master's level students.

3.4 Variables

The variables used in the research that have helped in obtaining the results are: Artificial intelligence (independent variable) and student performance (dependent variable)

3.5 Population and Sample

The selection of master's level students from various faculties is one of the population's criteria. A sample of 250 randomly selected students served as the basis for the data gathering for this study.

3.6 Research limitations/implications-

The sample was limited to survey participants only. As a result, the findings of this research cannot be generalized to the entire population. There are other factors that affect AI, but we have focused on the teaching and learning process, because only the master's level students are involved.

4. THE RESULTS

The data were analyzed using descriptive-research statistics, regression, correlation, etc. Regression was used to find the impact of artificial intelligence on the effectiveness of the education of master's level students studying in different fields.

4.1 Data Analysis

4.1.1 Descriptive Analyses

Table 1. Distribution of research participants by gender

Gender					
		Frequency	Percent	Valid Percent	Cumulative Percent
Valid	Male	90.0	36.0	36.0	36.0
	Female	160.0	64.0	64.0	100.0
	Total	250	100.0	*100.0	

The table above shows that 90 (36%) participants are male, while 160 (64%) participants are female.

Table 2. Distribution of research participants by age

Age					
		Frequency	Percent	Valid Percent	Cumulative Percent
Valid	18-25 years old	140.0	56.0	56.0	56.0
	26-35 years old	80.0	32.0	32.0	88.0
	36-45 years old	20.0	8.0	8.0	96.0
	Over 45 years old	10.0	4.0	4.0	100.0
	Total	250	100.0	100.0	

The table regarding the age variable shows that 140 participants (56%) are aged 18-25; 80 participants (32%) are aged 26-35; 20 participants (8%) are aged 36-45; 10 participants (4%) are over 45 years old.

Table 3. Distribution of research participants, according to marital status

Marital status					
		Frequency	Percent	Valid Percent	Cumulative Percent
Valid	Married	95.0	38.0	38.0	38.0
	Single	135.0	54.0	54.0	92.0
	Other	20.0	8.0	8.0	100.0
	Total	250	100.0	100.0	

Regarding information on marital status, 95 participants (38%) are married, 135 of them (54%) are single, and 20 participants (8%) have a marital status other than married or single.

Table 4. Distribution of participants in the research, according to the Faculty of the study

Faculty of the study					
		Frequency	Percent	Valid Percent	Cumulative Percent
Valid	Economic	75.0	30.0	30.0	30.0
	Legal/Law	36.0	14.4	14.4	44.4
	Natural Science	25.0	10.0	10.0	54.4
	Computer Science	60.0	24.0	24.0	78.4
	Philology	35.0	14.0	14.0	92.4
	Education	19.0	7.6	7.6	100.0
	Total	250	100.0	100.0	

The above table regarding the level of education shows that 75 participants (30%) are students studying at the Faculty of Economics, 36 participants (14.4%) are students studying at the Faculty of Law, 25 participants (10%) are students studying at the Faculty of Natural Sciences, 60 participants (24%) are students studying at the Faculty of Computer Sciences, 35 participants (14%) are students studying at the Faculty of Philology and 19 participants (7.6%) are students studying at the Faculty of Education.

4.1. Validity Analysis

Table 5. KMO dhe Bartlett's Test

KMO and Bartlett's Test		
Kaiser-Meyer-Olkin Measure of Sampling Adequacy.		**.576**
Bartlett's Test of Sphericity	Approx. Chi-Square	3356.728
	Df	435
	Sig.	.000

KMO indicates the suitability of the data set to perform factor analysis. If the KMO value is greater than 0.50 then we say that the data set is suitable for factorial analysis.

In our example, the KMO value 0.576 > 0.50. This indicates that the data set is suitable for factor analysis. This can also be understood from the Bartlett test, the Sig value. of which is 0.000. Because this value is less than 0.05 (5%), we can say that the data set is suitable for factorial analysis. In other words, there are high correlations between the variables

Table 6. Total Variance Explained

Total Variance Explained									
	Initial Eigenvalues			Extraction Sums of Squared Loadings			Rotation Sums of Squared Loadings		
Component	Total	% of Variance	Cumulative %	Total	% of Variance	Cumulative %	Total	% of Variance	Cumulative %
1	3.696	12.321	12.321	3.696	12.321	12.321	2.365	7.884	7.884
2	3.569	11.896	24.217	3.569	11.896	24.217	2.238	7.459	15.342
3	2.436	8.121	32.338	2.436	8.121	32.338	2.214	7.379	22.721
4	2.250	7.499	39.837	2.250	7.499	39.837	2.178	7.261	29.982
5	2.143	7.143	46.980	2.143	7.143	46.980	2.113	7.043	37.024
6	1.866	6.221	53.201	1.866	6.221	53.201	2.108	7.026	44.051
7	1.663	5.543	58.744	1.663	5.543	58.744	1.993	6.644	50.694
8	1.402	4.673	63.417	1.402	4.673	63.417	1.960	6.534	57.229
9	1.328	4.426	67.843	1.328	4.426	67.843	1.863	6.211	63.440
10	1.045	3.482	71.326	1.045	3.482	71.326	1.838	6.127	69.567
11	1.018	3.394	74.720	1.018	3.394	74.720	1.546	5.153	**74.720**
12	.919	3.063	77.783						
13	.851	2.835	80.618						
14	.774	2.580	83.198						
15	.634	2.115	85.312						
16	.606	2.019	87.331						
17	.456	1.521	88.852						
18	.452	1.508	90.360						
19	.425	1.416	91.776						
20	.377	1.258	93.033						
21	.307	1.024	94.058						
22	.286	.952	95.010						
23	.265	.883	95.893						
24	.245	.816	96.709						

continued on following page

Table 6. Continued

Total Variance Explained									
Component	Initial Eigenvalues			Extraction Sums of Squared Loadings			Rotation Sums of Squared Loadings		
	Total	% of Variance	Cumulative %	Total	% of Variance	Cumulative %	Total	% of Variance	Cumulative %
25	.210	.699	97.408						
26	.194	.645	98.053						
27	.160	.533	98.586						
28	.156	.519	99.105						
29	.141	.469	99.574						
30	.128	.426	100.000						

Extraction Method: Principal Component Analysis.

Total Variance Explained table summarizes information about the total variance explained. Using 30 statements, 11 factors with an Eigen value greater than 1 were formed. In total, the 11 factors describe 74.72% of the total variance, which represents a moderately high value. Where can we say these statements which have been used to measure the application of artificial intelligence in the performance of master's level students measure this at a level of 74.72%>50%.

Table 7. The final result of the factor analysis

Rotated Component Matrix[a]											
	Component										
	1	2	3	4	5	6	7	8	9	10	11
Artificial intelligence doen't eliminate human error	.825	.221	-.102	.183	.116	.061	.000	.037	-.022	.035	-.080
Artificial intelligence gives students more time for research	-.769	.145	-.176	.021	.259	-.026	.091	.024	.037	.033	.168
Artificial intelligence will increase the possibility of fraud	-.479	.023	-.141	-.407	.329	-.022	-.085	-.321	.255	-.139	-.100
The use of artificial intelligence increases cooperation with others	.460	.251	-.208	-.352	.221	.220	.120	.113	.160	.440	.048
Trainings and seminars for artificial intelligence will have a positive impact	.032	.776	-.062	-.144	-.016	-.124	-.102	-.117	-.141	.019	-.021
Artificial intelligence enables me to make the right decisions	.097	.636	.172	.146	.288	-.063	.373	-.016	.242	-.030	.012
Artificial intelligence enables me to be as creative as possible in lessons	-.062	.634	.106	.160	.204	.188	.253	.295	-.059	-.028	-.034
With the application of artificial intelligence, it will take more time	-.291	-.492	-.460	.049	-.030	-.238	.056	-.064	.129	.148	-.119
Artificial intelligence will provide data transparency	.039	.099	.839	-.165	-.072	.070	-.243	-.057	.064	.016	.065
Artificial intelligence will increase the level of youth unemployment	-.034	.013	.606	.354	.125	.207	.121	.114	.019	.295	-.257

continued on following page

Table 7. Continued

Rotated Component Matrix[a]											
	Component										
	1	**2**	**3**	**4**	**5**	**6**	**7**	**8**	**9**	**10**	**11**
Artificial intelligence will last for a short time	.123	-.013	-.083	.858	-.039	.020	.023	-.080	.038	-.114	.035
Artificial intelligence has an important role for students in facilitating tasks	-.088	.225	.091	.500	.112	.190	.091	.319	.495	.269	-.092
Artificial intelligence increases the possibility of social distancing	-.121	.127	-.034	-.006	.834	-.156	.072	.018	.029	.071	.053
Artificial intelligence makes us as student'shave greater opportunities in the proposal of programs	.190	-.221	-.429	.389	-.495	.197	-.158	.179	-.041	.037	-.070
The use of artificial intelligence increases the possibility of learning new things	.125	-.173	.054	.015	-.035	.666	.175	.218	.149	-.024	.153
Artificial intelligence will increase the number of applicants to study	.045	-.079	-.179	-.265	.041	-.656	.240	.151	-.162	.120	-.066
Artificial intelligence will replace classical learning	.049	.005	.173	.194	.136	-.639	.042	.092	.406	.031	.310
The use of artificial intelligence increases the effectiveness of the study	.314	.347	.186	.000	-.141	.548	-.284	.027	.089	.058	-.149
With the application of artificial intelligence, more commitment is required	-.009	.114	-.206	.124	.044	-.105	.786	.061	.069	.064	-.051
Artificial intelligence will not have much impact on my life as a student	-.140	.038	.059	-.399	.237	.050	.635	.104	-.361	.000	.171
Artificial intelligence makes students' performance increase	.302	.189	.037	.065	.303	.037	.023	.763	-.005	.089	.067
Artificial intelligence increases dependence on technological tools	.124	.175	.024	.090	.337	.066	-.121	-.719	-.149	.109	-.076
Artificial intelligence makes it easier for students to follow lectures and understand them	.108	-.103	.408	.124	.109	-.308	.417	-.494	.245	.020	.030
Using artificial intelligence increases my performance as a student	-.009	-.156	.081	.029	.075	.043	.015	.050	.827	-.078	-.024
Artificial intelligence enables me to have greater responsibility for studies	-.230	.119	-.334	-.149	-.310	.201	-.228	-.136	.518	.093	.108
Artificial intelligence requires infrastructure and costs	-.164	-.024	.098	-.145	-.027	.157	.049	-.071	.068	-.786	.078
Artificial intelligence makes me feel scared	.207	.188	-.275	.268	-.042	-.002	-.076	.090	-.085	-.686	.194
Artificial intelligence will have high application costs	-.017	.037	.245	-.219	-.132	.098	.400	-.309	-.119	.504	.318
Artificial intelligence shortens the time for making decisions	-.276	-.032	-.044	.062	.005	-.053	-.043	.109	-.014	-.138	.790
The use of artificial intelligence makes studying easier and faster	.146	.029	.058	-.128	.580	.139	.177	-.029	.030	-.020	.651

Extraction Method: Principal Component Analysis.
Rotation Method: Varimax with Kaiser Normalization.[a]
a. Rotation converged in 21 iterations.

4.1.1 Regression Analysis

Table 8. Model Summary

Model Summary[b]					
Model	R	R Square	Adjusted R Square	Std. Error of the Estimate	Durbin-Watson
1	.110[a]	.012	.008	.31335	.418

a. Predictors: (Constant),
b. Dependent Variable: Student performance (PS)

The Model Summary table presents the summary of the regression model. The R2 value indicates how much % of the variation in the dependent variable is explained by the independent variable. This value was found to be 0.012, which indicates that 1.2% of the variation in the dependent variable (student performance) is explained by the independent variable (the use of artificial intelligence in the educational process.).

Figure 2. Two variables relationship

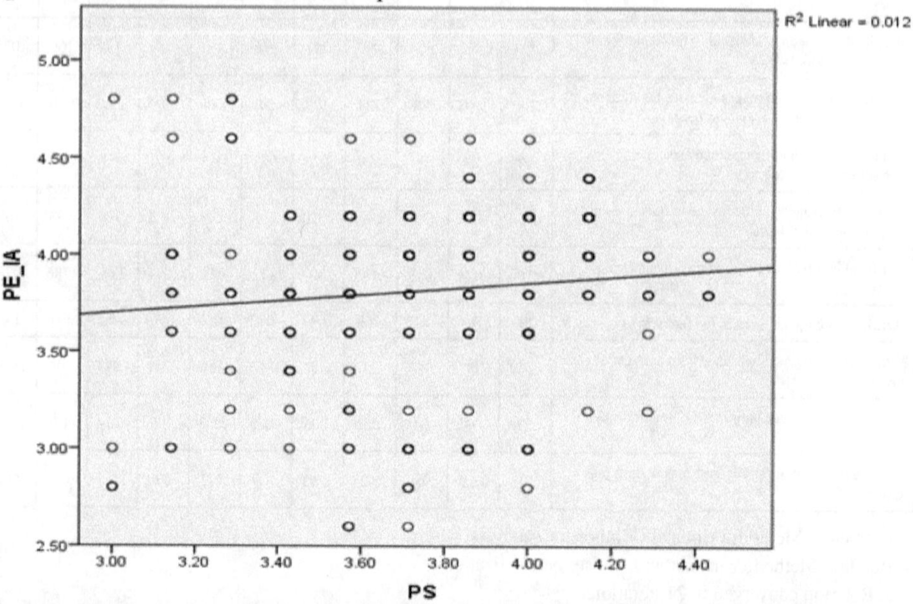

From the graph we can see that there is a negative relationship between the two variables selected for the study. This can also be seen by the distance of the points from the linear regression line.

Table 9. ANOVA

ANOVA[a]						
Model		Sum of Squares	df	Mean Square	F	Sig.
1	Regression	.300	1	.300	3.056	.082[b]
	Residual	24.351	248	.098		
	Total	24.651	249			

a. Dependent Variable: Student Performance (PS)
b. Predictors: (Constant), PE_IA

The ANOVA table summarizes the F value and sig, which explain the significance of the regression model. The value F=3.056 and p=.082>0.05 show that the regression model is not significant

Table 10. Coefficients

Coefficients[a]								
		Unstandardized Coefficients		Standardized Coefficients			Collinearity Statistics	
Model		B	Std. Error	Beta	T	Sig.	Tolerance	VIF
1	(Constant)	3.435	.171		20.030	.000		
	US_IA	.078	.045	.110	1.748	.082	1.000	1.000

a. Dependent Variable: PS

The Coefficients table summarizes the final result of the regression analysis. The constant shows how much the students' performance would be (dependent variable) if the use of artificial intelligence in their educational process would be zero (independent variable). In this case, the value of the constant is β 3.435,

So, the use of artificial intelligence in the educational process has an impact of 7.8% in increasing the performance of students.

$$y = \beta_0 + \beta_1 X + u$$

Students' performance= 3.435+ 0.078 using artificial intelligence

According to the analyzes made, we can say that the use of artificial intelligence for master's students has no impact on the level of performance. Since the hypothesis is not significant, then the hypothesis H_1 rejected.

So, claiming in these results, H_0 is successfully accepted

CONCLUSION

The research concluded that most master's students of various study areas, despite having knowledge about artificial intelligence, still struggled to apply its principles and understand how it works. Based on the data, we have determined that there is a not favorable correlation between the use of artificial intelligence in education and student performance measures. Most of the responding students have affirmed that the frequency of student-teacher meetings can bring positive results to the teaching and learning process. Artificial intelligence is a challenge and an opportunity for each of the institutions because it requires time for its adaptation and its application costs.

Due to the inadequate infrastructure on the part of institutions, staff, and students, such a thing cannot yet be supported to be put into operation. One of the reasons may be the need for a more professional, and trained staff with appropriate skills for this field. The research also concluded that the existence of artificial intelligence in the educational process has a positive correlation with the application of new methods. These data can be used as a benchmark and source of support for additional studies conducted in the same field. These studies can help educational institutions understand how certain aspects of artificial intelligence are developing to create a true and suitable environment

RECOMMENDATIONS

Master's level students of different fields of study in the country are recommended to first get informed more about the terms of artificial intelligence, and then about its impact on the performance and efficiency of education. With sufficient information, they can take initiatives that make it easier for them to accept innovations and avoid possible shortcomings that they may have in the educational process. All resources play an important role in artificial intelligence, and it is recommended to create a working group within the institution to create functionality and control the educational action. Each of the members of the working group should have adequate knowledge in this field to have real control in case of the application of intelligence in educational institutions. Trainings and seminars in this very challenging field should be organized for the students' performance to be at a high level. Institutions must make appropriate plans for the allocation of the budget in such a way that access to information is as easy as possible.

REFERENCES:

Abioye, S. O., Oyedele, L. O., Akanbi, L., Ajay, A., Delgado, J. D., Bilal, M., & Ahmed, A. (2021). Artificial intelligence in the construction industry: A review of present status,opportunities and future challenges. *Journal of Building Engineering Elsevier*https://www.sciencedirect.com/science/article/pii/S2352710221011578

Ali, M., & Abdel Haq, M. K. (2021). Bibliographical analysis of artificial intelligence learning in Higher Education: is the role of the human educator and educated a thing of the past? *IGI Global.* In Fostering Communication and Learning With Underutilized Technologies in Higher Education, 2021, 36-52. IGI Global. 7998-4846-2.ch003.https://www.igi-global.com/chapter/bibliographical-analysis-of-artificial-intelligence-learning-in-higher-education/262720

Baker, R. S., & Siemens, G. (2014). Educational data mining and learning analytics. 1-29DOI:. https://www.researchgate.net/publication/316628053_Educational_data_mining_and_learning_analytics/link/611682a60c2bfa282a41e893/download?_tp=eyJjb250ZXh0Ijp7ImZpcnN0UGFnZSI6InB1YmxpY2F0aW9uIiwicGFnZSI6InB1YmxpY2F0aW9uIn19DOI: 10.1017/CBO9781139519526.016

Bhatnagar, H. (2020). Artificial Intelligence-A New Horizon in Indian Higher Education. Journal of Learning and Teaching in Digital Age, 2020, 6(1), 30-34 ISSN: 2458-8350 pp 30-34 https://dergipark.org.tr/en/download/article-file/1184703

D'Mello, S., Olney, A., Williams, C., & Hays, P. (2012). Gaze tutor: A gaze-reactive intelligent tutoring system. *International Journal of Human-Computer Studies, 70(5), 377-398*, Retrieved from Gaze tutor: A gaze reactive intelligent tutoring system: https://www.sciencedirect.com/science/article/abs/pii/S1071581912000250?via%3DihubDOI: 10.1016/j.ijhcs.2012.01.004

Deng, X., & Yu, Z. (2023). A meta-analysis and systematic review of the effect of chatbot technology use in sustainable education. *Sustainability (Basel)*, 15(4), 2940. https://www.mdpi.com/2071-1050/15/4/2940. DOI: 10.3390/su15042940

. Francesc, Pedro. (2020). Applications of Artificial Intelligence to higher education: possibilities, evidence and challenges. *Journal of IUL University*, 61-76 DOI: .DOI: 10.57568/iulres.v1i1.43

Francesc, P., Subosa, M., Rivas, A., & Valverde, P. (2019). *Artificial Intelligence in Education Challenges and Opportunities for Sustainable Development.* Paris https://repositorio.minedu.gob.pe/handle/20.500.12799/6533: United Nations Educational, Scientific and Cultural Organization UNESCO.

Grajeda, A., Burgos, J., Cordova, P., & Sanjines, A. (2023). Assessing student-perceived impact of using artificial intelligence tools: Construction of a synthetic index of application in higher education. *Taylor and Francis Group*, 1-24 https://www.tandfonline.com/doi/full/10.1080/2331186X.2023.2287917

Kerr, K. (2020). Ethical considerations when using artificial intelligence-based assistive technologies in education. Ethical use of technology in digital learning environments: Graduates student perspectives., Pressbooks https://pressbooks.openeducationalberta.ca/educationaltechnologyethics/chapter/ethical-considerations-when-using-artificial-intelligence-based-assistive-technologies-in-education/

Kuleto, V., Ilić, M., Dumangiu, M., Ranković, M., Martins, O. M., Păun, D., & Mihoreanu, L. (2021). Exploring opportunities and challenges of artificial intelligence and machine learning in higher education institutions. *Sustainability (Basel)*, 13(18), 10424. https://www.mdpi.com/2071-1050/13/18/10424. DOI: 10.3390/su131810424

Luckin, R., Holmes, W., Griffiths, M., & Forcie. (2016). Intelligence unleashed: An argument for AI in education. London. *Retrievedfrom*https://static.googleusercontent.com/media/edu.google.com/en//pdfs/IntelligenceUnleashed-Publication.pdf

Owoc, M. L., Sawicka, A., & Weichbroth, P. (2021). *Artificial Intelligence Technologies in Education: Benefits, Challenges and Strategies of Implementation*. Springer., DOI: 10.1007/978-3-030-85001-2_4

Pedro, F. (2020). Applications of Artificial Intelligence to higher education: possibilities, evidence and challenges. https://iulresearch.iuline.it/index.php/IUL-RES/article/view/43, 61-76.

Wilson, J., & Daugherty, P. (2018). How humans and AI are working together in 1,500 companies. Harvard Business Review, July-August. Retrieved August 13, 2018, from https://hbr.org/2018/07/collaborative-intelligence-humans-and-ai-are-joining-forc. *Harvard Business Review, July-August*.

Winkler, R., & Sollner, M. (2018). Unleashing the potential of chatbots in education: A state-of-the-art analysis. *Proceedings - Academy of Management*, 2018(1), 1–40. DOI: 10.5465/AMBPP.2018.15903abstract

Chapter 8
The Role of AI in Enhancing Access to Justice and Legal Services

Rajesh Kanna Rajendran
https://orcid.org/0000-0001-7228-5031
Christ University, India

Ashok Immanuel V.
https://orcid.org/0000-0002-2422-6261
Christ University, India

Mohana Priya T.
Christ University, India

S. Vetrivel
SKP Arts and Science College, India

Wilfred Blessing N. R.
University of Technology and Applied Sciences-Ibri, Oman

ABSTRACT

Access to justice and legal services remains a critical issue in many societies, often hindered by high costs, complex procedures, and limited availability of legal professionals. This chapter explores the transformative potential of Artificial Intelligence (AI) in addressing these barriers and enhancing access to justice for all. AI technologies, including machine learning, natural language processing, and intelligent automation, are increasingly being integrated into legal systems to streamline processes and provide affordable legal assistance. It highlights key AI applications, such as AI-driven legal research tools, virtual legal assistants, and

DOI: 10.4018/979-8-3693-7205-0.ch008

online dispute resolution platforms, which democratize legal knowledge and services. These tools empower individuals with limited resources to understand their legal rights, receive preliminary legal advice, and navigate legal systems without the need for costly professional services.

INTRODUCTION

The legal profession is undergoing a profound transformation, driven by the rapid advancements in Artificial Intelligence (AI). As access to justice and legal services remains a significant challenge globally, AI offers innovative solutions to address these issues. Traditionally, legal services have been marked by high costs, slow processes, and limited accessibility, which often leaves underserved populations struggling to obtain necessary legal support. However, the integration of AI into the legal field is beginning to change this landscape, making legal services more efficient, affordable, and accessible.

AI technologies are revolutionizing how legal services are delivered by automating routine tasks, improving research accuracy, and providing instant support through virtual assistants and chatbots. These advancements are not only streamlining legal operations but also democratizing access to legal resources, enabling individuals who previously faced barriers to legal support to receive timely and effective assistance. By leveraging AI, the legal sector is moving towards a more inclusive and equitable system, where the promise of justice is extended to a broader audience. As we explore the various ways AI is enhancing access to justice, it becomes clear that these technologies are poised to play a crucial role in reshaping the future of legal services.

AI technologies have the potential to significantly improve document management practices in the legal field. By automating and streamlining tasks such as contract analysis and due diligence, AI tools, which utilize natural language processing and machine learning algorithms, can efficiently extract relevant information, categorize documents, and identify potential risks or anomalies. This not only reduces the need for manual effort but also speeds up the review process and enhances the accuracy of document analysis.

While the benefits of AI in legal decision-making are considerable, there are critical ethical issues that must be addressed before its widespread adoption in the judicial system. One major challenge is the lack of transparency and explainability in AI systems. Deep learning algorithms and other complex models often deliver accurate results without clear explanations of how they arrived at those conclusions, raising concerns about the reliability of AI-generated outcomes. To build trust in these systems, it is essential to develop AI models that offer interpretable explanations for their predictions, allowing legal professionals to understand and assess the underlying logic.

Another significant ethical concern is the potential for bias in AI-driven legal decision-making. AI systems trained on flawed or biased data can reinforce and exacerbate existing societal biases, leading to unfair and discriminatory outcomes. To ensure fairness, it is crucial to carefully select and audit training data, and to regularly check for and address any biases. Additionally, involving diverse and inclusive teams in the development and validation of AI systems is essential to minimize bias and ensure a broad range of perspectives are considered.

One significant advantage of AI-driven systems is their ability to significantly reduce the time needed for making legal judgments. By automating routine tasks and streamlining legal research, AI technologies can accelerate decision-making processes within the legal profession. These systems, equipped with AI algorithms, can efficiently process vast amounts of legal information, including case law, statutes, and regulations. Natural Language Processing (NLP) plays a crucial role here, as it helps extract relevant data, identify precedents, legal principles, and detailed specifics that can impact the outcome of legal cases. Overall, this advanced analysis not only improves the accuracy of legal research but also enhances the efficiency of legal professionals.

Literature Review

The integration of Artificial Intelligence (AI) into the legal field has garnered significant attention in recent years, particularly in its potential to enhance access to justice and improve the delivery of legal services. This literature review examines key studies and developments in AI technologies applied to the legal domain, exploring their impacts on efficiency, accessibility, and equity in legal services.

AI has revolutionized legal research and document review, tasks traditionally characterized by labor-intensive processes. Early research highlighted the potential of AI to expedite these processes through automated analysis. Katz et al. (2017) demonstrated how AI-powered tools could enhance legal research by rapidly sifting through vast amounts of case law and statutes, thereby significantly reducing the time required for legal research. Surden (2019) explored the use of machine learning algorithms for document review, emphasizing the efficiency gains and error reduction achieved through AI integration.

The automation of document drafting and contract analysis is another area where AI is making substantial contributions. Susskind (2020) indicated that AI systems, such as those employing natural language processing (NLP), could generate legal documents and contracts with high accuracy and speed, thereby lowering costs and improving accessibility. AI's ability to analyze and generate documents was further corroborated by Rodriguez and Gomez (2021), who found that AI tools could produce customized legal documents by interpreting user inputs and pre-defined templates.

Predictive analytics in legal practice, powered by AI, has been a significant focus of recent research. Katz, Bommarito, and Blackman (2018) explored how predictive models could forecast legal outcomes by analyzing historical case data and judicial behavior. Their findings highlighted the potential of predictive analytics to enhance strategic planning and decision-making in legal practice. Langer and Taylor (2022) examined the accuracy and utility of AI-driven predictions in various legal contexts, emphasizing how these tools could provide valuable insights into case outcomes and litigation strategies.

AI-powered chatbots and virtual assistants have emerged as vital tools for improving client interactions and accessibility. Research by Lin et al. (2019) highlighted how legal chatbots could provide immediate assistance and answer common legal questions, thus making legal information more accessible to the general public. McCarthy (2021) examined the role of virtual assistants in guiding users through legal processes and offering personalized support, demonstrating their potential to bridge gaps in access to legal services.

AI's application in case management and workflow automation has been extensively studied. According to McGinnis and Pearce (2021), AI-driven case management systems streamline administrative tasks such as scheduling, billing, and document management, thereby enhancing operational efficiency within legal practices. These systems not only improve internal workflows but also contribute to a more responsive and client-centered approach to legal service delivery.

AI's role in risk assessment and compliance management is gaining traction in the legal field. Research by McCormick (2022) explored how AI tools could analyze regulatory changes and identify potential risks, aiding organizations in maintaining compliance and mitigating legal risks. The study emphasized the value of AI in managing complex regulatory environments and enhancing proactive risk management strategies.

AI technologies are also playing a crucial role in expanding access to justice through online platforms and legal aid services. According to Wright and Schauer (2023), AI-powered platforms connect individuals with legal resources and pro bono services, improving access for underserved populations. These platforms leverage AI to match users with appropriate legal support and provide essential legal information, thereby addressing disparities in legal service availability.

The literature highlights the transformative impact of AI on the legal field, particularly in enhancing access to justice and improving the efficiency of legal services. From automating routine tasks and improving legal research to providing predictive insights and expanding access through chatbots and online platforms, AI technologies are reshaping how legal services are delivered. As AI continues to evolve, its integration into legal practice promises further advancements in accessibility, efficiency, and equity, addressing longstanding challenges in the legal profession and contributing to a more inclusive and effective legal system.

Examining the Various Ways AI is Transforming the Delivery of Legal Services

AI is rapidly transforming the delivery of legal services by introducing efficiencies, improving accessibility, and enhancing the quality of legal work. The integration of AI technologies into legal practice is reshaping how legal services are provided, making them more effective and affordable. Here, we explore the various ways AI is revolutionizing the legal field.

Enhanced Legal Research

AI-powered legal research tools leverage machine learning and natural language processing (NLP) to analyze vast amounts of legal data, including case law, statutes, and legal opinions. Traditional legal research methods can be time-consuming and labor-intensive. In contrast, AI tools quickly identify relevant precedents and provide comprehensive analyses, allowing legal professionals to find pertinent information with greater speed and accuracy. This capability not only reduces the time spent on research but also ensures that legal arguments are well-supported by the most relevant and recent case law.

Automated Document Drafting

Automated document drafting systems use AI to generate legal documents such as contracts, wills, and legal briefs based on predefined templates and user inputs. These systems employ NLP to understand user requirements and create customized documents efficiently. Automated drafting reduces the need for manual input and minimizes errors, thereby increasing the accuracy and speed of document creation. It also makes legal services more accessible by lowering the cost of routine document preparation.

Predictive Analytics

AI-driven predictive analytics tools analyze historical data and trends to forecast the outcomes of legal cases. By examining factors such as case precedents, judge rulings, and litigation strategies, these tools provide valuable insights into the likely success of legal actions. Predictive analytics assist legal professionals in developing more effective case strategies and offer clients a clearer understanding of their legal prospects. This technology enhances decision-making and helps manage expectations regarding case outcomes.

AI-Powered Legal Chatbots

Legal chatbots and virtual assistants use AI to interact with clients, answer legal questions, and guide users through legal processes. These tools employ NLP to understand and respond to user inquiries, providing immediate and accurate information. Legal chatbots can handle a range of tasks, from simple legal queries to complex procedural guidance, making legal assistance more accessible and convenient. They also free up time for legal professionals by handling routine inquiries and administrative tasks.

Intelligent Case Management

AI-enhanced case management systems streamline the administrative aspects of legal practice. These systems automate tasks such as scheduling, billing, and document management, enabling law firms to operate more efficiently. AI tools can track case progress, manage deadlines, and ensure that critical tasks are completed on time. By reducing the burden of administrative work, AI allows legal professionals to focus more on substantive legal issues and client interactions.

Advanced Due Diligence

AI technologies are increasingly used for due diligence in legal and corporate transactions. AI tools analyze vast quantities of data to identify potential risks and compliance issues. This includes reviewing contracts, financial statements, and other critical documents to uncover discrepancies or red flags. By automating due diligence processes, AI enhances the accuracy and efficiency of these tasks, reducing the likelihood of oversights and facilitating smoother transaction processes.

Enhanced Client Interaction

AI is transforming client interactions through personalized and efficient communication. AI tools can analyze client data to provide tailored advice and recommendations. For instance, AI systems can assess client needs and preferences to offer customized legal solutions or suggest relevant services. This personalized approach improves client satisfaction and helps build stronger client relationships.

Legal Analytics

Legal analytics tools use AI to analyze patterns and trends in legal data. By examining case law, judicial decisions, and litigation outcomes, these tools provide insights into legal trends and emerging issues. Legal analytics support strategic planning by offering data-driven insights into legal practice areas, helping firms and clients make informed decisions based on comprehensive analysis.

Risk Assessment and Management

AI is used to assess and manage legal and regulatory risks. AI tools analyze data from various sources, including legal texts and regulatory updates, to identify potential risks and compliance issues. These tools help organizations stay compliant with changing regulations and anticipate legal challenges before they arise. AI-driven risk management improves the ability to mitigate legal risks and avoid costly legal disputes.

Access to Justice

AI is playing a crucial role in improving access to justice by making legal services more affordable and accessible. Online platforms powered by AI connect individuals with legal resources, pro bono services, and legal aid organizations. AI tools can provide basic legal advice and document preparation services at a lower cost, bridging the gap for underserved populations and ensuring that more people can access legal help.

AI is significantly transforming the delivery of legal services by enhancing efficiency, accuracy, and accessibility. From automated document drafting and predictive analytics to advanced case management and client interaction, AI technologies are reshaping how legal services are provided and consumed. As AI continues to evolve, it promises to further revolutionize the legal field, making legal services more effective and accessible while driving improvements in legal practice and client outcomes. Embracing these innovations will be crucial for legal professionals seeking to stay competitive and meet the evolving needs of their clients in a rapidly changing landscape.

Bias Mitigation and Fairness in AI for Legal Decision-Making

As AI technologies become increasingly integral to legal decision-making, addressing bias and ensuring fairness are paramount concerns. AI systems, while offering significant advantages in efficiency and accuracy, can inadvertently perpetuate and amplify existing societal biases if not carefully managed. Here's a closer look at the key strategies for mitigating bias and promoting fairness in AI-driven legal systems. Bias in AI systems often originates from the data used to train these models. If the training data reflects historical biases or discriminatory practices, the AI system may reproduce and even exacerbate these biases. For instance, an AI model trained on historical sentencing data may inherit and replicate biases present in judicial decisions, potentially leading to unfair treatment of certain groups. This issue underscores the importance of addressing bias at every stage of AI development, from data collection to model deployment.

STRATEGIES FOR BIAS MITIGATION

Careful Data Selection and Preprocessing

Data Collection: Ensuring that the data used to train AI models is representative and free from discriminatory biases is crucial. This involves collecting diverse datasets that accurately reflect the populations and scenarios the AI will encounter in practice.

Data Preprocessing: Techniques such as data anonymization and de-biasing can help minimize the impact of biased data. This involves identifying and removing or correcting biased elements within the training data to prevent them from influencing the AI model.

Bias Detection and Regular Audits

Bias Detection Tools: Implementing tools and methodologies to detect bias in AI systems is essential. These tools analyze model outputs and identify disparities in how different groups are treated.

Regular Audits: Conducting regular audits of AI systems helps to identify and address emerging biases. These audits should be an ongoing process, not a one-time activity, to ensure that any new biases introduced over time are promptly addressed.

Transparent and Explainable AI

Explainability: Developing AI systems that provide clear, interpretable explanations for their predictions can help identify and address potential biases. Transparency in how decisions are made allows legal professionals to scrutinize and understand the rationale behind AI-driven outcomes.

Accountability: Ensuring that AI systems are accountable involves making the decision-making process transparent and open to review. This accountability helps build trust and ensures that any biased outcomes can be challenged and corrected.

Diverse and Inclusive Development Teams

Inclusive Design: Involving diverse teams in the development of AI systems can help mitigate bias. Diverse perspectives contribute to a more comprehensive understanding of potential biases and ensure that the AI model considers a wider range of viewpoints.

Stakeholder Engagement: Engaging with stakeholders, including community representatives and advocacy groups, can provide valuable insights into how AI systems impact different groups and help address any issues of bias.

Ethical Frameworks and Guidelines

Ethical Standards: Adopting ethical standards and guidelines for AI development and deployment ensures that fairness and bias mitigation are prioritized. These frameworks guide the design and implementation of AI systems to promote equitable outcomes.

Regulatory Compliance: Adhering to legal and regulatory requirements related to fairness and non-discrimination helps ensure that AI systems are developed and used in accordance with established ethical norms.

Promoting Fairness in AI Systems

Ensuring fairness in AI systems involves not only addressing bias but also striving for equitable outcomes. This means designing AI systems that provide fair treatment to all individuals, regardless of their background or characteristics. By implementing strategies such as data diversification, bias detection, and inclusive design, the legal field can harness the benefits of AI while promoting fairness and mitigating the risks of bias.

Bias mitigation and Fairness are critical components of developing AI systems for legal decision-making. By adopting comprehensive strategies to address bias, ensuring transparency and explainability, and fostering diversity within development teams, the legal sector can enhance the effectiveness of AI technologies while safeguarding the principles of justice and equality.

AI-Driven Legal Chatbots: Transforming Access to Legal Information for Low-Income Individuals

AI-driven legal chatbots are revolutionizing how low-income individuals access legal information and support. Traditionally, navigating legal issues required costly consultations with attorneys or limited access to legal aid services, which many low-income individuals could not afford. AI chatbots, however, provide a scalable solution by offering immediate, 24/7 access to legal information and guidance. These chatbots can handle a range of inquiries, from basic legal advice to more specific questions about legal processes and rights. By using natural language processing, they can understand and respond to user queries in a conversational manner, making legal information more accessible and user-friendly.

The impact of AI chatbots extends beyond just providing information. They help bridge the justice gap by offering preliminary legal advice, assisting with document preparation, and directing users to appropriate legal resources or services. For individuals facing financial constraints, this technology reduces the need for expensive consultations and makes it easier to navigate legal systems independently. As AI chatbots continue to evolve, they have the potential to enhance the reach and effectiveness of legal aid services, ensuring that more people receive the support they need without the burden of high costs.

Enhancing Legal Access for Non-English Speakers: AI Translation and Language Processing in Legal Services

In today's multicultural society, ensuring equitable access to legal services for non-English speakers is a critical challenge. Traditional legal systems often pose significant barriers for individuals who are not fluent in English, potentially leading to misunderstandings and inadequate representation. AI translation and language processing technologies are playing a transformative role in overcoming these barriers, making legal information and services more accessible to a diverse population. By leveraging sophisticated algorithms and natural language processing, AI tools can accurately translate legal documents, court proceedings, and informational materials into multiple languages, thereby facilitating clearer communication between legal professionals and non-English speaking clients.

AI-driven language processing tools extend beyond mere translation by offering contextual and nuanced understanding of legal jargon and complex terminology. These systems are designed to handle the intricacies of legal language, providing translations that retain the accuracy and intent of the original documents. For instance, AI can translate legal contracts, court filings, and legal advice into a user's native language while preserving the legal significance and context. This capability not only improves comprehension but also ensures that non-English speakers receive reliable and precise legal information, reducing the risk of misinterpretation and ensuring that their legal rights are upheld.

The integration of AI in legal services for non-English speakers promotes greater inclusivity and equality within the justice system. By removing language barriers, AI technologies enable a broader audience to access legal resources, seek assistance, and participate more fully in legal processes. This advancement is particularly beneficial in multicultural communities where diverse languages are spoken. As AI translation and language processing continue to evolve, they hold the promise of further enhancing legal access and support for non-English speakers, contributing to a more just and equitable legal system.

AI in Legal Services for Rural and Remote Areas: Bridging the Justice Gap Through Technology

Accessing legal services in rural and remote areas often presents significant challenges due to geographic isolation and a scarcity of local legal professionals. Many individuals in these regions face barriers such as long travel distances to the nearest legal office, limited availability of legal aid, and a lack of specialized legal support. AI technologies are emerging as a powerful tool to bridge this justice gap by providing remote legal assistance and resources. Through online platforms and AI-powered applications, individuals in underserved areas can now access legal information, guidance, and support without the need for extensive travel.

AI-driven legal services in rural and remote areas offer several key benefits. For instance, virtual legal assistants and chatbots can provide immediate, 24/7 access to legal information, answer common legal questions, and guide users through legal procedures. These tools can help individuals understand their rights, complete legal forms, and receive preliminary legal advice, all from the comfort of their own homes. AI systems can facilitate tele-law consultations, connecting clients with legal professionals via video calls or secure messaging, thus overcoming the limitations imposed by physical distance.

AI and Accessibility: Creating Inclusive Legal Services for Individuals with Disabilities

Screen Readers: AI-powered screen readers convert text into spoken words, aiding individuals with visual impairments in accessing legal documents and online resources.

Voice Recognition Software: Enables users with physical disabilities to interact with legal platforms and dictate documents hands-free.

Real-Time Transcription: Provides text transcriptions of verbal communications, such as court proceedings or consultations, benefiting individuals with hearing impairments.

Adaptive Features: AI systems can design user interfaces that cater to specific needs, such as larger text, high-contrast modes, and simplified navigation.

Personalized Content Delivery: Machine learning algorithms analyze user preferences and interactions to adjust the presentation of legal information, making it more accessible.

Automatic Captioning: AI generates real-time captions for video and audio content, ensuring that individuals with hearing impairments can follow legal discussions and presentations.

Speech-to-Text Services: Converts spoken language into written text, supporting individuals with hearing difficulties or those who prefer written communication.

Customizable Legal Tools: AI-driven legal platforms offer features that can be tailored to accommodate various disabilities, ensuring broader access to legal services.

Enhanced Accessibility Features: Integration of AI to include voice commands, gesture controls, and other accessibility options that support users with diverse needs.

Barrier Removal: AI technologies help eliminate physical and communicative barriers, allowing individuals with disabilities to fully participate in legal processes.

Equal Access: AI-driven solutions contribute to a more inclusive legal system, promoting fairness and ensuring that all individuals, regardless of their disabilities, can access the legal support they need.

Virtual Legal Assistants in Family Law

Virtual legal assistants are revolutionizing the field of family law by providing accessible, efficient, and cost-effective support to individuals navigating complex family-related legal issues. These AI-driven tools are designed to assist with various aspects of family law, including divorce, child custody, and spousal support, by offering personalized legal guidance and streamlining administrative tasks. With the integration of advanced natural language processing and machine learning technologies, virtual legal assistants are able to provide high-quality support that significantly enhances the client experience.

- **Personalized Legal Guidance**: Virtual legal assistants can offer tailored advice based on the specifics of a user's case. They analyze the information provided by users to deliver customized recommendations on legal procedures, document preparation, and potential outcomes. This personalized approach helps individuals understand their legal options and make informed decisions without needing immediate, expensive consultations with a lawyer.
- **Efficient Document Preparation**: One of the key benefits of virtual legal assistants is their ability to automate the preparation of legal documents. Users can input relevant details into the system, which then generates accurate and compliant legal forms, such as divorce petitions, custody agreements, and financial disclosures. This automation reduces the risk of errors and ensures that documents meet legal standards, saving time and reducing the need for manual intervention.
- **Streamlined Communication**: Virtual legal assistants facilitate better communication between clients and legal professionals. They can manage scheduling, send reminders for important deadlines, and provide updates on the progress of a case. Additionally, these tools can answer frequently asked questions and handle routine inquiries, allowing legal professionals to focus on more complex aspects of their cases.
- **24/7 Availability**: Unlike traditional legal services, virtual legal assistants are available around the clock. This constant accessibility means that individuals can seek legal assistance and obtain information outside of regular business hours, which is particularly beneficial for those with busy schedules or urgent issues. The ability to access support anytime also helps alleviate the stress and uncertainty associated with family law matters.
- **Cost-Effectiveness**: By reducing the need for extensive legal consultations and administrative work, virtual legal assistants help lower the overall cost of legal services. This is especially advantageous for individuals who may not have the financial resources to afford traditional legal fees. The reduced cost barrier makes it easier for a broader range of people to seek and receive the legal support they need during challenging family situations.

virtual legal assistants are transforming the landscape of family law by making legal support more accessible, efficient, and affordable. Their ability to provide personalized advice, automate document preparation, and facilitate communication represents a significant advancement in the way legal services are delivered, ultimately benefiting individuals navigating the complexities of family law.

Real-Time Implementation Scenario: AI in the Legal System

A mid-sized law firm specializing in commercial litigation is experiencing increased case volumes and complexity, leading to significant strain on its legal staff. Document review, a critical yet time-consuming aspect of legal work, has become a bottleneck. The firm decides to implement an AI-powered document review system to enhance efficiency and accuracy in processing legal documents.

AI System Integration

The law firm selects an AI-driven legal technology platform designed to automate and optimize document review. This platform incorporates natural language processing (NLP) and machine learning algorithms to analyze large volumes of legal documents, such as contracts, discovery materials, and case files.

Training and Customization

The AI system is customized to the firm's specific needs by training it on a dataset of previous legal documents and case files. This training helps the AI model understand legal terminology, recognize relevant clauses, and identify potential issues or discrepancies.

Deployment and Operation

The AI system is integrated into the firm's existing document management workflow. Legal staff begin by uploading documents into the platform, which then uses NLP to extract key information, categorize content, and highlight important clauses. The AI system also flags potential risks, such as inconsistent terms or compliance issues, and suggests relevant legal precedents based on the content of the documents.

Review and Validation

Human reviewers use the AI-generated summaries and alerts to conduct a more focused and efficient review. The AI system significantly reduces the time needed to sift through large volumes of documents, allowing legal professionals to concentrate on higher-level analysis and strategic decision-making.

Ongoing Learning and Improvement

The AI system continuously learns from user interactions and feedback. As legal professionals review and validate AI findings, the system refines its algorithms and improves accuracy over time. This iterative learning process enhances the system's performance and reliability in handling diverse types of legal documents.

AI in the Court System

AI technologies are increasingly being integrated into various aspects of the court system to improve efficiency, accuracy, and accessibility. Here are several real-time examples of how AI is being implemented in court systems around the world:

Case Prediction Tools in the U.S.: Some U.S. jurisdictions have begun using AI-powered predictive analytics to forecast case outcomes based on historical data. For example, tools like **PredPol** analyze past case data to predict future criminal activity and assess the likelihood of certain outcomes in criminal cases. By examining patterns and trends in data, these tools assist judges and attorneys in making more informed decisions about case strategy and resource allocation.

AI-Powered Legal Research

Ravel Law, now integrated into LexisNexis, uses AI to enhance legal research by analyzing judicial opinions and case law. The platform provides insights into how different judges interpret laws and identifies relevant precedents.

- Natural Language Processing (NLP): NLP algorithms analyze legal texts to extract key concepts, relationships, and precedents.
- User Interaction: Lawyers and judges use the platform to quickly find relevant case law and judicial opinions, improving the efficiency and thoroughness of legal research.

Automated Document Generation

ROSS Intelligence uses AI to help legal professionals draft legal documents and briefs. It can generate legal documents based on user input and available templates, streamlining the documentation process for court cases.

Virtual Courtrooms and AI Moderation

The UK court system has experimented with AI to assist in virtual court hearings. AI technologies are used to manage virtual courtrooms, facilitate real-time transcription, and ensure that all participants adhere to procedural rules.

- Virtual Court Platforms: AI is integrated into video conferencing platforms used for virtual hearings.
- Real-Time Transcription: AI-driven transcription services provide real-time text records of court proceedings.
- Moderation: AI tools assist in managing the virtual courtroom, including controlling participant access and monitoring adherence to court procedures.

AI for Sentencing and Risk Assessment

COMPAS (Correctional Offender Management Profiling for Alternative Sanctions): In the U.S., COMPAS is an AI tool used to assess the risk of reoffending. It provides risk scores that help judges make informed decisions about sentencing and parole.

- Risk Assessment: AI algorithms analyze factors such as criminal history, behavior patterns, and social factors to generate risk scores.
- Judicial Use: Judges use these risk scores to guide sentencing and parole decisions, aiming to balance public safety with rehabilitation opportunities.

AI for Court Case Scheduling

In some jurisdictions, AI systems are used to optimize court case scheduling. These systems analyze case details, judge availability, and courtroom resources to create efficient schedules and minimize delays.

- Data Integration: Data on case details, judge calendars, and courtroom availability is integrated into the AI system.
- Optimization Algorithms: AI algorithms generate optimal scheduling solutions, balancing case priorities and resource availability.
- Usage: Court administrators and scheduling officers use the system to create and adjust court schedules.

The integration of AI into court systems is transforming the legal landscape by improving efficiency, accuracy, and accessibility. From predictive analytics and legal research to automated document generation and virtual courtrooms, AI technologies are enhancing various aspects of the judicial process. These real-time implementation examples illustrate the potential of AI to streamline court operations, support legal professionals, and ultimately provide more equitable and effective justice.

List of AI tools in Legal Services

AI tools are increasingly becoming integral to the legal services industry, offering solutions that enhance efficiency, accuracy, and accessibility. Here are some notable AI tools and technologies transforming legal services:

Legal Research and Analytics

- **Ravel Law**: Uses AI to analyze judicial opinions and case law, providing insights into judicial behavior, case outcomes, and relevant precedents. It helps lawyers quickly locate pertinent case law and understand judicial trends.
- **LexisNexis**: Incorporates AI-powered tools like Lexis Answers to streamline legal research by providing direct answers to legal questions and highlighting relevant case law and statutes.

Document Review and Management

- **Kira Systems**: Utilizes machine learning to automate the extraction and analysis of key clauses from contracts and other legal documents. It speeds up due diligence, contract review, and compliance tasks.
- **Luminance**: An AI-powered document review platform that uses machine learning to analyze and categorize large volumes of documents, identifying critical information and potential risks.

Contract Analysis and Automation

- **LawGeex**: An AI tool that reviews contracts and compares them against predefined standards and legal best practices. It identifies issues and deviations, providing suggestions for amendments.
- **Evisort**: Uses AI to automate contract lifecycle management, including contract creation, review, and compliance monitoring. It helps manage and track contract obligations and deadlines.

Chatbots and Virtual Assistants

- **DoNotPay**: A virtual legal assistant that provides automated legal advice and assistance for various legal issues, including consumer rights, parking tickets, and small claims court matters.
- **LawBot**: An AI-powered chatbot that helps users navigate legal issues by providing information and guiding them through legal processes and document preparation.

Predictive Analytics and Risk Assessment

- **COMPAS**: A risk assessment tool used in the criminal justice system to predict the likelihood of reoffending. It aids in sentencing and parole decisions by analyzing various risk factors.
- **PsycApps**: Employs predictive analytics to assess mental health conditions and potential risks, which can be relevant in cases involving psychological evaluations and family law matters.

eDiscovery

- **Relativity Trace**: Uses AI to assist with electronic discovery by analyzing vast amounts of data to identify relevant documents, reduce review time, and ensure compliance with legal requirements.
- **Everlaw**: Provides AI-driven eDiscovery tools that automate document review, categorization, and analysis, helping legal teams manage large volumes of evidence more efficiently.

Contract Lifecycle Management

- **Ironclad**: An AI-based contract lifecycle management platform that automates the creation, negotiation, and execution of contracts. It includes features for tracking contract performance and compliance.
- **ContractPodAi**: Uses AI to streamline the entire contract lifecycle, from drafting and negotiation to execution and management, improving efficiency and reducing errors.

Legal Analytics

- **Premonition**: Offers predictive analytics on litigation outcomes by analyzing historical court data to predict how cases might be decided and the performance of legal professionals.
- **CaseText**: Employs AI to provide legal research and analytics, offering insights into case law, statutes, and legal trends that help lawyers build stronger cases and strategies.

AI-Powered Case Management

- **Clio**: Integrates AI to automate routine case management tasks, such as scheduling, billing, and client communication, enhancing overall practice efficiency.
- **Rocket Matter**: Uses AI to streamline case management processes, including time tracking, document management, and client interactions, facilitating smoother legal workflows.

Virtual Courtrooms

- **CourtCall**: Provides virtual courtroom solutions using AI to manage remote hearings, including scheduling, participant management, and real-time transcription services.
- **Zoom for Legal**: Integrates AI features for virtual hearings, including real-time language translation, automated transcription, and participant management to support remote legal proceedings.

AI tools are reshaping the legal services landscape by automating routine tasks, enhancing research and analytics, and improving client interactions. These technologies help legal professionals increase efficiency, reduce costs, and provide more accurate and accessible legal services. As AI continues to advance, its role in the legal industry is likely to expand, offering even more innovative solutions for legal challenges.

Impact of AI Tools on Legal Services

- AI tools automate repetitive and time-consuming tasks such as document review, contract analysis, and legal research. This automation significantly speeds up processes, allowing legal professionals to focus on more strategic and complex aspects of their work.

- Machine learning and natural language processing algorithms improve the precision of legal research and document analysis. AI tools can identify relevant case law, detect errors in documents, and ensure compliance with legal standards, reducing the likelihood of human error.
- By streamlining tasks and automating processes, AI tools help lower operational costs. Legal practices can reduce the need for extensive manual labor and cut down on the expenses associated with lengthy document review and research, making legal services more affordable.
- AI-driven chatbots and virtual assistants provide 24/7 access to legal information and support. This increased accessibility benefits individuals who might otherwise struggle to obtain legal assistance, including those in remote areas or with limited financial resources.
- Predictive analytics tools can forecast case outcomes and assess risks based on historical data. This insight helps legal professionals make informed decisions, develop better case strategies, and allocate resources more effectively.
- AI tools can handle large volumes of data and cases without a proportional increase in resources. This scalability allows legal practices to manage more cases and clients efficiently, adapting to fluctuating workloads and expanding their reach.

CONCLUSION

The integration of AI into the legal services sector is fundamentally transforming how legal work is conducted, offering a multitude of benefits that enhance the efficiency, accuracy, and accessibility of legal services. AI tools, ranging from document review and legal research to virtual assistants and predictive analytics, have streamlined numerous processes, significantly reducing the time and effort required for routine tasks. This efficiency not only accelerates case handling but also allows legal professionals to dedicate more time to complex and strategic aspects of their work, ultimately improving the quality of legal services provided.

AI's ability to automate and optimize document management and legal research has led to substantial cost savings. By minimizing the need for extensive manual labor and reducing the likelihood of human error, AI tools have made legal services more affordable and accessible. This is particularly advantageous for individuals with limited resources, as AI-driven chatbots and virtual assistants provide around-the-clock access to legal information and support, bridging gaps in access and ensuring that more people can receive the legal assistance they need.

As AI technology continues to advance, its impact on the legal field is expected to grow even further. The scalability and predictive capabilities of AI tools will enable legal practices to handle increasing workloads and complex cases with greater ease. Additionally, ongoing improvements in AI will enhance its ability to provide personalized and precise legal support, fostering a more equitable and efficient justice system. Overall, the integration of AI in legal services represents a significant step forward in modernizing the industry and addressing longstanding challenges.

REFERENCES

Brink, R., & Toth, C. (2021). Ethical considerations of AI in legal services: A critical review. *Journal of Legal Ethics*, 46(2), 256–279.

Goodman, B., & Flaxman, S. (2017). European Union regulations on AI: Implications for legal services. *European Journal of Law and Technology*, 8(1), 101–119.

Guszcza, J., & Kalinowski, M. (2021). AI and the future of legal services: Innovation and transformation. *Journal of Legal Technology*, 39(1), 23–45.

Hernandez, M., & Smith, D. (2022). AI-driven risk management in legal practice: A comprehensive overview. *Risk Management Journal*, 41(3), 174–192.

Katz, D. M., Bommarito, M. J., & Blackman, J. A. (2017). A first look at the empirical legal studies literature: AI in legal research and document review. *The Journal of Legal Studies*, 46(2), 123–156.

Katz, D. M., Bommarito, M. J., & Blackman, J. A. (2018). Predictive analytics in the legal field: Enhancing case outcomes. *The Journal of Law & Economics*, 61(3), 254–278.

Kim, S., & Cho, H. (2023). The role of AI in enhancing legal aid accessibility: Evidence from recent implementations. *International Journal of Legal Technology*, 33(1), 65–84.

Langer, D. M., & Taylor, A. (2022). The accuracy and utility of predictive legal analytics. *Law & Society Review*, 56(2), 312–340.

Lin, W., Cheng, M., & Xu, Q. (2019). Legal chatbots: Enhancing client interaction and accessibility. *AI & Law Journal*, 27(1), 77–99.

McCarthy, J. (2021). Virtual assistants in the legal field: Guiding users through legal processes. *Journal of Legal Innovation*, 34(3), 143–168.

McCormick, J. (2022). AI in risk assessment and compliance: Managing regulatory challenges. *The Regulatory Affairs Journal*, 39(2), 205–229.

McGinnis, J. O., & Pearce, R. (2021). Intelligent case management: AI in legal workflow automation. *Legal Practice Management Journal*, 42(4), 91–115.

Patel, S., & Garcia, L. (2022). Chatbots in legal services: Enhancing client engagement and accessibility. *AI & Society Journal*, 21(2), 143–160.

Robinson, K., & McDaniel, R. (2020). AI in law firms: Benefits, challenges, and the road ahead. *Law Firm Management Review*, 27(4), 112–130.

Rodriguez, A., & Gomez, M. (2021). The automation of legal document drafting: Benefits and challenges. *Legal Technology Review*, 29(4), 45–67.

Rosen, J., & Lyman, D. (2019). Predictive analytics in the legal sector: Use cases and impact. *Journal of Data Science and Law*, 30(3), 95–118.

Surden, H. (2019). Artificial intelligence and legal analytics: New tools for lawyers. *Harvard Journal of Law & Technology*, 32(1), 85–124.

Susskind, R. (2020). *Tomorrow's lawyers: An introduction to your future*. Oxford University Press.

Tsiros, M., & Mitchell, A. (2021). AI and the legal profession: Transformations and challenges. *Legal Innovation Quarterly*, 29(1), 22–39.

Wright, L., & Schauer, F. (2023). Expanding access to justice: AI-powered platforms and legal aid. *Journal of Access to Justice*, 25(1), 59–82.

Zarefsky, J., & Koonin, S. (2020). Legal document automation: Impact and future directions. *Stanford Technology Law Review : STLR : An Online High-Technology Law Journal from Stanford Law School*, 23(2), 89–112.

Chapter 9
Ethical and Regulatory Considerations in AI Adoption Within Legal Systems

Madhavi More
https://orcid.org/0009-0001-5236-8048
Department of Law, Christ University (Deemed), Pune, India

Samrudhee Shah
https://orcid.org/0009-0001-9238-5192
Dr. D. Y. Patil Law College Pimpri, Pune, India

Atmaram Shelke
Symbiosis Law School, Symbiosis International University (Deemed), Pune, India

Nitesh Behare
https://orcid.org/0000-0002-9338-8563
Balaji Institute of International Business, Sri Balaji University, Pune, India

ABSTRACT

As Artificial Intelligence (AI) continues to reshape the legal landscape, it is essential to address the accompanying ethical and regulatory considerations. This chapter investigates these critical dimensions, focusing on the ethical concerns of bias, transparency, accountability, and privacy within AI adoption in legal systems. It provides an in-depth analysis of the current regulatory landscape, including existing laws, guidelines, and international standards, and examines the challenges and opportunities in crafting effective regulatory frameworks. The chapter emphasizes the necessity of balancing innovation with ethical and social responsibility to ensure

DOI: 10.4018/979-8-3693-7205-0.ch009

public trust and confidence in AI applications. It concludes with best practices and recommendations for legal professionals, policymakers, and industry stakeholders, aiming to foster responsible AI adoption in legal systems. Through this exploration, the chapter contributes to the ongoing discourse on the integration of AI in law, offering insights and guidelines to navigate the complex ethical and regulatory terrain.

CHAPTER OBJECTIVES

- Identify and analyze the ethical considerations surrounding AI adoption in legal systems, including bias, transparency, accountability, and privacy.
- Examine the current regulatory landscape governing AI in legal systems, including existing laws, guidelines, and standards.
- Discuss the challenges and opportunities in developing regulatory frameworks that balance innovation with ethical and social responsibility.
- Provide best practices and recommendations for legal professionals, policymakers, and industry stakeholders to ensure responsible AI adoption in legal systems.

I. INTRODUCTION

The introduction of Artificial Intelligence (AI) has revolutionized numerous sectors, and the legal system is no exception. As AI technologies, like machine learning and natural language processing, continue to evolve, they are increasingly being integrated into various aspects of legal practice and judicial processes (Sheeba, 2023). These technologies promise to enhance efficiency, reduce costs, and potentially improve the accuracy of legal outcomes. However, the adoption of AI within legal systems is not without significant ethical and regulatory challenges. This chapter delves into these considerations, exploring the complexities and nuances that accompany the integration of AI in the legal domain.

AI's capabilities in automating repetitive tasks, analyzing vast datasets, and predicting legal outcomes have garnered considerable attention. For instance, AI-powered tools can assist lawyers in legal research, contract analysis, and even in predicting the likelihood of case outcomes based on historical data (Akash, 2022). In judicial systems, AI has the potential to aid judges in decision-making processes, ensuring consistency and reducing human biases. However, these benefits come hand in hand with ethical dilemmas and regulatory hurdles that must be meticulously addressed.

One of the foremost ethical concerns in the adoption of AI within legal systems is the issue of bias. AI systems are trained on historical data, which may inherently contain biases present in past legal decisions. If not carefully managed, these biases can be perpetuated or even exacerbated by AI algorithms, leading to unfair outcomes (Niral, 2022). For example, predictive policing algorithms, which are designed to forecast criminal activity, have been criticized for disproportionately targeting minority communities based on biased historical data. Addressing these biases requires a comprehensive approach, involving diverse data sets, transparent algorithms, and continuous monitoring to ensure fairness and equity in AI-driven legal processes.

Transparency and accountability are also critical ethical considerations. The decision-making processes of AI systems are often described as "black boxes" due to their complexity and the difficulty in understanding how they reach specific conclusions. In a legal context, where decisions can significantly impact individuals' lives, the opacity of AI algorithms poses a challenge to ensuring justice and accountability. Legal professionals and the public must be able to scrutinize and understand AI-driven decisions, necessitating the development of transparent and explainable AI models (George, 2023).

Privacy concerns further complicate the adoption of AI in legal systems (Praveen, 2024). AI technologies often require vast amounts of personal data to function effectively. The collection, storage, and use of this data must comply with stringent privacy regulations to protect individuals' rights. In legal contexts, where sensitive information is frequently handled, maintaining confidentiality and preventing unauthorized access to data is paramount. Regulatory frameworks must therefore be robust and adaptive to address the evolving nature of AI technologies and the associated privacy risks (OVIC, 2023).

Regulatory considerations extend beyond privacy to encompass the broader implications of AI in legal systems (ET, 2023) (Akash, 2022). The rapid pace of AI development often outstrips existing legal frameworks, creating a gap that must be bridged to ensure responsible AI adoption. Policymakers face the challenge of crafting regulations that foster innovation while safeguarding against potential harms (Lyytinen, Hekkert, Cheng, & Sovacool, 2022). This includes establishing standards for AI development, deployment, and oversight, as well as defining liability in cases where AI-driven decisions result in adverse outcomes (Adam, 2023).

Internationally, the regulatory landscape for AI in legal systems is diverse, with different countries adopting varied approaches based on their legal traditions, societal values, and levels of technological advancement (Mark, Simon, & Luisa, 2024). For instance, the European Union has been at the forefront of developing comprehensive AI regulations, emphasizing ethical considerations and human oversight. In contrast, other jurisdictions may prioritize economic growth and technological leadership, potentially at the expense of stringent regulatory measures. Understanding these global perspectives is crucial for developing cohesive and effective regulatory strategies.

II. ETHICAL CONSIDERATIONS

The integration of AI into legal systems brings with it a host of ethical considerations that are critical to ensuring that such technologies are deployed responsibly and fairly (Niral, 2022). As AI increasingly influences legal decision-making processes, it is essential to address concerns related to bias and discrimination, transparency and explainability, accountability and responsibility, and privacy and data protection.

- Bias and Discrimination

One of the most pressing ethical concerns in AI adoption within legal systems is the potential for bias and discrimination. AI algorithms are trained on historical data, which can contain biases reflective of past injustices and societal inequalities. When these biases are embedded in AI models, they can perpetuate or even exacerbate discriminatory practices (James, Jake, & Brittany, 2019).

For instance, predictive policing algorithms have been criticized for disproportionately targeting minority communities. These systems often rely on historical crime data, which may reflect existing biases in law enforcement practices (Jeena, 2024). As a result, areas with higher minority populations may be subject to increased police scrutiny, perpetuating a cycle of discrimination (Will Douglas, 2020), (Hung & Yen, 2023). Similarly, AI tools used in judicial decision-making, such as risk assessment algorithms for bail or sentencing, can unfairly disadvantage certain demographic groups if the underlying data is biased (Emilio, 2023).

To mitigate these risks, it is crucial to ensure that AI models are trained on diverse and representative datasets. Additionally, continuous monitoring and auditing of AI systems are necessary to identify and address any emerging biases. Developing fair and unbiased AI requires collaboration between technologists, legal experts, and ethicists to create frameworks that promote equity and justice.

- Transparency and Explainability

Transparency and explainability are critical to maintaining trust in AI-driven legal systems. AI algorithms often operate as "black boxes," with their decision-making processes hidden from users and stakeholders. In the context of legal decisions, where outcomes can significantly impact individuals' lives, this opacity is particularly problematic (George, 2023).

Legal professionals and the public must be able to understand and scrutinize AI-driven decisions. This requires the development of explainable AI models that provide clear and understandable rationales for their conclusions. Explainability not only fosters trust but also enables accountability, allowing stakeholders to challenge and appeal AI-driven decisions when necessary.

Moreover, transparency in the development and deployment of AI systems is essential. This includes clear documentation of the data sources, methodologies, and assumptions used in creating AI models. Transparent practices can help identify potential sources of bias and ensure that AI systems are developed in an ethical and responsible manner (Lyytinen, Hekkert, Cheng, & Sovacool, 2022).

- Accountability and Responsibility

The question of accountability and responsibility is a significant ethical consideration in AI adoption within legal systems. When AI-driven decisions lead to adverse outcomes, it is essential to determine who is responsible. This can be challenging, as AI systems involve multiple stakeholders, including developers, data providers, and end-users (Sheeba, 2023).

Establishing clear lines of accountability is crucial to ensuring that ethical standards are upheld. Legal frameworks need to define the responsibilities of various parties involved in the creation and deployment of AI systems. Developers should be accountable for ensuring that their models are fair, transparent, and secure. Legal professionals using AI tools must understand their limitations and use them responsibly. Regulatory bodies should oversee the deployment of AI in legal contexts, ensuring compliance with ethical and legal standards (Paul, 2023).

The concept of algorithmic accountability also involves the ability to audit and review AI systems. Independent audits can help identify biases, errors, and potential areas of improvement. Additionally, mechanisms for redress and appeal should be established to address grievances arising from AI-driven decisions.

- Privacy and Data Protection

Privacy and data protection are paramount in the context of AI adoption within legal systems. AI technologies often require access to vast amounts of personal and sensitive data to function effectively. However, the collection, storage, and use of this data must comply with stringent privacy regulations to protect individuals' rights (Mark van, 2023).

In legal contexts, where sensitive information such as criminal records, personal histories, and confidential communications are handled, ensuring data privacy is critical. Unauthorized access to or misuse of this data can have severe consequences for individuals' privacy and security. To address these concerns, robust data protection measures must be implemented. This includes encryption, anonymization, and strict access controls to safeguard personal data. Legal frameworks should also provide clear guidelines on data usage, retention, and sharing to ensure compliance with privacy laws (Komal, 2024).

Moreover, individuals should be informed about how their data is being used by AI systems and have the ability to consent or opt-out where appropriate. Transparency in data practices fosters trust and empowers individuals to make informed decisions about their privacy (Wanbil, Wolfgang, & Henry, 2016).

III. REGULATORY LANDSCAPE

The integration of Artificial Intelligence (AI) into legal systems necessitates a robust regulatory framework to address the complex ethical and operational challenges that arise. This section provides an overview of existing laws and regulations, discusses emerging guidelines and standards, and explores international perspectives and collaborations in regulating AI within the legal domain (Madaoui, 2024), (Praveen, 2024), (Ammar, 2024).

- Overview of Existing Laws and Regulations

The rapid advancement of AI technology has often outpaced the development of comprehensive legal frameworks. However, several existing laws and regulations provide a foundational basis for governing the use of AI in legal systems.

General Data Protection Regulation (GDPR):

The GDPR, implemented by the European Union in 2018, is one of the most significant regulations affecting AI. It emphasizes data protection and privacy, requiring organizations to ensure transparent data processing, obtain explicit consent, and implement data minimization principles (Anas & Maria, 2023). The GDPR also mandates that individuals have the right to not be subject to decisions based solely on automated processing, which includes AI-driven decisions, unless certain conditions are met (Scott, Rich, & Tréa, 2024).

Algorithmic Accountability Act:

In the United States, the Algorithmic Accountability Act, proposed in 2019, aims to require companies to conduct impact assessments of their automated decision systems. This includes evaluating the potential risks of bias, discrimination, and other adverse effects on individuals. While not yet enacted, this act signifies a move towards greater scrutiny of AI technologies (Jakob, Prathm, David, & Luciano, 2022).

AI Regulation Proposal by the European Commission:

In April 2021, the European Commission proposed a comprehensive regulatory framework for AI, known as the Artificial Intelligence Act. This proposal categorizes AI systems based on their risk levels (unacceptable, high, limited, and minimal risk) and sets out specific requirements for each category. High-risk AI systems, which include those used in critical infrastructure and judicial decision-making, would be subject to strict obligations regarding transparency, accountability, and human oversight (EU, 2024).

- Emerging Guidelines and Standards

As AI continues to evolve, emerging guidelines and standards are being developed to address the unique challenges posed by its adoption in legal systems.

Ethical Guidelines for Trustworthy AI:

The European Commission's High-Level Expert Group on AI released guidelines in 2019 outlining key requirements for trustworthy AI. These include human agency and oversight, technical robustness and safety, privacy and data governance, transparency, diversity, non-discrimination and fairness, societal and environmental well-being, and accountability. These guidelines serve a foundational framework for developing AI systems that are ethically sound and socially beneficial (European Commission, 2019).

ISO/IEC Standards:

The International Organization for Standardization (ISO) and the International Electro-Technical Commission (IEC) are working on developing international standards for AI. These standards aim to ensure the safety, security, and ethical implications of AI technologies are adequately addressed. For example, ISO/IEC

JTC 1/SC 42 is a committee focused on AI standardization, covering areas such as AI terminology, trustworthiness, and governance (ISO, 2024).

AI Ethics Guidelines from National Bodies:

Various countries have developed their own guidelines and frameworks to address the ethical use of AI. For instance, the United Kingdom's Centre for Data Ethics and Innovation (CDEI) has published principles for AI ethics, and Singapore has introduced its Model AI Governance Framework, which provides practical guidance on deploying AI responsibly.

- International Perspectives and Collaborations

The global nature of AI development and deployment necessitates international collaboration to ensure coherent and effective regulatory frameworks. Different countries and regions have adopted varied approaches based on their legal traditions, societal values, and technological priorities.

European Union:

The EU has been a frontrunner in developing comprehensive AI regulations. The proposed Artificial Intelligence Act represents a significant step towards creating a harmonized regulatory environment across member states. The EU also emphasizes the importance of ethical AI, as seen in its GDPR and AI ethics guidelines (EU, 2024).

United States:

In the US, the regulatory landscape is more fragmented, with various federal and state-level initiatives addressing AI. The National Institute of Standards and Technology (NIST) is working on developing AI standards, and several states have introduced their own regulations related to data privacy and AI. Collaboration between public and private sectors is key in shaping the future regulatory approach (Jakob, Prathm, David, & Luciano, 2022).

China:

China has adopted a proactive stance towards AI development, with significant investments and strategic plans to become a global leader in AI. The Chinese government has issued guidelines emphasizing ethical AI, data security, and the need for robust regulatory frameworks. However, the balance between innovation and regulation in China's approach differs from that of Western countries (FiscalNote, 2024).

Global Collaborations:

International collaborations are crucial for addressing the cross-border implications of AI. Organizations such as the OECD (Organisation for Economic Co-operation and Development) have developed AI principles that promote innovation while ensuring respect for human rights and democratic values. The G20 has also recognized the importance of global cooperation on AI ethics and regulation (OECD, 2023).

Multilateral Initiatives:

Initiatives like the Global Partnership on AI (GPAI) bring together governments, industry, academia, and civil society to foster responsible AI development and adoption. These collaborations aim to align global efforts and share best practices, ensuring that AI technologies benefit all of humanity (GPAI, 2024).

IV. REGULATORY CHALLENGES AND OPPORTUNITIES

The adoption of AI within legal systems presents both significant challenges and promising opportunities. The regulatory landscape must navigate the delicate balance between fostering innovation and ensuring ethical and social responsibility, addressing the lack of standardization and consistency, and ensuring public trust and confidence. Each of these areas poses unique challenges that need to be addressed to realize the full potential of AI in legal contexts while mitigating risks.

- Balancing Innovation with Ethical and Social Responsibility

One of the primary challenges in regulating AI in legal systems is finding the right balance between encouraging technological innovation and upholding ethical and social responsibilities. AI technologies have the potential to transform legal practices by enhancing efficiency, accuracy, and accessibility. However, without proper regulation, these advancements can lead to ethical dilemmas and social issues (Ciro, Umberto, Giuseppe, & Massimo, 2024).

Challenges:

Innovation vs. Regulation: Over-regulation can stifle innovation, making it difficult for AI developers to bring new and improved technologies to market. On the other hand, under-regulation can result in unethical practices, such as biased algorithms and unjust legal outcomes.

Ethical Concerns: AI systems in legal contexts must navigate complex ethical issues, including bias, fairness, and the potential for discrimination. Historical data used to train AI models may reflect existing societal biases, which can be perpetuated or amplified if not properly addressed.

Social Responsibility: Legal decisions have profound impacts on individuals' lives. Ensuring that AI systems uphold social responsibility requires rigorous oversight and continuous evaluation of their effects on various demographic groups.

Opportunities:

Ethical Innovation: By integrating ethical considerations into the development process, AI technologies can be designed to promote fairness and reduce biases. Ethical AI frameworks and guidelines, such as those proposed by the European Commission, can help developers create systems that align with societal values.

Collaborative Regulation: Policymakers, technologists, and ethicists can work together to develop regulatory frameworks that encourage innovation while safeguarding ethical standards. This collaboration can result in balanced regulations that promote both technological advancement and social good.

- Addressing the Lack of Standardization and Consistency

The rapid advancement of AI technologies has outpaced the development of standardized regulatory frameworks, leading to inconsistencies across jurisdictions. This lack of standardization poses significant challenges in ensuring that AI systems are developed and deployed in a fair, transparent, and accountable manner (Yoshija, 2024).

Challenges:

Fragmented Regulations: Different countries and regions have adopted varied approaches to AI regulation, resulting in a fragmented global regulatory landscape. This inconsistency can create challenges for multinational companies and complicate efforts to ensure that AI systems meet ethical and legal standards universally.

Technical Standards: The absence of universally accepted technical standards for AI development and deployment makes it difficult to ensure the quality and reliability of AI systems. Variations in data quality, algorithmic transparency, and performance metrics can lead to disparate outcomes in different legal contexts.

Opportunities:

International Collaboration: By fostering international collaboration, regulatory bodies can work towards harmonizing AI regulations and developing global standards. Initiatives such as the Global Partnership on AI (GPAI) and the OECD's AI principles provide platforms for countries to share best practices and align their regulatory approaches.

Standardization Efforts: Organizations such as the International Organization for Standardization (ISO) and the Institute of Electrical and Electronics Engineers (IEEE) are actively working on developing technical standards for AI. These standards can provide a foundation for ensuring consistency and interoperability across different AI systems.

- Ensuring Public Trust and Confidence

For AI technologies to be successfully integrated into legal systems, it is crucial to build and maintain public trust and confidence. AI-driven legal decisions must be perceived as fair, transparent, and accountable to gain widespread acceptance (Ciro, Umberto, Giuseppe, & Massimo, 2024).

Challenges:

Transparency Issues: AI systems are often described as "black boxes" due to their complex and opaque decision-making processes. This lack of transparency can undermine public trust, as individuals may not understand how decisions are made or have the ability to challenge them.

Accountability Gaps: Determining responsibility for AI-driven decisions is a complex issue. When adverse outcomes occur, it can be difficult to identify who is accountable – the developers, the users, or the AI system itself. This ambiguity can erode public confidence in AI technologies.

Opportunities:

Explainable AI: Developing explainable AI models that provide clear and understandable rationales for their decisions can enhance transparency and accountability. Explainability not only fosters trust but also enables stakeholders to scrutinize and challenge AI-driven outcomes.

Public Engagement: Engaging with the public to educate them about AI technologies and their implications can help build trust. Transparent communication about the benefits and risks of AI, as well as efforts to involve the public in the regulatory process, can foster a sense of shared responsibility and confidence.

Regulatory Oversight: Establishing robust regulatory oversight mechanisms can ensure that AI systems are deployed responsibly. Independent audits, impact assessments, and the ability to appeal AI-driven decisions are essential components of a trustworthy AI regulatory framework.

V. BEST PRACTICES AND RECOMMENDATIONS

The adoption of Artificial Intelligence (AI) within legal systems presents both significant opportunities and challenges. Ensuring ethical and responsible implementation requires a coordinated effort across various stakeholders, including legal professionals, policymakers and regulators, and industry stakeholders. This section outlines best practices and recommendations for each group to foster the ethical and effective integration of AI in legal contexts (Rowena, 2020).

- For Legal Professionals

Legal professionals play a crucial role in the deployment and use of AI in the legal system. They must ensure that these technologies are applied in a manner that upholds the principles of justice, fairness, and accountability.

Best Practices:

Continuous Education: Legal professionals should stay informed about the latest developments in AI technologies and their applications within the legal system. Continuous education programs and training can help lawyers and judges understand AI's capabilities and limitations (Bar&Bench, 2024).

Ethical Awareness: Lawyers and judges must be aware of the ethical implications of using AI in legal processes. This includes understanding issues related to bias, transparency, and accountability. Legal professionals should advocate for the use of ethical AI and challenge decisions that appear to be unfair or biased (Ammar, 2024).

Collaboration with Technologists: Legal professionals should work closely with AI developers and data scientists to ensure that AI systems are designed and deployed in a manner that aligns with legal standards and ethical principles. This collaboration can help identify potential biases and mitigate risks (Sreelatha & Gyandeep, 2023).

Transparency and Explainability: When using AI tools, legal professionals should demand transparency and explainability from AI providers. They should ensure that the AI systems they use provide clear and understandable rationales for their decisions, enabling them to explain these decisions to clients and the public (Oksana, 2024).

Advocacy for Robust Regulatory Frameworks: Legal professionals should advocate for comprehensive regulatory frameworks that govern the use of AI in legal contexts. These frameworks should include provisions for transparency, accountability, and redress mechanisms (Ammar, 2024).

- For Policymakers and Regulators

Policymakers and regulators are responsible for creating and enforcing the legal and regulatory frameworks that govern AI's use in the legal system. Their role is critical in ensuring that AI technologies are developed and deployed in a manner that protects individual rights and upholds the rule of law.

Best Practices:

Develop Comprehensive Regulations: Policymakers should develop comprehensive regulatory frameworks that address the ethical and social implications of AI. These frameworks should include clear guidelines on transparency, accountability, data protection, and bias mitigation (Keymaker, 2024).

Foster International Collaboration: Given the global nature of AI development, policymakers should engage in international collaboration to harmonize regulations and standards. This can help create a cohesive regulatory environment that facilitates innovation while ensuring ethical practices (Yoshija, 2024).

Stakeholder Engagement: Policymakers should engage with a broad range of stakeholders, including legal professionals, technologists, ethicists, and the public, to gather diverse perspectives and insights. This engagement can inform the development of balanced and effective regulations (Amanda, Jonathan, Gerald, & Anthony, 2020).

Promote Transparency and Accountability: Regulations should mandate transparency in AI development and deployment, requiring AI systems to be explainable and their decision-making processes to be auditable. Additionally, clear accountability frameworks should be established to assign responsibility for AI-driven decisions (Ben Chester, 2024).

Support Research and Innovation: Policymakers should support research into ethical AI and the development of technologies that promote fairness and reduce bias. Funding and incentives for research can drive innovation while ensuring that ethical considerations are prioritized (Ciro, Umberto, Giuseppe, & Massimo, 2024).

- For Industry Stakeholders

Industry stakeholders, including AI developers, tech companies, and data providers, play a pivotal role in creating and deploying AI technologies. Their practices and decisions have significant ethical and regulatory implications.

Best Practices:

Ethical Design and Development: Industry stakeholders should prioritize ethical considerations in the design and development of AI systems. This includes using diverse and representative datasets, implementing bias detection and mitigation techniques, and ensuring that AI systems are transparent and explainable.

Adherence to Standards: Industry stakeholders should adhere to established standards and guidelines for AI development. Participation in standard-setting organizations and compliance with international norms can enhance the reliability and trustworthiness of AI systems.

Transparency and Communication: Tech companies should be transparent about their AI technologies, including how they work, the data they use, and their potential impacts. Clear communication with users and stakeholders can build trust and facilitate informed decision-making.

Collaboration with Legal Professionals: Industry stakeholders should collaborate with legal professionals to ensure that AI systems are compatible with legal standards and practices. This collaboration can help identify and address potential legal and ethical issues early in the development process (Gloria, 2023).

Continuous Monitoring and Improvement: AI systems should be continuously monitored for performance, fairness, and bias. Industry stakeholders should implement feedback mechanisms to identify and address issues promptly, ensuring that AI technologies evolve in response to new challenges and insights (IITK, 2023).

Corporate Responsibility: Companies should embrace corporate social responsibility by actively contributing to the development of ethical AI practices and supporting initiatives that promote fairness and justice in AI applications.

VI. REAL WORLD APPLICATIONS

Here are some real-world examples of AI adoption in legal systems, along with the ethical and regulatory considerations involved:

1. Predictive Policing

Example: The Los Angeles Police Department (LAPD) used a predictive policing tool called PredPol, which analyzed historical crime data to forecast where crimes were likely to occur (Johana, 2021).

Ethical Considerations:

Bias and Discrimination: Critics argued that PredPol disproportionately targeted communities of color, as it relied on historical data that reflected past policing practices. This raised concerns about reinforcing systemic biases in law enforcement.

Transparency: The algorithms used by PredPol were not publicly disclosed, leading to calls for greater transparency regarding how predictions were made.

Regulatory Response: In some jurisdictions, there have been moves toward limiting the use of predictive policing tools or requiring audits to assess their impact on communities.

2. Risk Assessment Algorithms in Sentencing

Example: Tools like COMPAS (Correctional Offender Management Profiling for Alternative Sanctions) are used in several U.S. jurisdictions to assess the likelihood of a defendant reoffending, influencing bail and sentencing decisions (Tim & William, 2017).

Ethical Considerations:

Bias: Studies have shown that COMPAS can produce biased outcomes, where Black defendants were more likely to be incorrectly classified as high risk compared to white defendants, raising concerns about fairness in judicial decision-making.

Accountability: Questions arise about who is accountable for decisions influenced by these algorithms, especially when an AI tool leads to unjust outcomes.

Regulatory Response: Various states are considering legislation that mandates transparency in how risk assessments are conducted and allows defendants to challenge algorithmic decisions in court.

3. AI in Legal Research

Example: AI-powered legal research platforms like ROSS Intelligence and Casetext use natural language processing to help lawyers quickly find relevant case law and legal precedents (Akash, 2022).

Ethical Considerations:

Quality of Information: Ensuring the accuracy and reliability of the information retrieved by AI systems is crucial, as erroneous results can lead to flawed legal strategies.

Intellectual Property: Concerns exist about the proprietary nature of AI tools and whether the data used for training these models respect copyright and intellectual property laws.

Regulatory Response: Professional organizations and legal ethics boards are beginning to issue guidelines regarding the use of AI in legal research to ensure ethical practices and uphold professional standards.

4. Contract Review Automation

Example: Companies like Kira Systems and LawGeex use AI to automate the contract review process, identifying clauses and potential issues in legal documents more quickly than human reviewers (Maurice, 2023).

Ethical Considerations:

Data Privacy: These tools often require access to sensitive contractual data, raising concerns about data protection and privacy.

Accuracy and Accountability: There is a risk of relying too heavily on AI for legal judgments, which could lead to oversights if the AI misinterprets the data.

Regulatory Response: Legal tech companies are increasingly required to comply with data protection regulations like the GDPR, and clients may seek assurances regarding how their data is handled.

5. Chatbots for Legal Assistance

Example: Law firms and organizations like DoNotPay have developed AI chatbots that provide legal advice on issues such as small claims, consumer rights, and immigration (Milin, 2024).

Ethical Considerations:

Quality of Advice: Ensuring that the information provided by chatbots is accurate and legally sound is critical to prevent users from making uninformed decisions.

Access to Justice: While chatbots can increase access to legal information, there is a risk that they may not adequately address complex legal issues requiring professional legal advice.

Regulatory Response: Some jurisdictions are exploring regulations to govern the use of AI in legal services, including requirements for human oversight in legal advice dispensed by chatbots.

6. Blockchain for Legal Transactions

Example: Several jurisdictions are exploring the use of blockchain technology for smart contracts, which automatically execute transactions when certain conditions are met (Shivani, 2024).

Ethical Considerations:

Security and Trust: The immutability of blockchain can enhance trust in legal transactions, but vulnerabilities in the underlying technology could pose risks.

Legal Recognition: There are ongoing discussions about how to integrate blockchain-based transactions within existing legal frameworks, including issues of enforceability and jurisdiction.

Regulatory Response: Governments are beginning to formulate regulations to address the legal status of smart contracts, focusing on how they interact with traditional legal principles.

VII. CONCLUSION

The integration of Artificial Intelligence (AI) in legal systems presents both opportunities and challenges that necessitate careful consideration of ethical and regulatory frameworks. Key stakeholders—legal professionals, policymakers, and industry players—must collaborate to balance innovation with social responsibility, address the lack of standardization, and build public trust. Best practices, such as advocating for transparency, ensuring accountability, and promoting ethical AI development, are essential for responsible AI adoption. Real-world examples highlight the complexities involved, underscoring the need for robust regulations that mitigate bias and protect individual rights. By prioritizing ethical considerations and fostering dialogue among stakeholders, the legal system can harness the transformative potential of AI while upholding principles of justice, fairness, and accountability. This collaborative approach will ensure that AI serves as a tool for enhancing legal processes rather than compromising the core values of the legal profession.

REFERENCES

Adam, V. (2023, Nov 05). *New Frontier: AI Governance and Ethical Frameworks*. Retrieved Aug 14, 2024, from https://www.linkedin.com: https://www.linkedin .com/pulse/new-frontier-ai-governance-ethical-frameworks-adam-m-victor-qjotc/

Akash, T. (2022). *AI in legal businesses: Use cases, solution, benefits and implementation*. Retrieved Aug 01, 2024, from https://www.leewayhertz.com: https:// www.leewayhertz.com/ai-use-cases-in-legal-businesses/

Amanda, G., Jonathan, A., Gerald, M., & Anthony, H. (2020, May 16). Stakeholder identification and engagement in problem structuring interventions. *European Journal of Operational Research*, 283(01), 321–340. DOI: 10.1016/j.ejor.2019.10.044

Ammar, Z. (2024, April 15). Balancing the scale: Navigating ethical and practical challenges of artificial intelligence (AI) integration in legal practices. *Springer Link*, 04(27), 27. Advance online publication. DOI: 10.1007/s44163-024-00121-8

Anas, B., & Maria, K. (2023, Sep 29). *The Impact of the GDPR on Artificial Intelligence*. Retrieved Aug 15, 2024, from https://securiti.ai: https://securiti.ai/impact -of-the-gdpr-on-artificial-intelligence/

Bar&Bench. (2024, Aug 19). *AI Adoption and its Impact in the Legal Industry: An Indian Perspective*. Retrieved Aug 19, 2024, from https://www.barandbench.com: https://www.barandbench.com/law-firms/view-point/ai-adoption-and-impact-legal -industry-indian-perspective

Ben Chester, C. (2024, July 03). Transparency and accountability in AI systems: Safeguarding wellbeing in the age of algorithmic decision-making. *Frontiers in Human Dynamics*, 06, 1421273. Advance online publication. DOI: 10.3389/ fhumd.2024.1421273

Ciro, M., Umberto, M., Giuseppe, D. P., & Massimo, E. (2024, February 29). Ethical and regulatory challenges of AI technologies in healthcare: A narrative review. *Heliyon*, 10(04), e26297. Advance online publication. DOI: 10.1016/j.heliyon.2024. e26297 PMID: 38384518

Emilio, F. (2023, December 26). Fairness and Bias in Artificial Intelligence: A Brief Survey of Sources, Impacts, and Mitigation Strategies. *Sci*, 06(01), 3. Advance online publication. DOI: 10.3390/sci6010003

ET. (2023, Apr 25). *AI and Privacy: The privacy concerns surrounding AI, its potential impact on personal data*. Retrieved Aug 14, 2024, from https://economictimes.indiatimes.com: https://economictimes.indiatimes.com/news/how-to/ai-and-privacy-the-privacy-concerns-surrounding-ai-its-potential-impact-on-personal-data/articleshow/99738234.cms

EU. (2024, Jun 18). *EU AI Act: first regulation on artificial intelligence*. Retrieved Aug 14, 2024, from https://www.europarl.europa.eu: https://www.europarl.europa.eu/topics/en/article/20230601STO93804/eu-ai-act-first-regulation-on-artificial-intelligence

European Commission. (. (2019, Apr 08). *Ethics guidelines for trustworthy AI*. Retrieved Aug 04, 2024, from https://digital-strategy.ec.europa.eu: https://digital-strategy.ec.europa.eu/en/library/ethics-guidelines-trustworthy-ai

FiscalNote. (2024, Aug 07). *China's AI Policy & Development: What You Need to Know*. Retrieved Aug 19, 2024, from https://fiscalnote.com: https://fiscalnote.com/blog/china-ai-policy-development-what-you-need-to-know

George, B. M. (2023, Nov). *AI in the Legal System, Transparency, Interpretability and the Right to a Fair Trial: The Challenges and Implications for the Ghanaian Civil and Criminal Justice Systems*. Retrieved Aug 02, 2024, from https://www.researchgate.net: https://www.researchgate.net/publication/375640346_AI_in_the_Legal_System_Transparency_Interpretability_and_the_Right_to_a_Fair_Trial_The_Challenges_and_Implications_for_the_Ghanaian_Civil_and_Criminal_Justice_Systems

Gloria, M. (2023, December). Stakeholder roles in artificial intelligence projects. *Project Leadership and Society*, 03. Advance online publication. DOI: 10.1016/j.plas.2022.100068

GPAI. (2024). *The Global Partnership on Artificial Intelligence (GPAI)*. Retrieved Aug 05, 2024, from https://www.gpai.ai: https://www.gpai.ai/about/

Hung, T.-W., & Yen, C.-P. (2023, June). Predictive policing and algorithmic fairness. *Synthese*, 201(06), 206. Advance online publication. DOI: 10.1007/s11229-023-04189-0

IITK. (2023, Jul 28). *Understanding Bias in Artificial Intelligence: Challenges, Impacts, and Mitigation Strategies*. Retrieved Aug 15, 2024, from https://ifacet.iitk.ac.in: https://ifacet.iitk.ac.in/knowledge-hub/artificial-intelligence/understanding-bias-in-artificial-intelligence-challenges-impacts-and-mitigation-strategies/

ISO. (2024). *Artificial intelligence — Functional safety and AI systems*. Retrieved Aug 06, 2024, from https://www.iso.org: https://www.iso.org/obp/ui/en/#iso:std:iso-iec:tr:5469:ed-1:v1:en

Jakob, M., Prathm, J., David, S. W., & Luciano, F. (2022, August 18). The US Algorithmic Accountability Act of 2022 vs. The EU Artificial Intelligence Act: What can they learn from each other? *Minds and Machines*, 32(4), 751–758. DOI: 10.1007/s11023-022-09612-y

James, M., Jake, S., & Brittany, P. (2019, Oct 19). *What Do We Do About the Biases in AI?* Retrieved Aug 13, 2024, from https://hbr.org: https://hbr.org/2019/10/what-do-we-do-about-the-biases-in-ai

Jeena, J. (2024). Predicting crime or perpetuating bias? The AI dilemma. *Springer Link*. Retrieved Aug 15, 2024, from https://link.springer.com/article/10.1007/s00146-024-02032-9

Johana, B. (2021, Nov 08). *LAPD ended predictive policing programs amid public outcry. A new effort shares many of their flaws*. Retrieved Aug 14, 2024, from https://www.theguardian.com: https://www.theguardian.com/us-news/2021/nov/07/lapd-predictive-policing-surveillance-reform

Keymaker. (2024, Apr 02). *Ethical Considerations in AI Model Development*. Retrieved Aug 03, 2024, from https://keymakr.com: https://keymakr.com/blog/ethical-considerations-in-ai-model-development/

Komal, A. (2024, Jan 26). *Data protection and data privacy laws in India*. Retrieved Aug 08, 2024, from https://blog.ipleaders.in: https://blog.ipleaders.in/data-protection-laws-in-india-2/

Lyytinen, L., Hekkert, W., Cheng, Y., & Sovacool, S. (2022). Adaptive Legal Frameworks and Economic Dynamics in Emerging Technologies: Navigating the Intersection for Responsible Innovation. *Law and Economics*, 16(03), 202–220. DOI: 10.35335/laweco.v16i3.61

Madaoui, N. (2024, May). The Impact of Artificial Intelligence on Legal Systems: Challenges and Opportunities. *Problems of Legality*, 01(164), 2085–2303. DOI: 10.21564/2414-990X.164.289266

Mark, H., Simon, S., & Luisa, R. (2024, Jan 08). *Bridging the Gap Between Artificial Intelligence Implementation, Governance and Democracy: An Operational and Regulatory Perspective*. Retrieved Aug 15, 2024, from https://www.fticonsulting.com: https://www.fticonsulting.com/insights/articles/bridging-gap-between-artificial-intelligence-implementation-governance-democracy

Mark van. R. (2023, Feb 17). *Privacy in the Age of AI: Risks, Challenges and Solutions*. Retrieved Aug 13, 2024, from https://www.thedigitalspeaker.com: https://www.thedigitalspeaker.com/privacy-age-ai-risks-challenges-solutions/

Maurice, B. (2023, Sep 25). *Leveraging AI-Powered Tools for Streamlined Contract Analysis in Intellectual Property Law*. Retrieved Aug 12, 2024, from https://www.linkedin.com: https://www.linkedin.com/pulse/leveraging-ai-powered-tools-streamlined-contract-law-bretzfield-2c/

Milin, S. (2024, Mar 24). *Top five AI legal assistants to optimise your firms in 2024*. Retrieved Aug 12, 2024, from https://indiaai.gov.in: https://indiaai.gov.in/article/top-five-ai-legal-assistants-to-optimise-your-firms-in-2024

Niral, S. (2022, Aug 29). Bias and Ethical Concerns in Machine Learning. *ISACA, 04*, 01-04. Retrieved Aug 12, 2024, from https://www.isaca.org/resources/isaca-journal/issues/2022/volume-4/bias-and-ethical-concerns-in-machine-learning

OECD. (2023). *Artificial intelligence*. Retrieved Aug 19, 2024, from https://www.oecd.org: https://www.oecd.org/en/topics/policy-issues/artificial-intelligence.html

Oksana, Z. (2024, Jan 25). *Opening the Black Box: How to Create AI Transparency and Explainability to Build Trust*. Retrieved Aug 15, 2024, from https://shelf.io: https://shelf.io/blog/ai-transparency-and-explainability/

OVIC. (2023). *Artificial Intelligence and Privacy – Issues and Challenges*. Retrieved Aug 10, 2024, from https://ovic.vic.gov.au: https://ovic.vic.gov.au/privacy/resources-for-organisations/artificial-intelligence-and-privacy-issues-and-challenges/

Paul, V. (2023, Apr 20). *Accountability and Responsibility in AI: Assigning Responsibility in the Age of Autonomous AI Systems*. Retrieved Aug 19, 2024, from https://www.linkedin.com: https://www.linkedin.com/pulse/accountability-responsibility-ai-assigning-age-systems-paul-veitch/

Praveen, M. (2024, Feb 27). *AI And The Legal Landscape: Embracing Innovation, Addressing Challenges*. Retrieved Aug 03, 2024, from https://www.livelaw.in: https://www.livelaw.in/lawschool/articles/law-and-ai-ai-powered-tools-general-data-protection-regulation-250673

Rowena, R. (2020, December). Legal and human rights issues of AI: Gaps, challenges and vulnerabilities. *Journal of Responsible Technology*, 04, 100005. Advance online publication. DOI: 10.1016/j.jrt.2020.100005

Scott, R., Rich, C., & Tréa, L. (2024, Jul). *What is GDPR? Compliance and conditions explained*. Retrieved Aug 11, 2024, from https://www.techtarget.com: https://www.techtarget.com/whatis/definition/General-Data-Protection-Regulation-GDPR

Sheeba, N. (2023, July). Artificial Intelligence's Effects on the Legal Sector: Transforming Legal Practice. *International Journal for Legal Research & Analysis*, 02(07), 1–21. Retrieved August 12, 2024, from https://www.researchgate.net/publication/372343835_Artificial_intelligences_effects_On_the_legal_sector_transforming_Legal_practice

Shivani, T. (2024, Apr 02). *Smart Contracts Explained: Understanding Their Functionality on the Blockchain*. Retrieved Aug 10, 2024, from https://www.spydra.app: https://www.spydra.app/blog/smart-contracts-explained-understanding-their-functionality-on-the-blockchain#:~:text=Smart%20contracts%20are%20digital%20agreements,agreement%20are%20enforced%20by%20code

Sreelatha, A., & Gyandeep, C. (2023, Sep). *Exploring The Use of AI In Legal Decision Making: Benefits and Ethical Implications*. Retrieved Aug 15, 2024, from https://woxsen.edu.in: https://woxsen.edu.in/research/white-papers/exploring-the-use-of-ai-in-legal-decision-making-benefits-and-ethical-implications/

Tim, B., & William, D. (2017). Correctional Offender Management Profiles for Alternative Sanctions (COMPAS). In D. G. Jay P. Singh, *Handbook of Recidivism Risk/Needs Assessment Tools,* (pp. 49-75). Wiley Online Library. DOI: 10.1002/9781119184256

Wanbil, W. L., Wolfgang, Z., & Henry, C. (2016, Dec 24). *An Ethical Approach to Data Privacy Protection*. Retrieved Aug 09, 2024, from https://www.isaca.org: https://www.isaca.org/resources/isaca-journal/issues/2016/volume-6/an-ethical-approach-to-data-privacy-protection

Will Douglas, H. (2020, Jul 17). *Predictive policing algorithms are racist. They need to be dismantled.* Retrieved Aug 15, 2024, from https://www.technologyreview.com: https://www.technologyreview.com/2020/07/17/1005396/predictive-policing-algorithms-racist-dismantled-machine-learning-bias-criminal-justice/

Yoshija, W. (2024, February 26). Managing the race to the moon: Global policy and governance in Artificial Intelligence regulation—A contemporary overview and an analysis of socioeconomic consequences. *Springer Link*, 04(14), 14. Advance online publication. DOI: 10.1007/s44163-024-00109-4

Chapter 10
Harnessing Predictive Analytics and AI in Judicial Decisions

Vanita Mohod
https://orcid.org/0009-0005-4353-4250
Dr. D.Y. Patil Law College, Pune, India

Mayura Prakashrao Borde
Yashwantrao Chavan Law College, Pune, India

Trupti Rathi
National Institute of Construction Management and Research, NICMAR University, Pune, India

Madhavi More
https://orcid.org/0009-0001-5236-8048
Department of Law, Christ University (Deemed), Pune, India

Bhupesh Gopal Chintamani
Symbiosis Law School, Symbiosis International University (Deemed), Pune, India

Shrikant Waghulkar
https://orcid.org/0000-0002-3767-3765
Ramchandra Institute of Management Studies, Pune, India

Nitesh Behare
https://orcid.org/0000-0002-9338-8563
Balaji Institute of International Business, Sri Balaji University, Pune, India

Rashmi D. Mahajan
https://orcid.org/0000-0001-9082-6874
Balaji Institute of International Business, Sri Balaji University, Pune, India

ABSTRACT

This chapter explores the impact of predictive analytics and AI on judicial decision-making, tracing the evolution of technology in law from early data analysis to advanced AI techniques. It covers core concepts and applications, such as case outcome predictions, sentencing, and AI-powered legal research tools. The bene-

DOI: 10.4018/979-8-3693-7205-0.ch010

fits of AI—enhancing accuracy, efficiency, and consistency in legal decisions—are highlighted, along with ethical concerns like bias, accountability, and privacy. The chapter includes case studies demonstrating AI's global impact on legal systems and addresses challenges such as technical limitations and resistance to technology adoption. It concludes by discussing future trends, emerging technologies, and the need for ethical guidelines to create a more just, data-driven legal framework.

1. INTRODUCTION:

The judiciary, a cornerstone of democratic governance, has traditionally relied on human judgement, legal precedents, and statutory interpretations to deliver justice. However, the advent of technology, particularly predictive analytics and artificial intelligence (AI), is revolutionizing this age-old system (Chen, 2019). The integration of these advanced technologies into judicial decision-making processes promises to enhance the efficiency, consistency, and fairness of legal outcomes (Thomas, 2024).

Predictive analytics, which involves using statistical techniques and algorithms to analyse historical data and make predictions about future events, has found diverse applications across various sectors (Ashok Kumar, Sujatha, & Uma, 2022). In the legal domain, it offers significant potential to streamline case management, predict litigation outcomes, and even inform sentencing decisions. AI, encompassing machine learning and natural language processing, further augments these capabilities by processing vast amounts of legal texts, identifying patterns, and generating insights that can aid judges and lawyers in their decision-making processes (Chen, 2019).

One of the primary benefits of harnessing predictive analytics and AI in judicial decisions is the enhancement of efficiency. Courts around the world are grappling with overwhelming caseloads, leading to delays and backlogs that undermine the timely delivery of justice. By analysing historical case data, predictive analytics can help identify trends and predict case durations, allowing for better allocation of judicial resources. AI-powered tools can assist in automating routine tasks such as document review and legal research, freeing up valuable time for judges and legal practitioners to focus on more complex aspects of cases (Mustari, Sen, Banik, Mehedi, & Rasel, 2023).

Figure 1. Legal Analytics (Author Generated using Scopus AI)

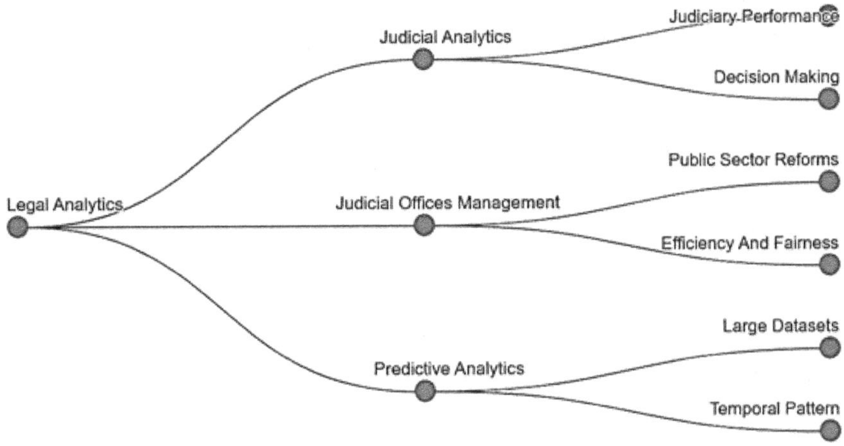

Consistency in judicial decisions is another critical area where predictive analytics and AI can make a substantial impact. Human judges, despite their best efforts, are susceptible to biases and inconsistencies. Predictive models, trained on extensive datasets, can help ensure that similar cases receive similar treatments, reducing the variability in judicial outcomes. This is particularly important in criminal justice, where sentencing disparities have long been a concern. AI systems can analyse a wide range of factors, including the nature of the crime, the defendant's history, and prevailing legal standards, to provide recommendations that are both consistent and aligned with established legal principles (Aletras, Tsarapatsanis, Preoţiuc-Pietro, & Lampos, 2016).

Moreover, the use of predictive analytics and AI can enhance the fairness and transparency of judicial decisions. These technologies can help uncover hidden biases in legal processes and highlight disparities that might otherwise go unnoticed. For instance, AI can be employed to analyse sentencing patterns across different demographic groups, providing insights that can inform policy reforms aimed at ensuring equitable treatment for all individuals. By making data-driven recommendations, predictive analytics can also increase the transparency of judicial reasoning, allowing stakeholders to better understand the basis for legal decisions (Valvoda, Thompson, Cotterell, & Teufel, 2024).

Despite the numerous advantages, the integration of predictive analytics and AI into judicial decision-making is not without challenges. Concerns about the ethical implications of AI, particularly related to privacy, accountability, and the potential for algorithmic bias, must be carefully addressed. Ensuring that AI systems are transparent, explainable, and subject to rigorous oversight is crucial to maintaining public trust in the judiciary. Additionally, the legal profession must grapple with questions about the extent to which AI should influence judicial decisions and the potential for over-reliance on technology at the expense of human judgement.

2. CORE CONCEPTS:

- Definition

Predictive analytics in the judicial system involves using statistical methods and machine learning algorithms to analyse historical legal data to forecast future outcomes. This process helps in making informed decisions by identifying patterns and trends within the data.

Predictive analytics in the judicial system refers to the application of data-driven techniques to predict case outcomes, streamline case management, and allocate judicial resources more effectively, thereby reducing backlogs and delays in the legal process.

In the judicial system, predictive analytics utilizes historical data and advanced algorithms to ensure consistent and unbiased judicial decisions. By analysing past cases and decisions, it aims to minimize disparities and enhance the fairness of legal outcomes.

Predictive analytics within the judicial context involves employing machine learning and statistical techniques to uncover and address biases in judicial decisions. By examining large datasets, it identifies patterns that may indicate systemic biases, promoting more equitable legal processes.

- Principles of predictive analytics.

Predictive analytics involves the application of statistical techniques and machine learning algorithms to historical data in order to make informed predictions about future events. This field of data science relies on various principles including data collection, model building, validation, and deployment.

Predictive Judicial Analytics

Assessing Extra-Legal Factors and Debiasing the Law: Predictive judicial analytics can evaluate extra-legal factors that influence judicial decisions, offering potential solutions for debiasing the law.

Evaluating Legal Bias with Machine Learning: Machine learning offers robust methods to assess bias within the legal system and evaluate the potential consequences of legal changes.

Integration of AI and Computer Science in Law: The incorporation of AI into legal decision-making improves efficiency and promotes standardization across legal procedures.

Learning Systems in Judicial Decision Making

Machine Learning as Decision Support: Machine learning methods can function as decision-support tools within the legal system, achieving over 70% accuracy in predicting court decisions.

Multi-Task Learning Networks: A novel multi-task learning network has been developed to unify multiple judicial prediction subtasks, significantly outperforming previous state-of-the-art methods.

Ethical and Data Protection Considerations

Processing Personal Data in Legal Analytics: Legal analytics and AI systems process personal data in judicial rulings for purposes like prediction, necessitating measures such as anonymization or pseudonymization to protect individuals' rights.

Predictive Analytics for Crime Data: Predictive analytics has been applied to analyse crime data, predicting crimes based on factors like time and location using machine learning techniques.

Risks of Bias and Lack of Transparency: The application of predictive analytics and machine learning to social problems can reflect existing biases and leave affected individuals unable to understand the basis of decisions.

Need for Ethical Guidelines: The use of predictive analytics in the judicial system necessitates professional ethical guidelines to ensure fairness and mitigate risks of social inequality, discrimination, and exclusion.

Data Protection Regulations: Improved data protection regulations are essential to counter the risks of abuse associated with predictive analytics in legal settings.

AI in the Judicial System

Revolutionizing Decision-Making: AI has the potential to revolutionize judicial decision-making processes, reducing human biases and improving efficiency.

Development of Predictive Models: The integration of AI and machine learning enables the development of predictive models for legal decision-making.

Addressing Challenges: Incorporating AI in the judicial domain presents challenges, such as the need for transparency, explainability, and ethical considerations regarding bias and privacy.

Improving Efficiency and Standardization: AI can enhance the efficiency of handling cases, promote standardization in legal procedures, and improve decision-making in complex legal situations.

Critiques and Risks: There are significant critiques concerning the unreflective application of predictive analytics and AI, particularly regarding biases and the potential impact on core rule-of-law values.

Future Implications: The use of AI and predictive analytics in the judicial system holds the promise of increasing efficiency and fairness, but it also requires careful consideration of its impact on legal practice and the rights of individuals.

Legal Factors and Equality of Arms

Epistemic Fragilities and Rights Violations: The use of predictive analytics in legal settings is affected by inherent epistemic fragilities and the risk of rights violations.

Impact on Judicial Efficiency: The integration of AI in legal decision-making improves the efficiency of handling cases and promotes standardization across legal procedures.

Data Processing and Individual Rights: Legal analytics techniques involve processing personal data, requiring careful assessment of the impact on individuals' rights and freedoms.

Case Outcome Prediction: Machine learning models can predict legal case outcomes based on both case-specific legal factors and extra-legal factors, such as the ideological direction of the court.

Figure 2. Key AI technologies used in legal contexts.

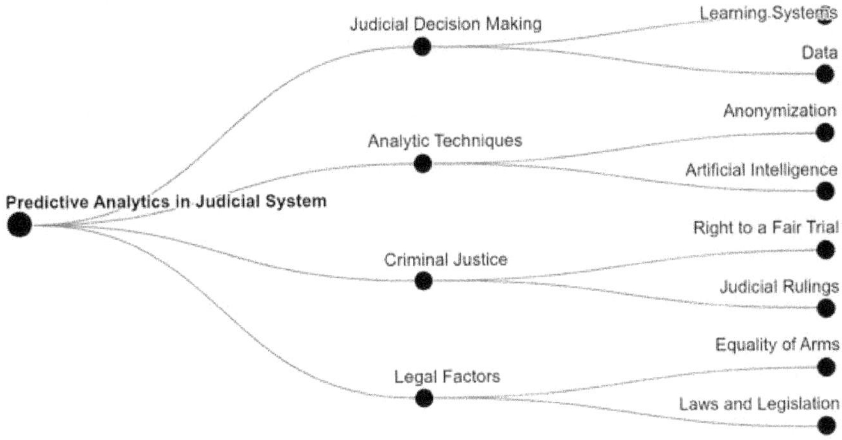

Machine Learning (ML):

Description: Machine learning is a subset of artificial intelligence that enables systems to learn from data and improve their performance over time without being explicitly programmed. In the legal context, ML algorithms can analyse historical case data to identify patterns, predict outcomes, and assess risks.

Applications: Predicting case outcomes, determining sentencing recommendations, and assessing recidivism risk.

Natural Language Processing (NLP):

Description: NLP focuses on the interaction between computers and human language, enabling machines to understand, interpret, and generate human language. This technology allows for the analysis of legal texts, documents, and case law.

Applications: Analysing legal documents for relevant information, automating contract review, and summarizing lengthy legal texts.

Expert Systems:

Description: Expert systems are AI programs that emulate the decision-making ability of a human expert. These systems rely on a knowledge base of legal rules and precedents to assist legal professionals.

Applications: Providing legal advice, automating compliance checks, and assisting in document drafting.

Predictive Analytics:

Description: Predictive analytics utilizes statistical techniques and machine learning to analyse historical data and forecast future outcomes. In legal contexts, it helps identify trends and patterns in judicial decisions.

Applications: Estimating the likelihood of case success, analysing past rulings for insights, and informing strategic legal decisions.

Case Management Systems (CMS):

Description: CMS software incorporates AI to enhance the efficiency of case management processes. These systems automate administrative tasks and improve the organization of case-related information.

Applications: Automating document management, scheduling hearings, and tracking case progress.

Sentiment Analysis:

Description: Sentiment analysis involves using NLP techniques to analyse text data and determine the sentiment expressed within it. In legal contexts, this can provide insights into the tone and sentiment of legal documents and opinions.

Applications: Evaluating the sentiment of judicial opinions or legal arguments to assess potential biases or emotional tones.

Decision Support Systems (DSS):

Description: DSS leverage AI and data analytics to assist judges and legal professionals in making informed decisions. These systems provide relevant data, case law references, and predictive insights.

Applications: Guiding judicial decision-making, recommending legal strategies, and providing insights based on historical data.

Anomaly Detection Algorithms:

Description: These algorithms identify unusual patterns or outliers in data that may indicate errors or biases. In the legal context, they can help detect inconsistencies in case handling or judicial decisions.

Applications: Identifying potential biases in sentencing patterns, detecting fraud in legal documentation, and ensuring compliance with legal standards.

Robotic Process Automation (RPA):

Description: RPA automates repetitive tasks and processes within legal workflows, allowing legal professionals to focus on higher-value work. This technology uses software robots to perform routine tasks.

Applications: Automating data entry, document generation, and case updates.

Chatbots and Virtual Assistants:

Description: AI-powered chatbots can provide legal information and assistance to users in real time. They can guide individuals through legal processes and answer common legal questions.

Applications: Offering legal advice for simple queries, assisting with document preparation, and providing information on legal rights.

- Overview of how predictive models work.

Predictive models in judicial decision-making employ techniques such as jurimetry, predictive analysis, and decision-making theories to analyse and forecast legal outcomes. These models detect patterns and trends within vast amounts of legal data, enabling more accurate predictions of court decisions. This process not only aids in identifying trends in the legal system but also supports a more systematic and efficient judicial process. By leveraging historical case data, these models enhance the accuracy and consistency of judicial decisions, thereby contributing to a more reliable legal system (Rwrsilany, Cleice De Pontes, Adriana, & Rogerio, 2023).

Figure 3. Decision making process

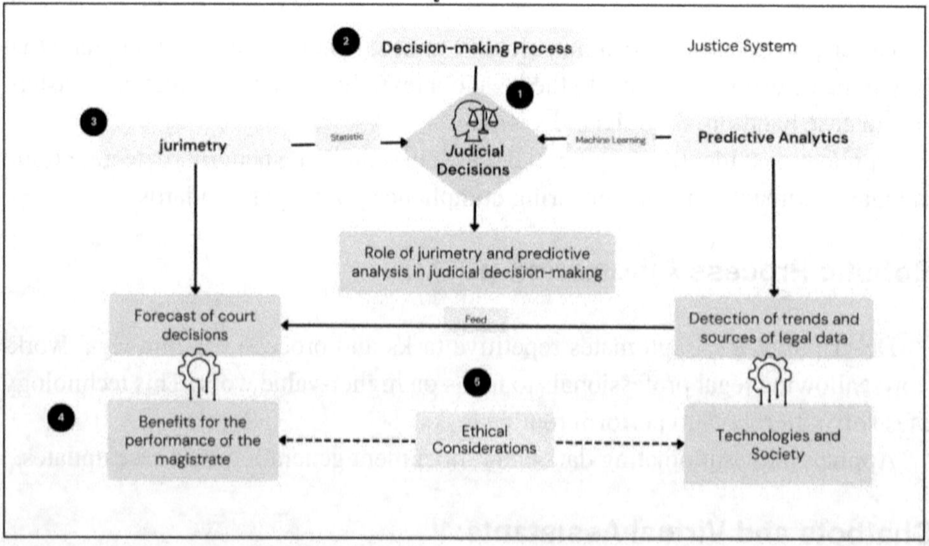

Source: https://login.semead.com.br/26semead/anais/arquivos/925.pdf

The benefits of these predictive techniques extend to both magistrates and society. For magistrates, they offer improvements in efficiency, decision systematization, and agility in handling cases. For society, the increased transparency and legal certainty fostered by these models enhance public trust in the justice system. However, the application of predictive models must be guided by strict ethical considerations to ensure fairness and impartiality (Liu, et al., 2024). Addressing issues such as data protection, bias minimization, and transparency is crucial for maintaining the integrity of the judicial process. Consequently, future research should focus on refining these techniques and exploring their implications further to enhance their effectiveness and ethical application in the legal domain.

- Predicting Case Outcomes and Sentencing

Predicting case outcomes is one of the most prominent applications of predictive analytics in judicial decision-making. By analysing historical data, predictive models can estimate the probability of various case outcomes based on specific case attributes. These attributes can include the nature of the case, the involved parties, the presiding judge, and previous similar cases. This information can help lawyers and litigants make strategic decisions, such as whether to settle a case or proceed to trial (Zhao, Gao, & Guo, 2023).

For judges, predictive analytics offers a tool to ensure consistency in sentencing. Sentencing disparities have long been a concern in the judicial system, with similar cases often receiving different sentences due to human biases or subjective interpretations (Zhao, Gao, & Guo, 2023). Predictive models can analyse a wide range of factors, including the severity of the crime, the defendant's criminal history, and relevant legal standards, to provide sentencing recommendations that are both consistent and aligned with established guidelines. This can reduce sentencing variability and enhance the fairness of the judicial process.

- Identifying High-Risk Recidivism and Optimizing Rehabilitation Strategies

Another critical application of predictive analytics in judicial decision-making is in the area of recidivism. Recidivism refers to the tendency of previously convicted individuals to reoffend. Predictive models can analyse data on past offenders, including their criminal records, socio-economic backgrounds, and rehabilitation efforts, to identify individuals at high risk of recidivism. This information is invaluable for parole boards, probation officers, and correctional facilities as they make decisions about parole, probation, and rehabilitation programs (Li, Duan, Zhou, & Yuan, 2022).

By identifying high-risk individuals, the judicial system can tailor rehabilitation strategies to address specific risk factors. For instance, individuals identified as high-risk due to substance abuse issues can be directed to specialized treatment programs, while those with unstable housing situations can receive support in finding stable accommodations. Optimizing rehabilitation strategies based on predictive insights can improve the effectiveness of these programs, reduce recidivism rates, and promote successful reintegration into society.

Furthermore, predictive analytics can assist in resource allocation within the criminal justice system. Correctional facilities and probation departments often operate with limited resources, and predictive models can help prioritize interventions for individuals most likely to benefit from them. This targeted approach ensures that resources are used efficiently and that high-risk individuals receive the support they need to avoid reoffending.

3. AI-POWERED LEGAL RESEARCH AND ANALYSIS:

Artificial Intelligence (AI) is transforming various sectors, and the legal domain is no exception. AI-powered legal research and analysis tools are revolutionizing how judges and lawyers conduct their work, making it more efficient, accurate, and insightful. These tools leverage machine learning algorithms and natural language processing to analyse vast amounts of legal data, identify patterns, and provide actionable insights.

- AI-Driven Legal Research Tools for Judges and Lawyers

Traditional legal research is often a time-consuming and labour-intensive process, requiring legal professionals to sift through numerous case laws, statutes, and legal texts to find relevant information. AI-driven legal research tools are designed to streamline this process by automating many of the manual tasks involved. These tools can quickly search through extensive legal databases, retrieve relevant documents, and provide summaries, saving significant time and effort (Wu, et al., 2022).

One of the key benefits of AI-driven legal research tools is their ability to understand the context and nuances of legal queries. Using natural language processing, these tools can interpret complex legal questions and provide precise answers. This capability is particularly useful for judges and lawyers who need to find specific precedents or legal interpretations quickly. By reducing the time spent on research, legal professionals can focus more on case strategy and decision-making.

Furthermore, AI-driven tools can assist in drafting legal documents. They can suggest relevant clauses, cite appropriate case laws, and even flag potential legal issues, ensuring that the documents are thorough and accurate. This not only enhances the quality of legal work but also reduces the likelihood of errors.

- Analysing Case Law and Statutes with Machine Learning Algorithms

Machine learning algorithms play a crucial role in analysing case law and statutes. These algorithms can process large volumes of legal texts, identify relevant information, and draw connections between different legal concepts. By doing so, they can uncover insights that might be difficult for humans to detect.

For example, machine learning algorithms can analyse past case rulings to predict the outcomes of similar cases. By examining factors such as the nature of the case, the involved parties, and the legal arguments presented, these algorithms can estimate the probability of different outcomes. This predictive capability is invaluable for lawyers as it helps them assess the strengths and weaknesses of their cases and devise effective legal strategies.

Additionally, machine learning algorithms can help in statutory analysis by identifying trends and patterns in legislation. They can track changes in laws over time, highlight the impact of new statutes on existing legal frameworks, and provide insights into legislative intent. This information is crucial for legal professionals who need to understand the broader context of the laws they are working with (Tsou, et al., 2022).

- Identifying Patterns and Biases in Judicial Decisions

One of the most significant contributions of AI in legal research and analysis is its ability to identify patterns and biases in judicial decisions. Bias in the judiciary is a critical concern, as it can undermine the fairness and integrity of the legal system. AI tools can help address this issue by providing objective analyses of judicial behaviour. By analysing a judge's past rulings, AI algorithms can detect patterns that may indicate bias. For instance, they can examine whether a judge consistently rules in favour of a particular type of litigant or whether their decisions are influenced by certain external factors. Identifying such patterns can prompt further investigation and potentially lead to corrective measures (Tsou, et al., 2022).

AI can also highlight disparities in sentencing, helping to ensure that similar cases receive consistent treatment. By comparing sentencing decisions across different cases, AI tools can identify anomalies and suggest adjustments to promote fairness. This capability is particularly important in criminal justice, where sentencing disparities have long been a concern. Moreover, AI-driven analysis can enhance transparency in the judicial process. By providing data-driven insights into judicial decisions, these tools can help the public and legal professionals better understand the reasoning behind rulings. This transparency can build trust in the legal system and ensure that judges are held accountable for their decisions (Feng, Li, Ge, Luo, & Ng, 2021).

4. AI-ASSISTED DECISION SUPPORT SYSTEMS:

Artificial Intelligence (AI) and predictive analytics are rapidly transforming various sectors, including the judicial system. AI-assisted decision support systems (DSS) are designed to aid judges in making more informed and consistent decisions. These systems leverage advanced technologies to analyse vast amounts of legal data, predict case outcomes, and provide insights that enhance the judicial decision-making process. This article explores the development of decision support systems for judges, the integration of predictive analytics and AI in judicial decision-making, and the importance of ensuring transparency and explainability in AI-driven decisions.

- Developing Decision Support Systems for Judges

The development of AI-assisted decision support systems for judges involves several key steps. Initially, it requires the aggregation and organization of extensive legal datasets, including past court rulings, statutes, legal precedents, and other relevant documents. This data forms the foundation upon which machine learning models and algorithms are trained.

The next step is to design and implement machine learning algorithms capable of analysing the data and extracting meaningful patterns. These algorithms can be trained to recognize various legal principles, understand the nuances of legal language, and identify correlations between different case attributes and outcomes. The goal is to create models that can accurately predict the outcomes of new cases based on historical data (Feng, Li, Ge, Luo, & Ng, 2021).

Additionally, the development process involves creating a user-friendly interface that allows judges to interact with the decision support system easily. The interface should provide clear and concise summaries of relevant cases, highlight pertinent legal precedents, and offer recommendations based on the analysis performed by the AI. This ensures that judges can quickly access the information they need to make informed decisions without being overwhelmed by excessive data.

- Integrating Predictive Analytics and AI in Judicial Decision-Making

Integrating predictive analytics and AI into judicial decision-making is a multifaceted process that requires careful planning and implementation. One of the primary applications of predictive analytics in this context is case outcome prediction. By analysing past rulings and identifying patterns, predictive models can estimate the likelihood of various outcomes for new cases. This information can be invaluable for judges, as it provides a data-driven basis for their decisions and helps reduce the potential for human bias (Huang & Lin, 2019).

AI can also assist in sentencing decisions by analysing a wide range of factors, including the nature of the crime, the defendant's criminal history, and applicable legal standards. Predictive models can offer sentencing recommendations that are consistent with past cases and aligned with established guidelines. This helps ensure that similar cases receive similar sentences, promoting fairness and reducing sentencing disparities.

Another critical application is the identification of high-risk recidivism. Predictive analytics can analyse data on past offenders to determine which individuals are at higher risk of reoffending. This information can guide parole boards and probation officers in making decisions about parole and probation, as well as inform rehabilitation strategies tailored to the needs of high-risk individuals. By optimizing these strategies, the judicial system can reduce recidivism rates and improve public safety.

- Ensuring Transparency and Explainability in AI-Driven Decisions

As AI-assisted decision support systems become more prevalent in the judicial system, ensuring transparency and explainability in AI-driven decisions is paramount. One of the main challenges with AI is the so-called "black box" problem, where the inner workings of the algorithms are not easily understood by users. This lack of transparency can lead to mistrust and reluctance to adopt AI technologies.

To address this issue, developers must prioritize creating explainable AI models. Explainable AI refers to systems that can provide clear and understandable justifications for their predictions and recommendations. This involves designing algorithms that not only produce accurate results but also offer insights into the factors and data points that influenced their decisions. By providing this level of transparency, AI-assisted decision support systems can help judges understand the rationale behind the AI's recommendations, fostering trust and confidence in the technology (Visentin, Nardotto, & Osullivan, 2019).

Moreover, it is crucial to implement robust validation and auditing processes to ensure the accuracy and fairness of AI models. Regular audits can help identify and mitigate biases that may be present in the data or algorithms. This is particularly important in the judicial system, where biases can have significant implications for justice and fairness. By continuously monitoring and refining AI models, developers can ensure that the systems remain reliable and equitable.

In addition to technical measures, there is a need for clear ethical guidelines and regulatory frameworks governing the use of AI in judicial decision-making. These guidelines should outline the responsibilities of developers, judges, and other stakeholders in ensuring that AI technologies are used ethically and responsibly. They should also address issues related to data privacy, security, and the protection of individuals' rights. Finally, education and training are essential to ensure that judges and legal professionals can effectively use AI-assisted decision support systems. Providing comprehensive training on how to interpret AI-generated recommendations, understand the underlying algorithms, and critically assess the information provided by these systems is crucial. This will empower judges to make informed decisions while leveraging the benefits of AI technology.

5. BENEFITS OF USING AI IN LEGAL DECISIONS:

The incorporation of Artificial Intelligence (AI) in legal decision-making processes offers transformative benefits, enhancing the efficiency, accuracy, and consistency of judicial outcomes. By leveraging advanced algorithms and data analytics, AI provides judges and legal professionals with powerful tools to streamline their work and improve the overall quality of legal proceedings. Here, we explore the significant advantages of using AI in legal decisions, focusing on improved accuracy and consistency in rulings, increased efficiency and reduced case backlog, enhanced ability to identify patterns and trends, and support for decision-making with data-driven insights.

- Improved Accuracy and Consistency in Rulings

One of the primary benefits of AI in legal decisions is the enhanced accuracy and consistency it brings to judicial rulings. Traditional judicial processes often suffer from human errors and biases, which can lead to inconsistent and sometimes unfair outcomes. AI algorithms, however, are capable of analysing vast amounts of data with a high degree of precision, ensuring that similar cases receive similar judgments based on established legal principles and precedents (Sivaranjani, Jayabharathy, & M., 2019).

Machine learning models, trained on historical case data, can identify patterns and correlations that may not be apparent to human judges. This capability helps in standardizing rulings and reducing the discrepancies that can arise from subjective interpretations of the law. By providing a more objective basis for decision-making, AI ensures that legal outcomes are fairer and more predictable, thereby enhancing the credibility and integrity of the judicial system.

- Increased Efficiency and Reduced Case Backlog

The integration of AI into the legal system significantly boosts efficiency and helps to alleviate the perennial issue of case backlog. Courts around the world are often inundated with cases, leading to prolonged delays and a sluggish judicial process. AI-powered tools can automate many routine tasks, such as document review, legal research, and the drafting of legal documents. This automation not only speeds up these processes but also allows legal professionals to focus on more complex and nuanced aspects of their work (Bi, Zhou, Pan, & Qi, 2023).

For instance, AI can quickly sift through large volumes of case law, statutes, and legal documents to find relevant information, a task that would take humans considerably longer. By streamlining these processes, AI reduces the time required to prepare for and conduct legal proceedings. Consequently, the judiciary can handle more cases within the same timeframe, effectively reducing the backlog and ensuring that justice is delivered more promptly (Barysė & Sarel, 2024).

- Enhanced Ability to Identify Patterns and Trends

AI's capacity to analyse extensive datasets and uncover hidden patterns and trends is particularly valuable in the legal domain. Legal professionals can use AI to analyse historical case data to identify trends that may influence future rulings. For example, AI can highlight shifts in judicial interpretations of certain laws, emerging legal issues, or changes in sentencing patterns over time.

This ability to identify patterns and trends provides judges and lawyers with deeper insights into the legal landscape. It helps them anticipate potential legal challenges, understand the evolving nature of legal standards, and adapt their strategies accordingly. Moreover, recognizing these trends can aid in the development of more effective legal policies and reforms, ensuring that the legal system evolves in line with societal changes and needs (Benyekhlef & Zhu, 2024).

- Support for Decision-Making with Data-Driven Insights

AI offers robust support for decision-making by providing data-driven insights that enhance the quality of judicial decisions. In complex cases where the stakes are high, having access to comprehensive and accurate data can be crucial. AI systems can analyse vast amounts of relevant data, including previous cases, legal statutes, expert opinions, and even social and economic factors that may influence the case outcome.

These data-driven insights enable judges to make more informed decisions based on a holistic understanding of the case. AI can present various possible outcomes and their probabilities, helping judges weigh different scenarios and consider all relevant factors before arriving at a decision. This comprehensive approach not only improves the quality of legal judgments but also fosters greater confidence in the judicial process among all stakeholders (Chen & Eagel, 2017).

Furthermore, AI-driven insights can help mitigate unconscious biases that might affect human judges. By relying on objective data and algorithmic analysis, AI can ensure that decisions are made based on facts and established legal principles rather than subjective opinions or prejudices. This contributes to a more equitable and just legal system.

6. ETHICAL AND LEGAL CONSIDERATIONS:

The integration of Artificial Intelligence (AI) in judicial decision-making has the potential to revolutionize the legal system by enhancing efficiency, accuracy, and consistency. However, the deployment of AI technologies in this sensitive domain also raises significant ethical and legal considerations. Addressing these issues is crucial to ensuring that AI-driven decisions are fair, transparent, and accountable.

- Addressing Bias in Data and Algorithms

Bias in data and algorithms is one of the most critical ethical challenges in the application of AI in the judiciary. AI systems learn from historical data, which may contain inherent biases reflecting past societal and judicial prejudices. If not properly addressed, these biases can be perpetuated or even amplified by AI models, leading to unfair or discriminatory outcomes.

To mitigate bias, it is essential to implement robust data pre-processing techniques that identify and correct biased data before it is used to train AI models. Additionally, ongoing monitoring and auditing of AI systems are necessary to detect and rectify biases that may emerge over time. Developing diverse and representative training datasets is also crucial to ensure that AI systems generalize well across different demographic groups and legal contexts (Ammar, 2024).

- Ensuring Accountability and Transparency in AI-Driven Decisions

Accountability and transparency are foundational to maintaining public trust in AI-driven judicial decisions. It is imperative that AI systems used in the judiciary are transparent about how they reach their conclusions. This involves providing clear explanations of the decision-making process, the factors considered, and the weight assigned to each factor (Ammar, 2024).

To ensure accountability, it is important to establish clear guidelines on the use of AI in judicial decision-making. This includes defining the roles and responsibilities of human judges and AI systems, ensuring that judges have the final authority to accept or override AI recommendations. Additionally, establishing mechanisms for external oversight and review can help ensure that AI systems operate within ethical and legal boundaries and are held accountable for their decisions.

- Fairness and Bias in AI Models

Ensuring fairness in AI models is essential to achieving just outcomes in the judicial system. Fairness in this context means that AI models should treat all individuals and cases equitably, without favouring or disadvantaging any particular group. Achieving fairness requires a multifaceted approach, including:

Bias Mitigation: Implementing techniques to detect and mitigate bias during model training and deployment.

Fairness Metrics: Developing and using fairness metrics to evaluate AI models' performance across different demographic groups.

Regular Audits: Conducting regular audits to assess and ensure the fairness of AI models.

Inclusive Design: Involving a diverse group of stakeholders, including legal experts, ethicists, and representatives from various demographic groups, in the design and evaluation of AI systems.

- Privacy and Data Security Concerns

The use of AI in the judiciary involves processing large volumes of sensitive and personal data, raising significant privacy and data security concerns. Ensuring that individuals' privacy rights are protected is paramount. This requires implementing stringent data protection measures, including:

Data Anonymization: Removing personally identifiable information from datasets to protect individuals' privacy.

Encryption: Using advanced encryption techniques to secure data at rest and in transit.

Access Controls: Implementing strict access controls to ensure that only authorized personnel can access sensitive data.

Compliance with Regulations: Adhering to relevant data protection regulations, such as the General Data Protection Regulation (GDPR), to ensure compliance with legal standards.

- Legal Regulations and Standards Governing AI Use in the Judiciary

The deployment of AI in judicial decision-making must be governed by comprehensive legal regulations and standards to ensure ethical and lawful use (Ammar, 2024). These regulations should address key aspects such as:

Transparency and Accountability: Establishing requirements for transparency in AI decision-making processes and accountability mechanisms for AI-driven decisions.

Bias and Fairness: Mandating regular audits and evaluations to ensure AI models are free from bias and operate fairly.

Privacy Protection: Setting stringent data protection standards to safeguard individuals' privacy.

Human Oversight: Ensuring that human judges have the ultimate authority in judicial decision-making and can override AI recommendations when necessary.

Ethical Standards: Developing ethical guidelines for the development and use of AI in the judiciary, including principles of justice, fairness, and impartiality.

Adopting such regulations and standards is crucial to building a legal framework that supports the ethical and responsible use of AI in the judiciary. It helps ensure that AI systems enhance, rather than undermine, the fairness and integrity of the judicial process.

By addressing these ethical and legal considerations, the judiciary can harness the benefits of AI while safeguarding the principles of justice, fairness, and transparency. The goal is to create a judicial system that is not only more efficient and accurate but also equitable and accountable to all members of society.

7. REAL-WORLD EXAMPLES OF AI INTEGRATION IN JUDICIAL SYSTEM

The integration of artificial intelligence (AI) in legal systems is transforming the landscape of law and justice. By enhancing legal research, streamlining case analysis, and supporting judicial decision-making, AI technologies offer significant efficiencies and insights. This evolution promises to improve accessibility, consistency, and accuracy in legal processes worldwide.

Here are five notable implementations of AI in legal systems around the world, with more details:

- ***ROSS Intelligence (United States):*** ROSS is an AI-powered legal research tool that leverages natural language processing to help lawyers conduct legal research more efficiently. Users can input questions in plain language, and ROSS analyses vast databases of legal texts to provide relevant case law, statutes, and legal precedents. This streamlines the research process, enabling attorneys to find information faster and focus more on strategic aspects of their cases (ROSS, 2023).
- ***DoNotPay (United Kingdom/United States):*** Originally created to help users contest parking tickets, DoNotPay has evolved into a broader AI-driven legal assistant. It offers guidance on various legal issues, including consumer rights, landlord-tenant disputes, and immigration matters. Users interact with the chatbot to receive tailored legal advice and generate documents, making legal assistance more accessible and affordable for individuals without legal representation (Joshua, 2015).
- ***Lex Machina (United States):*** Lex Machina employs AI to analyse litigation data across multiple jurisdictions. It provides insights into judges, attorneys, and case outcomes, allowing legal professionals to make informed decisions based on historical trends. By identifying patterns in litigation, lawyers can develop strategies, predict case outcomes, and assess the strengths and weaknesses of their arguments.
- ***Predictive Policing (Various Locations):*** Various law enforcement agencies worldwide utilize predictive policing tools, such as PredPol, which analyse historical crime data to forecast future criminal activity. By identifying

hotspots for potential crimes, police departments can allocate resources more effectively and implement preventative measures, ultimately aiming to reduce crime rates and improve public safety.

- ***AI in Sentencing (China):*** Some Chinese courts have begun implementing AI systems to assist judges in making sentencing decisions. These AI tools analyse past cases, judicial outcomes, and relevant laws to suggest appropriate penalties based on similar situations. This approach aims to promote consistency in sentencing and reduce human bias, although it raises ethical questions about the role of AI in the judicial process.
- Lessons learned and best practices.

The integration of artificial intelligence (AI) in legal systems is transforming the landscape of law and justice. By enhancing legal research, streamlining case analysis, and supporting judicial decision-making, AI technologies offer significant efficiencies and insights. This evolution promises to improve accessibility, consistency, and accuracy in legal processes worldwide.

The implementation of AI in legal systems has yielded valuable lessons and best practices that can guide future developments. One critical lesson is the importance of transparency in AI algorithms. Legal professionals must understand how AI systems generate recommendations and predictions to ensure trust in their outputs. Transparency fosters accountability and mitigates concerns regarding bias or errors in decision-making.

Another key takeaway is the need for collaboration between technologists and legal experts. Effective AI tools are developed when legal practitioners provide insights into their specific needs, ensuring that the technology aligns with real-world applications. This collaboration can lead to more intuitive interfaces and functionalities that enhance user experience.

Moreover, ongoing training and education for legal professionals are essential to maximize the benefits of AI tools. Lawyers and judges must be equipped with the skills to interpret AI-generated insights effectively, ensuring that they can leverage this technology to support their decision-making processes.

Lastly, it is crucial to continuously evaluate and refine AI applications based on feedback and performance metrics. This iterative approach helps identify areas for improvement and ensures that AI systems remain relevant and effective in the evolving legal landscape.

8. CHALLENGES AND LIMITATIONS

The integration of artificial intelligence (AI) in legal systems presents numerous challenges and limitations that must be addressed to harness its full potential.

- Technical Limitations and Data Quality Issues

One of the primary challenges is the technical limitations inherent in AI systems. Many legal AI applications rely on vast datasets to train their algorithms, but the quality and completeness of this data are often variable. Incomplete or biased datasets can lead to inaccurate predictions and unreliable outcomes, which can undermine the integrity of legal processes. Additionally, legal language is often nuanced and context-dependent, making it difficult for AI to accurately interpret and analyse cases. Natural language processing, while advancing, still struggles with complex legal terminology, leading to potential misinterpretations that could adversely affect case outcomes.

- Resistance to Technology Adoption

Another significant challenge is the resistance to technology adoption within the legal community. Many legal professionals are hesitant to embrace AI due to fears of job displacement, scepticism about the technology's reliability, and a general reluctance to change established practices. The legal profession has traditionally been slow to adopt new technologies, and this inertia can hinder the implementation of AI tools. Moreover, some practitioners may lack the technical skills necessary to effectively utilize AI, creating a barrier to entry. This resistance can limit the potential benefits of AI; as innovative solutions are not fully embraced or utilized within legal practices.

- The Gap Between AI Capabilities and Human Judgment

A critical limitation of AI in legal systems is the inherent gap between AI capabilities and human judgment. While AI can analyse large volumes of data and identify patterns more efficiently than humans, it lacks the ability to exercise judgment and consider the ethical implications of decisions. Legal professionals often rely on intuition, experience, and empathy—qualities that AI cannot replicate. For instance, in sensitive legal matters, such as family law or criminal cases, human judgment is crucial for understanding the nuances of individual circumstances and making compassionate decisions. Over-reliance on AI could lead to a depersonalized legal experience, where important contextual factors are overlooked.

9. IMPLEMENTING PREDICTIVE ANALYTICS AND AI IN JUDICIAL SYSTEMS:

Implementing predictive analytics and artificial intelligence (AI) in judicial systems requires a thoughtful and collaborative approach to maximize the benefits while minimizing potential risks. Key strategies include collaboration among legal stakeholders and technologists, developing ethical guidelines for AI use, and ensuring data privacy and security.

- Collaborating with Legal Stakeholders and Technologists

Successful implementation of AI in the judicial system necessitates strong collaboration between legal professionals, technologists, and policymakers. Legal stakeholders, including judges, lawyers, and court administrators, possess valuable insights into the specific needs and challenges within the judicial process. By working closely with technologists, these stakeholders can help design AI systems that align with the realities of legal practice and the intricacies of the law. This collaboration can lead to the development of user-friendly interfaces, tailored functionalities, and relevant data sources that enhance the overall effectiveness of AI applications. Engaging diverse legal perspectives also ensures that the technology serves the broader goals of justice, fairness, and accessibility.

- Developing Ethical Guidelines for AI in Judicial Decision-Making

Establishing ethical guidelines for the use of AI in judicial decision-making is paramount to maintain public trust and uphold the integrity of the legal system. These guidelines should address issues such as transparency, accountability, and bias mitigation. It is crucial to ensure that AI algorithms are designed to be interpretable, allowing legal professionals to understand how decisions are reached. Additionally, measures must be implemented to minimize bias in AI training data, as biased outcomes can perpetuate systemic inequalities. Engaging ethicists, legal experts, and community representatives in the development of these guidelines can foster a more inclusive and equitable approach to AI in the judiciary.

- Ensuring Data Privacy and Security in Legal Applications

Data privacy and security are critical considerations when implementing AI in judicial systems. Legal applications often handle sensitive information, including personal details and case-related data. Ensuring robust data protection measures is essential to prevent unauthorized access and maintain confidentiality. This includes employing encryption, secure data storage solutions, and stringent access controls. Moreover, organizations must adhere to relevant data protection regulations, such as the General Data Protection Regulation (GDPR) or local privacy laws, to safeguard individuals' rights.

10. FUTURE TRENDS AND INNOVATIONS:

The future of the legal industry is poised for significant transformation, driven by emerging technologies and advancements in predictive analytics and artificial intelligence (AI). These innovations promise to enhance the efficiency, accuracy, and accessibility of legal processes, ultimately reshaping how legal decisions are made.

- Emerging Technologies and Their Potential Impact on Legal Decisions

Emerging technologies such as blockchain, machine learning, and natural language processing (NLP) are set to have a profound impact on legal decision-making. Blockchain technology, known for its secure and transparent nature, can revolutionize contract management and dispute resolution. Smart contracts—self-executing contracts with terms encoded in the blockchain—can automate and enforce agreements, reducing the potential for disputes and the need for lengthy litigation. This technology enhances trust between parties and can streamline transactions in various sectors, including real estate and finance.

Machine learning, a subset of AI, will also play a critical role in legal decision-making. By analysing vast datasets, machine learning algorithms can identify patterns and trends that human practitioners may overlook. This capability allows for more informed decision-making and predictive outcomes, particularly in litigation and case management. For instance, machine learning models can analyse historical case data to assess the likelihood of success in litigation, enabling attorneys to advise clients more effectively on whether to pursue a case or settle.

- Predictive Analytics and AI Advancements on the Horizon

Predictive analytics is another area poised for growth in the legal sector. By leveraging advanced algorithms and data analysis, predictive analytics can forecast case outcomes based on historical trends. This capability allows legal professionals to assess risks and opportunities with greater precision. For example, courts may use predictive analytics to allocate resources more efficiently, prioritize cases with higher chances of resolution, or determine appropriate sentencing based on historical data.

Advancements in AI, particularly in natural language processing, are enhancing legal research and document review processes. Future AI systems will become increasingly adept at understanding context, intent, and nuance in legal language, making them more effective at providing relevant information and insights. This development will reduce the time attorneys spend on research, enabling them to focus on strategic aspects of their cases. Furthermore, AI-powered tools will assist in drafting legal documents, ensuring compliance with regulations and improving accuracy.

As these technologies evolve, they will enable greater collaboration between legal professionals and AI systems. Legal practitioners will increasingly rely on AI as a valuable partner in decision-making, utilizing its capabilities to enhance their own judgment and expertise.

- Long-term implications for the legal profession.

The future of AI implementation in judicial systems is marked by significant trends and innovations, particularly as countries like China, the UAE, and Saudi Arabia lead the way in integrating AI technologies. These nations are not only exploring AI as a supplementary tool but are also envisioning transformative applications that could reshape judicial processes.

- In China, the evaluation of AI in the court system has progressed through several transformative stages. Initially, AI served as a simple auxiliary tool, assisting judges in legal research and case analysis. However, the country's ambitious vision extends beyond this functionality. China is now developing autonomous agents capable of making judgments, referred to as "robot judges." These AI systems analyse case data, assess legal precedents, and render decisions in specific types of cases. While this innovation promises increased efficiency and reduced case backlogs, it also raises important ethical questions about accountability and the role of human judgment in legal decisions. As China continues to refine its AI capabilities, it will be crucial to balance technological advancements with the need for transparency and ethical oversight.
- UAE and Saudi Arabia are actively exploring the integration of AI into their judicial systems. Both countries recognize the potential for AI techniques to enhance judicial processes and improve access to justice. In the UAE, initiatives like the Dubai Courts' Smart Transformation Program aim to streamline court operations through AI-powered applications. These applications can automate routine tasks such as case filing and scheduling, ultimately enhancing efficiency and reducing delays in legal proceedings. Furthermore,

the UAE's emphasis on embracing technological innovation aligns with its broader goals of becoming a global hub for advanced technology.

- Saudi Arabia is also making strides in AI integration, with the Vision 2030 initiative promoting the use of technology to improve government services, including the judiciary. AI can play a crucial role in legal research, case management, and even in facilitating online dispute resolution. By leveraging AI, Saudi Arabia aims to modernize its judicial system, ensuring that it meets the demands of a rapidly evolving society.
- In the United States, AI is being leveraged to assist in various aspects of the legal system, from predictive analytics to improve case outcomes to AI-driven legal research tools. Companies like Lex Machina and ROSS Intelligence provide attorneys with insights from vast datasets, enhancing decision-making and legal strategy. Additionally, several jurisdictions are experimenting with AI in bail decisions and sentencing, using algorithms to analyse recidivism rates and other factors, although this has sparked debates about fairness and potential bias in these systems.
- United Kingdom is also exploring AI in the judiciary, particularly in the realm of dispute resolution. The UK's Ministry of Justice has been investigating the use of AI to streamline processes, improve access to legal information, and enhance online dispute resolution platforms. The adoption of AI in family law, for instance, could aid in providing more personalized legal advice to individuals navigating complex situations.
- In the European Union, initiatives are underway to develop ethical frameworks for AI in the legal sector. The EU's focus on establishing guidelines for trustworthy AI emphasizes transparency, accountability, and data protection. This approach aims to ensure that AI applications in judicial systems respect fundamental rights and promote fairness.

As these countries pioneer AI implementation in their judicial systems, the focus will be on creating frameworks that ensure ethical considerations, data privacy, and accountability. The potential for AI to enhance efficiency, reduce case backlogs, and improve access to justice is immense. However, addressing the challenges associated with autonomous decision-making and the implications for human oversight will be critical as these innovations unfold.

11. CONCLUSION:

The future of AI and emerging technologies in the judicial system holds tremendous potential for transforming legal processes and decision-making. Innovations such as blockchain, machine learning, and predictive analytics are set to enhance efficiency, accuracy, and accessibility in legal practices. By automating contract management through smart contracts and utilizing predictive analytics to forecast case outcomes, legal professionals can make more informed decisions and allocate resources effectively. Furthermore, advancements in natural language processing will streamline legal research and document preparation, allowing attorneys to focus on strategic elements of their cases. As these technologies evolve, they will foster greater collaboration between legal practitioners and AI systems, enhancing overall legal outcomes. However, ensuring ethical standards, data privacy, and human oversight will be essential as the legal community embraces these innovations. Ultimately, the integration of AI and emerging technologies promises to create a more responsive, equitable, and efficient judicial system for the future.

REFERENCES

Aletras, N., Tsarapatsanis, D., Preoţiuc-Pietro, D., & Lampos, V. (2016). Predicting judicial decisions of the European court of human rights: A natural language processing perspective. *PeerJ Computer Science, 2016*(10). DOI: 10.7717/peerj-cs.93

Ammar, Z. (2024, April 01). Balancing the scale: Navigating ethical and practical challenges of artificial intelligence (AI) integration in legal practices. *Discover AI*, 04(27), 27. Advance online publication. DOI: 10.1007/s44163-024-00121-8

Ashok Kumar, L., Sujatha, R., & Uma, M. B. (2022). Predictive Analytics for Data Driven Decision Making: Tools and Techniques for Solving Real World Problems. In *Predictive Analytics for Data Driven Decision Making: Tools and Techniques for Solving Real World Problems* (pp. 45-78). Nova Science Publishers, Inc. DOI: 10.52305/RZBM7280

Barysė, D., & Sarel, R. (2024, March). Algorithms in the court: Does it matter which part of the judicial decision-making is automated? *Artificial Intelligence and Law*, 32(01), 117–146. DOI: 10.1007/s10506-022-09343-6 PMID: 36643574

Benyekhlef, K., & Zhu, J. (2024). The judicial system and the work of judges and lawyers in the application of law and sanctions assisted by AI. In *Handbook of Artificial Intelligence at Work* (pp. 250-275). Edward Elgar Publishing Ltd. Retrieved Aug 15, 2024, from https://www.scopus.com/record/display.uri?origin=citedby&eid=2-s2.0-85189228691&noHighlight=false&relpos=2

Bi, S., Zhou, Z., Pan, L., & Qi, G. (2023, December). Judicial knowledge-enhanced magnitude-aware reasoning for numerical legal judgment prediction. *Artificial Intelligence and Law*, 31(04), 773–806. DOI: 10.1007/s10506-022-09337-4

Chen, D. L. (2019, March 15). Judicial analytics and the great transformation of American Law. *Artificial Intelligence and Law*, 27(01), 15–42. DOI: 10.1007/s10506-018-9237-x PMID: 32255924

Chen, D. L., & Eagel, J. (2017). Can machine learning help predict the outcome of asylum adjudications? *16th International Conference on Artificial Intelligence and Law, ICAIL 2017* (pp. 237-240). London: Association for Computing Machinery. DOI: 10.1145/3086512.3086538

Feng, Y., Li, C., Ge, J., Luo, B., & Ng, V. (2021, January 04). Recommending statutes: A portable method based on neural networks. *ACM Transactions on Knowledge Discovery from Data*, 15(02), 1–22. Advance online publication. DOI: 10.1145/3424671

Huang, D., & Lin, W. (2019). A model for legal judgment prediction based on multi-model fusion. *3rd IEEE International Conference on Electronic Information Technology and Computer Engineering, EITCE 2019* (pp. 892-895). Xiamen: IEEE. DOI: 10.1109/EITCE47263.2019.9094946

Joshua, B. (2015). *DoNotPay*. Retrieved Aug 10, 2024, from https://en.wikipedia.org: https://en.wikipedia.org/wiki/DoNotPay

Li, L., Duan, W., Zhou, D., & Yuan, J.-L. (2022, July). Law Article Recommendation Approach Based on Deep Semantic Matching. *Ruan Jian Xue Bao. Journal of Software*, 33(07), 2618–2632. DOI: 10.13328/j.cnki.jos.006287

Liu, Y., Wu, Y., Li, A., Zhang, Y., Sun, C., Lu, W., . . . Kuang, K. (2024). Unleashing the Power of LLMs in Court View Generation by Stimulating Internal Knowledge and Incorporating External Knowledge. In G. H. Duh K. (Ed.), *Findings of the Association for Computational Linguistics: NAACL 2024* (pp. 2782-2792). Mexico City: Association for Computational Linguistics (ACL). Retrieved Aug 10, 2024, from https://www.scopus.com/record/display.uri?eid=2-s2.0-85197949139&origin=resultslist&sort=plf-f&cite=2-s2.0-0040326619&src=s&imp=t&sid=23f8fb9656ff76b337ecc7e04b7aba2d&sot=cite&sdt=a&sl=0&relpos=7&citeCnt=0&searchTerm=

Mustari, N., Sen, S. K., Banik, A., Mehedi, M. H., & Rasel, A. A. (2023). Techniques to Estimate the Status of Legal Proceedings Considering Sequential Text Data. *5th International Conference on Emerging Smart Computing and Informatics, ESCI 2023*. Pune: Institute of Electrical and Electronics Engineers Inc. DOI: 10.1109/ESCI56872.2023.10099995

ROSS. (2023). *ROSS's AI Search*. Retrieved Aug 10, 2024, from https://www.rossintelligence.com: https://www.rossintelligence.com/what-is-ai

Rwrsilany, S., Cleice De Pontes, B., Adriana, B. N., & Rogerio, P. D. (2023, Nov 10). THE ROLE OF JURIMETRICS AND PREDICTIVE ANALYSIS IN JUDICIAL DECISIONMAKING: A CURRENT PANORAMA. *SemeAd*, 01-21. Retrieved Jul 30, 2024, from https://login.semead.com.br/26semead/anais/arquivos/925.pdf?

Sivaranjani, N., & Jayabharathy, J., & M., S. (2019). A Broad View of Automation in Legal Prediction Technology. *3rd International Conference on Electronics and Communication and Aerospace Technology, ICECA 2019* (pp. 180-185). Coimbatore: Institute of Electrical and Electronics Engineers Inc. DOI: 10.1109/ICECA.2019.8822019

Thomas, A. (2024). Exploring the power of AI-driven decision making in the judicial domain: Case studies, benefits, challenges, and solutions. In *Using Traditional Design Methods to Enhance AI-Driven Decision Making* (pp. 337–351). IGI Global., DOI: 10.4018/979-8-3693-0639-0.ch015

Tsou, J.-C., Hsieh, K.-Y., Huang, C.-H., Shih, Y.-A., Yu, H.-C., & Fan, Y.-C. (2022). Extracting Crime Prosecution Elements based on Neural Machine Reading Comprehension Model. *IEEE International Conference on Big Data, Big Data 2022* (pp. 3329 - 3335). Osaka: Institute of Electrical and Electronics Engineers Inc. DOI: 10.1109/BigData55660.2022.10020404

Valvoda, J., Thompson, A., Cotterell, R., & Teufel, S. (2024, June 02). The Ethics of Automating Legal Actors. *Transactions of the Association for Computational Linguistics*, 12, 700–720. DOI: 10.1162/tacl_a_00668

Visentin, A., Nardotto, A., & Osullivan, B. (2019). Predicting judicial decisions: A statistically rigorous approach and a new ensemble classifier. *31st IEEE International Conference on Tools with Artificial Intelligence, ICTAI 2019* (pp. 1820-1824). Portland: IEEE. DOI: 10.1109/ICTAI.2019.00275

Wu, Y., Liu, Y., Lu, W., Zhang, Y., Feng, J., Sun, C., & Kuang, K. (2022). Towards Interactivity and Interpretability: A Rationale-based Legal Judgment Prediction Framework. *Conference on Empirical Methods in Natural Language Processing, EMNLP 2022* (pp. 4787 - 4799). Abu Dhabi: Association for Computational Linguistics (ACL). DOI: 10.18653/v1/2022.emnlp-main.316

Zhao, Q., Gao, T., & Guo, N. (2023, September). LA-MGFM: A legal judgment prediction method via sememe-enhanced graph neural networks and multi-graph fusion mechanism. *Information Processing & Management*, 60(05), 103455. Advance online publication. DOI: 10.1016/j.ipm.2023.103455

Chapter 11
Predictive Justice in Criminal Proceedings: The Role of AI Jurimetrics

Abhinash Mohanta
https://orcid.org/0000-0002-8732-3202
KIIT University, India

Kyvalya Garikapati
https://orcid.org/0000-0003-0990-6514
KIIT University, India

Sneha
https://orcid.org/0000-0002-0158-2503
Xavier University, India

Sanskruti Mohanty
https://orcid.org/0009-0009-9530-0412
Utkal University, India

Shreya
https://orcid.org/0009-0008-3533-797X
KIIT University, India

ABSTRACT

This chapter explores the evolving role of AI and jurimetrics in criminal proceedings, highlighting their potential to enhance predictive justice and key challenges. It defines predictive justice and examines the foundations of jurimetrics and AI, including machine learning, data analytics, and NLP. Empirical findings reveal the effectiveness and limitations of tools like COMPAS, PredPol, and TrueAllele, emphasizing concerns about bias, transparency, and judicial discretion. The chapter

DOI: 10.4018/979-8-3693-7205-0.ch011

discusses AI's practical applications in law enforcement, courts, and legal procedures, illustrating how AI can streamline processes but also perpetuate biases. Ethical considerations, such as privacy threats and accountability, are critically examined. Trust dynamics, including stakeholder engagement and oversight, are stressed for responsible AI adoption. Future directions focus on advancing AI technologies, implementing robust policies, and prioritizing ethics to balance innovation with justice.

INTRODUCTION

The advancement of artificial intelligence and data analytics in the legal process and in the judicial system has revolutionised conventional approaches to law techniques. Such a technological push stimulates the generation of many new concepts and one of the most revolutionary concepts is the idea of predictive justice. The aim of predictive justice is to enhance the speed, fairness, accuracy of justice as well as the stability of the justice's output(Branovitskiy & Yarkov, 2022). However, its rising role raises issues of how to be fair in the sense of how one can design systems of accountability and justice that can address issues related to the role of complex technology in the production of judicial decision(Yulia & Sergiy, 2021).

As to the meaning of predictive justice, this is the concept of using data to seek the outcome of the cases. Through the use of case analysis, the predictive justice tools provide an estimation of the possible results that a certain case may necessitate hence helping the judges, lawyers, and policymakers in their decision making(Yang, 2021). They may well also be as diverse as determining the probability of committing a crime once again, or the probability of convincing an audience in a court of law. Thus, they are offered a chance to argue that the objective methodologies of predictive justice bring real values into the process, for instance, reduced docket load and accelerated proceedings.

However, one has to take into account that predictive justice in criminal trials also has certain disadvantages and challenges for implementation(Simmons, 2018). This paper identifies some of the problems that stem from the employment of AI and algorithms in the justice system including problems of legibility, accountability and the dehumanisation of the decision-making process. Some authors complained that depersonalised individuals are a real menace to focus on people as the subject of justice. Also, this data which is used in the development of these predictive models may itself be biased, thus, perpetuating or even magnifying biases within the legal system.

However, another point which can be raised within the discussion of predictive justice is the psychological impact on the judiciary made by the AI predicted outcome. Where computer analysis has suggested that a judge's decision will be 'such and such' in a given case or type of case, that will either force a Judge to make a decision in that manner because it is predetermined by fate or the Judge may make a contrary decision just to defy the computer analysis that seems to be guiding the decision to a certain direction(Eliot, 2020). If judges are aware of the predictive tools and their output then the perception of the output may creep into the judges' mind consciously or subconsciously and may interfere with the judicial duty.

In this chapter we shall endeavour to provide a critical analysis of the application and potential application of AI and jurimetrics in criminal trials under the umbrella of Predictive Justice. Jurimetrics or the application of quantitative methods in solving legal issues is very important for the achievement of the predictive justice(Abiodun & Lekan, 2020). Thus, jurimetrics enables one to reach conclusions on the conduct of legal subjects, the outcomes of the cases and performance of the legal system. Incorporated with AI, jurimetrics can be applied to enhance and refine current and existing predictive models; in this way, jurimetrics systems enable the prediction of legal decisions.

This chapter presents a historical overview of the concept of predictive justice, its evolution, and its applications in the field of criminal law. It will focus on specific applications of AI in the framework of the concept of predictive justice with an evaluation of the threats and benefits connected with their application. Also, the chapter will also examine the ethical, legal and policy concerns in the integration of AI and also the jurimetrics of the criminal trial process(Llinares, 2020).

Therefore, the chapter will use case-studies and real-world examples to describe how and with what outcomes the predictive tools have been employed. It will also look at the role of jurimetrics and predictive justice and how the it is used in legal situations and how AI enhances such numerical solutions.

The final section of the chapter will focus upon the ethical considerations of predictive justice. Issues of fairness, report and accountability towards artificial intelligence based decisions will be discussed. The chapter will also highlight some of the potential negative impacts of using the tools for prediction including the possibility of increasing biases and the impact on defendants' rights.

Lastly, the chapter shall also try to look at the future of predictive justice in criminal proceedings. Potential of AI and jurimetrics will be described and assessed potential of regulation to address the challenges of risks associated with those technologies. This chapter will also explain the meaning of the Predictive Justice for the legal system and if the system is shifting to another paradigm or if it is just trying to alter the concept of justice.

Finally, the present chapter provides a general overview of the notion of the predictive justice in the context of criminal trials with the focus on the AI and jurimetrics. However, as the focus of this chapter is on theoretical and practical aspects of the modern technologies and their ethical issues in the context of the future of justice in the data age, this chapter aims at presenting a conceptual framework for further discussions. Through this way the chapter will be able to articulate on the opportunities and the challenges that may occurred in the future given that AI has the potential to revolutionize the field of law..

THEORETICAL FOUNDATIONS

The development of the legal science has led to the appearance of new scientific disciplines which are aimed at predicting the development of legal operations. Jurimetrics is one such discipline and it concerns with the use of quantitative approach in which statistics and data analysis form part of the research methodology in law(Visser, 2006). Jurimetrics is an offspring of the early this century, when legal scholars seemed to be interested in the application of mathematical models to facilitate the solution of legal issues.

Over time, it has evolved into a robust approach that has incorporated diverse strategies, such as statistical analysis, empirical justice studies, and measurement techniques. The use of AI in combination with jurimetrics analysis included an additional level of development of the system since AI offers a more effective method of predicting legal precedents(Abiodun & Lekan, 2020). The topic of the section is as follows: This section will introduce the reader to the concept of jurimetrics, will discuss the history and development of jurimetrics and finally will describe current AI technologies in the legal system and the link between jurimetrics and AI.

Jurimetrics and Its Evolution

Jurimetrics emerged because the conventional ways of analyzing law which were chiefly referential and qualitative in its approach could be grounded on quantitative principles(Losano, 1971). Jurimetrics as a term was coined by Lee Loevinger in the 1940s when he tried to extend the reach of the term 'metrics' to include legal analysis, in the same manner as other fields of social science(Jurimetrics legal definition of jurimetrics, 2006). In other words, Loevinger added her voice to those of the legal realists who thought that decisions in the law could be made better by treating legal data statistically in order to reduce possibilities of arbitrary decisions.

The first use of jurimetrics was concerned with the use of statistical techniques for the description of legal decisions and definitions of legal norms. Legal scholar began collecting actual data from the court decisions in an effort of identifying which variables could be used to explain judicial decisions making. This first work laid the foundations for subsequent models which were to be able to make legal predictions on the basis of given input variables, or variables which included; the nature of the case, arguments from the legal point of view, and the judicial behaviour of the judges.

Jurimetrics has progressed from the early stages where it applied statistical analysis to other forms of quantification such as game theory, econometrics and computation among others. This has been due to advancement in technology where it has become much easier to acquire legal big data. Other changes that have been made are where jurimetrics can also build models that are capable of analyzing jurisprudential data and come up with certain results(Wu, 2018).

AI in the Legal System

Artificial intelligence is a new popular phenomenon that has been integrated into different sectors, and this includes the legal sector(AI in legal services: new trends in AI-enabled legal services - Service Oriented Computing and Applications, 2020). Application of AI in legal sector has been in high demand in areas such as machine learning, natural language processing, and data analysis. These technologies are in the process of transforming the manner that lawyers and other legal professionals search, assess and decide.

Subfield of artificial intelligence known as machine learning is focused on giving algorithms capability to learn from data and make the future prediction based on it(McKeown et al., 2020). In legal service, machine learning is used in processing of large data which encompasses court rulings, written and spoken word, as well as case laws with the aim of predicting trends and outcomes(Park & Ko, 2020). For instance, status assignment can be created by employing machine learning techniques in a bid to predict the likelihood of a particular case being typical of the positive status taking into account past cases. Consequently, this can be useful in areas of litigation since the legal team can be able to gauge their chances of winning a case through the model outcomes.

Another interesting field in the application of AI in the formulation of legal processes is the natural language processing (NLP). Since NLP concerns the meaning of text in the natural language of human, it becomes rather simple for the computer and relevant algorithms to work with legal documents(Nay, 2021). This is especially relevant in the legal domain as the NLP assists in the search of a large number of documents including statutes, legal cases and contracts. With this consideration, application of NLP assists in saving time for lawyers and other legal professions in law practice to search for legal information and it is accurate than manual work(Katz et al., 2023).

Analysis of data or the process of drawing conclusions from data can also be seen in the legal system as well(Stoykov & Chelebieva, 2019). The following are some of the advantages that legal professionals can get from the use of analytics in the legal processes: Legal professionals can be able to analyze various aspects of legal cases, patterns of judicial decisions and the assessment of legal changes. For instance, data analytics can be used in the examination of sentencing practices in criminal litigations where it is possible to establish that certain groups of people are treated differently depending on their race, gender or social status.

Thus, it could be suggested that application of the artificial intelligence in the scope of the legal system may lead to positive changes in the effectiveness of the legal processes. However, there are certain problems of ethical and legal nature which can be discussed, for instance, the problem of prejudice of the AI algorithm and the shift in the nature of legal work due to the automation(Khabibullina et al., 2019). These are the problems that will be discussed in detail in this chapter as follows.

Intersection of AI and Jurimetrics

The contemporary area of legal studies has thus been enriched by AI jurimetrics as an innovative and promising field. Legal scholars and practitioners can benefit from applying quantitative analysis of jurimetrics and qualitative analysis of AI in order to identify more accurate options for legal outcomes' prediction(Ashley, 2019). This integration has the potential of altering certain aspects of the legal system to a greater or lesser extent such as the judge or legal analysis and many others.

One of the areas that have equally been influenced by the practice of AI is the application of predictive modelling to enhance jurimetrics. Forecasting models use past events in order to make predictions as to what is likely to happen in the future. In the legal applications, the predictive models may be used in the delivery of outcomes expected in trial cases, rates of recidivism and impacts of legislations. It is also through the Machine Learning Model that a huge amount of legal data can be analyzed and patterns identified even by human analysts. This in a way make it easier to have informed prediction and assessment of legal outcomes and consequences.

For example, intelligent risk predictors are now used in criminal trials to assess the probability of an offender repeating his crime(Shah et al., 2021). These tools contain data about the former offenders in their records as well as their behaviour to assess their propensity to commit a crime. This information can assist the judges in coming up with the right decisions on the duration one is supposed to serve in jail, parole and even bailing out. These tools are capable to take a decision with reducing the chances of the biased and prejudices decision but there are some issues which are concerning the ethical and fairness of the Interactive AI solution and prediction.

Another way through which AI enhances jurimetrics is through data analysis since the data collected in the course of the process is huge and can be complicated. The use of tools like data analytics that is powered by artificial intelligence can handle and analyze such datasets in a better way than conventional methods this in turn helps legal professionals to have better understanding of the legal environment and its patterns(Vaissnave & Deepalakshmi, 2019). For example, AI can be used to look at thousands of court cases and determine factors that influence decisions such as the judge's personality, the facts presented by the parties and the arguments of law. Such information can be used to build better models depending on the legal decision and to organise the legal position(Sharma et al., 2021).

It is also important to point out that symbiosis of AI and jurimetrics can also be related to the issue of legal research. It is possible to find situation where NLP tools can be used for the purpose of analyzing the text of statutes and/or case laws. This makes it possible for the legal expert to make better research and get the most relevant legal authorities within a given case. Moreover, with the use of AI, it can assist in the creation of such documents as contract and briefs since the system is capable of analyzing previous documents and suggest certain terms or even inclusion of certain clauses(Zhong et al., 2020).

Thus, the combination of AI and jurimetrics is a significant step towards the enhancement of the methods that can be applied for the purpose of legal prediction and data processing within the system of legal knowledge. It has given rise to other useful ideas and contemplations but at the same time it has created ethical and legal questions that should be debated and solved as such tools are integrated into the legal system. The following sections of this chapter are devoted to the elaboration of these questions with reference to the consequences of the emergence of predictive justice for criminal trials and the legal systems in general.

EMPIRICAL RESEARCH FINDINGS

The empirical landscape of AI and jurimetrics in criminal proceedings reveals a complex interplay of benefits, challenges, and ethical dilemmas. Recent studies underscore the effectiveness of AI tools like PredPol, COMPAS, Live Facial Recognition (LFR), sentencing algorithms, and legal research platforms such as ROSS Intelligence and Lex Machina(Abiodun & Lekan, 2020). These technologies have been deployed in various capacities, ranging from crime prediction and risk assessment to aiding judges in decision-making and streamlining legal research. However, interviews with legal experts, such as Dr. Sonali Swetapadma, Assistant Professor at the School of Law, KIIT University, highlight significant challenges that accompany these technological advancements.

a. Case Studies of AI in Criminal Proceedings: Practical Applications and Challenges

AI applications in criminal justice, such as PredPol and COMPAS, have been extensively studied to evaluate their effectiveness in reducing crime rates and assisting in decision-making processes. PredPol, for instance, uses historical crime data to predict future hotspots of criminal activity, guiding law enforcement in resource allocation(Predictive Policing Technology, 2012). However, empirical evidence has shown that these tools often reinforce existing patterns of policing, leading to the over-surveillance of marginalized communities. Dr. Swetapadma points out that AI can inadvertently reinforce biases, especially when trained on skewed data, resulting in discriminatory outcomes. This aligns with findings from public documents revealing that LAPD's predictive policing programs, like PredPol and Operation Laser, validated existing biases, disproportionately targeting Black and brown communities, leading to public outcry and eventual discontinuation of these programs(PredPol is LAPD's Racist Predictive Policing Program, 2019).

Similarly, COMPAS, a tool used for recidivism risk assessment, has faced criticism for its opaque algorithms and questionable accuracy in predicting future criminal behaviour(Chouldechova, 2017). Although designed to assist in bail and sentencing decisions, COMPAS has been accused of racial bias, which raises concerns about fairness in the justice system(Dressel & Farid, 2021). Dr. Swetapadma emphasizes that while AI holds the potential to streamline legal processes, the application of such technologies must be coupled with rigorous oversight to ensure that biases do not compromise the integrity of judicial outcomes. The need for an empathetic and victim-sensitive approach in justice is underscored in her research on police responses to rape cases, which highlights the importance of context-specific and nuanced decision-making in legal proceedings(Swetapadma et al., 2023).

b. Effectiveness of Predictive Models: Balancing Benefits and Risks

The effectiveness of AI-driven predictive models in criminal justice hinges on their accuracy, transparency, and ability to complement human judgment rather than replace it. Tools like TrueAllele, which analyzes DNA evidence, and ROSS Intelligence, which assists with legal research, have proven valuable in enhancing efficiency and accuracy in court proceedings(Perlin et al., 2014). However, the reliability of these models is often questioned due to their "black box" nature, where decision-making processes are not fully transparent or understandable to users.

Dr. Swetapadma highlights that the legal community expresses cautious optimism about these technologies but remains wary of their potential to undermine nuanced human judgment. She notes that AI's role should be to support legal professionals, not to supplant their expertise, particularly in sensitive cases like sexual offenses, where judicial discretion plays a crucial role. AI models struggle to grasp the complex, contextual factors that influence judicial decisions, making it difficult for them to fully replace human judgment.

c. Impact on Judicial Decision-Making: Enhancing or Hindering Justice?

The integration of AI into judicial decision-making processes has sparked debate about the extent to which these technologies influence judges' rulings and the creation of reasoned orders. Sentencing algorithms, for example, provide data-driven recommendations that can assist judges in determining appropriate penalties based on risk assessments(Fortes, 2020). However, experts like Dr. Swetapadma argue that this raises concerns about over-reliance on technology and the potential erosion of judicial discretion.

In her interview, Dr. Swetapadma questions AI's ability to assess mitigating and aggravating factors in individual cases, which are often critical in crafting just outcomes. She suggests that AI lacks the capacity to fully understand the socio-legal nuances involved in judicial decisions, particularly in a diverse society like India, where cultural and contextual factors play significant roles in the justice process. This perspective underscores the importance of maintaining a human element in judicial decision-making, ensuring that AI tools serve as aids rather than authorities in legal proceedings.

d. Addressing Bias and Enhancing Fairness: The Need for Rigorous Oversight

Empirical findings consistently highlight the challenge of bias in AI-driven justice systems. Dr. Swetapadma emphasizes that the use of diverse datasets, regular audits, and transparent, explainable AI are essential measures to mitigate bias and enhance fairness. However, these solutions are still in their infancy and not uniformly applied across jurisdictions. Regulatory gaps further complicate the situation, as current laws often lag behind the rapid development of AI technologies, leaving critical issues of accountability and transparency unaddressed(Neznamov, 2020).

As Dr. Swetapadma notes, ethical oversight, public engagement, and legal reforms are vital to bridging these gaps. Stakeholders must collaborate to develop comprehensive guidelines that govern the ethical use of AI in criminal proceedings, ensuring that technology complements rather than compromises the principles of justice.

e. Moving Forward: Integrating AI Responsibly

The future of AI in criminal proceedings lies in striking a balance between technological innovation and ethical responsibility. While AI tools like Victor & Rafa chatbots have shown promise in assisting with legal queries and case management, their integration into the justice system must be approached with caution(Sanctis, 2021). Dr. Swetapadma underscores the need for clear regulations, continuous monitoring, and stakeholder involvement to ensure that AI serves as a force for good in the legal landscape.

Ultimately, the empirical research suggests that AI and jurimetrics hold transformative potential for criminal justice, but their successful implementation depends on overcoming challenges related to bias, transparency, and accountability. By addressing these issues head-on, the legal community can harness the power of AI to create a more efficient, equitable, and fair judicial system.

PRACTICAL APPLICATIONS

In this modern world where the legal system has begun to adapt the use of technological innovations, AI has become a significant and essential application in the practice of law enforcement, trial, and legal management. AI is not limited to helping the police solve crimes and prevent crimes but also helps the courts to work with cases and improve the legal process. This section continues with these applications and examines how the AI is applied in the police, courts, and legal procedures for the purpose of improving performance and reliability(Ramos et al., 2020).

AI Tools for Law Enforcement

The law enforcement agencies across the globe have now started exploring the potential of AI in enhancing their capabilities of investigation and crime prevention. The application of AI in the context of policing and intelligence is therefore premised on the strength of the technology in scanning through large databases, identifying trends and predicting future events, especially those that are criminal in nature(Gummadidala et al., 2020).

Among such areas, the use of artificial intelligence in policing, particularly so-called predictive policing, has attracted much attention. It is a policing strategy that utilizes AI algorithms to analyze the past crime trends with an aim of determining the future trends. This means that through identifying high-risk areas, the law enforcement agencies can marshal resources and prevent crime in those areas. For instance, the police departments in Los Angeles and Chicago have adopted the use of artificial intelligence in predictive policing whereby through analyzing the history of crimes such as the time, location and type of crime, the system is able to identify areas that are likely to be prone to crime in the future(Predicting crime, LAPD-style, 2023). These tools have been said to help in lowering the rates of crime, however, there has been concerns on issues concerning prejudice and infringement on people's rights.

Another field in which there has been great progress in the AI is facial recognition, which is something we use every day. This technology helps the police to recognize a suspect based on pictures taken from the cameras or from the social networks with the help of a database of individuals. Facial recognition has been used in different fields including in the police work to identify suspects and in events to control crowds(Petrescu, 2019). For instance, during events such as the Super Bowl, facial recognition has been employed to search through crowds for people who are on the watch lists. Nonetheless, issues to do with privacy, precision, and racial prejudices have forced people to demand the regulation of facial recognition technology(Lynch, 2020).

Cybercrime is also being impacted by AI, in terms of investigations. This means that the use of AI has become more and more significant in identifying and fighting cybercrime as these become more complex. AI assistances can help in the detection of cybercrimes, analyze large chunks of data and even track back the source of cyber incidents. For instance, AI based tools can identify trends in phishing emails or ransomware assaults to enable proseution of cyber criminals and stopping of the threats(Chandra, 2019). Also, in digital forensics, AI helps in the process of analyzing data from the seized electronic devices including smart phones and computers in order to find evidences in criminal cases.

For instance, natural language processing (NLP) that is a subspecialty of AI is also being used in intelligence gathering and counter terrorism. NLP algorithms can be used to analyze large volumes of text from social media platforms, online forums, and intercepted communications for instance to determine presence of threats(ALGORITHMS AND TERRORISM:, n.d). For instance, in the intelligence sector, NLP is applied to track conversations in the hope of identifying potential terrorist threats and prevent terrorists' attacks(Ahsan & Shah, 2008). These tools help in analyzing massive data and find keywords, phrases and patterns which are related to some criminal activities and thus help the police to act effectively.

However, like any other tools in the law enforcement, AI has its controversies. There are concerns of privacy, bias, and the possibility of profiling some communities excessively, among others, with the application of AI(Ezzeddine et al., 2023). This is because as the application of AI in law enforcement increases, these issues must be dealt with in a similar manner as other legal issues of the country.

Judicial Use of AI

The judicial branch has also embraced AI to a significant extent, with courts using AI in case management, legal research, and decision-making. These technologies are aimed at enhancing the performance and reliability of the judicial systems in order to fast track cases and reduce on the time taken in the judicial systems(Chen & Li, 2020).

Among the areas, where AI is used in the judiciary, the most important is the case management systems. There are numerous cases that are taken to the courts, and this means that the courts are always congested and hence justice delayed. These are aspects that can be easily automated by the case management systems that are powered by artificial intelligence to include arrangement of hearing dates, assignment of cases to judges and management of court diaries. For example, some courts employ the use of AI in identifying cases that require immediate attention or those that are complex so that such cases are not delayed(Dneprovskaya & Abramitov, 2020). These are some of the ways in which AI can be used in the courtroom and the result of these technologies is increased productivity of the judges and the court staff as they are relieved of some of the time-consuming tasks.

It is also applied in helping judges and lawyers in their research. The conventional methods of legal research can be quite cumbersome where lawyers and judges spend a lot of time searching through cases, statutes and other legal literature. Some of the examples include legal search engines and document analysis tools which are powered by AI to help in this process since they can easily help in the identification of legal precedents and information extraction from legal texts(Davis, 2020). The following are some examples, Ravel Law and ROSS Intelligence uses the AI to review legal texts and to present the lawyers with briefs of the cases, statutes and even predictions. These tools not only help in saving time, but also help in increasing the precision of the legal research as there is less chances of human mistakes.

The use of AI in the judiciary can therefore be well applied in decision support systems. These systems employ the use of Artificial Intelligence where the software breaks down previous cases and presents them to the judges in form of recommendations or insights that can help them in making their decisions. For instance, there are the AI-based tools for making recommendations on the proper sentences depending on the facts of the case, the offender's criminal history, the type of crime committed among others. An example of this is the COMPAS (Correctional Offender Management Profiling for Alternative Sanctions) that is used to predict the likelihood of an offender re-offending thus assisting in sentencing and parole(Dressel & Farid, 2021). Although these tools can be argued to increase objectivity and decrease the possibility of prejudice in the decision-making process, they have drawn criticism over their black box nature and the capacity to perpetuate current bias within the system.

Apart from decision making, AI is also in the process of being implemented in the solving of conflicts. There are some examples of jurisdictions which have tried to implement the use of AI in the form of online dispute resolution especially for the small claims and civil cases. These platforms work based on artificial intelligence where they assist the parties in the conflict resolution process, provide recommendations for the possible solutions and even create the drafts of the agreements. When applied to specific aspects of the conflict resolution process, AI will enable the reduction of the court's workload and give the parties faster and cheaper ways of resolving the conflicts.

Thus, AI has numerous opportunities for the improvement of the performance of the judiciary while, at the same time, there are potential risks that need to be managed. The application of AI in the judicial systems creates some issues such as the issue of explaining the results arrived at and the issue of fairness. This is due to the fact that as the courts gradually embrace the AI tools it becomes necessary to do so in a way that is consistent with justice and equity.

Optimization of Legal Procedures

Moving from law enforcement and courts, AI is also finding its application in much other aspects of the legal system to enhance legal processes. The use of ai in the legal processes has the potential of enhancing efficiency, reducing on the number of backlog cases.

In terms of improving the legal processes, AI is most efficient at eliminating repetitive tasks which would otherwise require much time and effort. For instance, there is the use of the AI in the creation of legal documents that includes contracts, pleadings, and briefs where the system fills the templates with appropriate data. This automation does not only make the drafting process faster but also minimises the chances of making a mistake. This way legal professionals can invest their time and effort in more complicated and important tasks(Marković & Gostojić, 2022).

AI also has an application in the E-Discovery, which entails the identification, collection and review of documents in electronic form in a given case. E-discovery can be a very tedious and costly activity especially where there is a large volume of data to go through. These are are automated e-discovery tools that employ machine learning to analyze electronic documents and extract useful data and to flag documents that may contain privileged information. There are several ways through which AI can help to lessen the time and costs involved in the e-discovery of the documents, as well as enhance the search(Cui et al., 2021).

Besides that, AI can assist in minimizing the number of pending cases by improving the utilization of available resources in the legal processes. For instance, using artificial intelligence, one can be able to analyze patterns in case loads and come up with ways through which judges and the court staff can work more effectively. These findings may be useful to the courts in the allocation of resources to areas of high demand with a view to improving the discharge of cases. Also, AI is employed in the detection of inefficiencies and other hurdles in the legal processes for instance delays in filing of documents or in the scheduling of cases among others, thus, improving on the backlogs.

Also, AI has the potential of increasing the availability and affordability of legal services in the society to increase access to justice. There are also AI based applications like online legal help, and chatbots which can help people in getting information about legal procedures and can also help in preparing legal documents. They can be useful in closing the gap for those people who cannot access the conventional legal services and thus assist them in receiving justice(Islam et al., 2018).

Although, there are numerous benefits that have been seen with the use of AI in the legal processes, it has to be noted that the technology is not without its drawbacks. AI tools harness data, and the quality of the data determines the performance of the tools; sometimes, the AI systems tend to reinforce bias and may not consider specific circumstances. It is important to keep on checking on how the use of the AI is being done in the legal system and how it is affecting the people involved.

Hence, the uses of AI in law enforcement, the judiciary and legal processes are evident that depict the possible impact of AI in the legal sector. Through increasing the efficiency and the reliability of legal procedures, AI brings the idea of improvement of the justice system. But like any other innovation, the use of AI in the judicial system must be done with consideration for the right and wrong doing in the society to maintain justice.

ETHICAL AND LEGAL CONSIDERATIONS

As artificial intelligence (AI) becomes increasingly integrated into criminal justice systems, it brings with it significant ethical and legal challenges. These challenges range from potential threats to privacy and data security to concerns about accountability, transparency, bias, and fairness in AI-driven decisions. Addressing these issues is essential to ensuring that the use of AI in criminal proceedings upholds the principles of justice and protects individual rights.

Digital Human Rights

One of the most important questions that arise with regard to the use of AI in the legal system is the threat to digital human rights, which concerns the violation of privacy, data protection, and people's rights(Bajgar & Horenovsky, 2022). This is because the majority of AI systems are data hungry, and thus the handling of data which includes aggregation, storage and analysis becomes crucial. This raises the questions as to how this data is gathered, utilised and secured.

Privacy is a primary human right while the AI applications require data which is a direct threat to privacy(Chatterjee & N.S., 2019). For example, the technologies applied in the practice of predictive policing or risk analysis may include details about a person such as criminal history, social media profiles, and biometric data. It is for this reason that the compilation of such data will result in intrusive surveillance where the activities of persons are monitored and analyzed in ways that do not require the individuals' permission. This again give rise to issues such as how much of the users' information should be made available to the police and judicial systems, and the risks of misusing this information.

Another issue that has compounds the problem is the issue of data security. As AI systems are involved with the processing of sensitive data, they are a tempting target for malicious attacks(Rankin, 2020). This means that privacy breaches of AI systems could result to release of private information to the public thus exposing the affected people to factors such as identity theft, discrimination, or even prosecution. Protection of data from hackers is a crucial element that must not be overlooked in order to guarantee the effectiveness of AI systems.

In addition, the application of AI in the justice system can also violate the rights of people by violating the requirements of due process and the right to presumption of innocence. For instance, there are the predictive policing algorithms that associate people with the likelihood of becoming criminals based on data sets and, although the people in question have not committed any crimes, they may be targeted by the police. Likewise, tools applied in risk assessment that determines the bail or sentencing may also distort the fairness of the legal process because these rely on actuarial analysis rather than the unique assessment of each person.

Thus, it is possible to state that there is a need to set up strong legal measures that guarantee and defend digital human rights within the context of AI. This encompasses rules dealing with data protection and usage and the right of the individuals to demand an explanation of AI based decisions that directly impact them.

Accountability and Transparency

Some of the issues that can be of concern include the fact that AI algorithms are complicated and impenetrable and this makes it hard for legal representatives and the public to know how decisions are being made which may lead to abuse or even mistakes.

In the context of AI applications accountability means the capability of determining who is to blame for the results provided by an AI system. In legal sense this implies that judges, police, and developers of AI must be made to answer for the outcomes reached by the AI based tools. For example, when an AI system suggests a specific statement, or a certain amount of cash to be paid for bail, it becomes crucial to identify who is to blame for that suggestion – the judge who acts based on the AI's suggestions, the developers who designed the given model, or the organization that has adopted the use of this technology(Kleinberg et al., 2017).

In order to establish accountability there should be ways of checking the AI systems and if they are working correctly or not. This entails periodic checks on the AI algorithms to check for biases or errors or other adverse impacts. In addition, there should be proper regulation on the use of the AI systems in legal processes; and mandates as to the roles and responsibilities of each party involved.

Nonetheless, the use of AI systems should be transparent so that the systems can be employed in a just manner. It means the capacity to give an account of how an AI system to arrive at its particular decision. However, the majority of the algorithms, and especially the ones based on machine learning, are often characterized as black boxes, due to the fact that the logic of their decision making is not easily understandable(Guidotti et al., 2018). Such an approach may raise concerns regarding fairness and justice of the AI system, and also erode the trust in the system.

To enhance transparency it is important that the AI systems developed must be able to explain their workings. This means that the legal practitioners and the persons who were impacted by the decision of the AI system should be able to explain the factors that led to the decision made by the system. For instance, if an AI tool suggests a certain sentence then one should be able to identify the data sets that went into the recommendation as well as the decision-making process that was used in the generation of the recommended sentence. Explainability is important not only in terms of gaining trust but also in terms of giving people tools to protest against the AI decisions that they find are unfair(Lima et al., 2022).

Also, transparency means that AI systems should be checked by other parties than their developers. This could include establishing of bodies or committees responsible for assessing the use of AI in the justice system. It is therefore possible to promote the development and use of AI systems in a manner which is compliant with the law and ethical principles.

Bias and Fairness

Among the most prominent ethical questions related to the use of artificial intelligence in criminal proceedings, the question of algorithmic bias is the most topical. Such systems are fed with data and if the data contains bias inherent in the legal system, the system is likely to reinforce this bias and even worsen it. This gives a lot of questions on the fairness of the use of AI in the legal system.

Bias in algorithm refers to a situation where AI systems results in outcomes that are prejudiced towards a given set of demographics including race, gender or income level. For example, the research has established that some of the algorithms used in predictive policing are likely to stimulate minority persons, even when other variables are held constant. Likewise, the risk assessment tools applied in the bail and sentencing have been accused of being prejudiced to deliver adverse impacts to the minority groups(Selbst, 2017).

If the AI systems are developed with the presence of a bias then it can act as a significant problem since it can result in stereotyping and thus hamper the credibility of the legal systems. When some categories of people are either specifically singled out or sidelined by AI in decision-making, it raises concerns on the perceived bias of the judiciary.

Among the approaches that can be used in order to solve the problem of algorithmic bias, several can be noted. First of all, there needs to be an understanding of the fact that the data set with which the AI systems are trained is devoid of any prejudice. This may mean gathering more varied data and deliberately seeking out and removing prejudice from the data sets. For instance, if the use is to predict recidivism, the data set should feature a diverse range of individuals, so the system does not overly focus on one demographic and thus contributes to the injustice of certain groups(Johndrow & Lum, 2017).

Second, fairness constraints should be included in the designs of AI by the developers. These constraints aim at preventing the AI systems from being prejudiced and thus, yielding unfair results for different categories of people. For instance, it is possible to apply fairness constraints to modify the risk scores in the predictive policing models to avoid the excessive focusing on the ethnic groups(Ferrara, 2023).

Third, it is necessary to provide the legal framework for the periodic assessment of the AI systems for the identification of the bias. Such audits should be performed by outside professionals capable of determining the pertinence of such applications and how it should be improved. Also, there is the need to ensure that legal professionals are equipped on how to handle bias in the AI recommendations(Schwartz et al., 2021).

Further, there has to be a commitment to human oversight to make sure that fairness is observed in the decisions made by the AI. Despite the fact that AI can create useful inputs and suggestions, it is important that the decision making power should remain with the legal professionals. For instance, judges need to look at the AI recommendations and come up with their decision while putting in mind other factors that surround a case. This human error is critical to make sure that the AI systems are not replacing the human judgment completely but are, in fact, there to assist the process.

Thus, while AI offers significant potential benefits in criminal proceedings, it also presents substantial ethical and legal challenges. Protecting digital human rights, ensuring accountability and transparency, and addressing bias and fairness are all critical to the responsible use of AI in the legal system. By carefully navigating these challenges, the legal system can harness the power of AI to improve justice while safeguarding the rights and dignity of individuals.

TRUST DYNAMICS IN AI ADOPTION

As artificial intelligence (AI) continues to gain traction in criminal proceedings and broader legal contexts, fostering trust in these systems becomes critical for their successful adoption. Trust in AI is not solely a technical matter but also involves legal professionals, policymakers, and the public, who must believe that these technologies can be relied upon to make fair and accurate decisions. This section explores the strategies for building trust in AI systems, the essential role of policymakers in ensuring ethical standards, and the importance of engaging various stakeholders in AI development and deployment.

Building Trust in AI Systems

To achieve this goal of raising trust in AI systems within the legal framework, there is a need to embrace transparency, reliability, fairness, and accountability.

Transparency can be considered as one of the most important factors that define trust. It is therefore necessary for Judges and Lawyers to have an understanding of how such AI systems work especially how they arrive at certain decisions or recommendations(Duenser & Douglas, 2023). This implies that AI systems must be interpretable, that is, they should be able to give reasons that are easy to understand about the output that they have generated. This also means that the data that are used to train these systems are also made available. If the legal professionals and the public know about the datasets and the methods used to create the AI models they will be more confident that the results generated are not biased or wrong.

The dependability of the AI systems is also as significant as the accuracy of the systems. This implies that for AI applications in criminal proceedings, they must always produce correct and reliable outcomes to enhance on the trust element. The following can help in the prevention of such scenarios; this is through proper testing and validation of AI systems before they are released for use in the real-world(Abiodun & Lekan, 2020). The consistent evaluation of AI performance and the making of adjustments for any problem that may be identified add on to the confidence that is placed in these technologies. Lawyers must be sure that the AI tools are going to improve their work and not bring new problems and challenges to the process.

This is followed by another significant factor of trust in AI which is fairness. This means that in order to avoid the so-called biased AI, the fairness should be addressed at the levels of both the architecture and the code of the systems. This includes ensuring that multiple datasets are used, there are no bias in the algorithms used and in fact the fairness constraints are integrated into the AI models. This is because the public always has doubts as to the biases that may influence the information they receive, therefore, the society must be assured of the neutrality of the media.

Accountability is a critical factor when it comes to AI systems. Responsibility for AI decisions should be well-defined especially when such decisions affect people's lives. If an AI system provides a recommendation or a decision which is wrong then it should be clear who is to blame whether it is the developers of the system, the legal professionals who applied the system or the institutions which implemented the system. This accountability helps to avoid the situation when AI can be perceived as making ultimate decisions on its own accord, instead, AI is a part of the legal process(Doshi-Velez et al., 2017).

Thus, the increase of trust in AI also presupposes raising awareness of legal professionals concerning the strengths and weaknesses of such technologies. In this way, they are better prepared to understand the potential and risks of AI to be able to trust and to properly apply these technologies in their work.

Role of Policymakers

Criminal justice systems are now relying on AI in the course of the proceedings and it is the role of the policymakers to oversee the use of the technology and enshrine ethical practices(Ré & Solow-Niederman, 2019). With the advancement of the AI technologies, legal and regulatory framework that governs their application is also expanding.

This is one of the most important tasks of the policymakers to provide a proper framework and legal framework for the application of AI in the legal sector. The following should be addressed by these guidelines: Data governance, Algorithmic disclosure, Equity, and Responsibility. For instance, rules should require that all AI tools applied in the course of a criminal case be periodically screened for the presence of bias and that the data which is employed for the training of AI systems is obtained in a legal and balanced manner and includes data from all groups of people(Boswell & Prakash, 2020).

It is also important for the policymakers to take measures to prevent harm on citizens' rights in case of applying the AI in the criminal justice system(Kauffman & Soares, 2020). This entails that people should have the ability to challenge decisions made by AI systems that impact on them directly and that there must be procedures that can be followed in order to make the challenge. In addition to the above, it is recommended that policies should provide that AI systems should not be used as replacing human decision-making discretion. This prevents the over-usage of AI which is essential in the justice system and maintains the aspect of human intervention.

Besides the regulation, the government has a responsibility to build the public's confidence in AI. This can be done by coming up with transparency measures that will inform the public on matters concerning use of AI in the legal system, measures that have been put in place to ensure that the use of AI does not prejudice the parties involved and the advantages of applying AI in the legal system. Availing public awareness campaigns and educational programs can reduce the fear that people have regarding artificial intelligence and its effects on privacy, fairness, and justice(Golbin et al., 2020).

It also means that policymakers have to fund and endorse the studies regarding the ethical implications and legal frameworks of AI. Through research on the ethical effects of AI and guidelines as to the proper use of AI, the policymakers can assist in the advancement of technology that complies with the legal systems and moral standards.

Also, there should be encouraging of the international cooperation in the management of the AI. This is the case because as AI technologies are being developed and used across the world there is need to come up with international standards and guidelines for the use of the technologies in criminal justice systems. This partnership can assist in proper coordination and standardization of laws across different jurisdictions, curb on the negative application of AI and encourage the right use of AI in the legal sector globally.

Stakeholder Engagement

Engaging a diverse range of stakeholders in the development and deployment of AI in the legal system is crucial to ensuring that these technologies are designed and implemented in ways that reflect the needs and values of society. Stakeholder engagement fosters collaboration, inclusivity, and shared responsibility, which are essential for building trust and ensuring the ethical use of AI.

The primary stakeholders in AI adoption within the legal system include legal professionals, technologists, policymakers, civil society organizations, and the general public.

Legal professionals, such as judges, lawyers, and court staff, are on the front lines of AI adoption in the criminal justice system. Their involvement in the development of AI tools is critical to ensuring that these technologies are designed with the practical needs of the legal system in mind. By involving legal professionals in the design and testing of AI systems, developers can create tools that are user-friendly, relevant, and capable of addressing real-world challenges in legal practice(Craigle, 2019).

Technologists and AI developers are responsible for creating the systems that will be used in criminal proceedings. Engaging them in discussions about ethical considerations, legal standards, and societal values is essential to ensuring that AI technologies are aligned with the principles of justice and fairness. Collaboration between technologists and legal experts can also help bridge the gap between technical capabilities and legal requirements, resulting in AI systems that are both innovative and legally sound.

Policymakers, as discussed earlier, have a key role in establishing the regulatory framework for AI adoption. Their engagement with other stakeholders ensures that policies are informed by a range of perspectives and that they address the concerns of all affected parties. This collaborative approach helps create a regulatory environment that balances innovation with ethical considerations and public trust.

Civil society organizations play an important role in representing the interests of marginalized communities and advocating for human rights in the context of AI adoption. Their involvement ensures that the voices of vulnerable populations are heard and that AI systems do not disproportionately impact certain groups. By engaging with civil society, developers and policymakers can identify potential biases and work to mitigate them before AI systems are deployed in the legal system(Chohlas-Wood et al., 2023).

The general public is ultimately affected by the use of AI in criminal proceedings, and their trust in the legal system is essential for its legitimacy. Public engagement through consultations, surveys, and educational initiatives helps ensure that AI technologies are aligned with societal values and that the public is informed about how these technologies will be used. Public input can also help identify potential concerns and areas where additional safeguards are needed.

Stakeholder engagement is not a one-time process but an ongoing dialogue that should continue throughout the lifecycle of AI technologies. This continuous engagement allows for the adaptation and improvement of AI systems based on feedback from all stakeholders and ensures that these technologies remain relevant, effective, and ethically sound.

The adoption of AI within the legal system is contingent upon the establishment of trust, which is shaped by factors such as transparency, reliability, fairness, and accountability. Policymakers play a crucial role in establishing regulations and promoting public trust, while stakeholder engagement ensures that AI technologies are developed and deployed in ways that reflect societal values. By addressing these factors, the legal system can harness the potential of AI to enhance justice while maintaining public trust and ethical integrity.

FUTURE DIRECTIONS AND RECOMMENDATIONS

The integration of Artificial Intelligence (AI) and jurimetrics into criminal proceedings has already transformed various facets of the legal system, offering unprecedented opportunities for enhancing judicial efficiency, consistency, and data-driven decision-making. However, as these technologies continue to evolve, there is a pressing need to consider future directions and formulate recommendations that ensure their ethical, fair, and effective application. This section explores potential advancements in AI and jurimetrics, proposes policies and regulatory frameworks to guide their use, and identifies key areas for further research to address the challenges highlighted in empirical findings.

Advancements in AI and Jurimetrics: Potential Future Developments and Implications

AI and jurimetrics stands to deepen the transformation of the legal system as technologies keep on being developed. Potential advancements in AI will likely centre on improving the precision, interpretability and the ethical application of predictive models; similarly, jurimetrics is expected to grow and include more elaborate data sets and techniques. All the above advances will have great impacts on the legal system and is likely to open new horizons while at the same time posing some threats(Burk, 2020).

There are more advanced techniques which are available as of now like deep learning and neural networks that can enhance the capability of AI models for better predictions. These technologies can sift through massive amounts of information that is not organized in a specific format like legal documents, case laws and previous judgments to find out the patterns and trends which are not easily discernible to human analysts. Being able to enhance the existing predictive models, AI will be able to calculate the risk more accurately, identify appropriate case-law and offer particular suggestions that correspond to the present legal framework.

Furthermore, there will be improvements in the natural language processing (NLP) which will improve the ability of AI in understanding and analysing legal documents. This may result in enhanced ways of searching for legal information, contract review and automated document creation, which will assist legal specialists in managing the abundance and constantly increasing amount of legal information. It can also help in identifying data from court records through NLP that will improve the empirical analysis of the behaviour of judges and their decisions.

However, as the use of AI increases in legal practice the questions of judicial discretion and the human touch need to be well thought through. However, it is crucial to underscore that the role of the judge is to make the final decision, and that is where AI cannot replace human judges because there are always factors that need to be considered, such as ethic, context and many other factors. The problem comes with the fact that AI-based decisions are efficient and consistent while people are emotional and unpredictable.

Policy and Regulatory Frameworks: Guiding the Ethical Use of AI in Criminal Proceedings

In order to prevent the misuse of AI and jurimetrics in criminal justice, strong policy and regulatory measures must be put in place. These frameworks should incorporate important considerations including; openness, accountability, bias management, and respect for individual rights in a bid to ensure that AI system delivers justice and not injustice.

The first recommendation that can be made is the creation of clear and complete set of rules that regulate the ethical integration of AI in the judiciary. These guidelines should contain the baseline for the quality of data, explainability of models, and non-bias in algorithms as well as the specifications for periodic checks and assessment of the AI systems. Policy makers should make it compulsory to use "explainable AI" so that the processes through which the AI tools arrive at the decisions can be easily understood by lawyers, accused persons, and people in the society(Ré & Solow-Niederman, 2019).

Also, there is the need to specify the legal responsibilities of the parties involved in the use of AI-based decisions. Where AI is seen to have played a part in the wrong or biased decision, then there must be a means of identifying culpability, in the developers of the system, the legal professionals applying the system or the regulatory authorities. This is important in enhancing the general public's confidence and to avoid the use of AI in a wrong manner, as a way of replacing the role of the judiciary.

It is also important that the regulatory bodies consider coming up with independent monitoring committees that will specifically monitor the use of AI in criminal justice. Such committees could periodically inspect the AI systems, check compliance of these systems with the certain ethical norms, and suggest possible modifications in the systems. It would also aid in the prevention of abuse and would be an opportunity to listen to the publics concerns about the use of AI in the legal system.

Public involvement is another essential element of regulatory frameworks that should be considered. Legal professionals, technologists, policymakers and community members should be involved in discussions that the regulators have with regard to the use of AI in criminal proceedings to ensure that different voices are heard in the making of decisions on AI tools. This is because with such collaboration, the society will have confidence in the AI technologies as well as the legal process(Smuha, 2021).

Research Agenda: Addressing Gaps and Challenges in AI Integration

Despite the advancements in AI and jurimetrics, significant gaps and challenges remain that warrant further research. Such challenges require a specific research agenda that would help determine the further steps in the integration of AI into the judiciary. This research agenda should primarily concern ethical issues that may arise with the use of AI, enhancement of technological tools and the human-technology interaction in the legal field.

Another open area is the analysis of the presence of bias in the training data for AI algorithms. For instance, research has been done on COMPAS and PredPol, where it was revealed that the use of AI only reinforces the prejudice and results in adverse effects on the minorities. Future work should focus on the identification of the sources of bias, the quantification of these sources and the possible ways of preventing them by focusing on the creation of new datasets as well as the improvement of the fairness of decision-making algorithms.

One more research question is about the effects of AI on the decision-making process of judges. Collective experiences like Dr. Sonali Swetapadma's research work that focuses on the details of legal decisions in sensitive matters like rape show that even as the use of AI in decision-making processes is encouraged, human input is still relevant and necessary; more research needs to be done to determine how AI can be of value without undermining human judgment(Swetapadma et al., 2023). Studies could look at the extent and nature of the tension between the use of AI driven recommendation and judicial discretion, and explore how AI impacts the thinking and production of reasoned orders.

The impacts of the AI-based models for prediction are also susceptible to continuous assessment. Further examinations should also measure the validity, practicality, and implications of these models in various legal systems. Thus, by following the development of the AI application in the legal profession and analyzing the cases, it is possible to determine the specific areas that have been improved and the areas that still require improvements.

Finally, there is a paucity of research studies examining the social impacts and consequences of AI integration within the criminal justice system, including an analysis of stakeholder attitudes and trust-related concerns(Hayward & Maas, 2020). This means that the perception of the various stakeholders such as the legal practitioners as well as the public on the use of AI in the judiciary can be of importance when it comes to building trust in the AI technologies. Further studies in this field may look into the ways on how AI is being explained, communicated, and promoted to the public and how communities can be engaged in understanding the advantages and disadvantages of AI.

It is for this reason that the future of AI and Jurimetrics in criminal proceedings will are reliant on the management of technological developments, the issues of ethics and the adequate checks and balances put in place through the legal frameworks. With the advancement of future AI technologies, defining the policies and enunciating the legislation the legal system can reap all the benefits while keeping the justice principles intact. Thus, there is a need for technologists, legal professionals, policymakers and the society as a whole to work towards creating a positive impact of AI in the delivery of justice.

CONCLUSION

The analysis of predictive justice, AI, and jurimetrics in criminal proceedings demonstrates the possibilities and risks of these technologies. The chapter starts with the concept of predictive justice which is the process of applying data analytics and artificial intelligence in order to improve the existing legal processes especially in criminal courts. It highlights how AI and jurimetrics are essential in the process of transforming the legal system and enhancing the capabilities of the judges, lawyers, and law enforcement agencies through the use of tools that can help in the automation of processes, increase the effectiveness of the decision-making process and support the analysis of data.

The theoretical foundation part of the paper demonstrates the development of jurimetrics that was initially proposed as a tool for using quantitative approaches in legal research. It has evolved hand in hand with the growth of the field of AI and some of the technologies that have fueled this include machine learning natural language processing and data analysis. This is due to the fact that it makes it possible for the system to make better predictions on recidivism rates, case outlooks as well as the patterns in legal judgments. There is therefore the possibility of changing the face of criminal justice system.

Real life application of AI in law enforcement, courts, and legal processes show that AI has found its place across the entire spectrum. Some of the applications of AI in the justice system include; PredPol, a predictive policing tool that uses crime data to predict crime occurrences; Lex Machina and ROSS Intelligence, legal tools that aid in research and case management respectively. These tools can therefore make the processes of decision making easier, reduce the pile up of cases and improve on the legal processes of delivery of justice. But, the findings of the research suggest that these technologies have the following drawbacks. Some of the important issues discussed in the interview with Dr. Sonali Swetapadma included; Bias in AI systems, potential reduction of the judicial discretion and the social impacts of over dependence on technology.

Thus, ethical and legal concerns are the most crucial factors that have to be taken into account when using AI in criminal proceedings. The chapter focuses on how AI affects the digital human rights, the impact on privacy, data protection and individual's rights. It highlights the aspects of openness, responsibility, and the actions to address the issues of bias in the algorithms. The risks of such predictive tools such as COMPAS which has been accused of perpetuating racial bias in the US justice system show how much more needs to be done to create better algorithms and better ways of monitoring their usage. The public needs to trust the AI systems and the processes that are based on them which is why there should be certain rules and the stakeholders should be involved in AI governance.

Trust factors in AI adoption relates with the legal integration of the AI where it plays a significant role. The chapter also explains how trust can be created, as in, for example, making the decisions of AI systems more understandable, raising public awareness, or creating policies together with stakeholders. The role of policymakers is very crucial in laying down the guidelines, monitoring AI application and enforcing ethical standards. Involving the society and particularly the legal industry in the development of AI is crucial in developing the best effective systems that are both technologically sound as well as socially fair.

Looking ahead, the chapter highlights future directions and recommendations for the integration of AI and jurimetrics in criminal proceedings. It requires development in the artificial intelligence technologies that makes it more precise in its predictions while considering the ethical issues. The importance of having policy and regulatory frameworks that set out best practices in relation to the sharing of information is highlighted including policy and regulatory frameworks related to transparency, accountability and equity. The research questions that should be addressed in the future include the analysis of biases, assessment of the effects of AI on the judicial decision, and perception of the public in regard to AI in the legal context.

The effects of AI and jurimetrics on the legal process are far-reaching as it touches each stage of the criminal process from police to the court. These technologies have the promise of enhancing the quality of justice by increasing its efficiency, reducing variability, and increasing its availability but they also present certain risks that need to be properly handled. On a positive note, AI can help in minimizing the human element, improve the reliability of risk assessment and offer better and meaningful information to help in decision making. For example, tools such as TrueAllele that analyze complex DNA evidence has made a positive impact in the criminal justice system since it provides accurate scientific information which assist in the assessment of who is guilty or not.

But AI has an impact that is not restricted to the technological aspect. This has been in light of the adoption of predictive policing strategies such as PredPol and Operation Laser. Recent developments such as the LAPD halting some of the predictive policing projects due to protests from the public show how wrong and even prejudiced such an approach can be. Based on the public records and reports, these programs only served to reinforce current practices of policing and contributed to the over policing of black and brown bodies with the call for the ethical use of AI in policing.

Moreover, the reliance on AI tools like COMPAS for sentencing and parole decisions has sparked debates about the balance between data-driven predictions and judicial discretion. This balance is well captured in the interview with Dr. Sonali Swetapadma where she explains the challenges that arise when it comes to making decisions based on algorithms even when the circumstances of the individual may be different. The increasing use of such tools in the course of criminal trials presents a challenge on how best to ensure that these technologies improve the quality of justice delivery systems rather than compounding the problems.

It is also important that the legal system look at the issues of the regulations and ethical dilemmas. The current legal systems have been seen to have failed to address the issue of accountability and transparency of artificial intelligence. Current there are no set guidelines in place which exposes the potential for abuse of AI technologies. These gaps can only be closed if there is positive policy intervention that provides policy direction on the application and use of AI, sets ethical standards and mandates mechanisms of control to avoid negative impacts.

The use of AI and jurimetrics in the criminal trials can be seen as a two sided sword. On one hand, the idea of improving the productivity, decreasing the backlog, and using the data analytics to drive decision making brings forth the possibility of a more effective legal system. On the other, there are issues of biasness, non-transparency and ethical concerns that are very important and cannot be overlooked. Therefore, there is need to ensure that the legal system integrates technology without compromise on the principles of justice, equity and human rights.

More specifically, technological developments should be followed with regards to the effects they can have on people. These tools should, therefore, be developed with the following ethical considerations in mind: there should be measures that help to address the issues of bias; there should be measures that are put in place so that accountability can be achieved; and finally, there should be measures that help to ensure that the human element remains an integral part of legal decision-making. Policymakers are important in defining the rules and providing the guidelines that will make the use of AI ethical, thus making sure that it is in line with the principles of the society and the laws.

Altogether, it is up to technologists, legal professionals, policymakers, and society in general to determine the fate of AI and jurimetrics in criminal trials. Through the promotion of the multistakeholder approach to the regulation of AI, supporting studies that help fill current gaps, and ensuring the primacy of human rights in AI-related regulation, the legal framework will be able to realize the potential of AI in the promotion of justice while maintaining the principles of justice. The future is not without its obstacles, yet, understanding the possibilities and risks of AI, it is possible to establish and use the technology for enhancing the fairness and effectiveness of the legal systems in the contemporary world.

REFERENCE

Abiodun, O. S., & Lekan, A. J. (2020, December 1). EXPLORING THE POTENTIALS OF ARTIFICIAL INTELLGIENCE IN THE JUDICIARY. *IJEAST*, 5(8). Advance online publication. DOI: 10.33564/IJEAST.2020.v05i08.004

Ahsan, S., & Shah, A. (2008, April 1). Data mining, semantic web and advanced information technologies for fighting terrorism. DOI: 10.1109/ISBAST.2008.4547644

ALGORITHMS AND TERRORISM. (n.d). https://www.un.org/counterterrorism/sites/www.un.org.counterterrorism/files/malicious-use-of-ai-uncct-unicri-report-hd.pdf

Ashley, K D. (2019, August 15). A Brief History of the Changing Roles of Case Prediction in AI and Law. Cambridge University Press, 36(1), 93-112. DOI: 10.26826/law-in-context.v36i1.88

Bajgar, O., & Horenovsky, J. (2022, January 1). Negative Human Rights as a Basis for Long-term AI Safety and Regulation. Cornell University. https://doi.org/DOI: 10.48550/arXiv.2208

Boswell, L., & Prakash, A. (2020, January 1). On the Fairness of 'Fake' Data in Legal AI. Cornell University. https://doi.org//arxiv.2009.04640DOI: 10.48550

Branovitskiy, K., & Yarkov, V. V. (2022, January 1). Some procedural aspects of the introduction of predictive justice in the civil procedure. *EDP Sciences*, 134, 00002–00002. DOI: 10.1051/shsconf/202213400002

Burk, D L. (2020, October 5). ALGORITHMIC LEGAL METRICS. DOI: 10.5210/spir.v2020i0.11184

Chandra, M. (2019, November 30). Reduction of Cyber Crimes by Effective Use of Artificial Intelligence Techniques. *Reduction of Cyber Crimes by Effective Use of Artificial Intelligence Techniques.*, 8(4), 8643–8645. DOI: 10.35940/ijrte.D8566.118419

Chatterjee, S., & N.S., S. (2019, July 1). Personal Data Sharing and Legal Issues of Human Rights in the Era of Artificial Intelligence. IGI Global, 15(3), 21-36. DOI: 10.4018/IJEGR.2019070102

Chen, M., & Li, S. (2020, June 1). Research on the application of artificial intelligence technology in the field of Justice. *Journal of Physics: Conference Series*, 1570(1), 012047–012047. DOI: 10.1088/1742-6596/1570/1/012047

Chohlas-Wood, A., Coots, M., Goel, S., & Nyarko, J. (2023, July 24). Designing equitable algorithms. *Nature Computational Science*, 3(7), 601–610. DOI: 10.1038/s43588-023-00485-4 PMID: 38177749

Chouldechova, A. (2017, June 1). Fair Prediction with Disparate Impact: A Study of Bias in Recidivism Prediction Instruments. Mary Ann Liebert. *Big Data*, 5(2), 153–163. DOI: 10.1089/big.2016.0047 PMID: 28632438

Craigle, V. (2019, January 1). Law Libraries Embracing AI. RELX Group (Netherlands). DOI: 10.2139/ssrn.3381798

Cui, L., Xu, Y., Lv, T., & Wei, F. (2021, January 1). Document AI: Benchmarks, Models and Applications. Cornell University. https://doi.org/DOI: 10.48550/arXiv.2111

Davis, A. E. (2020, January 1). The Future of Law Firms (and Lawyers) in the Age of Artificial Intelligence. Fundação Getúlio Vargas, Escola de Direito, 16(1). https://doi.org/DOI: 10.1590/2317-6172201945

Dneprovskaya, M., & Abramitov, S. (2020, January 1). Digital Technologies in Activities of Russian Courts: Prospects of Artificial Intelligence Application. DOI: 10.2991/aebmr.k.200502.034

Doshi-Velez, F., Kortz, M., Budish, R., Bavitz, C., Gershman, S., O'Brien, D. P., Scott, K. M., Schieber, S., Waldo, J., Weinberger, D., Weller, A., & Wood, A. (2017, January 1). Accountability of AI Under the Law: The Role of Explanation. Cornell University. https://doi.org//arxiv.1711.01134DOI: 10.48550

Dressel, J., & Farid, H. (2021, February 5). The Dangers of Risk Prediction in the Criminal Justice System. DOI: 10.21428/2c646de5.f5896f9f

Duenser, A., & Douglas, D. (2023, January 1). Who to Trust, How and Why: Untangling AI Ethics Principles, Trustworthiness and Trust. Cornell University. https://doi.org/DOI: 10.48550/arXiv.2309

Eliot, L. B. (2020, January 1). Legal Judgment Prediction (LJP) Amid the Advent of Autonomous AI Legal Reasoning. Cornell University. https://doi.org//arxiv.2009.14620DOI: 10.48550

Ezzeddine, Y., Bayerl, P. S., & Gibson, H. (2023, January 1). Citizen Perspectives on Necessary Safeguards to the Use of AI by Law Enforcement Agencies. Cornell University. https://doi.org/DOI: 10.48550/arXiv.2306

Ferrara, E. (2023, January 1). Fairness And Bias in Artificial Intelligence: A Brief Survey of Sources, Impacts, And Mitigation Strategies. Cornell University. https://doi.org/DOI: 10.48550/arXiv.2304

Fortes, P R B. (2020, September 15). Paths to Digital Justice: Judicial Robots, Algorithmic Decision-Making, and Due Process. Cambridge University Press, 7(3), 453-469. DOI: 10.1017/als.2020.12

Golbin, I., Rao, A S., Hadjarian, A., & Krittman, D. (2020, December 10). Responsible AI: A Primer for the Legal Community. DOI: 10.1109/BigData50022.2020.9377738

Guidotti, R., Monreale, A., Ruggieri, S., Turini, F., Pedreschi, D., & Giannotti, F. (2018, January 1). A Survey Of Methods For Explaining Black Box Models. Cornell University. https://doi.org//arxiv.1802.01933DOI: 10.48550

Gummadidala, P R., Karippur, N K., & Maddulety, K. (2020, January 1). Analysis of Factors Influencing the Adoption of Artificial Intelligence for Crime Management. Springer Science+Business Media, 3-9. DOI: 10.1007/978-3-030-64849-7_1

Hayward, K., & Maas, M. M. (2020, June 30). Artificial intelligence and crime: A primer for criminologists. *Crime, Media, Culture*, 17(2), 209–233. DOI: 10.1177/1741659020917434

Islam, M. A., Ferdaus, J., Khan, M A A., & Habib, M. T. (2018, October 30). Online Legal Service. *The Present and Future.*, 10(5), 13–20. DOI: 10.5121/ijcsit.2018.10502

Johndrow, J. E., & Lum, K. (2017, January 1). An algorithm for removing sensitive information: application to race-independent recidivism prediction. Cornell University. https://doi.org//arxiv.1703.04957DOI: 10.48550

Jurimetrics legal definition of jurimetrics. (2006, January 1). https://legal-dictionary .thefreedictionary.com/jurimetrics

Katz, D., Hartung, D., Gerlach, L., Jana, A., & Bommarito, M. J. (2023, January 1). Natural Language Processing in the Legal Domain. Cornell University. https:// doi.org/DOI: 10.48550/arXiv.2302

Kauffman, M E., & Soares, M N. (2020, October 18). AI in legal services: new trends in AI-enabled legal services. Springer Science+Business Media, 14(4), 223-226. DOI: 10.1007/s11761-020-00305-x

Khabibullina, A. S., Seleckaya, S. B., & Shpagonov, A. N. (2019, November 27). THE PROBLEMS OF ROBOTISATION OF LEGAL PROFESSION. *Federal University of Paraíba*, 8(6). Advance online publication. DOI: 10.22478/ufpb.2179-7137.2019v8n6.49311

Kleinberg, J., Lakkaraju, H., Leskovec, J., Ludwig, J., & Mullainathan, S. (2017, August 26). Human Decisions and Machine Predictions*. Oxford University Press. DOI: 10.1093/qje/qjx032

Lima, G., Grgić-Hlača, N., Jeong, J K., & Cha, M. (2022, June 20). The Conflict Between Explainable and Accountable Decision-Making Algorithms. DOI: 10.1145/3531146.3534628

Llinares, F M. (2020, January 23). INTELIGENCIA ARTIFICIAL Y JUSTICIA PENAL: MÁS ALLÁ DE LOS RESULTADOS LESIVOS CAUSADOS POR ROBOTS., 87-130. DOI: 10.5944/rdpc.20.2018.26446

Losano, M G. (1971, December 1). Juricybernetics: Genesis and Structure of a Discipline. Cambridge University Press, 19(76), 93-114. DOI: 10.1177/039219217101907605

Lynch, J. (2020, January 1). Face Off: Law Enforcement Use of Face Recognition Technology. RELX Group (Netherlands). DOI: 10.2139/ssrn.3909038

Marković, M., & Gostojić, S. (2022, November 16). Legal document assembly system for introducing law students with legal drafting. Springer Science+Business Media, 31(4), 829-863. DOI: 10.1007/s10506-022-09339-2

McKeown, T., Mustafina, J., Магизов, P., & Gataullina, C. (2020, December 14). AI in Law Practices. DOI: 10.1109/DeSE51703.2020.9450780

Nay, J J. (2021, February 18). Natural Language Processing for Legal Texts. Cambridge University Press, 99-113. DOI: 10.1017/9781316529683.011

Negri, K. M. E. S. M. (2020, October 18). AI in legal services: new trends in AI-enabled legal services - Service Oriented Computing and Applications. https://link.springer.com/article/10.1007/s11761-020-00305-x

Neznamov, A. (2020, January 1). Regulatory Landscape of Artificial Intelligence. DOI: 10.2991/assehr.k.200321.113

Park, S., & Ko, H. (2020, August 1). Machine Learning and Law and Economics: A Preliminary Overview. *De Gruyter*, 11(2), 20200034. Advance online publication. DOI: 10.1515/ajle-2020-0034

Perlin, M. W., Dormer, K. J., Hornyak, J. M., Schiermeier-Wood, L., & Greenspoon, S. A. (2014, March 25). TrueAllele Casework on Virginia DNA Mixture Evidence: Computer and Manual Interpretation in 72 Reported Criminal Cases. *PLoS One*, 9(3), e92837–e92837. DOI: 10.1371/journal.pone.0092837 PMID: 24667531

Petrescu, R. V. (2019, January 1).. . *Face Recognition as a Biometric Application.*, 3(1), 237–257. DOI: 10.3844/jmrsp.2019.237.257

Predicting crime, LAPD-style. (2023, February 6). https://perma.cc/2FEC-4TCS

Predictive Policing Technology. (2012, March 9). https://www.predpol.com/technology

PredPol is LAPD's Racist Predictive Policing Program. (2019, October 11). https://freerads.org/2019/10/11/a-guide-to-predpol-and-dismantling-it/

Ramos, S., López, J Á P., & Abreu, R. (2020, June 1). An Analysis of the Importance of the Artificial Intelligence on the Information System of Police Forces. DOI: 10.23919/CISTI49556.2020.9141006

Rankin, S. G. (2020, January 1). Technological Tethereds: Potential Impact of Untrustworthy Artificial Intelligence in Criminal Justice Risk Assessment Instruments. RELX Group (Netherlands). DOI: 10.2139/ssrn.3662761

Ré, R M., & Solow-Niederman, A. (2019, May 19). Developing Artificially Intelligent Justice

Sanctis, F M D. (2021, March 23). Artificial Intelligence and Innovation in Brazilian Justice. Cambridge University Press, 59(1), 1-10. DOI: 10.1017/cri.2021.4

Schwartz, R., Down, L., Jonas, A., & Tabassi, E. (2021, June 22). A Proposal for Identifying and Managing Bias in Artificial Intelligence. DOI: 10.6028/NIST.SP.1270-draft

Selbst, A. D. (2017, January 1). Disparate Impact in Big Data Policing. RELX Group (Netherlands). DOI: 10.2139/ssrn.2819182

Shah, N., Bhagat, N., & Shah, M. (2021, April 29). Crime forecasting: A machine learning and computer vision approach to crime prediction and prevention. *Visual Computing for Industry, Biomedicine, and Art*, 4(1), 9. Advance online publication. DOI: 10.1186/s42492-021-00075-z PMID: 33913057

Sharma, S., Shandilya, R., & Sharma, S. (2021, January 1). Predicting Indian Supreme Court Judgments, Decisions, Or Appeals. Cornell University. https://doi.org//arxiv.2110.09251DOI: 10.48550

Simmons, R. (2018, January 1). Big Data, Machine Judges, and the Legitimacy of the Criminal Justice System. RELX Group (Netherlands). DOI: 10.2139/ssrn.3156510

Smuha, N A. (2021, January 2). From a 'race to AI' to a 'race to AI regulation': regulatory competition for artificial intelligence. Taylor & Francis, 13(1), 57-84. DOI: 10.1080/17579961.2021.1898300

Stoykov, K., & Chelebieva, S. (2019, October 1). Legal data extraction and possible applications. *IOP Conference Series. Materials Science and Engineering*, 618(1), 012037–012037. DOI: 10.1088/1757-899X/618/1/012037

Swetapadma, S., Subudhi, R N., & Chattoraj, P. (2023, August 7). Are reporting and investigation of rape cases victim friendly? Responses of the police from a cross-sectional study conducted in three states of eastern India., 30, 576-595. DOI: 10.1177/02697580231185156

Vaissnave, V., & Deepalakshmi, P. (2019, December 30). An Artificial Intelligence based Analysis in Legal domain. Blue Eyes Intelligence Engineering and Sciences Publication, 9(2S2), 1046-1051. DOI: 10.35940/ijitee.B1113.1292S219

Visser, J. (2006, March 1). Jurimetrics, safety and security. Taylor & Francis, 20(1-2), 123-133. DOI: 10.1080/13600860600580801

Wu, Y. (2018, January 1). Research On the Mechanism Innovation Of The Cultivation Of Rule Of Law Talents In the View Of Big Data. DOI: 10.2991/asssd-18.2018.63

Yang, J. (2021, March 1). Analysis and Application of Judicial Data Based on Machine Learning. *Journal of Physics: Conference Series*, 1846(1), 012027–012027. DOI: 10.1088/1742-6596/1846/1/012027

Yulia, R., & Sergiy, R. (2021, April 29). Justice in the Digital Age: Technological Solutions. *Hidden Threats and Enticing Opportunities.*, 4(2), 104–117. DOI: 10.33327/AJEE-18-4.2-a000061

Zhong, H., Xiao, C., Tu, C., Zhang, T., Liu, Z., & Sun, M. (2020, January 1). How Does NLP Benefit Legal System: A Summary of Legal Artificial Intelligence. DOI: 10.18653/v1/2020.acl-main.466

ADDITIONAL READING

Atılgan, E. Ü. (2024). Will artificial intelligence sit on the judge's bench? In Al-Turjman, F. (Ed.), *Advanced studies in complex systems: Computational intelligence and blockchain in complex systems* (pp. 127–132). Morgan Kaufmann., DOI: 10.1016/B978-0-443-13268-1.00027-3

Dias, S. A. de J., & Sátiro, R. M. (2024). Artificial intelligence in the judiciary: A critical view. *Futures*, 103493, 103493. Advance online publication. DOI: 10.1016/j.futures.2024.103493

Javed, K., & Li, J. (2024). Artificial intelligence in judicial adjudication: Semantic biasness classification and identification in legal judgement (SBCILJ). *Heliyon*, 10(9), e30184. DOI: 10.1016/j.heliyon.2024.e30184 PMID: 38737247

McNally, P., & Inayatullah, S. (1988). The rights of robots: Technology, culture and law in the 21st century. *Futures*, 20(2), 119–136. DOI: 10.1016/0016-3287(88)90019-5

Rao, A. S. R. S., & Gore, A. P. (2023). Indian courts of law can benefit immensely by adopting artificial intelligence methods in bail applications for speedy and accurate justice. In Krantz, S. G., Rao, A. S. R. S., & Rao, C. R. (Eds.), *Handbook of statistics* (Vol. 49, pp. 227–236). Elsevier., DOI: 10.1016/bs.host.2023.04.002

Restrepo Amariles, D., & Baquero, P. M. (2023). Promises and limits of law for a human-centric artificial intelligence. *Computer Law & Security Report*, 48, 105795. DOI: 10.1016/j.clsr.2023.105795

Stuurman, K., & Lachaud, E. (2022). Regulating AI: A label to complete the proposed Act on Artificial Intelligence. *Computer Law & Security Report*, 44, 105657. DOI: 10.1016/j.clsr.2022.105657

KEY TERMS & DEFINITIONS

Artificial Intelligence (AI): It refers to the act of creating machines in which the raw ability to execute intelligent processes is incorporated and somewhat encoded. AI can further be applied in legal areas to assist in areas such as document research, risk analysis and decision propensity.

Digital Human Rights: Important powers in relation to protecting individual's data, privacy and their freedoms within the digital sphere with specific reference to AI solutions.

Jurimetrics: The employment of statistical quantitative analysis in legal matters and the application of statistics and probabilities in solving legal problems.

Machine Learning: A specific field of artificial intelligence that is aimed at designing algorithms and statistical models that would allow computers to get better at performing a given task as a result of experience.

Natural Language Processing (NLP): A branch of AI that comprises of the processes of modelling the communication between computers and humans through the use of natural language for computers to comprehend, process and also reply to natural language of humans.

Predictive Justice: The use of Artificial Intelligence and statistics to forecast the results in court cases, with the purpose of increasing the effectiveness and equality of the judicial system.

Chapter 12
Mathematical Approach: AI-Based Feature Selection in Machine Learning

Naren Kathirvel
Anand Institute of Higher Technology, India

Kathirvel Ayyaswamy
https://orcid.org/0000-0002-5347-9110
Department of Computer Science and Engineering, Tagore Engineering College, Chennai, India

N. Saravanan
MNM Jain Engineering College, India

P. Kaliappan
Department of Artificial Intelligence and Data Science, Panimalar Engineering College, Chennai, India

ABSTRACT

Search engine to identify the promising feature subset candidates and a criterion to identify the best candidate often comprise a feature selection framework. A crucial technique in the field of machine learning, feature selection is given new significance in information retrieval (IR) 5.0. This strategy, sometimes referred to as variable or attribute selection, selects a subset of important traits or predictors in order to construct a model. Selected as a crucial technique for dimensionality reduction, its main goal from the viewpoint of IR 5.0 is to carefully select a subset of features from the original set. Part of the curation process is eliminating anything that is noisy, superfluous, or redundant. In the IR 5.0 era, feature selection becomes a central role as information retrieval is marked by unprecedented sophistication. Feature set accelerates both the improvement of learning performance and increased accuracy

DOI: 10.4018/979-8-3693-7205-0.ch012

in the learning process.

1. INTRODUCTION

An artificial intelligence-based machine learning gives systems the competence to learn automatically from established knowledge without having to be hardcoded. The information at present in existence comprises data or observations from samples, direct experience, or instruction that is carefully examined to improve decisions on newly collected or forthcoming data (Hajamydeen and Helmi, 2020). Feature selection has become extensively used across various sectors (Zia et.al., 2015; Wu & Wang, 2015; Hajamydeen and Udzir, 2016; Salcedo-Sanz et.al., 2018; Rokad et.al., 2019; Álvarez et. al., 2019; Hajamydeen and Udzir, 2019; Samsuddin et.al., 2019; Sharma & Jain, 2020; Jaleel et.al., 2021; Pudjihartono et.al., 2022; Qiao et.al., 2022) and is remarkably critical when working with large datasets with dimensions up to thousands. A search engine to identify the promising feature subset candidates and a criterion to identify the best candidate often comprise a feature selection framework (Kotsiantis, 2011).

Information retrieval (IR) 5.0 places a novel importance on feature selection, a critical method in the discipline of machine learning. This scheme, which at times called variable or attribute selection, is choosing a subset of significant features or predictors for the purpose of building a model. Recognized as an essential method for reducing dimensionality, its primary objective in the perspective of IR 5.0 is to cautiously choose a subset of features from the original set. The curation process involves removing elements that are unnecessary, redundant, or loud. Feature selection becomes a pivotal role in the era of IR 5.0, where information retrieval is characterized by unparalleled sophistication. The enrichment of learning performance and intensified accuracy in the learning process are both accelerated by feature set optimization.

Knowing the predictive ability of every feature in relation to every other feature in a log/dataset assist in precisely identifying the important features (Saarela and Jauhiainen, 2021; Oh, 2022). Therefore, feature selection needs to perform by setting every feature in the log as class attributes to know the relationship of the set feature with other features. The selected features of all class attribute settings were summarized to find the unselected features (Sudha, D., & Kathirvel, A, 2023b) and every such unselected feature was removed from the respective logs/datasets before further processing.

As an alternative of performing feature selection, providing the whole set of features to the machine learning algorithm itself to resolve on the importance of features is not a viable choice (Sudha, D., & Kathirvel, A, 2022), because of the following reasons. The reasons are: (1) Having lesser number of instances than the number of features in a dataset does not provide the needed generalization, resulting in zero learning by the algorithm. (2) Models are to be simple and understandable and with lots of feature understandability is lost. (3) Most datasets contain no or less informative features leading to poor quality output.

2 FEATURE SELECTION METHODS

Feature selection methods are envisioned to condense the number of input variables so that the significant variables remain to predict the target variable. Feature selection methods are generally categorised as supervised and unsupervised. Supervised methods are used to recognise appropriate features on labelled instances to intensify the efficacy of supervised models especially regression and classification, whereas unsupervised methods act on unlabelled data. Systematically all these methods can be further categorised as filter, embedded, hybrid and wrapper methods. The key variation among supervised (Smialowski et.al, 2010; Huang, 2015) and unsupervised methods (Dy and Brodley, 2004; Solorio-Fernández et.al. 2020) is that supervised method chooses features based on their significance to a specific task, typically from discriminating collections of samples. On the other hand, unsupervised methods choose features that capture the maximum variability in the data, without considering any target variable.

The following is the taxonomy of the feature selection methods:

Feature Selection: Choose a subset of input features from the dataset.

- ***Unsupervised***: Does not make use of a target variable.
- Correlation
- ***Supervised***: Utilizes the target variable
- **Wrapper**: Search for well-performing (significant) subsets of features.
- **Filter:** Pick subsets of features based on their association with the target.
- **Intrinsic**: Methods that perform automatic feature selection in training phase.

2.1 Wrapper Methods

Wrapper methods (El Aboudi and Benhlima, 2016; Pudjihartono et.al., 2022; Liu et.al., 2023) were used to identify a subset of features from the provided dataset that assists in achieving the best performance of a predictive model. In other words, it tests every subset of the available variables for the model's accuracy. There are two kinds of wrapper methods for feature selection, forward selection, and backward elimination.

Forward Selection: This method (Gutlein, 2009; Wan et.al., 2018) starts with an empty set of features and those features providing the best performance were iteratively added to the result set. The competence of forward selection to systematically construct a model by considering the incremental influence of every feature is one of its highest advantages. This method extends insights into the relative value of the attributes in addition to assisting in the identification of the most relevant predictors. Forward selection seeks to achieve a balance between model complexity and forecast accuracy by beginning with an empty set and gradually adding features based on their respective contributions.

Backward Elimination: This method (Nguyen et. al., 2014; Wan et.al., 2018; Fu et. al., 2023) starts with all the features in the data set and the insignificant or trivial features were removed iteratively. Backward elimination is an iterative method that involves systematically evaluating every feature's influence on the model's performance and eliminating those features that do not have a significant impact. By keeping the most significant predictors, this strategy resolves multicollinearity problems and improving the final model's interpretability. Wan et al. (2018) highlighted the usefulness of backward elimination and its capability to enhance feature sets for intensified model efficiency. The difficulty with this approach is that the final group of characteristics varies depending on the significance levels chosen, and the elimination of features is determined by the statistical criteria.

2.2 Filter Methods

Filter methods (Sánchez-Maroño et.al., 2007, Rajab and Wang, 2020) for feature selection are typically pre-processing methods which autonomously consider every feature in the dataset. It employs a model on every feature and then estimates, which is then utilized to examine its effect on a predictive model. There are four primary filter methods which are statistical, information-theoretic, model-based and frequency based.

Statistical: Utilizes statistical measures to assess the significance of every feature independently of the other features. The method makes decisions about which features to adopt or disregard from a model based on a variety of statistical measures that estimate every feature's significance. The often-used statistical measure p-value assesses the likelihood of obtaining examined results under the assumption that the null hypothesis is true. Higher p-value features are deemed as less significant and removed. This approach is based on hypothesis testing, where the null hypothesis generally states that a certain attribute has no influence on the result.

Information-Theoretic: Measures the amount of information by every single feature about the target variable based on the concept of entropy and mutual information. A sign of a random variable's uncertainty is called as entropy. It is challenging to calculate the value that a random variable could take, when higher the entropy. A measure of the mutual reliance connecting two random variables, X and Y, is called mutual information. By observing the other random variable, it computes the amount of knowledge that can be learned about one random variable.

Model-Based: A learning model to value the magnitude of every feature in forecasting the target variable. By valuing the model's features using the observed data that is available, this method assists the model to forecast future values and offer insights into the association between the features and the target variable. A variety of methods, including meta-learning algorithms for time series forecast model performance prediction, can be used in the estimation process.

Frequency-Based: Rank features based on frequency of occurrence or occurrence rate in a dataset. Using this approach, features are rated according to how repeatedly they appear or exist in the dataset. The rationale behind this is that characteristics with higher frequency of occurrence across instances might have superior discriminating ability or significance. Generally, features are prioritised in descending order of frequency, with the most appearing features being listed highest.

2.3 Intrinsic Methods

Intrinsic methods have feature selection integrated in the algorithm itself and does not have a feature selection method explicitly (Sudha, D., & Kathirvel, A, 2023a). These methods are quick and simple to apply, and no separate algorithm is needed to filter features. Several such methods are available as follows:

Lasso Regression: Uses regularization to minimize the constants of inappropriate features to zero consequently eliminating these features from the model.

Ridge Regression: Penalizes the sum of squared values of the model constants reducing the influence of inappropriate features.

Elastic Net Regression: Mixture of Lasso and Ridge regression and uses regularization to choose appropriate features.

Decision Trees: Automatically pick appropriate features by separating data based on the most exposing features.

Random Forest: Employ decision trees to identify appropriate features and merge the outcomes from several trees to improve the accuracy of the model.

Principal Component Analysis (PCA): Transforms the initial features into a fresh set of uncorrelated features called principal components and are graded by their capability to explicate the variance in the data. The higher graded components are chosen as appropriate features.

3 FEATURE SELECTION ALGORITHMS

Feature selection algorithms (Molina et.al., 2002; Kumar & Minz, 2014; Li et.al., 2017) are a mixture of a search technique for suggesting new feature subsets, with an evaluation measure which scores the different feature subsets. The objective of feature selection in machine learning is to discover the ideal set of features to build useful models. Feature selection approaches encompasses two portions which includes an attribute evaluator and a search method. Attribute evaluator evaluates an attribute in a dataset in the context of the class variable or the class label, which carries the judgment/conclusion of all the attributes in that instance. Search method is the flow of navigation to various combination of attributes to conclude on the list of selected features. Moreover, every attribute evaluator is compatible with selected search method(s) and accordingly a particular search method should be chosen after selecting an attribute evaluator. For example, *CorrelationAttributeEval* uses only *RankerSearch* method. On the other hand, attribute evaluators like *CfsSubsetEval* works with multiple search methods like *BestFirst, GreedyStepwise* and *ExhaustiveSearch*. There are many supervised feature selection algorithms available, and those algorithms that were chosen to demonstrate the ability of feature selection are discussed.

3.1 Info Gain

Information Gain (Pereira et.al., 2015) calculates the ability of a specific feature towards contributing to the reduction of uncertainty in predicting the target variable or the class label. The information gained by including a particular feature in the model is evaluated, and those features that contributes more information are considered more informative for prediction and is selected. On the other hand, those features that are less information are discarded from selection. Weka's Information Gain (Thanoon et. al., 2019) encompasses comparing the distribution of the target variable earlier and later containing a feature. If a particular feature makes the target variable's distribution clearer and more different, then that feature is chosen automatically. These features have a solid influence on the target variable and less important features were excluded. Nevertheless, Information Gain inclines to prefer features with more values (categorical features with numerous choices), which may rarely lead to influenced selections.

3.2 Info Gain Ratio

Information Gain Ratio (Mohammad, 2018; Chauhan & Gangopadhyay, 2022; Qu et.al., 2023) is an improvement over Information Gain, that addresses the bias of towards features with numerous values for categorical features, and to avoid overfitting. It separates the Information Gain by a measure of specialized or genuine information for a particular feature characterised as split information. Split information considers the count of branches a feature generates when the data is split based on that feature. By partitioning Information Gain by split information, Information Gain Ratio strives to make the selection process more sensible, principally while dealing with features having different numbers of values. Weka's Information Gain Ratio regulates feature selection by assessing the potential complexity each attribute presents with the intelligibility each attribute supplements to predictions. Essentially, it facilitates in the detection of attributes that are both beneficial and informative thereby boosting predictive models.

3.3 OneR

OneR method (Zia et.al., 2015) evaluates by focusing on the capacity of a single attribute to ensure that the selected attribute gives predictions, likely with the most clarity. In other words, it looks at data to find the single most important feature to assist in making predictions precisely. This is accomplished, by analysing which feature has the strongest association to the outcome to predict and thus provides a clear rule to follow in making predictions (Kathirvel et. al, 2022a). OneR Feature Selection from Weka presents feature selection more useful by extending a direct solution without losing accuracy by aiming on one distinctive characteristic. It treats all numerical features as continuous and separate the range of values into several disjoint intervals and manages missing values by treating “missing” as an acceptable value. The method creates easy rules based on individual feature alone. Though it is a minimum classifier, but it is beneficial for deciding a baseline performance as a standard for other learning methods. Nevertheless, its simplified nature limits not to acquire complex relationships in data and doesn't treat connections between features.

3.4 ReliefF

ReliefF (Spolaôr, 2013; Wu & Wang, 2015) is a filter-based method that rates features based on their capability to differentiate between instances of dissimilar classes. The idea is to value the significance of every feature by comparing its values for instances inside the same class and across various classes. For every feature in an instance, calculate the difference between feature value of that instance with the feature value of it nearest neighbour within that class (Selvaraj Naveneethan et. Al, 2022). The value calculated as such is subtracted from the difference between the feature of that instance with the nearest neighbour of another class. The absolute difference is picked up and is counted towards feature score. Scores of every feature is accumulated over all instances in a dataset and those that have high scores are significant for classification.

3.5 CfsSubsetEval

CFS (Kumar et.al., 2017; Samsuddin et.al., 2019; Qiao et.al., 2022) is a feature selection algorithm chooses a subdivision of related features considering the correlation between features and its connection to the target feature. The objective is to discover a subset of features that are highly interrelated with the target feature and at the same has low correlation in between the features. In machine learning, feature selection plays a essential role in reducing the quantity of input variables, which decreases computational costs and occasionally improves model performance. The CFS algorithm fit in to the category of filter-based feature selection, which chooses subsets of properties corresponding to how they associate to the target variable and is one of the numerous feature selection techniques that are available.

3.6 ClassifierAttributeEval

Weka's *ClassifierAttributeEval* (Rokad et.al., 2019; Álvarez et. al., 2019; Qiao et.al., 2022) class is used to measure the extent of knowledge discovered about the class, that an attribute belongs to determine, how significant an attribute is. It evaluates a single attribute by determining the outcome of eliminating from the entire set. To perform this, the classifier is initially trained using the complete set of characteristics, and it is then reoriented after a particular attribute is eliminated. The change in classification accuracy or other performance markers gives an indication of how essential the missing feature is. The rationale is a significant decrease in performance implies the attribute's importance in providing useful data to the representation.

3.7 CorrelationAttributeEval

The *CorrelationAttributeEval* (Sugianela and Ahmad, 2020; Sharma and Jain, 2020; Jaleel et.al., 2021) class offers a rapid and elementary approach to discover which attributes have a substantial correlation with the target class. The Pearson's correlation between an attribute and the class is measured using the *CorrelationAttributeEval* class to ascertain the attribute's value. Each nominal attribute is considered as a marker, value by value, as it finds qualities that are highly associated with the target class, and still uncorrelated with each other. Due to the probability of related characteristics providing duplicate information and no additional perception to the model, this twofold factor is important for reducing redundancy in feature representation.

4. DETAILS OF DATASETS USED

Table 1. Datasets Details

No	Dataset Name	Features Excluding Class Labels	Instances	Remarks
1	Chord Progressions	4	29	Numeric (4)
2	Zoo	17	101	Numeric (16), Text (1)
3	Spine	12	310	Numeric
4	NIDS	41	10000	Numeric

To substantiate the ability of the feature selection algorithm in identifying the most significant features in a dataset (https://www.kaggle.com/datasets) that could contribute to building models, it needs to be evaluated with various datasets. Four datasets were chosen to be tested with various algorithms, which consists of various datatypes and varying number of instances and the details were tabulated in Table 1. The number of features mentioned for each dataset excludes the class label. The details of the features available in every dataset were listed in the Table 2, Table 3, Table 4 and Table 5.

Table 2. Chord

NIDS	
1	**duration**
2	protocol_type
3	service
4	flag
5	src_bytes
6	dst_bytes
7	land
8	wrong_fragment

continued on following page

Table 2. Continued

NIDS	
1	**duration**
9	urgent
10	hot
11	num_failed_logins
12	logged_in
13	num_compromised
14	root_shell
15	su_attempted
16	num_root
17	num_file_creations
18	num_shells
19	num_access_files
20	num_outbound_cmds
21	is_host_login
22	is_guest_login
23	count
24	srv_count
25	serror_rate
26	srv_serror_rate
27	rerror_rate
28	srv_rerror_rate
29	same_srv_rate
30	diff_srv_rate
31	srv_diff_host_rate
32	dst_host_count
33	dst_host_srv_count
34	dst_host_same_srv_rate
35	dst_host_diff_srv_rate
36	dst_host_same_src_port_rate
37	dst_host_srv_diff_host_rate
38	dst_host_serror_rate
39	dst_host_srv_serror_rate
40	dst_host_rerror_rate
41	dst_host_srv_rerror_rate

Table 3. Spine

Spine	
1	**pelvic_incidence**
2	pelvic_tilt
3	lumbar_lordosis_angle
4	sacral_slope
5	pelvic_radius
6	degree_spondylolisthesis
7	pelvic_slope
8	direct_tilt
9	thoracic_slope
10	cervical_tilt
11	sacrum_angle
12	scoliosis_slope

Table 4. Zoo

Zoo	
1	**animal_name**
2	hair
3	feathers
4	eggs
5	milk
6	airborne
7	aquatic
8	predator
9	toothed
10	backbone
11	breathes
12	venomous
13	fins
14	legs
15	tail
16	domestic
17	catsize

Table 5. NIDS

Chord Progressions	
1	**1st chord**
2	2nd chord
3	3rd chord
4	4th chord

This enables to interpret the results of the feature selection methods faster and easier. **Table 6** presents the rules that has been taken into consideration, while choosing several datasets to evaluate the ability of the feature selection methods in manipulating various datatypes, features, and instances.

Table 6. Rules and Categories

Category	Rule
1	Less Features, Less Instances
2	Less Features, More Instances
3	More Features, Less Instances
4	More Features, More Instances

Based on the criteria set in **Table 6,** the chosen datasets have been categorised in **Table 7**. This gives a clear understanding of which dataset belongs to which category.

Table 7. Categorisation of Dataset as per the Rules.

Dataset Name	Features Excluding Class Labels	Instances	Category	Rule
Chord Progressions	4	29	1	Less Features, Less Instances
Zoo	17	101	3	More Features, Less Instances
Spine	12	310	2	Less Features, More Instances
NIDS	41	10000	4	More Features, More Instances

5. APPLICATION AND PERFORMANCE OF FEATURE SELECTION ALGORITHMS ON MULTIVARIATE DATASETS

To envision the nature of data contained in the instances of the dataset, a sample instance was tabulated (**Table 8**) excluding the class label, for each dataset used for evaluation.

Table 8. Sample Data

No	Name of the Dataset	Feature Name	Sample data	Remarks
1	Chord Progressions	1st chord, 2nd chord, 3rd chord, 4th chord	6, 4, 1, 5	Numeric (4)
2	Zoo	animal_name, hair, feathers, eggs, milk, airborne, aquatic, predator, toothed, backbone, breathes, venomous, fins, legs, tail, domestic, catsize	aardvark, 1, 0, 0, 1, 0, 0, 1, 1, 1, 1, 0, 0, 4, 0, 0, 1	Numeric (16), Text (1)
3	Spine	pelvic_incidence, pelvic_tilt, lumbar_lordosis_angle, sacral_slope, pelvic_radius, degree_spondylolisthesis, pelvic_slope, direct_tilt, thoracic_slope, cervical_tilt, sacrum_angle, scoliosis_slope	63.0278175, 22.55258597, 39.60911701, 40.47523153, 98.67291675, -0.254399986, 0.744503464, 12.5661, 14.5386, 15.30468, -28.658501, 43.5123	Numeric
4	NIDS	duration, protocol_type, service, flag, src_bytes, dst_bytes, land, wrong_fragment, urgent, hot, num_failed_logins, logged_in, num_compromised, root_shell, su_attempted, num_root, num_file_creations, num_shells, num_access_files, num_outbound_cmds, is_host_login, is_guest_login, count, srv_count, serror_rate, srv_serror_rate, rerror_rate, srv_rerror_rate, same_srv_rate, diff_srv_rate, srv_diff_host_rate, dst_host_count, dst_host_srv_count, dst_host_same_srv_rate, dst_host_diff_srv_rate, dst_host_same_src_port_rate, dst_host_srv_diff_host_rate, dst_host_serror_rate, dst_host_srv_serror_rate, dst_host_rerror_rate, dst_host_srv_rerror_rate	0,tcp,ftp_data,SF,491,0, 0,0,0,0,0,0,0,0,0,0,0,0,0,0,0,0,2,2,0, 0,0,0,1,0,0,150,25,0.17,0.03,0.17,0,0,0, 0.05,0	Numeric (38), Text (3)

Various datasets were tested with a set of feature selection algorithms and the results of the selected features were tabulated. The performance of the algorithms in selecting features for various datasets were discussed.

5.1 Evaluation of Feature Selection Algorithm with Class Labels

Supervised feature selection algorithms in Weka requires a class label for each of the data set to predict the significant features for that dataset. Therefore, the datasets were used with the class labels. All the four chosen feature selection algorithms were evaluated with all the four datasets. Basically, all the features in a particular dataset were given a score based on the ability of the feature to predict the class label. **Table 9** presents the number of the feature in order of the scores achieved from higher to lower.

Table 9. Selected Features: Feature Selection with Class Labels

Name of the Dataset	Selected Attributes			
	InfoGain	**InfoGain Ratio**	**OneR**	**ReliefFAttribute**
Chord Progressions	1,3,4,2: **4**	1,3,4,2: **4**	4,3,2,1: 4	1,2,3,4: 4
Zoo	1,14,5,9,4,2,3,10,11,15,6,13,7,17,8,12,16: 17	10,3,5,9,4,11,2,13,14,15,6,7,1,17,16,8,12: 17	14,3,5,4,9,2,6,11,10,13,7,17,15,1,8,16,12:17	5,4,9,2,3,10,11,15,6,13,17,7,14,8,12,1,16: 17
Spine	6,1,3,5,2,4,9,10,11,7,8,12: 12	6,1,3,2,4,5,9,10,11,7,8,12: 12	6,5,12,9,1,2,4,10,8,3,11,7: 12	6,1,5,2,3,10,4,8,11,9,12,7: 12
NIDS	5,3,6,30,4,29,33,34,35,12,38,39,25,23,26,37,36,32,31,24,41,2,40,27,28,1,10,8,13,16,19,22,15,14,7,11,20,9,18,17,21: 41	12,6,26,25,4,39,30,5,29,38,37,33,3,34,35,23,31,8,32,36,41,28,27,40,16,15,2,10,1,19,13,24,22,11,20,18,7,14,9,17,21: 41	5,3,6,4,29,30,34,33,35,12,23,25,38,39,26,36,32,37,24,31,41,40,27,28,2,8,10,13,1,14,11,19,20,22,18,17,7,15,9,16,21: 41	3,4,29,32,38,39,33,26,34,36,12,23,31,35,30,40,25,2,24,37,41,10,8,27,28,1,22,11,13,6,14,19,9,18,5,15,7,20,21,16,17: 41

For example, the order of the features for the dataset *Chord Progressions* with *InfoGain* are 1,3,4,2 which signifies, the feature 1 has the highest score and the feature 2 having the lowest score. The details of the scores achieved by each algorithm with every dataset is available in **Appendix 1**. *InfoGain* and *GainRatio* provided the same ranking with the dataset *Chord Progressions* and *Spine*, where both the dataset has numerical features for all the values in an instance. Therefore, it was concluded that, both algorithms have a similar evaluation strategy when dealing with numerical dataset, irrespective of the number of features and the number of instances. i.e., *Chord Progressions* has four features and 29 instances whereas *Spine* has 12 features and 310 instances. Alternatively, with datasets i.e., Zoo and NIDS, containing both numeric and non-numeric values for the features, *InfoGain* and *GainRatio* generated altogether a different ranking. This shows that, *InfoGain* and *GainRatio* treats numerical valued and non-numerical valued features contrarily.

As for *OneR* and *ReliefF* is concerned, in terms of feature ranking, there were no similarities between *OneR* and *ReliefF* for both numerical and non-numerical features. Both the algorithms exposed a dissimilar ranking order amongst each other and very distinct from the other two algorithms (*InfoGain* and *GainRatio*) that were tested.

5.2 Evaluation of Feature Selection Algorithms without Class Labels.

Unsupervised feature selection methods facilitate in discovering the most significant and useful features from a dataset without depending on a class labels. These methods focus on patterns and connections within the feature space, permitting to reduce dimensionality and exclude redundant or unrelated features. Four algorithms namely *CfsSubsetEval, ClassifierAttributeEval, CorrelationAttributeEval* and *ReliefFAttributeEval* were tested with the same four datasets used earlier, by just removing or excluding the last feature (class label) from the dataset. **Table 10** provides the features selected by these algorithms. The details of the scores achieved by each algorithm with every dataset is available in **Appendix 2.**

Table 10. Selected Features: Feature Selection without Class Labels

Name of the Dataset	Features Selected			
	CfsSubsetEval	ClassifierAttributeEval	CorrelationAttributeEval	ReliefFAttributeEval
Chord Progressions	1,2,3: 3	3,2,1: 3	3,1,2: 3	2,3,1: 3
Zoo	1,2,5,6,10,12: 6	6,15,6,5,4,3,2,7,8,9,13,14,12,10,11,1: 16	5,2,10,9,15,11,8,1,14,13,16,7,3,12,6,4: 16	6,5,4,3,10,15,1,9,13,11,14,12,16,8,2,7: 16
Spine	2,7: 2	11,3,2,5,4,6,10,9,8,7,1: 11	4,10,11,9,1,8,5,6,3,2,7: 11	2,3,9,1,10,7,4,6,8,11,5: 11
NIDS	2,27,28,30,40: 5	40,13,12,39,14,15,16,17,18,11,10,9,4,2,3,5,8,6,7,19,20,21,35,33,34,36,31,37,38,32,30,22,25,23,24,26,29,27,28,1: 40	28,27,40,4,35,30,1,2,23,3,32,36,37,11,5,21,20,7,13,16,9,17,15,18,6,14,19,10,22,8,31,24,29,25,38,39,26,33,34,12: 40	3,40,4,28,37,32,39,33,26,36,34,12,38,27,1,31,35,25,5,19,17,11,30,10,15,13,16,14,6,2,21,7,20,22,9,18,8,24,29,23: 40

WrapperSubsetEval is exceedingly time consuming in evaluating the datasets having more features and instances, hence not appropriate to handle larger datasets. As tabulated (Table 10), the algorithms *CfsSubsetEval, ClassifierAttributeEval, CorrelationAttributeEval* and *ReliefFAttributeEval* were tested with the chosen datasets. These algorithms took less than 5 seconds to select features irrespective of the size of the dataset which makes these algorithms more viable for real production environment.

6. SUMMARY

This chapter discusses the essentials of feature selection especially on the various selection methods and the various algorithms involving various methods. To evaluate the capability of various feature selection algorithms, several datasets of varying number of features and instances were tested. Criteria on choice of the datasets to

REFERENCES

Álvarez, J. D., Matias-Guiu, J. A., Cabrera-Martín, M. N., Risco-Martín, J. L., & Ayala, J. L. (2019). An application of machine learning with feature selection to improve diagnosis and classification of neurodegenerative disorders. *BMC Bioinformatics*, 20(1), 1–12. DOI: 10.1186/s12859-019-3027-7 PMID: 31601182

Ayyaswamy, K. (2024b). Enhancing Digital Technology Planning, Leadership, and Management to Transform Education. In Bhatia, M., & Mushtaq, M. T. (Eds.), *Navigating Innovative Technologies and Intelligent Systems in Modern Education* (pp. 1–9). IGI Global., DOI: 10.4018/979-8-3693-5370-7.ch001

Chauhan, S., & Gangopadhyay, S. (2022, June). Design of Intrusion Detection System Based on Logical Analysis of Data (LAD) Using Information Gain Ratio. In *International Symposium on Cyber Security, Cryptology, and Machine Learning* (pp. 47-65). Cham: Springer International Publishing. DOI: 10.1007/978-3-031-07689-3_4

Dy, J. G., & Brodley, C. E. (2004). Feature selection for unsupervised learning. *Journal of Machine Learning Research*, 5(Aug), 845–889.

El Aboudi, N., & Benhlima, L. (2016, September). Review on wrapper feature selection approaches. In 2016 International Conference on Engineering & MIS (ICEMIS) (pp. 1-5). IEEE. DOI: 10.1109/ICEMIS.2016.7745366

Fu, G. H., Wang, J. B., & Lin, W. (2023). An adaptive loss backward feature elimination method for class-imbalanced and mixed-type data in medical diagnosis. *Chemometrics and Intelligent Laboratory Systems*, 236, 104809. DOI: 10.1016/j.chemolab.2023.104809

Gobinath, V., Ayyaswamy, K., & Kathirvel, N. (2024). Information Communication Technology and Intelligent Manufacturing Industries Perspective: An Insight. *Asian Science Bulletin*, 2(1), 36–45. DOI: 10.3923/asb.2024.36.45

Gobinath, V. M., Kathirvel, A., Rajesh Kanna, S. K., & Annamalai, K. "Chapter 5: Smart Technology in Management Industries: A Useful Perspective", Artificial Intelligence Applied to Industry 4.0, Wiley Publiser, USA, 1st Edition, July 2024g, pp.93-106, , ISBN 978-1-394-21611-6, DOI eBook ISBN, https://www.wiley.com/en-us/Topics+in+Artificial+Intelligence+Applied+to+Industry+4+0-p-9781394216116DOI: 10.1002/9781394216147.ch5

Gutlein, M., Frank, E., Hall, M., & Karwath, A. (2009). *Large-scale attribute selection using wrappers. In 2009 IEEE symposium on computational intelligence and data mining*. IEEE.

. Hajamydeen, A. I., & Helmi, R. A. A. (2020). Performance of Supervised Learning Algorithms on Multi-Variate Datasets. *Machine Learning and Big Data: Concepts, Algorithms, Tools and Applications*, 209-232.

Hajamydeen, A. I., & Udzir, N. I. (2016). A refined filter for UHAD to improve anomaly detection. *Security and Communication Networks*, 9(14), 2434–2447. DOI: 10.1002/sec.1514

Hajamydeen, A. I., & Udzir, N. I. (2019). A detailed description on unsupervised heterogeneous anomaly based intrusion detection framework. *Scalable Computing: Practice and Experience*, 20(1), 113–160. DOI: 10.12694/scpe.v20i1.1465

Huang, S. H. (2015). Supervised feature selection: A tutorial. *Artificial Intelligence Research*, 4(2), 22–37. DOI: 10.5430/air.v4n2p22

Jaleel, R. A., Burhan, I. M., & Jalookh, A. M. (2021). A proposed model for prediction of COVID-19 depend on k-nearest neighbors classifier: iraq case study. In *2021 International Conference on Electrical, Communication, and Computer Engineering (ICECCE)* (pp. 1-6). IEEE.

Kathirvel, A. (2024a). Applications of Serverless Computing: Systematic Overview. In Aluvalu, R., & Maheswari, U. (Eds.), *Serverless Computing Concepts, Technology and Architecture* (Vol. 221-233). IGI Global., DOI: 10.4018/979-8-3693-1682-5.ch014

Kathirvel, A. (2024c). Innovation and Industry Application: IoT-Based Robotics Frontier of Automation in Industry Application. In Satishkumar, D., & Sivaraja, M. (Eds.), *Internet of Things and AI for Natural Disaster Management and Prediction* (pp. 83–105). IGI Global., DOI: 10.4018/979-8-3693-4284-8.ch004

Kathirvel, A., & Gobinath, V. M. (2024f) "Chapter 1: A Review on Additive Manufactuing in Industrial", Modern Hybird Machince and Super Finishing Process: Technology and Application, CRC Publiser/Chapman and Hall, New York, 1st Edition, ISBN 1032354291, DOI eBook ISBN 9781032354293, https://books.google.co.in/books/about/Modern_Hybrid_Machining_and_Super_Finish.html?id=I_VW0AEACAAJ&source=kp_book_description&redir_esc=y

Kathirvel, A., Gopinath, V. M., Naren, K., Nithyanand, D., & Nirmaladevi, K. (2024i). Manufacturing Smart Industry Perspective an Overview. *American Journal of Engineering and Applied Sciences*, 17(1), 33–39. DOI: 10.3844/ajeassp.2024.33.39

Kathirvel, A., & Maheswaran, C. P. (2023a), "Chapter 8: Enhanced AI-Based Intrusion Detection and Response System for WSN", Artificial Intelligence for Intrusion Detection Systems, CRC Publiser/Chapman and Hall, New York, 1st Edition, ISBN 978-100096755-5, 978-103238665-2 DOI eBook ISBN 9781003346340, https://www.taylorfrancis.com/chapters/edit/10.1201/9781003346340-8/enhanced-ai-based-intrusion-detection-response-system-wsn-kathirvel-maheswaranDOI: 10.1201/9781003346340-8

. Kathirvel A, Maheswaran C P, Subramaniam M, and Naren A K, (March 2023b). "Chapter 25: Quantum Computers Based on Distributed Computing Systems for the Next Generation: Overview and Applications", Quantum Computers Based on Distributed Computing Systems for the Next Generation, Handbook of Research on Quantum Computing for Smart Environments, IGI Global Publiser, Hershey, Pennsylvania, USA, ISBN13: 9781668466971 ISBN10: 166846697X EISBN13: 9781668466988, DOI: Quantum Computers Based on Distributed Computing Systems for the Next Generation: Overview and Applications: Computer Science & IT Book Chapter | IGI Global (igi-global.com)DOI: 10.4018/978-1-6684-6697-1.ch025

Kathirvel, A., & Naren, A. K. (2024). Critical Approaches to Data Engineering Systems Innovation and Industry Application Using IoT. In *Critical Approaches to Data Engineering Systems and Analysis*. IGI Global. DOI: 10.4018/979-8-3693-2260-4.ch005

Kathirvel, A., & Naren, A. K. (2024d). Diabetes and Pre-Diabetes Prediction by AI Using Tuned XGB Classifier. In Khang, A. (Ed.), *Medical Robotics and AI-Assisted Diagnostics for a High-Tech Healthcare Industry* (pp. 52–64). IGI Global., DOI: 10.4018/979-8-3693-2105-8.ch004

Kathirvel, A., Naren, K., Nithyanand, D., & Santhoshi, B. (2024h). Overview of 5G Technology: Streamlined Virtual Event Experiences. *Advances of Robotic Technology*, 2(1), 1–8. DOI: 10.23880/art-16000109

Kathirvel, A., Rithik, G., & Naren, A. K. "Chapter 11: Automation of IOT Robotics." In *Predicting Natural Disasters With AI and Machine Learning,* edited by D. Satishkumar and M. Sivaraja, 224-249. ISBN 9798369322802, eBook ISBN 9798369322819, Hershey, PA: IGI Global, 2024e. https://doi.org/DOI: 10.4018/979-8-3693-2280-2.ch011

Kathirvel, A., Subramaniam, M., Navaneethan, S., & Sabarinath, C. (2021a). "Improved IDR Response System for Sensor Network", Journal of Web Engineering, Vol. 20 1, 53–88, Publisher: © River Publishers, 15 Feb 2021, ISSN: 1540-9589 (Print Version). ISSN: 1544-5976 (Online Version), https://doi.org/DOI: 10.13052/jwe1540-9589.2013

Kathirvel, A., Sudha, D., Naveneethan, S., Subramaniam, M., Das, D., & Kirubakaran, S. (2022a). AI Based Mobile Bill Payment System using Biometric Fingerprint. *American Journal of Engineering and Applied Sciences*, 15(1), 23–31. DOI: 10.3844/ajeassp.2022.23.31

Kotsiantis, S. (2011). Feature selection for machine learning classification problems: A recent overview. *Artificial Intelligence Review*, 42(1), 157–176. DOI: 10.1007/s10462-011-9230-1

Kumar, C. A., Sooraj, M. P., & Ramakrishnan, S. (2017). A comparative performance evaluation of supervised feature selection algorithms on microarray datasets. *Procedia Computer Science*, 115, 209–217. DOI: 10.1016/j.procs.2017.09.127

Kumar, V., & Minz, S. (2014). Feature selection: A literature review. *SmartCR*, 4(3), 211–229. DOI: 10.6029/smartcr.2014.03.007

Li, J., Cheng, K., Wang, S., Morstatter, F., Trevino, R. P., Tang, J., & Liu, H. (2017). Feature selection: A data perspective. *ACM Computing Surveys*, 50(6), 1–45. DOI: 10.1145/3136625

Liu, Z., Yang, J., Wang, L., & Chang, Y. (2023). A novel relation aware wrapper method for feature selection. *Pattern Recognition*, 140, 109566. DOI: 10.1016/j.patcog.2023.109566

Mohammad, A. H. (2018). Comparing Two Feature Selections Methods (Information Gain And Gain Ratio) On Three Different Classification Algorithms Using Arabic Dataset. *Journal of Theoretical and Applied Information Technology*, 96(6).

Molina, L. C., Belanche, L., & Nebot, À. (2002). Feature selection algorithms: A survey and experimental evaluation. In *2002 IEEE International Conference on Data Mining, 2002. Proceedings.* (pp. 306-313). IEEE. DOI: 10.1109/ICDM.2002.1183917

Naveneethan, S. Madhan E.S., Kathirvel A. (2022) Identifying and Eliminating the Misbehavior Nodes in the Wireless Sensor Network. In: Reddy V.S., Prasad V.K., Wang J., Reddy K. (eds) Soft Computing and Signal Processing. ICSCSP 2021. Advances in Intelligent Systems and Computing, vol 1413. Springer International Publishing, Springer, Singapore. https://doi.org/DOI: 10.1007/978-981-16-7088-6_36

. Nguyen, H. B., Xue, B., Liu, I., & Zhang, M. (2014, July). Filter based backward elimination in wrapper based PSO for feature selection in classification. In 2014 IEEE congress on evolutionary computation (CEC) (pp. 3111-3118). IEEE.

Oh, S. (2022). Predictive case-based feature importance and interaction. *Information Sciences*, 593, 155–176. DOI: 10.1016/j.ins.2022.02.003

. Pereira, R. B., Carvalho, A. P. D., Zadrozny, B., & Merschmann, L. H. D. C. (2015). Information gain feature selection for multi-label classification.

Pudjihartono, N., Fadason, T., Kempa-Liehr, A. W., & O'Sullivan, J. M. (2022). A review of feature selection methods for machine learning-based disease risk prediction. *Frontiers in Bioinformatics*, 2, 927312. DOI: 10.3389/fbinf.2022.927312 PMID: 36304293

Qiao, Q., Yunusa-Kaltungo, A., & Edwards, R. E. (2022). Feature selection strategy for machine learning methods in building energy consumption prediction. *Energy Reports*, 8, 13621–13654. DOI: 10.1016/j.egyr.2022.10.125

Qu, K., Xu, J., Hou, Q., Qu, K., & Sun, Y. (2023). Feature selection using Information Gain and decision information in neighborhood decision system. *Applied Soft Computing*, 136, 110100. DOI: 10.1016/j.asoc.2023.110100

Rajab, M., & Wang, D. (2020). Practical challenges and recommendations of filter methods for feature selection. *Journal of Information & Knowledge Management*, 19(01), 2040019. DOI: 10.1142/S0219649220400195

Rokad, B., Karumudi, T., Acharya, O., & Jagtap, A. (2019). Survival of the Fittest in PlayerUnknown BattleGround. *arXiv preprint arXiv:1905.06052*.

Saarela, M., & Jauhiainen, S. (2021). Comparison of feature importance measures as explanations for classification models. *SN Applied Sciences*, 3(2), 1–12. DOI: 10.1007/s42452-021-04148-9

Salcedo-Sanz, S., Cornejo-Bueno, L., Prieto, L., Paredes, D., & García-Herrera, R. (2018). Feature selection in machine learning prediction systems for renewable energy applications. *Renewable & Sustainable Energy Reviews*, 90, 728–741. DOI: 10.1016/j.rser.2018.04.008

Samsuddin, S., Shah, Z. A., Saedudin, R. R., Kasim, S., & Seah, C. S. (2019). Analysis of attribute selection and classification algorithm applied to hepatitis patients. *International Journal on Advanced Science, Engineering and Information Technology*, 9(3), 967–971. DOI: 10.18517/ijaseit.9.3.5041

Sánchez-Maroño, N., Alonso-Betanzos, A., & Tombilla-Sanromán, M. (2007). Filter methods for feature selection–a comparative study. In *International Conference on Intelligent Data Engineering and Automated Learning* (pp. 178-187). Berlin, Heidelberg: Springer Berlin Heidelberg. DOI: 10.1007/978-3-540-77226-2_19

. Sharma, S., & Jain, A. (2020). An empirical evaluation of correlation based feature selection for tweet sentiment classification. *Advances in Cybernetics, Cognition, and Machine Learning for Communication Technologies*, 199-208.

Smialowski, P., Frishman, D., & Kramer, S. (2010). Pitfalls of supervised feature selection. *Bioinformatics (Oxford, England)*, 26(3), 440–443. DOI: 10.1093/bioinformatics/btp621 PMID: 19880370

Solorio-Fernández, S., Carrasco-Ochoa, J. A., & Martínez-Trinidad, J. F. (2020). A review of unsupervised feature selection methods. *Artificial Intelligence Review*, 53(2), 907–948. DOI: 10.1007/s10462-019-09682-y

Spolaôr, N., Cherman, E. A., Monard, M. C., & Lee, H. D. (2013). ReliefF for multi-label feature selection. In *2013 Brazilian Conference on Intelligent Systems* (pp. 6-11). IEEE. DOI: 10.1109/BRACIS.2013.10

Subramaniam, M., Kathirvel, A., Sabitha, E., & Anwar Basha, H. "Modified Firefly Algorithm and Fuzzy C-Mean Clustering Based Semantic Information Retrieval", Journal of Web Engineering, Vol. 20 1, 33–52, 2021b. Publisher: © River Publishers, 15 Feb 2021, ISSN: 1540-9589 (Print Version). ISSN: 1544-5976 (Online Version), https://doi.org/DOI: 10.13052/jwe1540-9589.2012

Sudha, D., & Kathirvel, A. An Intrusion Detection System to Detect and Mitigating Attacks Using Hidden Markov Model (HMM) Energy Monitoring Technique. Stochastic Modeling an Applications, 26(3) (January – June, Special Issue 2022 Part – 9), 467-476, 2022a. ISSN: 0972-3641.

Sudha, D., & Kathirvel, A. The performance enhancement of Aodv protocol using GETUS. International Journal of Early Childhood Special Education (INT-JECSE), Vol. 15, Issue 2, 2023a. Pp. 115-125. ISSN: 1308-5581. DOI:DOI: 10.48047/INTJECSE/V15I2.11

Sudha, D., & Kathirvel, A. The effect of ETUS in various generic attacks in mobile ad hoc networks to improve the performance of Aodv protocol. International Journal of humanities, law, and social sciences, Kanpur philosophers, Vol. 9 Issue 1, 2023b, N0.1, 467-476, 2022. ISSN: 2348-8301.

Sugianela, Y., & Ahmad, T. (2020, February). Pearson correlation attribute evaluation-based feature selection for intrusion detection system. In *2020 International Conference on Smart Technology and Applications (ICoSTA)* (pp. 1-5). IEEE. DOI: 10.1109/ICoSTA48221.2020.1570613717

Wah, Y. B., Ibrahim, N., Hamid, H. A., Abdul-Rahman, S., & Fong, S. (2018). Feature selection methods: Case of filter and wrapper approaches for maximising classification accuracy. *Pertanika Journal of Science & Technology*, 26(1).

Wu, M., & Wang, Y. (2015). A feature selection algorithm of music genre classification based on ReliefF and SFS. In *2015 IEEE/ACIS 14th International Conference on Computer and Information Science (ICIS)* (pp. 539-544). IEEE. DOI: 10.1109/ICIS.2015.7166651

Zia, T., Akhter, M. P., & Abbas, Q. (2015). Comparative study of feature selection approaches for Urdu text categorization. *Malaysian Journal of Computer Science*, 28(2), 93–109.

KEY TERMS AND DEFINITIONS

Scalability: scalability refers to the capacity of a system to maintain or improve its performance under increasing operational demands.

Security: In order to ensure confidentiality, integrity, and availability, security refers to the use of procedures and policies to protect systems, data, and information against damage, interruption, or unauthorised access. It is an all-encompassing strategy to guard against possible dangers and weaknesses across a range of sectors.

Ethereum: With smart contract features, Ethereum is a decentralisedblockchain. The platform's native coin is called ether. Bitcoin has a larger market capitalization than ether among cryptocurrencies. Open-source software is what it is. 2013. Programmer VitalikButerin came up with the idea for Ethereum.

Sharding: A single dataset can be sharded and distributed among several databases, allowing it to be kept on several servers.

Blockchain: A blockchain is a public ledger that is digitally distributed and decentralised via a network.

Consensus: The fundamental goal of the consensus algorithm, which is to come to a consensus and guarantee the network's dependability, can be created with a variety of features. a mechanism that certifies a transaction as genuine.

Leadger: A distributed ledger that uses blocks of data connected in a chain using encryption, making it difficult to change.

APPENDIX 1

Table 11

Name of the Dataset	InfoGain	InfoGain Ratio	OneR	ReliefF Attribute
Chord Progressions	Ranked attributes: 1.514 1 1st chord 0.869 3 3rd chord 0 4 4th chord 0 2 2nd chord Selected attributes: 1,3,4,2: 4	Ranked attributes: 1 1 1st chord 0.924 3 3rd chord 0 4 4th chord 0 2 2nd chord Selected attributes: 1,3,4,2: 4	Ranked attributes: 0 4 4th chord 0 3 3rd chord 0 2 2nd chord 0 1 1st chord Selected attributes: 4,3,2,1: 4	Ranked attributes: 0.328 1 1st chord 0.302 2 2nd chord 0.202 3 3rd chord 0.165 4 4th chord Selected attributes: 1,2,3,4: 4
Zoo	Ranked attributes: 2.391 1 animal_name 1.311 14 legs 0.974 5 milk 0.866 9 toothed 0.83 4 eggs 0.791 2 hair 0.718 3 feathers 0.676 10 backbone 0.614 11 breathes 0.5 15 tail 0.47 6 airborne 0.467 13 fins 0.389 7 aquatic 0.308 17 catsize 0 8 predator 0 12 venomous 0 16 domestic Selected attributes: 1,14,5,9 ,4,2,3,10,11,15,6,13,7,17,8 ,12,16: 17	Ranked attributes: 1.000000000000001 10 backbone 1 3 feathers 1 5 milk 0.8937704169438974 9 toothed 0.8475416839425929 4 eggs 0.8332240281860931 11 breathes 0.8035061888568452 2 hair 0.7136511261800152 13 fins 0.6876433108844757 14 legs 0.6082134356057161 15 tail 0.5937588425125653 6 airborne 0.4144874290882562 7 aquatic 0.360110306749591 1 animal_name 0.3122320668253054 17 catsize 0 16 domestic 0 8 predator 0 12 venomous Selected attributes: 10,3,5,9 ,4,11,2,13,14,15,6,7,1,17,1 6,8,12: 17	Ranked attributes: 73.267 14 legs 60.396 3 feathers 60.396 5 milk 59.406 4 eggs 59.406 9 toothed 58.416 2 hair 54.455 6 airborne 53.465 11 breathes 50.495 10 backbone 49.505 13 fins 47.525 7 aquatic 45.545 17 catsize 43.564 15 tail 42.574 1 animal_name 40.594 8 predator 40.594 16 domestic 40.594 12 venomous Selected attributes: 14,3,5,4 ,9,2,6,11,10,13,7,17,15,1,8 ,16,12: 17	Ranked attributes: 0.68355 5 milk 0.60931 4 eggs 0.59256 9 toothed 0.57493 2 hair 0.41986 3 feathers 0.36974 10 backbone 0.35019 11 breathes 0.31386 15 tail 0.28171 6 airborne 0.27653 13 fins 0.25026 17 catsize 0.24831 7 aquatic 0.22401 14 legs 0.07196 8 predator 0.0319 12 venomous 0.0066 1 animal_name -0.00218 16 domestic Selected attributes: 5,4,9,2, 3,10,11,15,6,13,17,7,14,8,1 2,1,16: 17

Table 12

Name of the Dataset	InfoGain	InfoGain Ratio	OneR	ReliefF Attribute
Spine	Ranked attributes: 0.3394 6 degree_ spondylolisthesis 0.1222 1 pelvic_ incidence 0.1044 3 lumbar_ lordosis_angle 0.0933 5 pelvic_radius 0.0758 2 pelvic_tilt 0.716 sacral_slope 0 9 thoracic_slope 0 10 cervical_tilt 0 11 sacrum_angle 0 7 pelvic_slope 0 8 direct_tilt 0 12 scoliosis_ slopeSelected attributes: 6,1,3,5,2,4,9,10,11,7,8,12: 12	Ranked attributes: 0.3405 6 degree_ spondylolisthesis 0.1363 1 pelvic_ incidence 0.1138 3 lumbar_ lordosis_angle 0.1015 2 pelvic_tilt 0.0936 4 sacral_slope 0.0935 5 pelvic_radius 0 9 thoracic_slope 0 10 cervical_tilt 0 11 sacrum_angle 0 7 pelvic_slope 0 8 direct_tilt 0 12 scoliosis_slope Selected attributes: 6,1,3,2,4,5,9,10,11,7,8,12: 12	Ranked attributes:73.871 6 degree_spondylolisthesis70 5 pelvic_radius65.1613 12 scoliosis_slope64.5161 9 thoracic_slope63.5484 1 pelvic_incidence63.2258 2 pelvic_tilt62.5806 4 sacral_slope60.6452 10 cervical_tilt60.6452 8 direct_tilt60.3226 3 lumbar_lordosis_angle60.3226 11 sacrum_angle58.0645 7 pelvic_slopeSelected attributes: 6,5,12,9,1,2,4,10,8,3,11,7: 12	Ranked attributes: 0.03227 6 degree_ spondylolisthesis 0.02446 1 pelvic_incidence 0.02361 5 pelvic_radius 0.02087 2 pelvic_ tilt 0.02013 3 lumbar_lordosis_ angle 0.01104 10 cervical_tilt 0.01086 4 sacral_slope 0.00839 8 direct_tilt 0.00617 11 sacrum_angle 0.00485 9 thoracic_slope 0.00417 12 scoliosis_slope 0.00142 7 pelvic_slopeSelected attributes: 6,1,5,2,3,10,4,8,11,9,12,7: 12

Table 13

Name of the Dataset	InfoGain	InfoGain Ratio	OneR	ReliefF Attribute
NIDS	Ranked attributes: 0.799504 5 src_bytes 0.680859 3 service 0.630331 6 dst_bytes 0.523111 30 diff_srv_rate 0.520748 4 flag 0.506251 29 same_srv_rate 0.463738 33 dst_host_srv_count 0.437121 34 dst_host_same_srv_rate 0.411122 35 dst_host_diff_srv_rate 0.408868 12 logged_in 0.405893 38 dst_host_serror_rate 0.401416 39 dst_host_srv_serror_rate 0.390922 25 serror_rate 0.386138 23 count 0.37819 26 srv_serror_rate 0.268861 37 dst_host_srv_diff_host_rate 0.193854 36 dst_host_same_src_port_rate 0.193148 32 dst_host_count 0.146976 31 srv_diff_host_rate 0.087967 24 srv_count 0.08547 41 dst_host_srv_rerror_rate 0.062902 2 protocol_type 0.047804 40 dst_host_rerror_rate 0.0477 27 rerror_rate 0.046853 28 srv_rerror_rate 0.029177 1 duration 0.011305 10 hot 0.010729 8 wrong_fragment 0.005196 13 num_compromised 0.004385 16 num_root 0.001897 19 num_access_files 0.000892 22 is_guest_login 0.000735 15 su_attempted 0 14 root_shell 0 7 land 0 11 num_failed_logins 0 20 num_outbound_cmds 0 9 urgent 0 18 num_shells 0 17 num_file_creations 0 21 is_host_login Selected attributes: 5,3,6,30,4,29,33,34,35,12,38,39,25,23,26,37,36,32,31,24,41,2,40,27,28,1,10,8,13,16,19,22,15,14,7,11,20,9,18,17,21: 41	Ranked attributes: 0.4233 12 logged_in 0.3914 6 dst_bytes 0.3792 26 srv_serror_rate 0.3568 25 serror_rate 0.3392 4 flag 0.3363 39 dst_host_srv_serror_rate 0.3361 30 diff_srv_rate 0.3272 5 src_bytes 0.3145 29 same_srv_rate 0.2844 38 dst_host_serror_rate 0.1792 37 dst_host_srv_diff_host_rate 0.1762 33 dst_host_srv_count 0.1745 3 service 0.159 34 dst_host_same_srv_rate 0.1463 35 dst_host_diff_srv_rate 0.1375 23 count 0.1364 31 srv_diff_host_rate 0.135 8 wrong_fragment 0.1184 32 dst_host_count 0.1105 36 dst_host_same_src_port_rate 0.1077 41 dst_host_srv_rerror_rate 0.09 28 srv_rerror_rate 0.0869 27 rerror_rate 0.0835 40 dst_host_rerror_rate 0.0817 16 num_root 0.0783 15 su_attempted 0.073 2 protocol_type 0.0722 10 hot 0.0658 1 duration 0.0609 19 num_access_files 0.0551 13 num_compromised 0.0309 24 srv_count 0.0115 22 is_guest_login 0 11 num_failed_logins 0 20 num_outbound_cmds 0 18 num_shells 0 7 land 0 14 root_shell 0 9 urgent 0 17 num_file_creations 0 21 is_host_login Selected attributes: 12,6,26,25,4,39,30,5,29,38,37,33,3,34,35,23,31,8,32,36,41,28,27,40,16,15,2,10,1,19,13,24,22,11,20,18,7,14,9,17,21: 41	Ranked attributes: 96.19 5 src_bytes 91.53 3 service 91.09 6 dst_bytes 88.05 4 flag 87.24 29 same_srv_rate 87.14 30 diff_srv_rate 85.22 34 dst_host_same_srv_rate 84.15 33 dst_host_srv_count 83.57 35 dst_host_diff_srv_rate 83.16 12 logged_in 82.77 23 count 81.69 25 serror_rate 81.53 38 dst_host_serror_rate 80.79 39 dst_host_srv_serror_rate 80.69 26 srv_serror_rate 72.68 36 dst_host_same_src_port_rate 72.47 32 dst_host_count 72.16 37 dst_host_srv_diff_host_rate 63.35 24 srv_count 63.12 31 srv_diff_host_rate 61.51 41 dst_host_srv_rerror_rate 60.74 40 dst_host_rerror_rate 60.49 27 rerror_rate 60.33 28 srv_rerror_rate 57.49 2 protocol_type 53.9 8 wrong_fragment 53.74 10 hot 53.45 13 num_compromised 53.36 1 duration 52.92 14 root_shell 52.92 11 num_failed_logins 52.92 19 num_access_files 52.92 20 num_outbound_cmds 52.92 22 is_guest_login 52.92 18 num_shells 52.92 17 num_file_creations 52.92 7 land 52.92 15 su_attempted 52.92 9 urgent 52.92 16 num_root 52.92 21 is_host_login Selected attributes: 5,3,6,4,29,30,34,33,35,12,23,25,38,39,26,36,32,37,24,31,41,40,27,28,2,8,10,13,1,14,11,19,20,22,18,17,7,15,9,16,21: 41	Ranked attributes: 0.52712 3 service 0.24188 4 flag 0.2277068 29 same_srv_rate 0.22040337 32 dst_host_count 0.1822717 38 dst_host_serror_rate 0.1577717 39 dst_host_srv_serror_rate 0.13871451 33 dst_host_srv_count 0.1361603 26 srv_serror_rate 0.1182087 34 dst_host_same_srv_rate 0.1151233 36 dst_host_same_src_port_rate 0.11478 12 logged_in 0.10926394 23 count 0.0691059 31 srv_diff_host_rate 0.0669537 35 dst_host_diff_srv_rate 0.0537703 30 diff_srv_rate 0.0507087 40 dst_host_rerror_rate 0.0466386 25 serror_rate 0.03867 2 protocol_type 0.02855802 24 srv_count 0.01891 37 dst_host_srv_diff_host_rate 0.0168571 41 dst_host_srv_rerror_rate 0.01109805 10 hot 0.01019667 8 wrong_fragment 0.0074104 27 rerror_rate 0.0068358 28 srv_rerror_rate 0.00653293 1 duration 0.00645 22 is_guest_login 0.002035 11 num_failed_logins 0.00116682 13 num_compromised 0.00061377 6 dst_bytes 0.00043 14 root_shell 0.00027667 19 num_access_files 0.00026 9 urgent 0.00014 18 num_shells 0.00012542 5 src_bytes 0.000025 15 su_attempted 0 7 land 0 20 num_outbound_cmds 0 21 is_host_login -0.00000979 16 num_root -0.00002207 17 num_file_creations Selected attributes: 3,4,29,32,38,39,33,26,34,36,12,23,31,35,30,40,25,2,24,37,41,10,8,27,28,1,22,11,13,6,14,19,9,18,5,15,7,20,21,16,17: 41

APPENDIX 2

Table 14

Name of the Dataset	CfsSubsetEval	ClassifierAttributeEval	CorrelationAttributeEval	ReliefFAttributeEval
Chord Progressions	1st chord 2nd chord 3rd chord Selected attributes: 1,2,3: 3	0 3 3rd chord 0 2 2nd chord 0 1 1st chord Selected attributes: 3,2,1: 3	0.206 3 3rd chord -0.107 1 1st chord -0.122 2 2nd chord Selected attributes: 3,1,2: 3	0.0335 2 2nd chord 0.0185 3 3rd chord 0.0145 1 1st chord Selected attributes: 2,3,1: 3
Zoo	animal_name hair milk airborne backbone venomous Selected attributes: 1,2,5,6,10,12: 6	0 16 domestic 0 15 tail 0 6 airborne 0 5 milk 0 4 eggs 0 3 feathers 0 2 hair 0 7 aquatic 0 8 predator 0 9 toothed 0 13 fins 0 14 legs 0 12 venomous 0 10 backbone 0 11 breathes 0 1 animal_name Selected attributes: 16,15,6,5,4, 3,2,7,8,9,13,14,12,10,11,1: 16	0.5749 5 milk 0.455 2 hair 0.357 10 backbone 0.344 9 toothed 0.2433 15 tail 0.2041 11 breathes 0.1448 8 predator 0.0999 1 animal_name 0.0688 14 legs 0.0317 13 fins 0.0201 16 domestic -0.1119 7 aquatic -0.1359 3 feathers -0.1837 12 venomous -0.3498 6 airborne -0.5147 4 eggs Selected attributes: 5,2,10,9,15, 11,8,1,14,13,16,7,3,12,6,4: 16	0.04186 6 airborne 0.03745 5 milk 0.02882 4 eggs 0.02113 3 feathers 0.01612 10 backbone 0.00929 15 tail 0.00301 1 animal_name 0.00118 9 toothed -0.01327 13 fins -0.02617 11 breathes -0.03712 14 legs -0.03732 12 venomous -0.04269 16 domestic -0.04313 8 predator -0.05507 2 hair -0.06438 7 aquatic Selected attributes: 6,5,4,3,10,1 5,1,9,13,11,14,12,16,8,2,7: 16

Table 15

Name of the Dataset	CfsSubsetEval	ClassifierAttributeEval	CorrelationAttributeEval	ReliefFAttributeEval
Spine	pelvic_tilt pelvic_slope Selected attributes: 2,7: 2	0 11 sacrum_angle 0 3 lumbar_lordosis_angle 0 2 pelvic_tilt 0 5 pelvic_radius 0 4 sacral_slope 0 6 degree_ spondylolisthesis 0 10 cervical_tilt 0 9 thoracic_slope 0 8 direct_tilt 0 7 pelvic_slope 0 1 pelvic_incidence Selected attributes: 11,3,2,5,4,6,10,9,8,7,1: 11	0.03285 4 sacral_slope 0.02124 10 cervical_tilt 0.01534 11 sacrum_angle 0.00954 9 thoracic_slope -0.00725 1 pelvic_incidence -0.02402 8 direct_tilt -0.03014 5 pelvic_radius -0.04102 6 degree_ spondylolisthesis -0.04905 3 lumbar_ lordosis_angle -0.05655 2 pelvic_tilt -0.07389 7 pelvic_slope Selected attributes: 4,10,11,9,1,8,5,6,3,2,7: 11	0.0036665 2 pelvic_tilt 0.0035729 3 lumbar_ lordosis_angle 0.0019125 9 thoracic_slope 0.0012583 1 pelvic_ incidence 0.0009948 10 cervical_tilt 0.000549 7 pelvic_slope -0.0000498 4 sacral_slope -0.0009218 6 degree_ spondylolisthesis -0.0014791 8 direct_tilt -0.0019185 11 sacrum_ angle -0.0032223 5 pelvic_radius Selected attributes: 2,3,9,1,10,7,4,6,8,11,5: 11

Table 16

Dataset	CfsSubsetEval	ClassifierAttributeEval	CorrelationAttributeEval	ReliefFAttributeEval
NIDS	protocol_type rerror_rate srv_rerror_rate diff_srv_rate dst_host_rerror_ rate Selected attributes: 2,27,28,30,40: 5	0 40 dst_host_rerror_rate 0 13 num_compromised 0 12 logged_in 0 39 dst_host_srv_serror_rate 0 14 root_shell 0 15 su_attempted 0 16 num_root 0 17 num_file_creations 0 18 num_shells 0 11 num_failed_logins 0 10 hot 0 9 urgent 0 4 flag 0 2 protocol_type 0 3 service 0 5 src_bytes 0 8 wrong_fragment 0 6 dst_bytes 0 7 land 0 19 num_access_files 0 20 num_outbound_cmds 0 21 is_host_login 0 35 dst_host_diff_srv_rate 0 33 dst_host_srv_count 0 34 dst_host_same_srv_rate 0 36 dst_host_same_src_port_rate 0 31 srv_diff_host_rate 0 37 dst_host_srv_diff_host_rate 0 38 dst_host_serror_rate 0 32 dst_host_count 0 30 diff_srv_rate 0 22 is_guest_login 0 25 serror_rate 0 23 count 0 24 srv_count 0 26 srv_serror_rate 0 29 same_srv_rate 0 27 rerror_rate 0 28 srv_rerror_rate 0 1 duration Selected attributes: 40,13,12,39,14, 15,16,17,18,11,10,9,4,2,3,5,8,6,7,1 9,20,21,35,33,34,36,31,37,38,32,3 0,22,25,23,24,26,29,27,28,1: 40	0.97503 28 srv_rerror_rate 0.97102 27 rerror_rate 0.92567 40 dst_host_rerror_rate 0.40039 4 flag 0.37899 35 dst_host_diff_srv_rate 0.27628 30 diff_srv_rate 0.20401 1 duration 0.16772 2 protocol_type 0.15711 23 count 0.095 3 service 0.07375 32 dst_host_count 0.0364 36 dst_host_same_src_ port_rate 0.02777 37 dst_host_srv_diff_ host_rate 0.0134 11 num_failed_logins 0.01109 5 src_bytes 0 21 is_host_login 0 20 num_outbound_cmds 0 7 land -0.00225 13 num_compromised -0.00293 16 num_root -0.00374 9 urgent -0.00436 17 num_file_creations -0.00577 15 su_attempted -0.00916 18 num_shells -0.01336 6 dst_bytes -0.01359 14 root_shell -0.01535 19 num_access_files -0.02907 10 hot -0.03156 22 is_guest_login -0.03608 8 wrong_fragment -0.08042 31 srv_diff_host_rate -0.1125 24 srv_count -0.20867 29 same_srv_rate -0.22925 25 serror_rate -0.23024 38 dst_host_serror_rate -0.23487 39 dst_host_srv_serror_ rate -0.23554 26 srv_serror_rate -0.25039 33 dst_host_srv_count -0.25668 34 dst_host_same_ srv_rate -0.27077 12 logged_in Selected attributes: 28,27,40,4,35,3 0,1,2,23,3,32,36,37,11,5,21,20,7,1 3,16,9,17,15,18,6,14,19,10,22,8,31 ,24,29,25,38,39,26,33,34,12: 40	0.1511746 3 service 0.1275031 40 dst_host_rerror_rate 0.111461 4 flag 0.0786506 28 srv_rerror_rate 0.0577873 37 dst_host_srv_diff_ host_rate 0.0516599 32 dst_host_count 0.0451897 39 dst_host_srv_ serror_rate 0.041171 33 dst_host_srv_count 0.036967 26 srv_serror_rate 0.0296859 36 dst_host_same_src_ port_rate 0.0294 34 dst_host_same_srv_rate 0.0281593 12 logged_in 0.0236743 38 dst_host_serror_rate 0.0211623 27 rerror_rate 0.0135177 1 duration 0.0133825 31 srv_diff_host_rate 0.0111552 35 dst_host_diff_ srv_rate 0.0092948 25 serror_rate 0.0050919 5 src_bytes 0.0043386 19 num_access_files 0.0036875 17 num_file_creations 0.0035182 11 num_failed_logins 0.0027011 30 diff_srv_rate 0.0024741 10 hot 0.0023503 15 su_attempted 0.0021743 13 num_compromised 0.0018677 16 num_root 0.0011181 14 root_shell 0.0003739 6 dst_bytes 0.0002015 2 protocol_type 0 21 is_host_login 0 7 land 0 20 num_outbound_cmds -0.0000101 22 is_guest_login -0.000111 9 urgent -0.0001974 18 num_shells -0.000612 8 wrong_fragment -0.0037437 24 srv_count -0.0046926 29 same_srv_rate -0.0131934 23 count Selected attributes: 3,40,4,28,37,32 ,39,33,26,36,34,12,38,27,1,31,35,2 5,5,19,17,11,30,10,15,13,16,14,6,2 ,21,7,20,22,9,18,8,24,29,23: 40

Chapter 13
The Impact of AI on Elderly Inmates in Central Prison

S. Srinivasan
https://orcid.org/0009-0002-0179-9849
Humanities and Social Sciences, Graphic Era University (Deemed), Dehradun, India

N. Rajavel
https://orcid.org/0000-0001-7270-7708
Department of Social Work, Bharathidasan University, India

Nicamil K. Sanchez
St. Mary's College Quezon, University of Makati, Philippines

ABSTRACT

This study investigates the impact of digitalization and Artificial Intelligence (AI) on prison administration, criminal records, and offenders' re-entry, particularly on elderly convicts. International research in countries like Australia, Japan, Sweden, Canada, France, and the UK highlights the increasing challenges posed by ageing prison populations. The study, conducted in central prisons in Tamil Nadu, India, employed a descriptive research design and purposive sampling method, involving 259 participants across five central jails. Utilizing qualitative and quantitative analysis methods, including SPSS software, the study identifies post-release challenges faced by elderly inmates in society and the workplace, emphasizing issues of diversity, equity, inclusion, and social justice. It concludes with insights into the coping strategies adopted by older offenders to navigate these challenges, underscoring the need for societal understanding and support for their successful reintegration.

DOI: 10.4018/979-8-3693-7205-0.ch013

INTRODUCTION

The impact of AI on elderly inmates in Central Prison can be both positive and negative aspects but here there are some potential implications. AI has a positive effect on the central prison, providing emotional support for elderly inmates and reducing feelings of loneliness among elderly inmates. AI can help healthcare and wellness among older individuals and it increases health outcomes and provides a better quality of life (Bacanoiu & Danoiu, 2022). AI can support elderly inmates with access to important information related to legal resources, education and environmental support (Chu et al., 2022). AI can always monitor and the system can support the safety and security of elderly inmates to reduce the risk of and abuse neglect. AI on elderly inmates hurts their social isolation. They use only machines, like AI-powered tools, which reduces face-to-face interaction and leads to social isolation due to the lack of human connections. The lack of human touch means AI lacks empathy and emotional intelligence, which contributes to feelings of frustration among elderly inmates (Ertl et al., 2019). Elderly inmates may face numerous struggles with technological complexities and are unable to assess the AI tools. There is discrimination leading to unequal treatment of elderly inmates in central prisons. It is used for more types of offenders and different types of crimes in this digitalization for Artificial Intelligence in prison administration and criminal records and re-entry offender particular data (Tayumi Ishiy & Marcondes Ramos, 2023). AI implements human interaction rather than replacing it. Providing support for elderly inmates to use AI-powered tools is effective, in monitoring and addressing potential decision-making, AI can enhance rather than replace human care and support (Fedorczyk, 2024).

A lot of focus on the handling of elderly convicts has grown dramatically during the last few decades. International experts in correctional research have conducted various studies in countries such as Australia (Grant, 1999; Dawes, 2009), Japan (Johnson, 2000), Sweden (Fazel & Grann, 2002), Canada (Gal, 2002), France (Steiner, 2003) UK (Howse, 2003; Wahidin & Cain, 2006). According to individual investigations, several nations and the United Nations are dealing with problems linked to an ageing prison population. This chapter emphasizes the post-release challenges faced by elderly inmates in society and the workplace, including issues related to diversity, equity, inclusion, and social justice. The research was conducted in various central prisons of Tamil Nadu, India. The study utilized a descriptive research design and purposive sampling method, with a total sample size of 259 participants. The research was conducted in five central prisons namely, Central Prison for Men, Special Prison for Women, and Open Prison, Tamil Nadu, India. The outcomes of the research were analyzed using qualitative and quantitative methods (Statistical Package for the Social Sciences) SPSS software. The study concludes with suggestions that older offenders confront issues of social justice, diversity, equity, and inclusion following their release from central prison, which affects how they are viewed by the public. This study also explored coping strategies employed by these individuals to handle these situations.

AI plays a vital role in predicting and reducing recidivism rates, as the main causes of convicted criminals are reoffending. AI plays a significant role in risk assessment by maintaining vast amounts of criminal data and analyzing the socio-economic status of prisoners, as well as the behavioural status of prison inmates, to determine individual reoffending patterns (Vilasenor & Foggo, 2020). AI is more useful in making decisions about release conditions for prison inmates, providing rehabilitation support, and offering post-release support to maximize AI benefits. Lifetime convicts require early intervention support from AI machine learning to identify high risks of incarceration (Zivanai & Mahlangu, 2022). AI can facilitate counselling and therapy for those experiencing severe conditions such as substance abuse, mental health problems, lack of awareness, and educational barriers. Prisons can intervene with highly affected convicts by providing awareness campaigns, counselling, vocational training, and expert motivational talks covering legal, intervention, medical, welfare, psychological, and recreational aspects to support the inmates. In rehabilitation programs, AI plays a major role based on individual needs and risk factors for inmates.

By analyzing incarceration data, AI algorithms can suggest specific interventions and treatment support to reduce recidivism. Post-release support continues through machine learning after release from prison, including community resources, mental health support, and employment opportunities to facilitate inmates' better transition into society (Shand, 1996). AI proves more useful in reducing the risk of reoffending and supporting full and successful recovery for elderly inmates. AI can help policy-makers identify trends in recidivism data and develop strength-based policies and interventions. Analyses are more useful for making systematic strategic plans and creating policies addressing poverty, lack of education, and social support (Monica, 2024). Elderly inmates, when they are released or leave prison, are happy, but they face an uncertain future. Most people, after a long time, re-enter society and may face many challenges in starting a life free of criminal intentions. Bearing in mind that many inmates come to prison for various reasons and disadvantages, not all of their problems will have been addressed during incarceration. Their expectations, worries, and concerns vary, but the majority express concerns regarding their family, housing situation, finding employment, and re-establishing family bonds upon release (Ekunwe & Jones, 2011). The study mainly focused on smart prisons to understand the emergence of digital technologies. The prison context reveals certain contradictions and paradoxes in the digital imperative (Kaun & Stiernstedt, 2020).

Background of the Study

The study highly emphasizes the impact of AI on elderly inmates in Central Prison and involves exploring AI technologies in various aspects to enhance incarceration and rehabilitation services. This study aims to examine how AI can be used to manage and monitor elderly inmates both pre-and post-release. It also assesses the effectiveness of AI-driven interventions in addressing the unique challenges and needs of elderly inmates. AI can play a vital role in improving elderly inmates' well-being and reintegration. The study clearly explains the challenges faced by elderly inmates in the criminal justice system, both pre- and post-release, and how AI technology can support the reduction of individual issues faced by this group.

Significant of the study

The chapter emphasizes the post-release challenges faced by elderly inmates, including rehabilitation service support, healthcare support, financial support, stigma, and discrimination due to legal barriers.

I) **Rehabilitation Support:** Ageing inmates regularly face reintegrating into society due to limited support services and their specific needs. This includes various accesses to housing facilities, employment opportunities, health care support and mental health support services. Without sufficient support, most ageing individuals face a high risk of unemployment, homelessness, and reoffending. II) **Healthcare Support:** Ageing inmates may not have significant healthcare needs, such as chronic illness, disabilities and mental health incarcerated aged people. However, there are often faced some of the barriers such as inadequate health care services and released elderly inmates it is including lack of insurance, financial sources and transportation it is included. It can be unfair for the ageing inmates unable to access medical conditions and issues of impaired health disparities. III) **Financial Instability:** The majority of the ageing inmates who worked in the prison inmates' life there faced some financial instability upon release; they have limited savings or job skills to secure employment. Discrimination based on their criminal history further complicates their ability to find stable employment; ageing inmates are socially and economically deprived marginalized communities. The financial strain can hinder their ability to meet basic needs and contribute to social isolation. IV) **Stigma and Discrimination:** Incarceration elderly inmates face stigma and discrimination in their lives including family, working places and social interactions. This stigma includes social exclusion, reduced opportunities and psychological distress it is impacting their overall well-being and sense of belonging to the community. V) **Legal Barriers:** Elderly Inmates encounter legal barriers to post-release, such as restrictions on voting rights, and public assistance programs.

The legal barriers include marginalization community including elderly inmates incarcerated. Addressing the challenges requires comprehensive reforms to promote diversity, equity, inclusion and social justice for elderly individuals in post-release. It is implementing policies to support successful rehabilitation, to access healthcare and social services, to promote fair hiring and stigma and discrimination based on criminal history. Alternative incarceration and restorative justice approach to prevent and protect the incarceration of ageing individuals in the community.

Objective of the Study

1. To investigating the pre-offending of elderly inmates
2. To determine the post-release conditions of elderly inmates
3. To understand the social justice challenges faced by elderly inmates.

LITERATURE REVIEW

A Global Perspective on Elderly Inmates in Prison: Age Differences

The review clearly explains that the elderly inmate population is increasing globally, with the number of incarcerated individuals rising due to the ageing boom. The study discusses the challenges and implications of this trend, providing a comprehensive country-wise and year-wise distribution of the population, along with the available resources.

Demographic and Trends

Country-wise, the United States of America has one of the fastest-growing populations of elderly prisoners. This increase in ageing inmates parallels the ageing of the general population (Mehmood & Ahmad, 2016). Some states in the USA have double the percentage of elderly inmates compared to others. In Europe, countries such as the UK and Germany have also seen a rise in the number of elderly inmates. While the general population is increasing in the USA, European countries often have more social welfare systems to support elderly people, including post-release support for elderly inmates. In Asia, Japan is also experiencing a rapid increase in elderly prisoners, partly due to an ageing population and rising crime rates among the elderly, often related to issues like poverty and social isolation (Tonry, 2022).

Figure 1. Number of Arrest

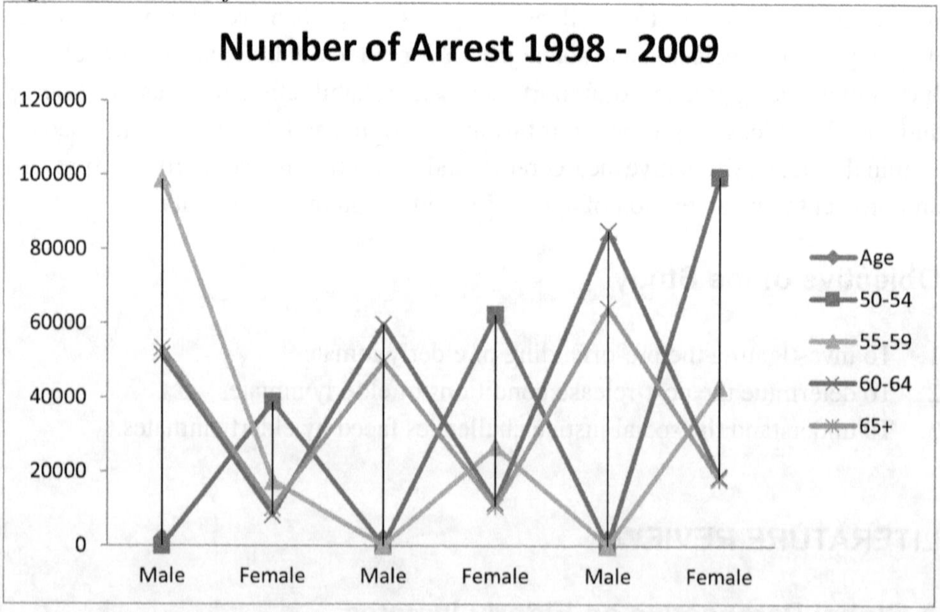

Source: U.S. Department of Justice, Bureau of Justice Statistics (1998, 2004, 2009) Source book criminal Justice Statistics (Harnsberger, 2011).

Table 1 shows an overall increasing trend for elderly inmates across all age groups and genders from 1998 to 2009. The number of male elderly inmates is higher than that of female elderly inmates, as the trend indicates. The figure emphasizes the age-wise trend, with the 50 to 55 age group being the most substantial, and it shows a rising trend for younger elderly people. The table highlights the increasing trend among elderly inmates and provides insights and challenges related to this demographic.

Figure 2. Number of Arrest

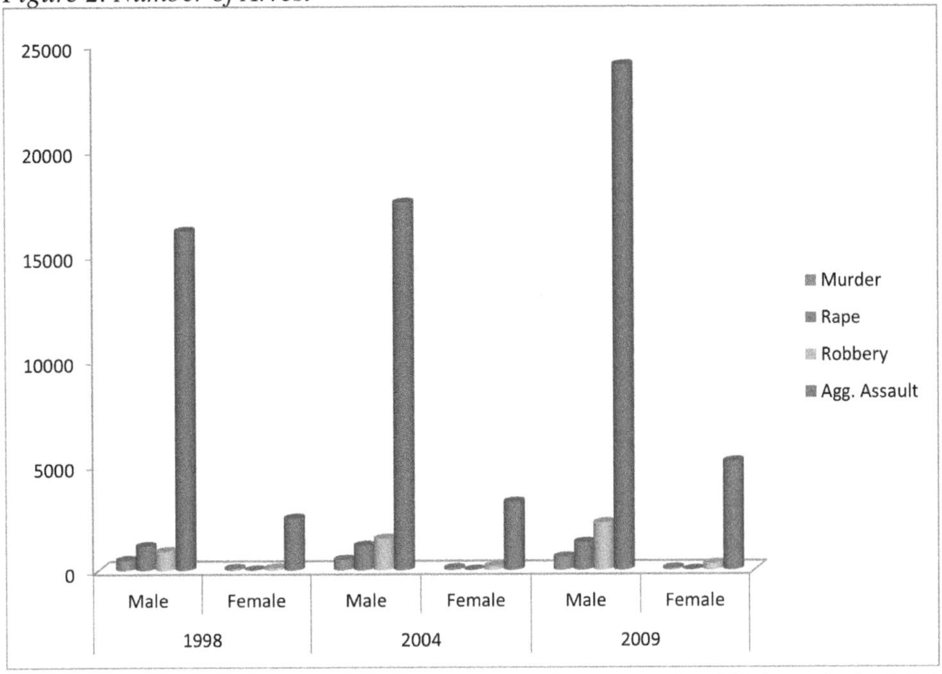

Source: U.S. Department of Justice, Bureau of Justice Statistics (1998, 2004, 2009) Source book criminal Justice Statistics

Table 2 on violent crime and gender-wise data shows details for the period from 1998 to 2009. The murder rate among male inmates is approximately 29% during this period, compared to a 4% murder rate among female offenders. This reflects an increasing trend in female inmate numbers relative to males from 1998 to 2009. There are gender disparities, with male inmates consistently representing the majority of murders compared to females, with 137 male offender cases from 1998 to 2009. There is a significant difference between male and female offenders for robbery, with male offenders rising by 153% and female offenders by 193% from 1998 to 2009. The gender disparities in robbery offences show a notable increase among both genders over the years. Aggravated assault increased significantly for both male and female offenders, with male offenders increasing by 49% and female offenders by more than 108%, which is highly alarming for females, as reflected in the period between 1998 and 2009.

Figure 3. Violent Crime

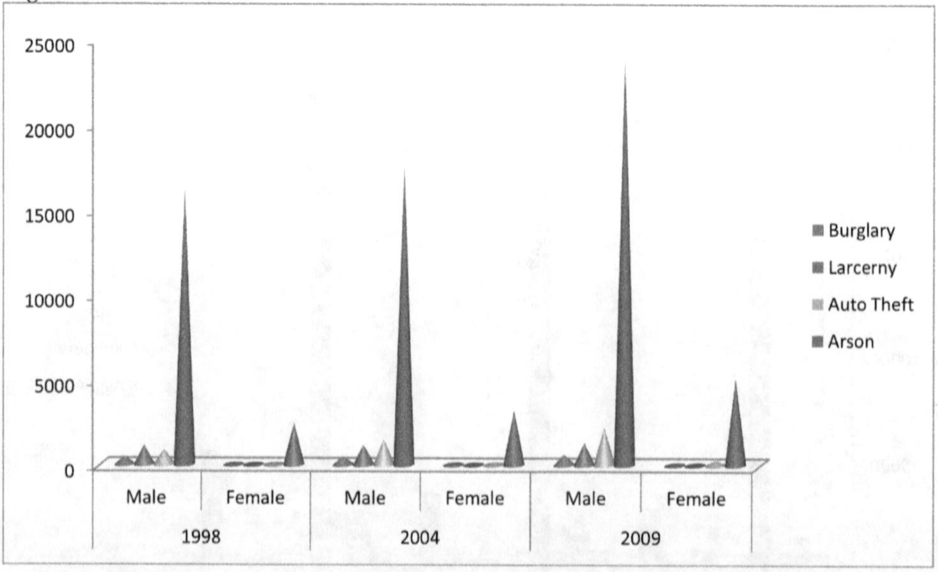

Source: U.S. Department of Justice, Bureau of Justice Statistics (1998, 2004, 2009) Source book criminal Justice Statistics

Table 3 visualizes violent crimes over the period from 1998 to 2009. These violent crimes include burglary, larceny, auto theft, and arson. Over the years, the number of crimes across various categories increased for both males and females. There have been gender disparities among male and female inmates throughout the years. The increase in arson is significant for both males and females, with a substantial rise noted.

The table emphasizes drug-related offences and other assaults. There was a significant increase in drug-related offences and other assaults over the period, affecting both male and female offenders. Gender-wise, males consistently committed more crimes compared to females throughout the period. Drug-related offences doubled in rate from 1998 to 2009. The increase in the number of other assaults is notable, with a significant rise, particularly among male offenders over the years.

Older Adults in Prison: Health and Well-Being

The author highlights the health-related problems faced by elderly inmates in prison settings. Due to insufficient care, loneliness, and constant reflection on their past offenses, elderly inmates often feel they do not receive a proper diet. They also worry about their families, which contributes to higher morbidity and mortality rates, including issues like diabetes and heart attacks, among other health-related problems.

Dementia is a common problem among the elderly prison population (Cipriani & Carkesu, 2017). To improve the quality of life for elderly inmates, they need proper care, regular medical check-ups, opportunities to share their feelings with peers, and the chance to form good friendships. Regular motivation from psychologists and counselors is also crucial for enhancing their well-being (Schlanger, 2017).

Inmates' Legal Rights and Human Rights

Elderly inmates are often unable to receive proper legal support for parole and to utilize the legal benefits available to them. The legal system provides provisions to help elderly inmates become eligible for parole. Even the UN Assembly has emphasized the importance of dignity and humane treatment for elderly inmates (Maschi et al., 2021).

Rehabilitation and Reentry

After release elderly inmates needs special care support healthcare, housing facility and social integrate improve the life enhancement. The study focus significant reentry challenges for release elderly person it include their of family support and difficult to access the health and challenges it obtain the employment opportunities. It additionaly increase social isolation and stigma for elderly inmates it can lead for recidivism for the elderly inmates (DiTomas et al., 2022). To explore the research ideas, it focuses on the impact of social reentry on individuals released from prison and the specific needs of these released prisoners during their resettlement (Partington, 2017; Wahidin & Cain, 2006). The correlation between the health and well-being of older and younger inmates is comparatively higher when preparing for and receiving release (Travis et al., 2001).

Maintain the Criminal Records

Maintaining all types of criminal data is useful for analyzing offender history and diagnosing inmates' behavior. AI can support saving and analyzing data by age, gender, type of offense, health status, and recidivism, helping to track repeat offenders and focus on regular recidivism. AI can play a crucial role in improving the living conditions and health support of elderly inmates, making it easier to identify, rehabilitate, and reintegrate them (Khoei & Singh, 2024).

AI application support for Elderly Inmates Dataset

AI can protect elderly inmates from disease and aid in early diagnosis. AI supports monitoring elderly inmates' behavior and attitudes toward their peers. AI is instrumental in protecting and preventing various chronic illnesses before and after inmates enter prison, as well as in providing periodical check-ups, identifying mental health problems, and offering medical support for elderly inmates. AI can also identify recidivism rates, address issues, monitor specific offenders, and provide rehabilitation and regular counseling for individual offenders. Additionally, AI can assist prison administration in reintegrating elderly inmates and reducing re-offense rates (Lee, 2019; Rodolfa et al., 2020).

Types of Dataset use in Prison Administration

The prison administration maintains records on a regular basis, including inmate details such as socio-economic status, age, previous occupation, gender, and period of incarceration. They also track various aspects of health status, including mental health conditions, medical history, and past histories. Disciplinary records are regularly maintained to monitor inmates and their release. Data is collected and maintained on those with regular recidivism, previous offenses, and re-incarceration, all of which are documented by the prison administration. This data is particularly useful for identifying family connections within the incarcerated population. AI can support the identification of inmates' characteristics through algorithms, which are useful for assessing prison life and improving the quality of life (Galassi & Athanasou, 2015, Lockwood et al., 2015).

Offenders' lives After They are Released from Prison

The life of an offender can be classified into various aspects such as well-being, social relationships, and reintegration into society. The impact of both positive and negative aspects on elderly inmates' lives after release, and how this influences their support within society, is crucial. Factors such as individual mental health, physical health, societal perception, and the effectiveness of reentry into society are key considerations (Visher & Travis, 2003).

Psychological Impact

Elderly inmates face numerous psychological issues such as anxiety, depression, stress, and post-traumatic stress disorder, along with mental health challenges after their release from prison. The transition from a structured prison environment to the outside world can be overwhelming. Ex-offenders often encounter social stigma, which affects their self-esteem (Markina, 2019). The study indicates various aspects of psychological problems experienced after release, including feelings of shame and guilt among the inmates. Their friends' and family members' misbehavior, as well as the elderly inmates' struggles with social adjustment within both their families and the community, are significant challenges (Harding et al., 2016).

Legal and Administration Challenges

The study examined parole and probation for elderly inmates, which are very difficult to obtain, though there are provisions to utilize the legal service system. Many ex-offenders, after release, are often under surveillance to help reduce recidivism. Ex-offenders face challenges in obtaining unique identification, such as an Aadhaar card, voter ID, or voting rights. They also struggle to open bank accounts due to difficulty in providing surety, and they are often unable to access social security schemes from government departments (Aukerman, 2003).

Society Perception

From a social perspective, ex-offenders are neglected by society, and the public is often afraid and avoids involving them in social functions, feeling unsafe to interact with them. The current system aims to improve the effectiveness of support systems for ex-offenders. Due to economic burdens and difficulty in finding employment, ex-offenders may fall back into recidivism. Addressing these issues can lead to improvements in public perception and the criminal justice system, ultimately providing better services for ex-offenders (Paulson, 2013).

Strategies to Improve the Outcomes

The study highlights the importance of providing reentry support for ex-offenders, such as housing support, mental health services, and job creation, which can significantly benefit them. Arranging educational support, vocational or livelihood training, and creating employment opportunities through partnerships with small-scale industries can help elderly inmates after their release (Gaes, 2008). A crucial aspect of supporting ex-offenders is community care and support, which plays a significant role in their successful reintegration. The study suggests that these efforts can lead to better outcomes by reducing recidivism and benefiting society (Denney et al., 2008).

Pre and Post Rehabilitation for the Elderly Inmates

The chapter highlights the experiences of elderly inmates before and after their release. The study addresses the physical, mental, and social support needed for elderly inmates. It aims to help them reintegrate into society for a successful aging life.

Pre-Rehabilitation for Elderly Inmates

Health Care and Wellness Programs

To provide healthcare facilities for elderly inmates, it is essential to address various diseases affecting them, such as diabetes, hypertension, arthritis, and cardiovascular disease. Pre-rehabilitation should include comprehensive health support for these elderly inmates.

Mental health services are crucial for addressing issues such as depression, anxiety, stress, dementia, and PTSD, with a particular emphasis on promoting CBT therapy to provide counselling and improve the elderly inmates' mental health and well-being. Regular exercise and improved physical fitness activities are essential to reducing the risk of falls for elderly inmates and enhancing overall health and well-being (Lares & Montogomery, 2020; Srinivasan, 2021).

Education and Skill Development

The prison setting provides comprehensive education for elderly inmates to increase their mental stability and self-confidence. Increasing the number of vocational training programs, such as arts and crafts, supports job opportunities for elderly inmates. Life skill training supports elderly inmates for later life or after release.

Psychological Support

A psychological support program is essential for elderly inmates to reduce stress related to reentry, manage stigma-related problems, and rebuild a sense of identity. Regular motivational programs should be conducted to enhance the lifestyle of elderly inmates and facilitate their rehabilitation.

Social and Family Support

Family and social support programs are essential to enhance reintegration for elderly inmates. Peer group support always plays a vital role in improving mental strength, fostering community, and increasing mutual support.

Legal and Administrative Assistance

Legal assistance supports parole and release planning, helping elderly inmates meet with their family members to reduce stress. It also ensures they have a clear and realistic plan for housing, healthcare, and social support within the community and family (Srinivasan, 2021).

Post-Rehabilitation for Elderly Inmates

Health Care Continuity Support

Post-rehabilitation for elderly inmates involves ensuring continued healthcare support within community services. It is essential to coordinate with local healthcare providers to maintain their treatment and provide proper health services without any challenges. Arrangements should be made for regular and periodic checkups to help elderly ex-offenders engage in healthcare activities.

Housing and Financial Stability

To ensure proper and appropriate housing options, it is important to assist with living facilities at the community level, whether they are supported by family members or other relations. Additionally, it is necessary to manage financial support, such as social security, pensions, or other social financial assistance for those eligible. After release, it is crucial to explore employment or volunteer opportunities that suit their capabilities.

Social Reintegration

Social reintegration support should include counselling for their families if needed. Regarding community involvement, it is important to consider how they participate and engage in community programs, such as old age centres or religious organizations, to help rebuild their social networks.

Mental and Emotional Well-being

After release, how elderly people cope with their mental and emotional well-being through continuous counselling or therapy is crucial in helping them adapt to the system and face isolation or depression. It is important to identify peer support for elderly ex-offenders, where they can share experiences and receive encouragement, helping to reduce feelings of isolation (Srinivasan, & Ilango, 2015).

Monitoring and Support

Monitoring support for released elderly people through social workers and caseworkers is essential. They will provide regular follow-ups to identify the needs of elderly ex-offenders and offer the necessary care and support. Additionally, it is important to ensure that elderly ex-offenders on parole receive the appropriate support to meet their conditions.

Ageing Related Challenges in Prison Pre and Post

There are many challenges that elderly inmates face both pre- and post-release. Before entering the prison system, they often struggle with mental health issues and psychological behavior, making it difficult for them to interact with peer inmate groups, leading to feelings of isolation. After release, they face a lack of respect from society, difficulty in adapting to the system, and rejection from both the community and family. The prison system must provide a proper strategic plan to improve their lives and enhance healthy aging in society.

The main reasons for recidivism among elderly inmates are the lack of financial support, unemployment, and rejection by family and community, which lead them to re-offend (Antwi, 2015). To reduce this risk, strategies must be adopted within the prison system, and the community must also support and care for them. Rehabilitation is required to address their physical, mental, emotional, and social needs. Pre- and post-rehabilitation efforts should be coordinated and continuous to ensure that elderly ex-offenders are reintegrated into society with dignity. Targeted programs and services can help elderly inmates live fulfilling lives post-incarceration, including providing regular treatment for those affected by health issues, offering counselling support, motivating them to engage in yoga and physical activities, and encouraging involvement in any job or livelihood activities. These measures can prevent recidivism and benefit society as a whole (Srinivasan, 2014; Among, 2007).

Social Justice Post-Released Elderly Inmates

The authors examined post-released elderly inmates should be treated humanely within the criminal justice system, according to a research study that focused largely on diversity, equity, inclusion, and social justice. Policy Reform enhancing policies to recognize the unique vulnerabilities and needs of elderly inmates is crucial. This includes promoting alternatives to incarceration for elderly individuals by providing healthcare support and social services (Aday & Krabil, 2012; Williams & Abraldes, 2007).

Support for Elderly Prisoners after Release from Government, Voluntary Organizations

Reintegration for elderly prisoners after release often involves both government and voluntary organizations to support them. It can help elderly ex-offenders and their family members by providing education and support to facilitate their transition back into society. Addressing their unique needs and challenges can reduce the likelihood of recidivism and support elderly inmates effectively.

Government support for ex-offenders post-release includes parole or probation support for elderly inmates. When elderly inmates are released, individual support and necessary services must be provided. Age-related challenges, such as the need for specialized healthcare and mental health services, should be addressed, along with providing proper housing conditions. There should be flexibility in parole conditions for elderly inmates, taking into account their physical limitations and the need for specialized care and support. The government can also support vocational and livelihood training to enhance their living conditions. This can improve their lifestyle and help them gain new skills or adapt existing ones for employment. The government should take necessary steps to conduct periodical health check-ups and disease-related diagnoses to identify health issues among elderly inmates and provide support for diagnosis and early intervention.

Role of Voluntary Organization

Limited organizations are working for inmates, especially elderly inmates, and even fewer providing holistic reentry programs for elderly ex-offenders to address their health, social, and emotional needs. This includes personalized case management to help individuals navigate reentry and access various services. Non-governmental organizations support the mental health aspects of elderly inmates by providing comprehensive mental health services. Additionally, voluntary organizations assist elderly ex-offenders in connecting with others facing similar problems, reducing feelings of isolation. Many service organizations provide housing support and arrange temporary shelters as part of long-term services for ex-offenders. Voluntary aid services also offer legal support to help elderly ex-offenders with housing, employment, and benefits. Advocacy efforts include reforming housing and parole conditions for elderly ex-offenders. Faith-based support and spiritual motivation in both house and community settings can also help reduce feelings of isolation among elderly ex-offenders.

Successful reintegration support for elderly inmates after their release involves coordination between government and voluntary organizations. The government provides healthcare support, financial assistance, housing, basic needs, and rations.

Voluntary organizations support reentry programs, social support, and advocacy efforts to address the unique challenges faced by elderly ex-offenders. These combined efforts can improve the transition back into society, ultimately reducing recidivism and improving the quality of life for elderly individuals.

Material Methods

The proposed research is to conduct qualitative and quantitative research methods. This research study gathered information and analysed both numerical data and quantitative data mixed methods used for the present study to understand the research topic, complementing the strengths and weaknesses of each method. The present study adopted a description of the descriptive research design. Specific details about the research study itself, such as the research question, objectives, population of interest, and number of variables included in this research study. The research might be implementing a purposive sampling method with a total sample size of 259 participants' elderly inmate convicts across the five central prisons in Central Prison for Men, Special Prison for Women, Open Prison, Tamil Nadu, India and analyzed the using SPSS software.

Result and Discussion

Socio-Demographic characteristics of the respondents

Table 1 portrays the socio-demographic characteristics of the respondents, who are the convicted inmates of the selected central prisons, special prisons for women and open-air prisons, in terms of their characteristics such as gender, age, religion, caste, educational qualification before imprisonment, state of birth, place of origin and marital status.

Table 1. Personal Characteristics of the Respondents

Sl. No.	Item	Frequency N = 259	Per cent
1	**Gender**		
	Male	190	73
	Female	69	27
2.	**Age**		
	51-60	181	70
	Above 60	78	30

continued on following page

Table 1. Continued

Sl. No.	Item	Frequency N = 259	Per cent
3.	**Religion**		
	Hindu	172	66
	Muslim	36	14
	Christian	51	20
4.	**Caste**		
	SC	124	48
	ST	5	2
	MBC	59	23
	BC	71	27
5.	**Educational Qualification Before Imprisonment**		
	Non-literate	126	49
	Primary	66	25
	High School	38	15
	Higher Studies	29	11
6.	**Place of Origin**		
	Urban	22	47
	Semi-Urban/Rural	48	36
	Rural	62	17
7.	**Marital Status**		
	Unmarried Married/Remarried	198	76
	Widow/Widower/Divorcee/	8	3
	Separated	53	21

This data seems to represent a study of a specific population, possibly prisoners or another group, based on demographic and social characteristics. Here's an interpretation of each section: Gender Distribution Male: (73%), Female (27%), Interpretation: The majority of the population in this study is male, with males making up nearly three-quarters of the sample. This indicates a significant gender imbalance within the group. 2. Age Distribution 51-60 years (70%) Above 60 years (30%), Interpretation: Most individuals in the study fall within the 51-60 age range, making up 70% of the population. A smaller portion, 30%, is above 60 years old. This suggests that the population is generally older, with the majority being in their late middle age. Religion, Hind (66%), Muslim (14%), Christian (20%). The majority of the population identifies as Hindu, followed by a significant Christian minority and a smaller Muslim minority. This distribution could reflect the religious demographics of the region or the specific population being studied. Caste SC (Scheduled Caste) (48%), ST (Scheduled Tribe) (2%), MBC (Most Backward Classes) (23%), BC (Backward Classes) (27%).

The population is predominantly from the Scheduled Castes, followed by Backward Classes and Most Backward Classes. There are very few individuals from Scheduled Tribes. This data suggests a significant representation of socially disadvantaged groups in the study. Educational Qualification before Imprisonment Non-literate (49%), Primary (25%), High School (15%), Higher Studies (11%). Nearly half of the population is non-literate, with only a small percentage having completed higher studies. This indicates a low level of educational attainment among the group, which could have implications for their social and economic status. Place of Origin Urban (47%), Semi-Urban/Rural (36%), Rural (17%). The population is nearly evenly split between those from urban areas and those from semi-urban or rural areas, with a slightly higher proportion coming from urban regions. A smaller segment comes from rural areas. This suggests a diverse range of origins within the group. Marital Status Unmarried (76%), Married/Remarried (3%), widow/Widower/Divorcee/Separated (21%).

A large majority of the population is unmarried, with a smaller proportion being widowed, divorced, or separated. Only a very small percentage is currently married or remarried. This could reflect social circumstances that influence marital status within this population. Overall Interpretation This study seems to focus on a population that is predominantly male, older, and from lower social and educational backgrounds. The data suggests significant social disadvantage, with high rates of non-literacy and a large representation of socially marginalized groups. The high proportion of unmarried individuals might indicate social isolation or other factors influencing marital status. The religious and regional diversity also provides insight into the background of the individuals studied.

Table 2. Health Characteristics of the Respondents

Sl. No.	Health Problems	Frequency N = 259	Per cent
1.	**Health Problems**		
	Has health problems	82	32.0
	Does not have health problems	177	68.0
1.	**Mental Illness**		
	Yes	22	9.0
	No	237	92.0
2.	**Tuberculosis**		

continued on following page

Table 2. Continued

Sl. No.	Health Problems	Frequency N = 259	Per cent
	Yes	3	1.0
	No	256	99.0
3.	**HIV**		
	Yes	3	1.0
	No	256	99.0
4.	**Cancer**		
	Yes	4	2.0
	No	255	98.0
5.	**Blood Pressure**		
	Yes	52	20.1
	No	207	79.9
6.	**Diabetes**		
	Yes	52	10.4
	No	232	89.6
7.	**Skin Disease**		
	Yes	6	2.3
	No	253	97.7
8.	**Heart Problem**		
	Yes	11	4.2
	No	248	95.8
9.	**Lung Related problems**		
	Yes	4	1.4
	No	255	98.6
10.	**Surgery**		
	Yes	6	2.1
	No	253	97.9
11.	**Disability**		
	Yes	4	2.0
	No	255	98.0

The fact that 45 persons(9 per cent) interviewed had episodes of mental illness reveals the poor psychological well-being of prison inmates. As many as 16 per cent of the world population suffer from mental disorders. In Tamil Nadu, the population of persons with mental disorders is found to be 77 lakhs (www.tnhealth.org). Yasmeen and Pandey (2018) reported that according to the National Mental Health

Survey conducted by the National Institute of Mental Health and Neuro Sciences (NIMHANS), Bengaluru, 13.7 per cent of India's general population and 11.8 per cent of the general population of Tamil Nadu suffer from mental disorders. Among the 5203 prison inmates who suffer from mental illness in India, 2744 (52.7 per cent) inmates are convicts. Among the 51 respondents who suffer from mental illness in Tamil Nadu, 19 prisoners (37. 3 per cent) are convicts (National Crime Records Bureau, 2016). As per this study, among the 259 respondents, 45 prison inmates (9 per cent) reported having a history of mental illness. The fact that the three highest reported health problems are blood pressure, diabetes and mental illness indicates the prevalence of stress among these prison inmates. It also indicates the need for diet food.

Table 3. Offence Related Characteristics of the Respondents

Sl. No.	Offence Related Characteristics	Frequency N = 259	Per cent
1.	**Type of Prison**		
	Central Prison for Men	181	69.7
	Special Prison for Women	58	22.6
	Open Air Prison	40	7.7
2.	**Number of Times Sentenced to Imprisonment**		
	First offender	244	94.4
	< 2-3 times	10	3.9
	>3 times	5	1.7
3.	**Frequency of Crime Based Category**		
	First Offender	244	94.4
	Sentenced more than once	25	5.6
4.	**Legal Category**		
	Criminal Prisoner	256	99.0
	Civil Prisoner	1	0.4
	Political Prisoner	2	0.6
5.	**Duration of Sentence Based Category**		
	Determinate Imprisonment	97	37.3
	Life time Imprisonment	162	62.7
6.	**Locality of Offence**		
	Rural	148	57.0
	Urban	78	30.0
	Semi-Urban	33	13.0

continued on following page

Table 3. Continued

Sl. No.	Offence Related Characteristics	Frequency N = 259	Per cent
7.	**Term of Imprisonment Completed**		
	<5 years	123	47.7
	6 to 10 years	88	33.8
	11 to 15 years	42	16.2
	>16 years	6	2.3

Table 3 provides information regarding Central Prisons, Special Prison, and Open Air Prison, with 69.7%, 22.6%, and 7.7% of the respondents, respectively. The predominant concentration of elderly inmates is in the Central Prison for Men, highlighting its primary role in housing this demographic. The Special Prison for Women and Open Air Prison serve a smaller fraction, indicating a need for targeted programs in these less-utilized facilities. Regarding the number of times sentenced to imprisonment, the majority of respondents are first-time offenders (94.4%), while those with 2-3 offences make up 3.9%, and those with more than 3 offences constitute 1.7%. This suggests that interventions should focus on preventing initial offences to control crime levels and manage repeat offences effectively. In terms of crime-based categories, 94.4% of respondents are first-time offenders, while 5.6% have been sentenced more than once. This high percentage of first-time offenders among elderly inmates underscores the critical need for preventive measures and support to address issues before incarceration.

The legal category of the respondents shows that 99% are criminal prisoners, 0.4% are civil prisoners, and 0.6% are political prisoners. The data indicates that elderly inmates are predominantly criminal prisoners, with minimal representation as political prisoners. This suggests that the offences committed are primarily criminal rather than political or civil. The study highlights that 37.3% of the respondents are serving determinate imprisonments, while the majority, 62.7%, are serving life sentences. This indicates that most elderly inmates are serving life sentences, reflecting a high proportion of long-term confinement. The majority of crimes committed by respondents occurred in rural areas, with 57% of respondents indicating this. This suggests that illiteracy or lack of resources in rural areas may contribute to higher crime rates. Therefore, localized interventions could benefit rural communities by addressing their specific needs. Most elderly inmates have completed less than 5 years or 6 to 10 years of imprisonment. This highlights the need for transitional support for inmates serving longer terms and suggests that many have not yet reached extreme periods of confinement.

Table 4. Leisure Time Activities – Before Imprisonment and After Imprisonment

Sl. No.	Leisure time activities after Imprisonment		Leisure time activities Before Imprisonment				Total		Statistical Significance
			Yes		No				
			No.	Per cent	No.	Per cent	No.	Per cent	
	Reading	Yes	53	84.1	34	17.1	87	33.4	χ^2 192.631 = df = 1 Sig. (2-sided) = .000** P<.01 **Significant**
		No	10	15.9	162	82.9	172	66.6	
	Total		63	100	196	100	259	100	
2	Listening to music	Yes	32	51.6	65	32.9	97	37.5	χ^2 14.202 = df = 1 Sig. (2-sided) = .000** P<.01 **Significant**
		No	31	48.4	131	67.1	162	62.5	
	Total		63	100	196	100	259	100	
3	Watching TV/Movie	Yes	114	74.8	22	20.7	136	52.5	χ^2 147.180 = df = 1 Sig. (2-sided) = .000** P<.01 **Significant**
		No	39	25.2	84	79.3	123	47.5	
	Total		153	100	106	100	259	100	
4	Games	Yes	38	56.3	18	9.7	56	21.8	χ^2 127.282 = df = 1 Sig. (2-sided) = .000** P<.01 **Significant**
		No	30	43.7	173	90.3	203	78.2	
	Total		68	100	191	100	259	100	
5	Prayer	Yes	76	87.9	47	27.5	123	47.7	χ^2 168.083 = df = 1 Sig. (2-sided) = .000** P<.01 **Significant**
		No	11	12.1	125	72.5	136	52.3	
	Total		87	100	172	100	259	100	
6	Exercise/ Yoga/ Gym	Yes	26	86.7	48	21.0	74	28.6	χ^2 112.226 = df = 1 Sig. (2-sided) = .000** P<.01 **Significant**
		No	4	13.3	181	79.0	185	72.4	
	Total		30	100	229	100	259	100	
7	Drawing/ Handicrafts	Yes	10	100.0	13	5.4	23	8.9	χ^2 202.380 = df = 1 Sig. (2-sided) = .000**; p<.01 **Not Significant** {One cell has expected count less than five (25%)
		No	0	0	236	94.6	236	91.1	
	Total		10	100	249	100	259	100	
8	Cultural Activities	Yes	15	65.2	16	6.8	31	12.0	χ^2 135.850 = df = 1 Sig. (2-sided) = .000** P<.01 **Significant**
		No	8	34.8	220	93.2	228	88.0	
	Total		23	100	236	100	259	100	
9	Nature	Yes	5	55	7	2.6	12	4.6	χ^2 119.437 = df = 1 Sig. (2-sided) = .000**; p<.01 **Not Significant** {One cell has expected count less than five (25%)}
		No	5	45	242	97.4	247	95.4	
	Total		10	100	249	100	259	100	

continued on following page

Table 4. Continued

Sl. No.	Leisure time activities after Imprisonment		Leisure time activities Before Imprisonment				Total		Statistical Significance
			Yes		No				
			No.	Per cent	No.	Per cent	No.	Per cent	
10	Social Service	Yes	9	62.1	4	1.4	13	4.8	χ^2 219.145 = df = 1 Sig. (2-sided) = .000**; p<.01 **Not Significant** {One cell has expected count less than five (25%)}
		No	5	37.9	241	98.6	246	95.2	
	Total		14	100	245	100	259	100	
11	No Interest/No Opportuniti es for Leisure Time Activities	Yes	54	74.8	30	16.3	84	32.4	χ^2 161.994 = df = 1 Sig. (2-sided) = .000** P<.01 **Significant**
		No	18	25.2	157	83.7	175	67.6	
	Total		72	100	187	100	259	100	
12	Being with family/work and Talking	Yes	5	19.0	15	6.5	20	7.9	χ^2 10.943 = df = 1 Sig. (2-sided) = .001** **Not Significant** {One cell has expected count less than five (25%)}
		No	24	81.0	215	93.5	239	92.1	
	Total		29	100	230	100	259	100	
13	Being with family/work	Yes	18	62.1	41	17.8	59	22.8	χ^2 57.314 = df = 1 Sig. (2-sided) = .000** P<.01 **Significant**
		No	11	37.9	189	82.2	200	77.2	
	Total		29	100	230	100	259	100	
14	No Interest/ No Opportunities for Leisure Time Activities	Yes	54	74.8	30	16.3	84	32.4	χ^2 161.994 = df = 1 Sig. (2-sided) = .000** P<.01 **Significant**
		No	18	25.2	157	83.7	175	67.6	
	Total		72	100	187	100	259	100	

The study recommended seeking work and leisure that engages your skills. Leisure time activities enhance the flow experience of being absorbed in a task activity or game without overwhelming them. Many a time less expensive leisure time activities such as gardening, craft work, drawing and socializing can result in a higher level of flow experience. The prison inmates were asked about their leisure time activities to understand if they had such happiness before imprisonment, whether they have such happiness at present and whether there is an association between the recreational habits before and after imprisonment (Marti, 2022).

The chi-squared test in Table 4 reflects a high level of significant dependence between the variables -leisure time activities before imprisonment and after imprisonment indicating the interests and options for spending leisure time before imprisonment impacted their interest towards leisure time activities in the prison. Before imprisonment a majority of 375 respondents (72.39 per cent) did not enjoy any leisure time activities, the reasons given being lack of time as they always had work to do and lack of opportunities. Their main activity was socializing and talking which some of them continue even in the prison. After imprisonment a majority of the respondents (67.6 per cent) do not enjoy leisure time activities such as drawing/ handicrafts (91.1 per cent), cultural activities (88 per cent), games (78.2 per cent), exercise/yoga (72.4 per cent), reading (66.6 per cent), listening to music (62.5 per cent). As many as 47.7 per cent of the respondents spend time in prayer and 52.5 per cent of them watch television inferring *prayer and watching television* as the preferred leisure time activities of prison inmates. Some inmates also mentioned that they spend their leisure time doing some work, talking with others and socializing (7.9 per cent), enjoying nature (4.6 per cent) and social service by helping other prisoners in need (4.8 per cent). The need to motivate prison inmates to engage in recreational activities that enhance the flow of experience and well-being is reflected in the findings.

Outcome of the Study

To study expected the following outcomes;

1. Identification of Challenges: The study may have identified specific challenges faced by older inmates post-release, such as difficulties accessing housing, employment, healthcare, and social support networks. The study highlights the challenges it is considering various factors age, race, gender and socioeconomic status.
2. Post-Release Interventions: The study addresses the various aspects of older inmates' release intervention to promote reintegration, and support services and to address various health issues. This study identifies the gaps and intervention-based improvement strengthen.
3. Diversity and Social Justice: The study to provide insights into social diversity, equality, inclusion and social justice to intersect among older inmates and post-release. This study analyses the disparities among elderly inmates as well as the impact of systemic inequalities in the criminal justice system.
4. Policy Implications: The expected finding of the study is to increase the policy and practice for development and tailored effective intervention and older individuals transitioning out of incarceration. The study adopts the holistic and intersectional approach to address the needs of this population and to promote the successful reintegration of society. Overall, the outcome of the study likely contributes to a deeper understanding of the challenges faced by older inmates post-release and provides valuable insights for advancing equity, inclusion, and social justice within the criminal justice system. Elderly inmates utilize

resources such as healthcare support, and educational support. AI is used for various purposes for information and assistance to the needs of elderly people and disabilities. Health Care supports AI healthcare technologies to monitor predictive analytics, healthcare outcomes for the elderly inmate's health issues early personalized care. AI is used for monitoring and surveillance support AI to use reentry and rehabilitation for elderly inmates and reintegrate them into society. Overall this research study identified the impact of diversity, equity and inclusion for elderly inmates in Central Prisons.

CONCLUSION

In conclusion, the study contributes to the multifaceted challenges faced by older individuals transitioning out of incarceration. Our findings highlight the intersecting dynamics of age, race, gender, and socio-economic status in shaping post-release experiences, revealing systemic inequities within the criminal justice system. Despite existing efforts, our analysis indicates persistent barriers to reintegration, including limited access to essential resources and support networks. Moving forward, it is imperative to adopt a holistic approach that addresses the diverse needs of older inmates, promotes equity, and fosters social justice. This necessitates the development of tailored interventions, informed by collaboration between researchers, policymakers, and community stakeholders, to ensure the successful reintegration of older individuals into society and advance broader goals of diversity, equity, inclusion, and social justice within the criminal justice system.

Future Research Study

Longitudinal experimental studies can be carried out to understand the impacts of faith-based, life skills-based counseling services and other relevant support programmes among prison inmates over time. Such studies can be effective baseline sources for designing and updating reformation programs in prisons. In-depth qualitative studies or quantitative studies focusing on particular prison categories such as central prisons, special prisons for women, open-air prisons, district prisons and sub-jails or particular prisoner categories such as under trials, young offenders, first offenders, women offenders, A class prisoners, prisoners undergoing life imprisonment, prisoners in high-security cells, prisoners sentenced to death, elderly prisoners, unemployed and employed prisoners and prisoners with symptoms of mental disorders such as suicidal tendency, self-mutilation, depressive episodes and other mental illness can be undertaken by future researchers.

Some of the other researchable areas are the effectiveness of welfare programs and the functioning of prison industries in facilitating the rehabilitation of prison inmates, problems faced by families of prison inmates including women, and children as well as the impact of the absence of female or male inmates upon family well-being and situation of family members who come to visit prison inmates and their opinions on visiting system. The situation of released prisoners and the problems faced by them is another area of enquiry. Research studies on working conditions and stress levels of prison staff and prison officials and resource management in prison industries are other areas of research open to future researchers.

The future directions of the study could pathway towards significant implications for both academia and policy guidelines. Primarily, the investigation of older inmates navigating post-release life through the lens of diversity, equity, inclusion, and social justice could shed light on systemic inequalities within the criminal justice system. This study reveals the disparities in access to human and other resources, social networks and opportunities for reintegration, thereby informing targeted interventions to address these gaps and promote equitable outcomes for older individuals re-entering society after incarceration. This study addresses the intersectional identities of older inmates it considers the factors of social and economic background and it could deepen the understanding of post-release challenges of older inmates from central prisons. Moreover, this research brings direction towards post-release challenges and rehabilitation and support services for older inmates of prison for future research.

Further future studies on the impact of AI on elderly inmates in Central Prison should consider the following areas:

Explore various applications of AI technologies within Central Prison to support elderly inmates. Investigate how AI tools can assist elderly inmates in various aspects such as health monitoring, rehabilitation, and security. Examine how AI can enhance safety, and rehabilitation services, and improve healthcare support for elderly inmates. Evaluate how AI can address technical issues and ethical concerns, including reducing privacy violations. Study how AI can support the rehabilitation and reintegration process of elderly inmates, including improving and reducing barriers to their reintegration into society post-release. Conduct a comparative analysis of elderly inmates exposed to AI technologies versus those who are not. Assess the impact on recidivism rates, mental and physical health, and overall well-being. Explore how AI technologies can advance the capabilities of prison staff and healthcare providers, and how they can be effectively utilized to impact inmates. Provide a comprehensive understanding of AI's impact on elderly inmates in Central Prison to contribute to more informed decision-making and improve policy development.

There are several future recommendations are addressed based on the present study including;

1. They will provide a better guideline for the post-released older inmates of prison. Because the basic profile of the socio-economic status of the older inmates provides insights about effective post-release interventions and the requirement for comprehensive support systems.
2. The theme of post-released older inmates from the central prisons is not popular in academic and research discussions. The study will give directions for the development of a framework among correctional settings to ensure the quality of life and well-being of older inmates.
3. The study is trying to explore the unique challenges faced by older inmates from marginalized communities that can help tailor interventions to address their specific needs. The study provides suggestions to prevent the vulnerabilities of elderly prisoners after their release from central prisons.
4. Collaborative and collective efforts of individuals and stakeholders can transform into policy and practice in correctional settings.
5. The academic aspects of correctional settings and police science can be incorporated into the humanitarian values towards older inmates and future concerns for them.
6. The study is expected to provide suggestions for best practices and their design, development and implementation for older inmates and promote greater equity and social justice within the criminal justice system.

To conclude, the present study has the potential to address justice for older inmates after release from central prison. It gives directions to policymakers for access to resources, and support services tailored to the needs of older inmates.

AUTHOR CONTRIBUTION

It is confirmed by authors that S. Srinivasan is the author. The study was conceived by S. Srinivasan Direction and planning were handled results were discussed, the article was reviewed, and the final draft was approved.

FUNDING

None.

DATA AVAILABILITY

The corresponding author will provide the datasets as per your request.

DECLARATIONS

Ethics approval and consent to participate Participants gave their informed consent, and the experimental protocol was developed by the S. Srinivasan Declaration's ethical criteria.

CONFLICTS OF INTEREST

Conflicts of interest the authors declare they have no conflicts of interest that are directly or indirectly related to the research.

ACKNOWLEDGEMENTS

Mr. S. Srinivasan fieldworkers contributed greatly to the data collection in his Ph. D work.

REFERENCES

Aday, R. H., & Krabill, J. J. (2012). Older and geriatric offenders: Critical issues for the 21st century. *Special needs offenders in correctional institutions, 1*, 203-233. https://books.google.co.in/books?hl=en&lr=&id=wct1AwAAQBAJ&oi=fnd&pg=PA203&dq=International+experts+in+correctional+research+have+conducted+various+studies+in+countries+such+as+Australia+(Grant,+1999%3B+Dawes,+2009),+Japan+(Johnson,+2000),+Sweden+(Fazel+%26+Grann,+2002),+Canada+(Gal,+2002),+France+(Steiner,+2003)+UK+(Howse,+2003%3B+Wahidin+%26+Cain,+2006).&ots=L4HJ4fiyxT&sig=qaWkrKhiLXQ-Q3qf-nxGRKwmOkY&redir_esc=y#v=onepage&q&f=false

Among, H. I. V. (2007). Module for Prison Intervention: South Asia. https://www.unodc.org/documents/southasia/Trainingmanuals/Module_for_Prison_Intervention_-_South_Asia.pdf

Antwi, A. L. E. X. (2015). *Social reintegration of offenders and recidivism in Ghana. Unpublished doctoral thesis*. University of Ghana., https://ugspace.ug.edu.gh/server/api/core/bitstreams/7af9f24e-d7b1-4108-9d03-d7bcc5ebd480/content

Aukerman, M. J. (2003). Barriers to reentry: Legal strategies to reduce recidivism and promote the success of ex-offenders. *Michigan Criminal Law Annual Journal, 1*, 4-11. https://waynecountydefendertraining.com/cap-archives/2006/handouts/2006-09-15_05_barriers.pdf

Bacanoiu, M. V., & Danoiu, M. (2022). New strategies to improve the quality of life for normal aging versus pathological aging. *Journal of Clinical Medicine*, 11(14), 4207. DOI: 10.3390/jcm11144207 PMID: 35887969

Chu, C. H., Nyrup, R., Leslie, K., Shi, J., Bianchi, A., Lyn, A., McNicholl, M., Khan, S., Rahimi, S., & Grenier, A. (2022). Digital ageism: Challenges and opportunities in artificial intelligence for older adults. *The Gerontologist*, 62(7), 947–955. DOI: 10.1093/geront/gnab167 PMID: 35048111

Cipriani, G., Danti, S., Carlesi, C., & Di Fiorino, M. (2017). Old and dangerous: Prison and dementia. *Journal of Forensic and Legal Medicine*, 51, 40–44. DOI: 10.1016/j.jflm.2017.07.004 PMID: 28750353

Dawes, J. (2009). Ageing prisoners: Issues for social work. *Australian Social Work*, 62(2), 258–271. DOI: 10.1080/03124070902803475

Denney, A. S., Tewksbury, R., & Jones, R. S. (2014). Beyond Basic Needs: Social Support and Structure for Successful O ender Reentry. *Journal of Qualitative Criminal Justice & Criminology*, 2(1). Advance online publication. DOI: 10.21428/88de04a1.d95029f6

DiTomas, M., Augustine, D., & Williams, B. A. (2022). Growing older: challenges of prison and reentry for the aging population. *Public Health Behind Bars: From Prisons to Communities*, 63-87. DOI: 10.1007/978-1-0716-1807-3_5

Ekunwe, I., & Jones, R. S. (2011). *Global perspectives on re-entry: Exploring the challenges facing ex-prisoners.* University of Tampere. Re entry, recidivism, and life after prison. *Cogent Social Sciences*, 9(2), 2246706. DOI: 10.1080/23311886.2023.2246706

Ertl, T., Taugerbeck, S., Esau, M., Aal, K., Tolmie, P., & Wulf, V. (2019). The social mile-How (psychosocial) ICT can help to promote resocialization and to overcome prison. *Proceedings of the ACM on Human-Computer Interaction, 3*(GROUP), 1-31. DOI: 10.1145/3370270

Fahey, J., Roberts, C., & Engel, L. (2006). Employment of ex-offenders: Employer perspectives. *Crime and Justice Institute, 55*(4), 297-305. https://www.crj.org/assets/2017/07/Employer_Perspectives.pdf

Fedorczyk, F. (2024). Navigating the dichotomy of smart prisons: Between surveillance and rehabilitation. *Law, Innovation and Technology*, 16(1), 243–260. DOI: 10.1080/17579961.2024.2313793

Gaes, G. G. (2008). The impact of prison education programs on post-release outcomes. *Reentry Roundtable on Education, John Jay College of Criminal Justice, New York, March, 31*. http://www.antoniocasella.eu/nume/Gaes_2008.pdf

Gal, M. (2003). The physical and mental health of older offenders. []. Correctional Service of Canada. Physical and Mental Health of Older Offenders | Office of Justice Programs] [ojp.gov]. *Forum on Corrections Research*, 14(2), 15–19.

Galassi, A., Mpofu, E., & Athanasou, J. (2015). Therapeutic community treatment of an inmate population with substance use disorders: Post-release trends in re-arrest, re-incarceration, and drug misuse relapse. *International Journal of Environmental Research and Public Health*, 12(6), 7059–7072. DOI: 10.3390/ijerph120607059 PMID: 26103591

Grant, A. (1999). Elderly Inmates: Issues for Australia. []. Elderly inmates: issues for Australia] [psu.edu]. *Trends and Issues in Crime and Criminal Justice*, •••, 115.

Harding, D. J., Morenoff, J. D., Dobson, C. C., Lane, E. B., Opatovsky, K., Williams, E. D. G., & Wyse, J. (2016). Families, prisoner reentry, and reintegration. *Boys and men in African American families*, 105-160. DOI: 10.1007/978-3-319-43847-4_8

Harnsberger, R. S. (2011). *A Guide to Sources of Texas Criminal Justice Statistics* (No. 6). University of North Texas Press.

Howse, K. (2003). Growing old in prison. *A Scoping Study on Older Prisoners. London: Prison Reform Trust.* Growing Old in Prison - a scoping study.pdf (prisonreformtrust.org.uk) https://books.google.co.in/books?hl=en&lr=&id=MyFnFsI9wL4C&oi=fnd&pg=PA7&dq=International+Perspective+of+the+Review+Adults+in+prison:&ots=QXLzVobNDo&sig=sfIlWLI89F-zWuIMdWZ5-aufY7k&redir_esc=y#v=onepage&q=International%20Perspective%20of%20the%20Review%20Adults%20in%20prison%3A&f=falsehttps://www.google.co.in/books/edition/A_Guide_to_Sources_of_Texas_Criminal_Jus/VLZvBni_p7kC?hl=en&gbpv=0

Johnson, E. H. (2000). Elders and Japanese corrections. *Elders, crime, and the criminal justice system*, 222-235.

Kaun, A., & Stiernstedt, F. (2020). Doing time, the smart way? Temporalities of the smart prison. *New Media & Society*, 22(9), 1580–1599. DOI: 10.1177/1461444820914865

Khoei, T. T., & Singh, A. (2024). A survey of Emotional Artificial Intelligence and crimes: Detection, prediction, challenges and future direction. *Journal of Computational Social Science*, 7(3), 1–44. DOI: 10.1007/s42001-024-00313-3

Lares, L. A., & Montgomery, S. (2020). Psychosocial needs of released long-term incarcerated older adults. *Criminal Justice Review*, 45(3), 358–377. DOI: 10.1177/0734016820913101

Lee, L. M. (2019). The impact of prison programming on recidivism. *Corrections : Policy, Practice and Research*, 4(4), 252–271. DOI: 10.1080/23774657.2017.1399095

Lockwood, S. K., Nally, J. M., Ho, T., & Knutson, K. (2015). Racial disparities and similarities in post-release recidivism and employment among ex-prisoners with a different level of education. *Journal of Prison Education and Reentry*, 2(1), 16–31. DOI: 10.15845/jper.v2i1.703

Mahlangu, G., & Zivanai, E. (2023). Offender eLearning: A systematic literature review on re-Markina, A. (2019). Problems related to reintegration of young ex-offenders in Estonia. *Kriminologijos studijos, 7*, 56-74. DOI: 10.15388/CrimLithuan.2019.7.3

Marti, I. (2022). During Leisure Time. In *Doing Indefinite Time: An Ethnography of Long-Term Imprisonment in Switzerland* (pp. 235–328). Springer International Publishing., DOI: 10.1007/978-3-031-12590-4_6

Maschi, T., Morgen, K., Hintenach, A., & Kaye, A. (2021). Aging in prison and correction policy in global perspectives. In *Oxford Research Encyclopedia of Criminology and Criminal Justice*. DOI: 10.1093/acrefore/9780190264079.013.648

Mehmood, S., Ahmad, Z., & Khan, A. A. (2016). Dynamic relationships between tourist arrivals, immigrants, and crimes in the United States. *Tourism Management*, 54, 383–392. DOI: 10.1016/j.tourman.2015.12.010

Monica, M., & Geeta, D. (2024). The Future of Rehabilitation: AI And The Transformation Of Education In Prisons. *Educational Administration: Theory and Practice*, 30(2), 916–922. DOI: 10.53555/kuey.v30i2.2996

Partington, S. T. (2017). *Age, imprisonment and social re-entry: Exploring the needs and experiences of older offenders following release and resettlement from prison* (Doctoral dissertation, University of Huddersfield). https://eprints.hud.ac.uk/id/eprint/34149/

Paulson, P. (2013). The Role of Community Based Programs in Reducing Recidivism in Ex-Offenders. https://library.stkate.edu/archives/sophia

Rodolfa, K. T., Salomon, E., Haynes, L., Mendieta, I. H., Larson, J., & Ghani, R. (2020). Case study: predictive fairness to reduce misdemeanor recidivism through social service interventions. In *Proceedings of the 2020 Conference on Fairness, Accountability, and Transparency* (pp. 142-153). DOI: 10.1145/3351095.3372863

Schlanger, M. (2017). Prisoners with disabilities. https://repository.law.umich.edu/book_chapters/114/

Shand, R. A. (1996). Pre-release/transition: Inmate programs and support upon entry, during incarceration, and after release. *Journal of Correctional Education*, •••, 20–40. https://www.jstor.org/stable/23292010

Srinivasan, S. (2014). The Rights of Prisoners: An Overview. https://papers.ssrn.com/sol3/papers.cfm?abstract_id=2704761

Srinivasan, S. (2021). Health problem faced by Elderly inmates' in Central prisons India. https://papers.ssrn.com/sol3/papers.cfm?abstract_id=3962980

Srinivasan, S. (2021). Mental Health problems faced by Aged Inmates due to Overcrowding of Central prison in Tamil Nadu.

Srinivasan, S., & Ilango, P. (2015). The Elderly Inmates in the Indian Prisons–A Psychosocial Perspective. In *The 2nd International Social Work Conference*. https://papers.ssrn.com/sol3/papers.cfm?abstract_id=2704808

Steiner, E. (2003). Early release for seriously ill and elderly prisoners: Should French practice be followed? *Probation Journal*, 50(3), 267–276. DOI: 10.1177/0264550503503013

Tayumi Ishiy, K., & Marcondes Ramos, J. R. (2023). Access to justice and the new technologies applied during the implementation of prison sentences.

Tonry, M. (2022). Punishments, politics, and prisons in Western countries. *Crime and Justice*, 51(1), 7–57. DOI: 10.1086/721278

Travis, J., Solomon, A., & Waul, M. (2001). *From prison to home*. The Urban Institute., https://d1wqtxts1xzle7.cloudfront.net/53679164/FROM_PRISON_TO_HOME20170627-4007-5rbnzk-libre.pdf?1498577786=&response-content-disposition=inline%3B+filename%3DFrom_Prison_to_Home.pdf&Expires=1723569654&Signature=N5esnCFuwnkIGupnufzk3FKoTw~wpW1RcAlqc774a~peCLXke0ynvXZΛtdTBGV5IAIluhJZEHIXi8O9xaJxHeQWhaUEXYuvJcNdubScO4PM0ZZdsAjJ2d1bRCNW6iybVylJrbQjIR33JhPcQJd25Fmwfay-Ud4obGyCtzBjTnAfLtcsKW-uOwHWep-x2EXwYYGdBseG6InVyAY3llhUVfmqOsOmHZsw~tHhqH3TohfTn2tpjABv2EAjAvUCfyyYSOk9UO6a6oIlsI2fhcM6Q8qrlekrks4iJpmDZ665QHOwH~tB75WAVMJavR9HIXkYSDJ1q7AmAc6O6Xpsb00lZ2w__&Key-Pair-Id=APKAJLOHF5GGSLRBV4ZA

Villasenor, J., & Foggo, V. (2020). Artificial Intelligence, Due Process and Criminal Sentencing. *Mich. St. L. Rev.*, 295. https://heinonline.org/HOL/LandingPage?handle=hein.journals/mslr2020&div=11&id=&page=

Visher, C. A., & Travis, J. (2003). Transitions from prison to community: Understanding individual pathways. *Annual Review of Sociology*, 29(1), 89–113. DOI: 10.1146/annurev.soc.29.010202.095931

Wahidin, A., & Cain, M. E. (Eds.). (2006). *Ageing, crime and society*. Cullompton: Willan. 10.4324_9781843925729_previewpdf (1).pdf

Williams, B., & Abraldes, R. (2007). Growing older: Challenges of prison and reentry for the aging population. In *Public health behind bars: From prisons to communities* (pp. 56–72). Springer New York., DOI: 10.1007/978-0-387-71695-4_5

Yasmin, N., & Pandey, R. (2018). Prospective memory, working memory, planning, and attention in schizophrenia and bipolar disorder: A comparative study. *Applied Cognitive Psychology*, 32(4), 487–498. DOI: 10.1002/acp.3423

Zivanai, E., & Mahlangu, G. (2022). Digital prison rehabilitation and successful re-entry into a digital society: A systematic literature review on the new reality on prison rehabilitation. *Cogent Social Sciences*, 8(1), 2116809. DOI: 10.1080/23311886.2022.2116809

Compilation of References

. de los Riscos, A. M., & D'Haro, L. F. (2021). Toxicbot: A conversational agent to fight online hate speech. *Conversational dialogue systems for the next decade*, 15-30.

. Francesc, Pedro. (2020). Applications of Artificial Intelligence to higher education: possibilities, evidence and challenges. *Journal of IUL University*, 61-76 DOI: .DOI: 10.57568/iulres.v1i1.43

. Hajamydeen, A. I., & Helmi, R. A. A. (2020). Performance of Supervised Learning Algorithms on Multi-Variate Datasets. *Machine Learning and Big Data: Concepts, Algorithms, Tools and Applications*, 209-232.

. Kathirvel A, Maheswaran C P, Subramaniam M, and Naren A K, (March 2023b). "Chapter 25: Quantum Computers Based on Distributed Computing Systems for the Next Generation: Overview and Applications", Quantum Computers Based on Distributed Computing Systems for the Next Generation, Handbook of Research on Quantum Computing for Smart Environments, IGI Global Publiser, Hershey, Pennsylvania, USA, ISBN13: 9781668466971 ISBN10: 166846697X EISBN13: 9781668466988, DOI: Quantum Computers Based on Distributed Computing Systems for the Next Generation: Overview and Applications: Computer Science & IT Book Chapter | IGI Global (igi-global.com)DOI: 10.4018/978-1-6684-6697-1.ch025

. Nguyen, H. B., Xue, B., Liu, I., & Zhang, M. (2014, July). Filter based backward elimination in wrapper based PSO for feature selection in classification. In 2014 IEEE congress on evolutionary computation (CEC) (pp. 3111-3118). IEEE.

. Pereira, R. B., Carvalho, A. P. D., Zadrozny, B., & Merschmann, L. H. D. C. (2015). Information gain feature selection for multi-label classification.

. Rossini, P. (2020). Beyond toxicity in the online public sphere: understanding incivility in online political talk. *A research agenda for digital politics*, 160-170.

. Sharma, S., & Jain, A. (2020). An empirical evaluation of correlation based feature selection for tweet sentiment classification. *Advances in Cybernetics, Cognition, and Machine Learning for Communication Technologies*, 199-208.

. Singh, B., & Kaunert, C. (2024). Future of Digital Marketing: Hyper-Personalized Customer Dynamic Experience with AI-Based Predictive Models. *Revolutionizing the AI-Digital Landscape: A Guide to Sustainable Emerging Technologies for Marketing Professionals*, 189.

. Srba, I., Lenzini, G., Pikuliak, M., & Pecar, S. (2021). Addressing hate speech with data science: an overview from computer science perspective. *Hate Speech-Multidisziplinäre Analysen und Handlungsoptionen: Theoretische und empirische Annäherungen an ein interdisziplinäres Phänomen*, 317-336.

. Trott, V., Beckett, J., & Paech, V. (2020). Tuning out hate speech on Reddit: Automating moderation and detecting toxicity in the manosphere. *AoIR Selected Papers of Internet Research.*

'AI for Lawyers Guide: Do Artificial Attorneys Dream of Electric Practice?' (*RSS*) <https://growlawfirm.com/blog/ai-for-lawyers-guide> accessed 23 October 2023

Abiodun, O. S., & Lekan, A. J. (2020, December 1). EXPLORING THE POTENTIALS OF ARTIFICIAL INTELLGIENCE IN THE JUDICIARY. *IJEAST*, 5(8). Advance online publication. DOI: 10.33564/IJEAST.2020.v05i08.004

Abioye, S. O., Oyedele, L. O., Akanbi, L., Ajay, A., Delgado, J. D., Bilal, M., & Ahmed, A. (2021). Artificial intelligence in the construction industry: A review of present status,opportunities and future challenges. *Journal of Building Engineering Elsevier*https://www.sciencedirect.com/science/article/pii/S2352710221011578

Adam, V. (2023, Nov 05). *New Frontier: AI Governance and Ethical Frameworks.* Retrieved Aug 14, 2024, from https://www.linkedin.com: https://www.linkedin.com/pulse/new-frontier-ai-governance-ethical-frameworks-adam-m-victor-qjotc/

Aday, R. H., & Krabill, J. J. (2012). Older and geriatric offenders: Critical issues for the 21st century. *Special needs offenders in correctional institutions, 1*, 203-233. https://books.google.co.in/books?hl=en&lr=&id=wct1AwAAQBAJ&oi=fnd&pg=PA203&dq=International+experts+in+correctional+research+have+conducted+various+studies+in+countries+such+as+Australia+(Grant,+1999%3B+Dawes,+2009),+Japan+(Johnson,+2000),+Sweden+(Fazel+%26+Grann,+2002),+Canada+(Gal,+2002),+France+(Steiner,+2003)+UK+(Howse,+2003%3B+Wahidin+%26+Cain,+2006).&ots=L4HJ4fiyxT&sig=qaWkrKhiLXQ-Q3qf-nxGRKwmOkY&redir_esc=y#v=onepage&q&f=false

Ahsan, S., & Shah, A. (2008, April 1). Data mining, semantic web and advanced information technologies for fighting terrorism. DOI: 10.1109/ISBAST.2008.4547644

Ahuja, V. K. (2020). Artificial Intelligence and Copyright: Issues and Challenges. ILI Law Review, *Winter Issue*. 270-285. https://ili.ac.in/pdf/vka.pdf

Akash, T. (2022). *AI in legal businesses: Use cases, solution, benefits and implementation*. Retrieved Aug 01, 2024, from https://www.leewayhertz.com: https://www.leewayhertz.com/ai-use-cases-in-legal-businesses/

AlEmadi, M. M., & Zaghouani, W. (2024, May). Emotional Toll and Coping Strategies: Navigating the Effects of Annotating Hate Speech Data. In *Proceedings of the Workshop on Legal and Ethical Issues in Human Language Technologies@ LREC-COLING 2024* (pp. 66-72).

Aletras, N., Tsarapatsanis, D., Preoţiuc-Pietro, D., & Lampos, V. (2016). Predicting judicial decisions of the European court of human rights: A natural language processing perspective. *PeerJ Computer Science, 2016*(10). DOI: 10.7717/peerj-cs.93

ALGORITHMS AND TERRORISM. (n.d). https://www.un.org/counterterrorism/sites/www.un.org.counterterrorism/files/malicious-use-of-ai-uncct-unicri-report-hd.pdf

Ali, M., & Abdel Haq, M. K. (2021). Bibliographical analysis of artificial intelligence learning in Higher Education: is the role of the human educator and educated a thing of the past? *IGI Global.* In Fostering Communication and Learning With Underutilized Technologies in Higher Education, 2021, 36-52. IGI Global. 7998-4846-2.ch003.https://www.igi-global.com/chapter/bibliographical-analysis-of-artificial-intelligence-learning-in-higher-education/262720

Ali, S. (2024). *Youth, social media, and online safety: a holistic approach towards detecting and mitigating risks in online conversations* (Doctoral dissertation).

Al-Qusi, H. (2018). The Problem of the Person Responsible for Operating the Robot - A Prospective Analytical Study in the European Civil Law Rules for Robots (In Arabic), *Generation Journal of In-Depth Legal Research*, May 2018 Issue, Generation Scientific Research Center, Lebanon, pp.89-93.

Álvarez, J. D., Matias-Guiu, J. A., Cabrera-Martín, M. N., Risco-Martín, J. L., & Ayala, J. L. (2019). An application of machine learning with feature selection to improve diagnosis and classification of neurodegenerative disorders. *BMC Bioinformatics*, 20(1), 1–12. DOI: 10.1186/s12859-019-3027-7 PMID: 31601182

Amanda, G., Jonathan, A., Gerald, M., & Anthony, H. (2020, May 16). Stakeholder identification and engagement in problem structuring interventions. *European Journal of Operational Research*, 283(01), 321–340. DOI: 10.1016/j.ejor.2019.10.044

Ammar, Z. (2024, April 15). Balancing the scale: Navigating ethical and practical challenges of artificial intelligence (AI) integration in legal practices. *Springer Link*, 04(27), 27. Advance online publication. DOI: 10.1007/s44163-024-00121-8

Among, H. I. V. (2007). Module for Prison Intervention: South Asia. https://www.unodc.org/documents/southasia/Trainingmanuals/Module_for_Prison_Intervention_-_South_Asia.pdf

Anas, B., & Maria, K. (2023, Sep 29). *The Impact of the GDPR on Artificial Intelligence*. Retrieved Aug 15, 2024, from https://securiti.ai: https://securiti.ai/impact-of-the-gdpr-on-artificial-intelligence/

Anjum, & Katarya, R. (2024). Hate speech, toxicity detection in online social media: a recent survey of state of the art and opportunities. *International Journal of Information Security, 23*(1), 577-608.

Antwi, A. L. E. X. (2015). *Social reintegration of offenders and recidivism in Ghana. Unpublished doctoral thesis*. University of Ghana., https://ugspace.ug.edu.gh/server/api/core/bitstreams/7af9f24e-d7b1-4108-9d03-d7bcc5ebd480/content

Appel, G., Neelbauer, J., & Schweidel, D. A. (2023, April 7). Generative AI has an intellectual property problem. *Harvard Business Review*. https://hbr.org/2023/04/generative-ai-has-an-intellectual-property-problem

Armour, J., & Sako, M. (2020). AI-enabled business models in legal services: From traditional law firms to next-generation law companies? *Journal of Professions and Organization*, 7(1), 27–46.

Artechouse, (n.d.). Artechouse announces the return of the ground breaking exhibition machine hallucinations: NYC with refik anadol for a special limited-duration run in New York City. *Artechouse.*https://www.artechouse.com/news/artechouse-announces-return-of-machine-hallucination-nyc/

Ashley, K D. (2019, August 15). A Brief History of the Changing Roles of Case Prediction in AI and Law. Cambridge University Press, 36(1), 93-112. DOI: 10.26826/law-in-context.v36i1.88

Ashok Kumar, L., Sujatha, R., & Uma, M. B. (2022). Predictive Analytics for Data Driven Decision Making: Tools and Techniques for Solving Real World Problems. In *Predictive Analytics for Data Driven Decision Making: Tools and Techniques for Solving Real World Problems* (pp. 45-78). Nova Science Publishers, Inc. DOI: 10.52305/RZBM7280

Assibong, P., Wogu, I. A., Sholarin, M. A., Misra, S., Damasevičius, R., & Sharma, N. (2019). The Politics of Artificial Intelligence Behaviour and Human Rights Violation Issues in the 2016 US Presidential Elections: An Appraisal. In Sharma, N. C. (Ed.), *Advances in Intelligent Systems and Computing* (pp. 295–309). Springer.

Aukerman, M. J. (2003). Barriers to reentry: Legal strategies to reduce recidivism and promote the success of ex-offenders. *Michigan Criminal Law Annual Journal, 1*, 4-11. https://waynecountydefendertraining.com/cap-archives/2006/handouts/2006-09-15_05_barriers.pdf

Ayyaswamy, K. (2024b). Enhancing Digital Technology Planning, Leadership, and Management to Transform Education. In Bhatia, M., & Mushtaq, M. T. (Eds.), *Navigating Innovative Technologies and Intelligent Systems in Modern Education* (pp. 1–9). IGI Global., DOI: 10.4018/979-8-3693-5370-7.ch001

Azumah, S. W., Elsayed, N., ElSayed, Z., Ozer, M., & La Guardia, A. (2024). Deep Learning Approaches for Detecting Adversarial Cyberbullying and Hate Speech in Social Networks. *arXiv preprint arXiv:2406.17793*.

Bacanoiu, M. V., & Danoiu, M. (2022). New strategies to improve the quality of life for normal aging versus pathological aging. *Journal of Clinical Medicine*, 11(14), 4207. DOI: 10.3390/jcm11144207 PMID: 35887969

Bajgar, O., & Horenovsky, J. (2022, January 1). Negative Human Rights as a Basis for Long-term AI Safety and Regulation. Cornell University. https://doi.org/DOI: 10.48550/arXiv.2208

Baker, R. S., & Siemens, G. (2014). Educational data mining and learning analytics. 1-29DOI:. https://www.researchgate.net/publication/316628053_Educational_data_mining_and_learning_analytics/link/611682a60c2bfa282a41e893/download?_tp=eyJjb250ZXh0Ijp7ImZpcnN0UGFnZSI6InB1YmxpY2F0aW9uIiwicGFnZSI6InB1YmxpY2F0aW9uIn19DOI: 10.1017/CBO9781139519526.016

Bar&Bench. (2024, Aug 19). *AI Adoption and its Impact in the Legal Industry: An Indian Perspective*. Retrieved Aug 19, 2024, from https://www.barandbench.com: https://www.barandbench.com/law-firms/view-point/ai-adoption-and-impact-legal-industry-indian-perspective

Barbosa, F., & Valadares, L. (2023). Artificial intelligence: a claim for strict liability for human rights violation. *Revista de Direito Internacional*, 150.

Barbosa, R. G. (2009). The Philosophical Approaches to Intellectual Property and Legal Transplants - The Mexican Supreme Court and NAFTA Article 1705. *Houston Journal of International Law*, 31(3), 515–564.

Barfield, W. (2006). Intellectual Property Rights in Virtual Environments: Considering the Rights of Owners, Programmers and Virtual Avatars. *Akron Law Review*, 39(3), 649–700.

Barfield, W., & Pagallo, U. (2021). *Advanced Introduction to Law and Artificial Intelligence*. Edward Elgar Publishing Ltd.

Barysė, D., & Sarel, R. (2024, March). Algorithms in the court: Does it matter which part of the judicial decision-making is automated? *Artificial Intelligence and Law*, 32(01), 117–146. DOI: 10.1007/s10506-022-09343-6 PMID: 36643574

Beck, S. (2019). Autonomous Systems and Criminal Law – new impulses for the concept of responsibility? https://www.inf.uni-hamburg.de/en/inst/ab/eit/about/newsfeed/2019/ 20190703-beck.html

Bellaiche, L., Shahi, R., Turpin, M. H., Ragnhildstveit, A., Sprockett, S., Barr, N., Christensen, A., & Seli, P. (2023). Humans versus AI: Whether and why we prefer human-created compared to AI-created artwork. *Cognitive Research: Principles and Implications*, 8(1), 42. DOI: 10.1186/s41235-023-00499-6 PMID: 37401999

Bellamy, R., Dey, K., Hind, M., Hoffman, S., Houde, S., Kannan, K., Lohia, P., Martino, J., Mehta, S., Mojsilovic, A., Nagar, S., Ramamurthy, K. N., Richards, J., Saha, D., Sattigeri, P., Singh, M., Varshney, K. R., & Zhang, Y. (2019). AI Fairness 360: An extensible toolkit for detecting and mitigating algorithmic bias. *IBM Journal of Research and Development*, 63(4/5), 63. DOI: 10.1147/JRD.2019.2942287

Ben Chester, C. (2024, July 03). Transparency and accountability in AI systems: Safeguarding wellbeing in the age of algorithmic decision-making. *Frontiers in Human Dynamics*, 06, 1421273. Advance online publication. DOI: 10.3389/fhumd.2024.1421273

Benyekhlef, K., & Zhu, J. (2024). The judicial system and the work of judges and lawyers in the application of law and sanctions assisted by AI. In *Handbook of Artificial Intelligence at Work* (pp. 250-275). Edward Elgar Publishing Ltd. Retrieved Aug 15, 2024, from https://www.scopus.com/record/display.uri?origin=citedby&eid=2-s2.0-85189228691&noHighlight=false&relpos=2

Bhatnagar, H. (2020). Artificial Intelligence-A New Horizon in Indian Higher Education. Journal of Learning and Teaching in Digital Age, 2020, 6(1), 30-34 ISSN: 2458-8350 pp 30-34 https://dergipark.org.tr/en/download/article-file/1184703

Bilal, A. (2010). *Principles of the Egyptian Penal Code - General Section.* Dar Al-Nahda Al-Arabiya. (In Arabic)

Binu, D., & Rajakumar, B. R. (2021). *Artificial intelligence in data mining: Theories and applications.* Academic Press.

Bi, S., Zhou, Z., Pan, L., & Qi, G. (2023, December). Judicial knowledge-enhanced magnitude-aware reasoning for numerical legal judgment prediction. *Artificial Intelligence and Law*, 31(04), 773–806. DOI: 10.1007/s10506-022-09337-4

Biswas, P., & Paul, C. (2020). Review paper on hate speech inside the context of online social networks. [TURCOMAT]. *Turkish Journal of Computer and Mathematics Education*, 11(1), 352–365.

Bowker, J., & Ophoff, J. (2022, July). Reducing exposure to hateful speech online. In *Science and Information Conference* (pp. 630-645). Cham: Springer International Publishing.

Brandtzaeg, P., Heim, J., & Karahasanovic, A. (2011). Understanding the new digital divide-A typology of Internet users in Europe Author Links open overlay panel. *International Journal of Human-Computer Studies*, 69(3), 123–138. DOI: 10.1016/j.ijhcs.2010.11.004

Branovitskiy, K., & Yarkov, V. V. (2022, January 1). Some procedural aspects of the introduction of predictive justice in the civil procedure. *EDP Sciences*, 134, 00002–00002. DOI: 10.1051/shsconf/202213400002

Brink, R., & Toth, C. (2021). Ethical considerations of AI in legal services: A critical review. *Journal of Legal Ethics*, 46(2), 256–279.

Buccafusco, C. (2016). A theory of copyright authorship. *Virginia Law Review*, 102(5), 1229–1295. https://www.jstor.org/stable/43923336

Buey, M. G., Garrido, A. L., Bobed, C., & Ilarri, S. (2016, February). The AIS project: Boosting information extraction from legal documents by using ontologies. In *ICAART (2)* (pp. 438-445).

Burk, D L. (2020, October 5). ALGORITHMIC LEGAL METRICS. DOI: 10.5210/spir.v2020i0.11184

Caldwell, M. (2023). What is an "author"? -Copyright authorship of ai art through a philosophical lens. *Houston Law Review*, 61(2), 411–442. https://houstonlawreview.org/article/92132-what-is-an-author-copyright-authorship-of-ai-art-through-a-philosophical-lens

Casula, P., Anupam, A., & Parvin, N. (2021, June). "We found no violation!": Twitter's Violent Threats Policy and Toxicity in Online Discourse. In *Proceedings of the 10th International Conference on Communities & Technologies-Wicked Problems in the Age of Tech* (pp. 151-159).

Chakraborty, T., & Masud, S. (2022). Nipping in the bud: detection, diffusion and mitigation

Chandra, M. (2019, November 30). Reduction of Cyber Crimes by Effective Use of Artificial Intelligence Techniques. *Reduction of Cyber Crimes by Effective Use of Artificial Intelligence Techniques.*, 8(4), 8643–8645. DOI: 10.35940/ijrte.D8566.118419

Chang, R. C., May, J., & Lerman, K. (2023, September). Feedback Loops and Complex Dynamics of Harmful Speech in Online Discussions. In *International Conference on Social Computing, Behavioral-Cultural Modeling and Prediction and Behavior Representation in Modeling and Simulation* (pp. 85-94). Cham: Springer Nature Switzerland. DOI: 10.1007/978-3-031-43129-6_9

Chatterjee, S., & N.S., S. (2019, July 1). Personal Data Sharing and Legal Issues of Human Rights in the Era of Artificial Intelligence. IGI Global, 15(3), 21-36. DOI: 10.4018/IJEGR.2019070102

Chaudhary, M., Saxena, C., & Meng, H. (2021). Countering online hate speech: An nlp perspective. *arXiv preprint arXiv:2109.02941*.

Chauhan, S., & Gangopadhyay, S. (2022, June). Design of Intrusion Detection System Based on Logical Analysis of Data (LAD) Using Information Gain Ratio. In *International Symposium on Cyber Security, Cryptology, and Machine Learning* (pp. 47-65). Cham: Springer International Publishing. DOI: 10.1007/978-3-031-07689-3_4

Chen, X., Xie, H., Zou, D., & Hwang, G. (2020). Application and theory gaps during the rise of Artificial Intelligence in Education. *Computers and Education: Artificial Intelligence*.

Chen, D. L. (2019, March 15). Judicial analytics and the great transformation of American Law. *Artificial Intelligence and Law*, 27(01), 15–42. DOI: 10.1007/s10506-018-9237-x PMID: 32255924

Chen, D. L., & Eagel, J. (2017). Can machine learning help predict the outcome of asylum adjudications? *16th International Conference on Artificial Intelligence and Law, ICAIL 2017* (pp. 237-240). London: Association for Computing Machinery. DOI: 10.1145/3086512.3086538

Chen, M., & Li, S. (2020, June 1). Research on the application of artificial intelligence technology in the field of Justice. *Journal of Physics: Conference Series*, 1570(1), 012047–012047. DOI: 10.1088/1742-6596/1570/1/012047

Chen, X., Zou, D., Xie, H., Cheng, G., & Caixia, L. (2022). Two Decades of Artificial Intelligence in Education. *Journal of Educational Technology & Society*, •••, 28–47.

Chesterman, S. (2024). Good models borrow, great models steal: Intellectual property rights and generative AI. *Policy and Society*, •••, puae006. Advance online publication. DOI: 10.1093/polsoc/puae006

Chohlas-Wood, A., Coots, M., Goel, S., & Nyarko, J. (2023, July 24). Designing equitable algorithms. *Nature Computational Science*, 3(7), 601–610. DOI: 10.1038/s43588-023-00485-4 PMID: 38177749

Choudhary, V. & Ali, Aamir S. M. (2023). ChatGPT and Copyright Concerns. *Economic and Political Weekly*, 58(16), 4–5.

Chouldechova, A. (2017, June 1). Fair Prediction with Disparate Impact: A Study of Bias in Recidivism Prediction Instruments. Mary Ann Liebert. *Big Data*, 5(2), 153–163. DOI: 10.1089/big.2016.0047 PMID: 28632438

Chu, C. H., Nyrup, R., Leslie, K., Shi, J., Bianchi, A., Lyn, A., McNicholl, M., Khan, S., Rahimi, S., & Grenier, A. (2022). Digital ageism: Challenges and opportunities in artificial intelligence for older adults. *The Gerontologist*, 62(7), 947–955. DOI: 10.1093/geront/gnab167 PMID: 35048111

Cipriani, G., Danti, S., Carlesi, C., & Di Fiorino, M. (2017). Old and dangerous: Prison and dementia. *Journal of Forensic and Legal Medicine*, 51, 40–44. DOI: 10.1016/j.jflm.2017.07.004 PMID: 28750353

Ciro, M., Umberto, M., Giuseppe, D. P., & Massimo, E. (2024, February 29). Ethical and regulatory challenges of AI technologies in healthcare: A narrative review. *Heliyon*, 10(04), e26297. Advance online publication. DOI: 10.1016/j.heliyon.2024.e26297 PMID: 38384518

Corazza, M., Menini, S., Cabrio, E., Tonelli, S., & Villata, S. (2020). A multilingual evaluation for online hate speech detection. *ACM Transactions on Internet Technology*, 20(2), 1–22. DOI: 10.1145/3377323

Correa, P. R., Grandón, E., & Cataluna, J. (2020). *Users segmentation based on the Technological Readiness Adoption Index in emerging countries: The case of Chile.* Technological Forecasting AND Social Change.

Costa, S., da Silva, B. M., & Tavares, M. (2021, December). Tackling online hate speech? play your role! In *International Conference on ArtsIT, Interactivity and Game Creation* (pp. 79-93). Cham: Springer International Publishing.

Cotter, T. (2010). Transformative use and cognizable harm. *Vanderbilt Journal of Entertainment and Technology Law*, 12(4), 701–753. https://scholarship.law.vanderbilt.edu/jetlaw/vol12/iss4/3

Craigle, V. (2019, January 1). Law Libraries Embracing AI. RELX Group (Netherlands). DOI: 10.2139/ssrn.3381798

Cristiano ALMONTE vs. AVERNA VISION & ROBOTICS, INC.; United States District Court, W.D. New York. No. 11-CV-1088 EAW, 128 F.Supp.3d 729 (2015), Signed August 31, 2015.

Cui, L., Xu, Y., Lv, T., & Wei, F. (2021, January 1). Document AI: Benchmarks, Models and Applications. Cornell University. https://doi.org/DOI: 10.48550/arXiv.2111

D'Mello, S., Olney, A., Williams, C., & Hays, P. (2012). Gaze tutor: A gaze-reactive intelligent tutoring system. *International Journal of Human-Computer Studies, 70(5), 377-398*, Retrieved from Gaze tutor: A gaze reactive intelligent tutoring system: https://www.sciencedirect.com/science/article/abs/pii/S1071581912000250?via%3DihubDOI: 10.1016/j.ijhcs.2012.01.004

Dahshan, Y. (2020). *Criminal Responsibility for Artificial Intelligence Crimes, Sharia and Law Journal, Issue 82, April 2020.* College of Law, Emirates University.

Dar, A. A., & Anuradha, N. (2020a). Use of Taguchi method for optimisation of process parameters of option pricing model. *International Journal of Services. Economics and Management*, 11(1), 1–20.

Dar, A. A., & Anuradha, N. (2020b). Studies on European call option of binomial option pricing model using Taguchi's L27 orthogonal array. *International Journal of Intelligent Enterprise*, 7(1-3), 234–249. DOI: 10.1504/IJIE.2020.104663

Dar, A. A., Gulzar, Z., Babu, R. A., Ali, L., & Shreedevi, G. (2024). Comparison: Taguchi method and full factorial design in WACC. *International Journal of Intelligent Enterprise*, 11(3), 300–315. DOI: 10.1504/IJIE.2024.139777

Davis, A. E. (2020, January 1). The Future of Law Firms (and Lawyers) in the Age of Artificial Intelligence. Fundação Getúlio Vargas, Escola de Direito, 16(1). https://doi.org/DOI: 10.1590/2317-6172201945

Dawes, J. (2009). Ageing prisoners: Issues for social work. *Australian Social Work*, 62(2), 258–271. DOI: 10.1080/03124070902803475

Deng, X., & Yu, Z. (2023). A meta-analysis and systematic review of the effect of chatbot technology use in sustainable education. *Sustainability (Basel)*, 15(4), 2940. https://www.mdpi.com/2071-1050/15/4/2940. DOI: 10.3390/su15042940

Denney, A. S., Tewksbury, R., & Jones, R. S. (2014). Beyond Basic Needs: Social Support and Structure for Successful O ender Reentry. *Journal of Qualitative Criminal Justice & Criminology*, 2(1). Advance online publication. DOI: 10.21428/88de04a1.d95029f6

Dimitrova, R. (2023). Liability Associated with AI Systems under the Bulgarian Criminal Code: Requirements, Approaches and Proposals. *2023 XXXII International Scientific Conference Electronics (ET)*, 1-6. https://doi.org/DOI: 10.1109/ET59121.2023.10279266

Dirican, C. (2015). The Impacts of Robotics, Artificial Intelligence On Business and Economics. *Procedia: Social and Behavioral Sciences*, 195, 564–573. DOI: 10.1016/j.sbspro.2015.06.134

DiTomas, M., Augustine, D., & Williams, B. A. (2022). Growing older: challenges of prison and reentry for the aging population. *Public Health Behind Bars: From Prisons to Communities*, 63-87. DOI: 10.1007/978-1-0716-1807-3_5

Djugumanov, I., & Janev, M. H. (2022). *Practical Applications of Advanced Technologies for Enhancing security and defense capabilities: perspectives and challenges for the Western Balkans*. IOS Press.

Dneprovskaya, M., & Abramitov, S. (2020, January 1). Digital Technologies in Activities of Russian Courts: Prospects of Artificial Intelligence Application. DOI: 10.2991/aebmr.k.200502.034

Dollens, D. (2014). Alan Turing's Drawings, Autopoiesis and Can Buildings Think? *Leonardo*, 47(3), 249–253. https://www.jstor.org/stable/43834182. DOI: 10.1162/LEON_a_00766

Dorn, R., Kezar, L., Morstatter, F., & Lerman, K. (2024). Harmful Speech Detection by Language Models Exhibits Gender-Queer Dialect Bias. *arXiv preprint arXiv:2406.00020*. DOI: 10.1145/3689904.3694704

Dremliuga, R., & Prisekina, N. (2020). The Concept of Culpability in Criminal Law and AI Systems. *Journal of Politics and Law*, 13(3), 256. DOI: 10.5539/jpl.v13n3p256

Dressel, J., & Farid, H. (2021, February 5). The Dangers of Risk Prediction in the Criminal Justice System. DOI: 10.21428/2c646de5.f5896f9f

Duenser, A., & Douglas, D. (2023, January 1). Who to Trust, How and Why: Untangling AI Ethics Principles, Trustworthiness and Trust. Cornell University. https://doi.org/DOI: 10.48550/arXiv.2309

Dy, J. G., & Brodley, C. E. (2004). Feature selection for unsupervised learning. *Journal of Machine Learning Research*, 5(Aug), 845–889.

Editor's Introduction'. (1995). 3. *Artificial Intelligence and Law*, •••, 1.

Eichner, S. V. (2023). *The Copyright Implications of Generative AI* [Paper presentation]. AIPLA Annual Meeting 2023

Ekunwe, I., & Jones, R. S. (2011). *Global perspectives on re-entry: Exploring the challenges facing ex-prisoners*. University of Tampere. Re entry, recidivism, and life after prison. *Cogent Social Sciences*, 9(2), 2246706. DOI: 10.1080/23311886.2023.2246706

El Aboudi, N., & Benhlima, L. (2016, September). Review on wrapper feature selection approaches. In 2016 International Conference on Engineering & MIS (ICEMIS) (pp. 1-5). IEEE. DOI: 10.1109/ICEMIS.2016.7745366

El-Kady, R. (2022). Criminal confrontation of encrypted digital currencies and artificial intelligence crimes Analytical study in Egyptian and comparative legislation, *Journal Sharia and Law*: Vol. 2022: No. 89, Article 6. Available at: https://scholarworks.uaeu.ac.ae/sharia_and_law/vol2022/iss89/6

El-Kady, R. (2021). Towards approving rules for criminal liability and punishment for misuse of artificial intelligence applications. *Journal of Legal and Economic Research (Mansoura)*, 11(1), 875–924. DOI: 10.21608/mjle.2022.217213

El-Kady, R. (2024). Artificial Intelligence and Criminal Law. In Tavares, M., Azevedo, G., Vale, J., Marques, R., & Bastos, M. (Eds.), *Artificial Intelligence Approaches to Sustainable Accounting* (pp. 34–52). IGI Global., DOI: 10.4018/979-8-3693-0847-9.ch003

El-Kady, R. (2024). Artificial Intelligence from a Criminal Law Perspective. *Al-Zaytoonah University of Jordan Journal for Legal Studies*, 2024(Special Issue), 186–210.

El-Kady, R. (2024). Navigating the Legal Maze: Electric Self-Driving Cars and the Complexities of Criminal Law. In Shaik, M. (Ed.), *Solving Fundamental Challenges of Electric Vehicles* (pp. 215–247). IGI Global., DOI: 10.4018/979-8-3693-4314-2.ch009

Ellamey, Y., & Elwakad, A. (2023). *The criminal responsibility of artificial intelligence systems: A prospective analytical study*. Corporate Law and Governance Review., DOI: 10.22495/clgrv5i1p8

Emilio, F. (2023, December 26). Fairness and Bias in Artificial Intelligence: A Brief Survey of Sources, Impacts, and Mitigation Strategies. *Sci*, 06(01), 3. Advance online publication. DOI: 10.3390/sci6010003

Enholm, I., Papagiannidis, E., Mikalef, P., & Krogstie, J. (2021). Artificial Intelligence and Business Value: A Literature Review. *Information Systems Frontiers*, •••, 1709–1734.

Ertl, T., Taugerbeck, S., Esau, M., Aal, K., Tolmie, P., & Wulf, V. (2019). The social mile-How (psychosocial) ICT can help to promote resocialization and to overcome prison. *Proceedings of the ACM on Human-Computer Interaction, 3*(GROUP), 1-31. DOI: 10.1145/3370270

ET. (2023, Apr 25). *AI and Privacy: The privacy concerns surrounding AI, its potential impact on personal data*. Retrieved Aug 14, 2024, from https://economictimes.indiatimes.com: https://economictimes.indiatimes.com/news/how-to/ai-and-privacy-the-privacy-concerns-surrounding-ai-its-potential-impact-on-personal-data/articleshow/99738234.cms

EU. (2024, Jun 18). *EU AI Act: first regulation on artificial intelligence*. Retrieved Aug 14, 2024, from https://www.europarl.europa.eu: https://www.europarl.europa.eu/topics/en/article/20230601STO93804/eu-ai-act-first-regulation-on-artificial-intelligence

European Commission. (. (2019, Apr 08). *Ethics guidelines for trustworthy AI*. Retrieved Aug 04, 2024, from https://digital-strategy.ec.europa.eu: https://digital-strategy.ec.europa.eu/en/library/ethics-guidelines-trustworthy-ai

European Police. "Europol" & Darktrace "company specialized in information security" (2019). How Technology Will Shape the Future of Cybercrime? Published on the website darktrace.com, Cyber Attacks Managed by Artificial Intelligence, a report published with an article entitled: Powered by Artificial Intelligence and Technology the Fifth Generation - European Police and "Dark Trace" warn of new patterns of cybercrime, published on the Internet on 7/23/2019, at: https://www.emaratalyoum.com/

Ezzeddine, Y., Bayerl, P. S., & Gibson, H. (2023, January 1). Citizen Perspectives on Necessary Safeguards to the Use of AI by Law Enforcement Agencies. Cornell University. https://doi.org/DOI: 10.48550/arXiv.2306

Fahey, J., Roberts, C., & Engel, L. (2006). Employment of ex-offenders: Employer perspectives. *Crime and Justice Institute, 55*(4), 297-305. https://www.crj.org/assets/2017/07/Employer_Perspectives.pdf

Febriani, R., Sholahuddin, M., & Kuswati, R. (2022). Do Artificial Intelligence and Digital Marketing Impact Purchase Intention Mediated by Perceived Value? *Journal of Business and Management Studies*, 184-196.

Fedorczyk, F. (2024). Navigating the dichotomy of smart prisons: Between surveillance and rehabilitation. *Law, Innovation and Technology*, 16(1), 243–260. DOI: 10.1080/17579961.2024.2313793

Feng, Y., Li, C., Ge, J., Luo, B., & Ng, V. (2021, January 04). Recommending statutes: A portable method based on neural networks. *ACM Transactions on Knowledge Discovery from Data*, 15(02), 1–22. Advance online publication. DOI: 10.1145/3424671

Ferrara, E. (2023, January 1). Fairness And Bias in Artificial Intelligence: A Brief Survey of Sources, Impacts, And Mitigation Strategies. Cornell University. https://doi.org/DOI: 10.48550/arXiv.2304

FiscalNote. (2024, Aug 07). *China's AI Policy & Development: What You Need to Know*. Retrieved Aug 19, 2024, from https://fiscalnote.com: https://fiscalnote.com/blog/china-ai-policy-development-what-you-need-to-know

Fortes, P R B. (2020, September 15). Paths to Digital Justice: Judicial Robots, Algorithmic Decision-Making, and Due Process. Cambridge University Press, 7(3), 453-469. DOI: 10.1017/als.2020.12

Foster, W. E., & Lawson, A. L. (2017). When to Praise the Machine: The Promise and Perils of Automated Transactional Drafting. *South Carolina Law Review*, 69, 597.

Francesc, P., Subosa, M., Rivas, A., & Valverde, P. (2019). *Artificial Intelligence in Education Challenges and Opportunities for Sustainable Development.* Paris https://repositorio.minedu.gob.pe/handle/20.500.12799/6533: United Nations Educational, Scientific and Cultural Organization UNESCO.

Francesc, P., Miguel, S., Axel, R., & Paula, V. (2019). *Artificial intelligence in education: challenges and opportunities for sustainable development.* Ministerio de Educación del Perú.

Franklin, R., & Mohana. (2024). Traffic Signal Violation Detection using Artificial Intelligence and Deep Learning. *2024 International Conference on Cognitive Robotics and Intelligent Systems*, (pp. 425-431).

Freitas, P. M., Andrade, F., & Novais, P. (2014). Criminal liability of autonomous agents: From the unthinkable to the plausible. In *AI Approaches to the Complexity of Legal Systems: AICOL 2013 International Workshops, AICOL-IV@ IVR, Belo Horizonte, Brazil, July 21-27, 2013 and AICOL-V@ SINTELNET-JURIX, Bologna, Italy, December 11, 2013, Revised Selected Papers* (pp. 145-156). Springer Berlin Heidelberg.

Frey, T. (2023, April 27). The difference between human creativity and generative AI creativity. *Futurist Speaker*. https://futuristspeaker.com/artificial-intelligence/the-difference-between-human-creativity-and-generative-ai-creativity/

Fu, G. H., Wang, J. B., & Lin, W. (2023). An adaptive loss backward feature elimination method for class-imbalanced and mixed-type data in medical diagnosis. *Chemometrics and Intelligent Laboratory Systems*, 236, 104809. DOI: 10.1016/j.chemolab.2023.104809

Gaes, G. G. (2008). The impact of prison education programs on post-release outcomes. *Reentry Roundtable on Education, John Jay College of Criminal Justice, New York, March, 31*. http://www.antoniocasella.eu/nume/Gaes_2008.pdf

Galassi, A., Mpofu, E., & Athanasou, J. (2015). Therapeutic community treatment of an inmate population with substance use disorders: Post-release trends in re-arrest, re-incarceration, and drug misuse relapse. *International Journal of Environmental Research and Public Health*, 12(6), 7059–7072. DOI: 10.3390/ijerph120607059 PMID: 26103591

Gal, M. (2003). The physical and mental health of older offenders. [). Correctional Service of Canada. Physical and Mental Health of Older Offenders | Office of Justice Programs] [ojp.gov]. *Forum on Corrections Research*, 14(2), 15–19.

Garg, T., Masud, S., Suresh, T., & Chakraborty, T. (2023). Handling bias in toxic speech detection: A survey. *ACM Computing Surveys*, 55(13s), 1–32. DOI: 10.1145/3580494

George, B. M. (2023, Nov). *AI in the Legal System, Transparency, Interpretability and the Right to a Fair Trial: The Challenges and Implications for the Ghanaian Civil and Criminal Justice Systems*. Retrieved Aug 02, 2024, from https://www.researchgate.net: https://www.researchgate.net/publication/375640346_AI_in_the_Legal_System_Transparency_Interpretability_and_the_Right_to_a_Fair_Trial_The_Challenges_and_Implications_for_the_Ghanaian_Civil_and_Criminal_Justice_Systems

Ghaitas, G. (2017). Internet and Digital Transformation Department (In Arabic), *International Policy Journal*, Issue 180, Cairo, April 2017.

Ghose, A. & Ali, Aamir S. M. (2023). Amplifying Music with Artificial Intelligence. *Economic and Political Weekly*, 58(17), 4–6.

Ghose, A., Ali, S. M., & Mishra, A. M. (2024). Artistic Expressions, Generative AI, and Legal Tapestry: Exploring the Dynamics of Copyright Laws in the Confluence of AI and Artistic Creation. In Hai-Jew, S. (Ed.), *Making Art With Generative AI Tools* (pp. 198–214). IGI Global., DOI: 10.4018/979-8-3693-1950-5.ch011

Ghose, A., & Gilda, A. (2023). Decussating aspects of intellectual property rights and private international law in India. *Journal of Intellectual Property Rights*, 28(6), 510–517. DOI: 10.56042/jipr.v28i6.762

Giuseppe, C., Francesca, L., Marco, L., Wolfgang, M., Przemyslaw, P., & Giovanni, S. (2018). Towards Consumer-Empowering Artificial Intelligence. *Proceedings of the Twenty-Seventh International Joint Conference on Artificial Intelligence*, (pp. 5150-5157). Stochkholm.

Gloria, M. (2023, December). Stakeholder roles in artificial intelligence projects. *Project Leadership and Society*, 03. Advance online publication. DOI: 10.1016/j.plas.2022.100068

Gobinath, V. M., Kathirvel, A., Rajesh Kanna, S. K., & Annamalai, K. "Chapter 5: Smart Technology in Management Industries: A Useful Perspective", Artificial Intelligence Applied to Industry 4.0, Wiley Publiser, USA, 1st Edition, July 2024g, pp.93-106, , ISBN 978-1-394-21611-6, DOI eBook ISBN, https://www.wiley.com/en-us/Topics+in+Artificial+Intelligence+Applied+to+Industry+4+0-p-9781394216116DOI: 10.1002/9781394216147.ch5

Gobinath, V., Ayyaswamy, K., & Kathirvel, N. (2024). Information Communication Technology and Intelligent Manufacturing Industries Perspective: An Insight. *Asian Science Bulletin*, 2(1), 36–45. DOI: 10.3923/asb.2024.36.45

GOELDNER. (2015). M. & HERSTATT, C. TIETZE, F. (2015). The emergence of care robotics – A patent and publication analysis. *Technological Forecasting and Social Change*, 92(March), 115–131.

Golbin, I., Rao, A S., Hadjarian, A., & Krittman, D. (2020, December 10). Responsible AI: A Primer for the Legal Community. DOI: 10.1109/BigData50022.2020.9377738

Goodman, B., & Flaxman, S. (2017). European Union regulations on AI: Implications for legal services. *European Journal of Law and Technology*, 8(1), 101–119.

GPAI. (2024). *The Global Partnership on Artificial Intelligence (GPAI)*. Retrieved Aug 05, 2024, from https://www.gpai.ai: https://www.gpai.ai/about/

Grajeda, A., Burgos, J., Cordova, P., & Sanjines, A. (2023). Assessing student-perceived impact of using artificial intelligence tools: Construction of a synthetic index of application in higher education. *Taylor and Francis Group*, 1-24 https://www.tandfonline.com/doi/full/10.1080/2331186X.2023.2287917

Grant, A. (1999). Elderly Inmates: Issues for Australia. []. Elderly inmates: issues for Australia] [psu.edu]. *Trends and Issues in Crime and Criminal Justice*, •••, 115.

Griffin, R. (2022). New school speech regulation as a regulatory strategy against hate speech on social media: The case of Germany's NetzDG. *Telecommunications Policy*, 46(9), 102411. DOI: 10.1016/j.telpol.2022.102411

Grimmelmann, J. (2015). Copyright for Literate Robots. *Iowa Law Review*, 101(2), 657–681. https://ilr.law.uiowa.edu/sites/ilr.law.uiowa.edu/files/2023-02/ILR-101-2-Grimmelmann.pdf

Guadamuz, A. (2017). Artificial intelligence and copyright. *WIPO Magazine*. https://www.wipo.int/wipo_magazine/en/2017/05/article_0003.html

Gummadidala, P R., Karippur, N K., & Maddulety, K. (2020, January 1). Analysis of Factors Influencing the Adoption of Artificial Intelligence for Crime Management. Springer Science+Business Media, 3-9. DOI: 10.1007/978-3-030-64849-7_1

Guszcza, J., & Kalinowski, M. (2021). AI and the future of legal services: Innovation and transformation. *Journal of Legal Technology*, 39(1), 23–45.

Gutlein, M., Frank, E., Hall, M., & Karwath, A. (2009). *Large-scale attribute selection using wrappers. In 2009 IEEE symposium on computational intelligence and data mining*. IEEE.

Hacker, P. (2022). The European AI Liability Directives - Critique of a Half-Hearted Approach and Lessons for the Future. *ArXiv*, abs/2211.13960. https://doi.org//arXiv.2211.13960.DOI: 10.48550

Hajamydeen, A. I., & Udzir, N. I. (2016). A refined filter for UHAD to improve anomaly detection. *Security and Communication Networks*, 9(14), 2434–2447. DOI: 10.1002/sec.1514

Hajamydeen, A. I., & Udzir, N. I. (2019). A detailed description on unsupervised heterogeneous anomaly based intrusion detection framework. *Scalable Computing: Practice and Experience*, 20(1), 113–160. DOI: 10.12694/scpe.v20i1.1465

Halevy, M., Harris, C., Bruckman, A., Yang, D., & Howard, A. (2021, October). Mitigating racial biases in toxic language detection with an equity-based ensemble framework. In *Proceedings of the 1st ACM Conference on Equity and Access in Algorithms, Mechanisms, and Optimization* (pp. 1-11). DOI: 10.1145/3465416.3483299

Hallevy, G. (2010). The criminal liability of artificial intelligence entities-from science fiction to legal social control. *Akron Intell. Prop. J.*, 4, 171.

Hallevy, G. (2013). *When robots kill: Artificial intelligence under criminal law*. Northeastern University Press.

Hallevy, G. (2022, April). The basic models of criminal liability of AI systems and outer circles. In *International Conference on Autonomous Systems and the Law* (pp. 69-82). Cham: Springer International Publishing.

Hangartner, D., Gennaro, G., Alasiri, S., Bahrich, N., Bornhoft, A., Boucher, J., Demirci, B. B., Derksen, L., Hall, A., Jochum, M., Munoz, M. M., Richter, M., Vogel, F., Wittwer, S., Wüthrich, F., Gilardi, F., & Donnay, K. (2021). Empathy-based counterspeech can reduce racist hate speech in a social media field experiment. *Proceedings of the National Academy of Sciences of the United States of America*, 118(50), e2116310118. DOI: 10.1073/pnas.2116310118 PMID: 34873046

Hanif, M., Khalid, F., Putra, R., Rehman, S., & Shafique, M. (2018). Robust Machine Learning Systems: Reliability and Security for Deep Neural Networks. *IEEE*, 257-260.

Harding, D. J., Morenoff, J. D., Dobson, C. C., Lane, E. B., Opatovsky, K., Williams, E. D. G., & Wyse, J. (2016). Families, prisoner reentry, and reintegration. *Boys and men in African American families*, 105-160. DOI: 10.1007/978-3-319-43847-4_8

Harnsberger, R. S. (2011). *A Guide to Sources of Texas Criminal Justice Statistics* (No. 6). University of North Texas Press.

Hayward, K., & Maas, M. M. (2020, June 30). Artificial intelligence and crime: A primer for criminologists. *Crime, Media, Culture*, 17(2), 209–233. DOI: 10.1177/1741659020917434

Hearn, J. (2022). 'A Library is a Growing Organism': Redefining Artificial Intelligence and the Role of the Information Professional in the Corporate Legal World. *Legal Information Management*, 22(2), 81–87.

Hencz, A. (2022, August 19). Digitized memories and machine hallucinations. *Artland Magazine*. https://magazine.artland.com/refik-anadol/

Hernandez, M., & Smith, D. (2022). AI-driven risk management in legal practice: A comprehensive overview. *Risk Management Journal*, 41(3), 174–192.

Hisam, M. W., Dar, A. A., Elrasheed, M. O., Khan, M. S., Gera, R., & Azad, I. (2024). The Versatility of the Taguchi Method: Optimizing Experiments Across Diverse Disciplines. *Journal of Statistical Theory and Applications : JSTA*. Advance online publication. DOI: 10.1007/s44199-024-00093-9

Howse, K. (2003). Growing old in prison. *A Scoping Study on Older Prisoners. London: Prison Reform Trust*. Growing Old in Prison - a scoping study.pdf (prisonreformtrust.org.uk) https://books.google.co.in/books?hl=en&lr=&id=MyFnFsI9wL4C&oi=fnd&pg=PA7&dq=International+Perspective+of+the+Review+Adults+in+prison:&ots=QXLzVobNDo&sig=sfIlWLI89F-zWuIMdWZ5-aufY7k&redir_esc=y#v=onepage&q=International%20Perspective%20of%20the%20Review%20Adults%20in%20prison%3A&f=falsehttps://www.google.co.in/books/edition/A_Guide_to_Sources_of_Texas_Criminal_Jus/VLZvBni_p7kC?hl=en&gbpv=0

Hristov, K. (2017). Artificial Intelligence and the Copyright Dilemma. *IDEA: The Journal of the Franklin Pierce Center for Intellectual Property*, 57(3), 431–454.

Huang, J., Saleh, S., & Liu, Y. (2021). A Review on Artificial Intelligence in Education . *Academic Journal of Interdisciplinary Studies*, 206-2017.

Huang, D., & Lin, W. (2019). A model for legal judgment prediction based on multi-model fusion. *3rd IEEE International Conference on Electronic Information Technology and Computer Engineering, EITCE 2019* (pp. 892-895). Xiamen: IEEE. DOI: 10.1109/EITCE47263.2019.9094946

Huang, E. J., Sarma, A., Hwang, S., Chandrasekharan, E., & Chancellor, S. (2024, July). Opportunities, tensions, and challenges in computational approaches to addressing online harassment. In *Proceedings of the 2024 ACM Designing Interactive Systems Conference* (pp. 1483-1498). DOI: 10.1145/3643834.3661623

Huang, S. H. (2015). Supervised feature selection: A tutorial. *Artificial Intelligence Research*, 4(2), 22–37. DOI: 10.5430/air.v4n2p22

Hung, T.-W., & Yen, C.-P. (2023, June). Predictive policing and algorithmic fairness. *Synthese*, 201(06), 206. Advance online publication. DOI: 10.1007/s11229-023-04189-0

Hutchison, C. (1993). Artificial Intelligence in Business and Industry. *Managing with Information Technology*, 101-117.

Hu, Y. (2018). Robot criminals. *University of Michigan Journal of Law Reform. University of Michigan. Law School*, 52, 487.

Ibrahim, A. (2020). *Criminal Liability Resulting from Artificial Intelligence Errors in UAE Legislation - A Comparative Study* (In Arabic), Doctoral dissertation, Ain Shams University.

IITK. (2023, Jul 28). *Understanding Bias in Artificial Intelligence: Challenges, Impacts, and Mitigation Strategies*. Retrieved Aug 15, 2024, from https://ifacet.iitk.ac.in: https://ifacet.iitk.ac.in/knowledge-hub/artificial-intelligence/understanding-bias-in-artificial-intelligence-challenges-impacts-and-mitigation-strategies/

Ijiga, A. C., Aboi, E. J., Idoko, I. P., Enyejo, L. A., & Odeyemi, M. O.Amina Catherine IjigaEnoch Joseph AboiIdoko Peter IdokoLawrence Anebi EnyejoMicheal Olumubo Odeyemi. (2024). Collaborative innovations in Artificial Intelligence (AI): Partnering with leading US tech firms to combat human trafficking. *Global Journal of Engineering and Technology Advances*, 18(3), 106–123. DOI: 10.30574/gjeta.2024.18.3.0046

Information and Decision Support Center of the Egyptian Cabinet (IDSC), (2020). Artificial intelligence is the most essential element of the Fourth Industrial Revolution, Bulletin of Future Directions, Year (1), Issue (1), January 2020.

International Labour Organization. (2017). Global estimates of modern slavery: Forced labour and forced marriage. *International Labour Organization*. Citaristi, I. (2022). United Nations Office on Drugs and Crime—UNODC. In *The Europa Directory of International Organizations 2022* (pp. 248-252). Routledge.

Islam, M. A., Ferdaus, J., Khan, M A A., & Habib, M. T. (2018, October 30). Online Legal Service. *The Present and Future.*, 10(5), 13–20. DOI: 10.5121/ijcsit.2018.10502

ISO. (2024). *Artificial intelligence — Functional safety and AI systems*. Retrieved Aug 06, 2024, from https://www.iso.org: https://www.iso.org/obp/ui/en/#iso:std:iso-iec:tr:5469:ed-1:v1:en

Jabbarpour, M. R., Saghiri, A., & Sookhak, M. (2021). A Framework for Component Selection Considering Dark Sides of Artificial Intelligence: A Case Study on Autonomous Vehicle. *Electronics (Basel)*, 10(4), 384. DOI: 10.3390/electronics10040384

Jakob, M., Prathm, J., David, S. W., & Luciano, F. (2022, August 18). The US Algorithmic Accountability Act of 2022 vs. The EU Artificial Intelligence Act: What can they learn from each other? *Minds and Machines*, 32(4), 751–758. DOI: 10.1007/s11023-022-09612-y

Jaleel, R. A., Burhan, I. M., & Jalookh, A. M. (2021). A proposed model for prediction of COVID-19 depend on k-nearest neighbors classifier: iraq case study. In *2021 International Conference on Electrical, Communication, and Computer Engineering (ICECCE)* (pp. 1-6). IEEE.

James, M., Jake, S., & Brittany, P. (2019, Oct 19). *What Do We Do About the Biases in AI?* Retrieved Aug 13, 2024, from https://hbr.org: https://hbr.org/2019/10/what-do-we-do-about-the-biases-in-ai

Jeena, J. (2024). Predicting crime or perpetuating bias? The AI dilemma. *Springer Link*. Retrieved Aug 15, 2024, from https://link.springer.com/article/10.1007/s00146-024-02032-9

Johana, B. (2021, Nov 08). *LAPD ended predictive policing programs amid public outcry. A new effort shares many of their flaws*. Retrieved Aug 14, 2024, from https://www.theguardian.com: https://www.theguardian.com/us-news/2021/nov/07/lapd-predictive-policing-surveillance-reform

Johnson, E. H. (2000). Elders and Japanese corrections. *Elders, crime, and the criminal justice system*, 222-235.

Joshua, B. (2015). *DoNotPay*. Retrieved Aug 10, 2024, from https://en.wikipedia.org: https://en.wikipedia.org/wiki/DoNotPay

Jurimetrics legal definition of jurimetrics. (2006, January 1). https://legal-dictionary.thefreedictionary.com/jurimetrics

Kathirvel, A., & Gobinath, V. M. (2024f) "Chapter 1: A Review on Additive Manufactuing in Industrial", Modern Hybird Machince and Super Finishing Process: Technology and Application, CRC Publiser/Chapman and Hall, New York, 1st Edition, ISBN 1032354291, DOI eBook ISBN 9781032354293, https://books.google.co.in/books/about/Modern_Hybrid_Machining_and_Super_Finish.html?id=I_VW0AEACAAJ&source=kp_book_description&redir_esc=y

Kathirvel, A., & Maheswaran, C. P. (2023a), "Chapter 8: Enhanced AI-Based Intrusion Detection and Response System for WSN", Artificial Intelligence for Intrusion Detection Systems, CRC Publiser/Chapman and Hall, New York, 1st Edition, ISBN 978-100096755-5, 978-103238665-2 DOI eBook ISBN 9781003346340, https://www.taylorfrancis.com/chapters/edit/10.1201/9781003346340-8/enhanced-ai-based-intrusion-detection-response-system-wsn-kathirvel-maheswaranDOI: 10.1201/9781003346340-8

Kathirvel, A., Rithik, G., & Naren, A. K. "Chapter 11: Automation of IOT Robotics." In *Predicting Natural Disasters With AI and Machine Learning,* edited by D. Satishkumar and M. Sivaraja, 224-249. ISBN 9798369322802, eBook ISBN 9798369322819, Hershey, PA: IGI Global, 2024e. https://doi.org/DOI: 10.4018/979-8-3693-2280-2.ch011

Kathirvel, A., Subramaniam, M., Navaneethan, S., & Sabarinath, C. (2021a). "Improved IDR Response System for Sensor Network", Journal of Web Engineering, Vol. 20 1, 53–88, Publisher: © River Publishers, 15 Feb 2021, ISSN: 1540-9589 (Print Version). ISSN: 1544-5976 (Online Version), https://doi.org/DOI: 10.13052/jwe1540-9589.2013

Kathirvel, A. (2024a). Applications of Serverless Computing: Systematic Overview. In Aluvalu, R., & Maheswari, U. (Eds.), *Serverless Computing Concepts, Technology and Architecture* (Vol. 221-233). IGI Global., DOI: 10.4018/979-8-3693-1682-5.ch014

Kathirvel, A. (2024c). Innovation and Industry Application: IoT-Based Robotics Frontier of Automation in Industry Application. In Satishkumar, D., & Sivaraja, M. (Eds.), *Internet of Things and AI for Natural Disaster Management and Prediction* (pp. 83–105). IGI Global., DOI: 10.4018/979-8-3693-4284-8.ch004

Kathirvel, A., Gopinath, V. M., Naren, K., Nithyanand, D., & Nirmaladevi, K. (2024i). Manufacturing Smart Industry Perspective an Overview. *American Journal of Engineering and Applied Sciences*, 17(1), 33–39. DOI: 10.3844/ajeassp.2024.33.39

Kathirvel, A., & Naren, A. K. (2024). Critical Approaches to Data Engineering Systems Innovation and Industry Application Using IoT. In *Critical Approaches to Data Engineering Systems and Analysis*. IGI Global. DOI: 10.4018/979-8-3693-2260-4.ch005

Kathirvel, A., & Naren, A. K. (2024d). Diabetes and Pre-Diabetes Prediction by AI Using Tuned XGB Classifier. In Khang, A. (Ed.), *Medical Robotics and AI-Assisted Diagnostics for a High-Tech Healthcare Industry* (pp. 52–64). IGI Global., DOI: 10.4018/979-8-3693-2105-8.ch004

Kathirvel, A., Naren, K., Nithyanand, D., & Santhoshi, B. (2024h). Overview of 5G Technology: Streamlined Virtual Event Experiences. *Advances of Robotic Technology*, 2(1), 1–8. DOI: 10.23880/art-16000109

Kathirvel, A., Sudha, D., Naveneethan, S., Subramaniam, M., Das, D., & Kirubakaran, S. (2022a). AI Based Mobile Bill Payment System using Biometric Fingerprint. *American Journal of Engineering and Applied Sciences*, 15(1), 23–31. DOI: 10.3844/ajeassp.2022.23.31

Katz, D. M., Bommarito, M. J., & Blackman, J. A. (2017). A first look at the empirical legal studies literature: AI in legal research and document review. *The Journal of Legal Studies*, 46(2), 123–156.

Katz, D. M., Bommarito, M. J., & Blackman, J. A. (2018). Predictive analytics in the legal field: Enhancing case outcomes. *The Journal of Law & Economics*, 61(3), 254–278.

Katz, D., Hartung, D., Gerlach, L., Jana, A., & Bommarito, M. J. (2023, January 1). Natural Language Processing in the Legal Domain. Cornell University. https://doi.org/DOI: 10.48550/arXiv.2302

Kauffman, M E., & Soares, M N. (2020, October 18). AI in legal services: new trends in AI-enabled legal services. Springer Science+Business Media, 14(4), 223-226. DOI: 10.1007/s11761-020-00305-x

Kaun, A., & Stiernstedt, F. (2020). Doing time, the smart way? Temporalities of the smart prison. *New Media & Society*, 22(9), 1580–1599. DOI: 10.1177/1461444820914865

Kerr, K. (2020). Ethical considerations when using artificial intelligence-based assistive technologies in education. Ethical use of technology in digital learning environments: Graduates student perspectives., Pressbooks https://pressbooks.openeducationalberta.ca/educationaltechnologyethics/chapter/ethical-considerations-when-using-artificial-intelligence-based-assistive-technologies-in-education/

Keymaker. (2024, Apr 02). *Ethical Considerations in AI Model Development*. Retrieved Aug 03, 2024, from https://keymakr.com: https://keymakr.com/blog/ethical-considerations-in-ai-model-development/

Khabibullina, A. S., Seleckaya, S. B., & Shpagonov, A. N. (2019, November 27). THE PROBLEMS OF ROBOTISATION OF LEGAL PROFESSION. *Federal University of Paraíba*, 8(6). Advance online publication. DOI: 10.22478/ufpb.2179-7137.2019v8n6.49311

Khalifa, M. (2018). Artificial Intelligence in the Balance of Legislation (In Arabic), *Dubai Legal Journal*, issued by the Dubai Public Prosecution, Issue 28, March 2018, Dubai, United Arab Emirates.

Khisamova, Z., & Begishev, I. (2019). Criminal Liability and Artificial Intelligence: Theoretical and Applied Aspects. *Russian Journal of Criminology*. https://doi.org/ .DOI: 10.17150/2500-4255.2019.13(4).564-574

Khoei, T. T., & Singh, A. (2024). A survey of Emotional Artificial Intelligence and crimes: Detection, prediction, challenges and future direction. *Journal of Computational Social Science*, 7(3), 1–44. DOI: 10.1007/s42001-024-00313-3

Kim, S., & Cho, H. (2023). The role of AI in enhancing legal aid accessibility: Evidence from recent implementations. *International Journal of Legal Technology*, 33(1), 65–84.

Kingston, J. (2016). Artificial Intelligence and Legal Liability, *International Conference on Innovative Techniques and Applications of Artificial Intelligence*, November 2016.

Kiritchenko, S., Nejadgholi, I., & Fraser, K. C. (2021). Confronting abusive language online: A survey from the ethical and human rights perspective. *Journal of Artificial Intelligence Research*, 71, 431–478. DOI: 10.1613/jair.1.12590

Kleinberg, J., Lakkaraju, H., Leskovec, J., Ludwig, J., & Mullainathan, S. (2017, August 26). Human Decisions and Machine Predictions*. Oxford University Press. DOI: 10.1093/qje/qjx032

Koltys, H. (1992). CORPORATE COUNSEL CUT COSTS WITH AI: Legal Knowledge-Based Systems. *Information Systems Management*, 9(1), 82–85.

Komal, A. (2024, Jan 26). *Data protection and data privacy laws in India.* Retrieved Aug 08, 2024, from https://blog.ipleaders.in: https://blog.ipleaders.in/data-protection-laws-in-india-2/

Kotsiantis, S. (2011). Feature selection for machine learning classification problems: A recent overview. *Artificial Intelligence Review*, 42(1), 157–176. DOI: 10.1007/s10462-011-9230-1

Kuleto, V., Ilić, M., Dumangiu, M., Ranković, M., Martins, O. M., Păun, D., & Mihoreanu, L. (2021). Exploring opportunities and challenges of artificial intelligence and machine learning in higher education institutions. *Sustainability (Basel)*, 13(18), 10424. https://www.mdpi.com/2071-1050/13/18/10424. DOI: 10.3390/su131810424

Kumar, C. A., Sooraj, M. P., & Ramakrishnan, S. (2017). A comparative performance evaluation of supervised feature selection algorithms on microarray datasets. *Procedia Computer Science*, 115, 209–217. DOI: 10.1016/j.procs.2017.09.127

Kumar, V., & Minz, S. (2014). Feature selection: A literature review. *SmartCR*, 4(3), 211–229. DOI: 10.6029/smartcr.2014.03.007

Lagioia, F., & Sartor, G. (2019). AI Systems Under Criminal Law: A Legal Analysis and a Regulatory Perspective. *Philosophy & Technology*, 33(3), 433–465. DOI: 10.1007/s13347-019-00362-x

Lalic, D., Popovski, K., Gecevska, V., & Vasilevska, S. (2011). *Analysis of the opportunities and challenges for renewable energy market in the Western Balkan countries*. ScienceDirect. DOI: 10.1016/j.rser.2011.04.011

Langer, D. M., & Taylor, A. (2022). The accuracy and utility of predictive legal analytics. *Law & Society Review*, 56(2), 312–340.

Lares, L. A., & Montgomery, S. (2020). Psychosocial needs of released long-term incarcerated older adults. *Criminal Justice Review*, 45(3), 358–377. DOI: 10.1177/0734016820913101

Lath, A. (2022, October 10). *AI Art and Indian Copyright Registration.* Spicy IP. https://spicyip.com/2022/10/ai-art-and-indian-copyright-registration.html

Latonero, M. (2011). Human trafficking online: The role of social networking sites and online classifieds. *Available at* SSRN *2045851*. Bales, K., & Soodalter, R. (2010). *The slave next door: Human trafficking and slavery in America today*. Univ of California Press. DOI: 10.2139/ssrn.2045851

Lee, L. M. (2019). The impact of prison programming on recidivism. *Corrections : Policy, Practice and Research*, 4(4), 252–271. DOI: 10.1080/23774657.2017.1399095

LEEMANS, T. & JACQUEMIN, H. (2017). *La Responsabilité Extracontractuelle de l'Intelligence Artificielle*, Master en droit, Faculté de droit et de criminologie (DRT), Université Catholique de Louvain.

Li, J., Cheng, K., Wang, S., Morstatter, F., Trevino, R. P., Tang, J., & Liu, H. (2017). Feature selection: A data perspective. *ACM Computing Surveys*, 50(6), 1–45. DOI: 10.1145/3136625

Li, L., Duan, W., Zhou, D., & Yuan, J.-L. (2022, July). Law Article Recommendation Approach Based on Deep Semantic Matching. *Ruan Jian Xue Bao. Journal of Software*, 33(07), 2618–2632. DOI: 10.13328/j.cnki.jos.006287

Lima, G., Grgić-Hlača, N., Jeong, J K., & Cha, M. (2022, June 20). The Conflict Between Explainable and Accountable Decision-Making Algorithms. DOI: 10.1145/3531146.3534628

Lim, D. (2023). Generative AI and copyright: Principles, priorities and practicalities. *Journal Of Intellectual Property Law and Practice*, 18(12), 841–842. DOI: 10.1093/jiplp/jpad081

Lin, W., Cheng, M., & Xu, Q. (2019). Legal chatbots: Enhancing client interaction and accessibility. *AI & Law Journal*, 27(1), 77–99.

Liu, Y., Wu, Y., Li, A., Zhang, Y., Sun, C., Lu, W., . . . Kuang, K. (2024). Unleashing the Power of LLMs in Court View Generation by Stimulating Internal Knowledge and Incorporating External Knowledge. In G. H. Duh K. (Ed.), *Findings of the Association for Computational Linguistics: NAACL 2024* (pp. 2782-2792). Mexico City: Association for Computational Linguistics (ACL). Retrieved Aug 10, 2024, from https://www.scopus.com/record/display.uri?eid=2-s2.0-85197949139&origin=resultslist&sort=plf-f&cite=2-s2.0-0040326619&src=s&imp=t&sid=23f8fb9656ff76b337ecc7e04b7aba2d&sot=cite&sdt=a&sl=0&relpos=7&citeCnt=0&searchTerm=

Liu, Z., Yang, J., Wang, L., & Chang, Y. (2023). A novel relation aware wrapper method for feature selection. *Pattern Recognition*, 140, 109566. DOI: 10.1016/j.patcog.2023.109566

Llinares, F M. (2020, January 23). INTELIGENCIA ARTIFICIAL Y JUSTICIA PENAL: MÁS ALLÁ DE LOS RESULTADOS LESIVOS CAUSADOS POR ROBOTS., 87-130. DOI: 10.5944/rdpc.20.2018.26446

Lockwood, S. K., Nally, J. M., Ho, T., & Knutson, K. (2015). Racial disparities and similarities in post-release recidivism and employment among ex-prisoners with a different level of education. *Journal of Prison Education and Reentry*, 2(1), 16–31. DOI: 10.15845/jper.v2i1.703

Losano, M G. (1971, December 1). Juricybernetics: Genesis and Structure of a Discipline. Cambridge University Press, 19(76), 93-114. DOI: 10.1177/039219217101907605

Loureiro, S., Guerreiro, J., & Tussyadiah, I. (2021). Artificial intelligence in business: State of the art and future research agenda. *Journal of Business Research*, 129, 911–926. DOI: 10.1016/j.jbusres.2020.11.001

Luckin, R., Holmes, W., Griffiths, M., & Forcie. (2016). Intelligence unleashed: An argument for AI in education. London. *Retrievedfrom*https://static.googleusercontent.com/media/edu.google.com/en//pdfs/IntelligenceUnleashed-Publication.pdf

Lupu, Y., Sear, R., Velásquez, N., Leahy, R., Restrepo, N. J., Goldberg, B., & Johnson, N. F. (2023). Offline events and online hate. *PLoS One*, 18(1), e0278511. DOI: 10.1371/journal.pone.0278511 PMID: 36696388

Lynch, J. (2020, January 1). Face Off: Law Enforcement Use of Face Recognition Technology. RELX Group (Netherlands). DOI: 10.2139/ssrn.3909038

Lyytinen, L., Hekkert, W., Cheng, Y., & Sovacool, S. (2022). Adaptive Legal Frameworks and Economic Dynamics in Emerging Technologies: Navigating the Intersection for Responsible Innovation. *Law and Economics*, 16(03), 202–220. DOI: 10.35335/laweco.v16i3.61

Madaoui, N. (2024, May). The Impact of Artificial Intelligence on Legal Systems: Challenges and Opportunities. *Problems of Legality*, 01(164), 2085–2303. DOI: 10.21564/2414-990X.164.289266

Mahlangu, G., & Zivanai, E. (2023). Offender eLearning: A systematic literature review on re-Markina, A. (2019). Problems related to reintegration of young ex-offenders in Estonia. *Kriminologijos studijos, 7*, 56-74. DOI: 10.15388/CrimLithuan.2019.7.3

Manwaring, K. (2017). Emerging Information Technologies: Challenges for Consumers. *Oxford University Commonwealth Law Journal*, 265-279.

Mariani, m., Machado, I., & Nambisan, S. (2023). Types of innovation and artificial intelligence: A systematic quantitative literature review and research agenda Author links open overlay panel. *Journal of Business Research.*

Marie, P., & Yvette, M. (2020). AI in the Home: Artificial Intelligence and Consumer Protection. *Cambridge University Press*, 1-15.

Mark van. R. (2023, Feb 17). *Privacy in the Age of AI: Risks, Challenges and Solutions*. Retrieved Aug 13, 2024, from https://www.thedigitalspeaker.com: https://www.thedigitalspeaker.com/privacy-age-ai-risks-challenges-solutions/

Mark, H., Simon, S., & Luisa, R. (2024, Jan 08). *Bridging the Gap Between Artificial Intelligence Implementation, Governance and Democracy: An Operational and Regulatory Perspective*. Retrieved Aug 15, 2024, from https://www.fticonsulting.com: https://www.fticonsulting.com/insights/articles/bridging-gap-between-artificial-intelligence-implementation-governance-democracy

Marković, M., & Gostojić, S. (2022, November 16). Legal document assembly system for introducing law students with legal drafting. Springer Science+Business Media, 31(4), 829-863. DOI: 10.1007/s10506-022-09339-2

Marti, I. (2022). During Leisure Time. In *Doing Indefinite Time: An Ethnography of Long-Term Imprisonment in Switzerland* (pp. 235–328). Springer International Publishing., DOI: 10.1007/978-3-031-12590-4_6

Maschi, T., Morgen, K., Hintenach, A., & Kaye, A. (2021). Aging in prison and correction policy in global perspectives. In *Oxford Research Encyclopedia of Criminology and Criminal Justice*. DOI: 10.1093/acrefore/9780190264079.013.648

Maurice, B. (2023, Sep 25). *Leveraging AI-Powered Tools for Streamlined Contract Analysis in Intellectual Property Law*. Retrieved Aug 12, 2024, from https://www.linkedin.com: https://www.linkedin.com/pulse/leveraging-ai-powered-tools-streamlined-contract-law-bretzfield-2c/

McCann, J., Quinn, L., McGrath, S., & Connell, E. (2018). Towards the distributes Edge – An IoT review. *12th International Conferences on Sensing Technology,* (pp. 263-263). Ireland: Limerich.

McCarthy, J. (2021). Virtual assistants in the legal field: Guiding users through legal processes. *Journal of Legal Innovation*, 34(3), 143–168.

McClain, N. M., & Garrity, S. E. (2011). Sex trafficking and the exploitation of adolescents. *Journal of Obstetric, Gynecologic, and Neonatal Nursing*, 40(2), 243–252. DOI: 10.1111/j.1552-6909.2011.01221.x PMID: 21284727

McCormick, J. (2022). AI in risk assessment and compliance: Managing regulatory challenges. *The Regulatory Affairs Journal*, 39(2), 205–229.

McGinnis, J. O., & Pearce, R. (2021). Intelligent case management: AI in legal workflow automation. *Legal Practice Management Journal*, 42(4), 91–115.

McKeown, T., Mustafina, J., Magizov, R., & Gataullina, C. (2020, December). AI in law practices. In *2020 13th International Conference on Developments in eSystems Engineering (DeSE)* (pp. 27-32). IEEE.

McKeown, T., Mustafina, J., Магизов, Р., & Gataullina, C. (2020, December 14). AI in Law Practices. DOI: 10.1109/DeSE51703.2020.9450780

Mehmood, S., Ahmad, Z., & Khan, A. A. (2016). Dynamic relationships between tourist arrivals, immigrants, and crimes in the United States. *Tourism Management*, 54, 383–392. DOI: 10.1016/j.tourman.2015.12.010

Mester, G. (2017). *Ranking of Croatian researchers from several disciplines using Google Scholar database*. Interdisciplinary Description of Complex System.

Metz, C., & Weise, K. (2023, January 23). Microsoft to invest $10 billion in openai, the creator of chatgpt. *The New York Times*. https://www.nytimes.com/2023/01/23/business/microsoft-chatgpt-artificial-intelligence.html

Migliorini, S., & Moreira, J. I. (2024). The case for nurturing AI literacy in Law schools. *Asian Journal of Legal Education*, 23220058241265613.

Milin, S. (2024, Mar 24). *Top five AI legal assistants to optimise your firms in 2024*. Retrieved Aug 12, 2024, from https://indiaai.gov.in: https://indiaai.gov.in/article/top-five-ai-legal-assistants-to-optimise-your-firms-in-2024

Militsyna, K. (2023). Human creative contribution to ai-based output – one just can('t) get enough. *GRUR International*, 72(10), 939–949. DOI: 10.1093/grurint/ikad075

Mirzazadeh, I. (2023). Artificial Intelligence (AI) and Violation of Human Rights. *SSRN*. DOI: 10.2139/ssrn.4310188

Mohamed, S. (2020). Legal Aspects of Artificial Intelligence and Robotics, *Arab Democratic Center's periodical website*, on 29/2/2020, at: https://democraticac.de/?p=64965

Mohammad, A. H. (2018). Comparing Two Feature Selections Methods (Information Gain And Gain Ratio) On Three Different Classification Algorithms Using Arabic Dataset. *Journal of Theoretical and Applied Information Technology*, 96(6).

Mohammed, S., Dar, A. A., Khan, M. S., Azad, I., Jayaraman, G., & Albalawi, O. (2024). Goodwill Valuation Enhancement through Capitalization Method and Statistical Impact Analysis. *Journal of Risk and Financial Management*, 17(6), 226. DOI: 10.3390/jrfm17060226

Mohsin, K. (2020). Regulation of AI and AI Crimes. https://doi.org/DOI: 10.2139/ssrn.3552140

Molina, L. C., Belanche, L., & Nebot, À. (2002). Feature selection algorithms: A survey and experimental evaluation. In *2002 IEEE International Conference on Data Mining, 2002. Proceedings.* (pp. 306-313). IEEE. DOI: 10.1109/ICDM.2002.1183917

Monica, M., & Geeta, D. (2024). The Future of Rehabilitation: AI And The Transformation Of Education In Prisons. *Educational Administration: Theory and Practice*, 30(2), 916–922. DOI: 10.53555/kuey.v30i2.2996

Mozafari, M., Farahbakhsh, R., & Crespi, N. (2020). Hate speech detection and racial bias mitigation in social media based on BERT model. *PLoS One*, 15(8), e0237861. DOI: 10.1371/journal.pone.0237861 PMID: 32853205

Munn, L. (2020). Angry by design: Toxic communication and technical architectures. *Humanities & Social Sciences Communications*, 7(1), 1–11. DOI: 10.1057/s41599-020-00550-7

Murray, M. D. (2022). *A Short and Happy Guide to Copyright* (2nd ed.). West Academic Publishing.

Murray, M. D., & DuBoff, L. D. (2023). *Art Law: Cases and Materials* (3rd ed.). Aspen Publishing.

Mustari, N., Sen, S. K., Banik, A., Mehedi, M. H., & Rasel, A. A. (2023). Techniques to Estimate the Status of Legal Proceedings Considering Sequential Text Data. *5th International Conference on Emerging Smart Computing and Informatics, ESCI 2023*. Pune: Institute of Electrical and Electronics Engineers Inc. DOI: 10.1109/ESCI56872.2023.10099995

Nagy, S., & Hajdu, N. (2021). Consumer acceptance of the use of artificial intelligence in online shopping: Evidence from Hungary. *Amfiteatru Economic*, 23(56), 155–173. DOI: 10.24818/EA/2021/56/155

Naik, N., Hameed, B. Z., Shetty, D. K., Swain, D., Shah, M., Paul, R., & Somani, B. K. (2022). Legal and ethical consideration in artificial intelligence in healthcare: Who takes responsibility? *Frontiers in Surgery*, 9, 862322.

Nanos, A. (2023). Criminal Liability of Artificial Intelligence. *Charles University in Prague Faculty of Law Research Paper No.*

Nascimento, F. R., Cavalcanti, G. D., & Da Costa-Abreu, M. (2022). Unintended bias evaluation: An analysis of hate speech detection and gender bias mitigation on social media using ensemble learning. *Expert Systems with Applications*, 201, 117032. DOI: 10.1016/j.eswa.2022.117032

National Harbor. MD Ramalho, A. (2022). *Intellectual Property Protection for AI-generated Creations Europe, United States, Australia and Japan*. Routledge, Taylor & Francis Group.

Naveneethan, S. Madhan E.S., Kathirvel A. (2022) Identifying and Eliminating the Misbehavior Nodes in the Wireless Sensor Network. In: Reddy V.S., Prasad V.K., Wang J., Reddy K. (eds) Soft Computing and Signal Processing. ICSCSP 2021. Advances in Intelligent Systems and Computing, vol 1413. Springer International Publishing, Springer, Singapore. https://doi.org/DOI: 10.1007/978-981-16-7088-6_36

Nay, J J. (2021, February 18). Natural Language Processing for Legal Texts. Cambridge University Press, 99-113. DOI: 10.1017/9781316529683.011

Nedbálek, K. (2018). The Future Inclusion of Criminal Liability of the Robots and Artificial Intelligence in the Czech Republic, Paradigm of Law and Public Administration, Interregional Academy for Personnel Management, Ukraine, 2018, available at https://maup.com.ua/assets/files/expert/1/the-future-inclusion-of-criminal.pdf

Negri, K. M. E. S. M. (2020, October 18). AI in legal services: new trends in AI-enabled legal services - Service Oriented Computing and Applications. https://link.springer.com/article/10.1007/s11761-020-00305-x

NEVEJANS, N. (2016). Dirctorate-General for Internal Policies, Policy Department C: Citizens' Rights and Constitutional Affairs, Legal Affairs, European Civil Law Rules in Robotics, No. EA n° 2471, October 2016.

Neznamov, A. (2020, January 1). Regulatory Landscape of Artificial Intelligence. DOI: 10.2991/assehr.k.200321.113

Nguyen, A., Rai, A., & Maruping, L. (2024). Understanding the Unintended Effects of Human-Machine Moderation in Addressing Harassment within Online Communities. *Journal of Management Information Systems*, 41(2), 341–366. DOI: 10.1080/07421222.2024.2340831

Nguyen, T. (2024). Merging public health and automated approaches to address online hate speech. *AI and Ethics*, 4(2), 441–450. DOI: 10.1007/s43681-023-00281-w PMID: 37360146

Niral, S. (2022, Aug 29). Bias and Ethical Concerns in Machine Learning. *ISACA, 04*, 01-04. Retrieved Aug 12, 2024, from https://www.isaca.org/resources/isaca-journal/issues/2022/volume-4/bias-and-ethical-concerns-in-machine-learning

No, J. D., & Stearns, D. (2015). UNITED STATES DISTRICT COURT DISTRICT OF MASSACHUSETTS CIVIL ACTION NO. 14-13870-RGS.

OECD. (2023). *Artificial intelligence*. Retrieved Aug 19, 2024, from https://www.oecd.org: https://www.oecd.org/en/topics/policy-issues/artificial-intelligence.html

Oh, S. (2022). Predictive case-based feature importance and interaction. *Information Sciences*, 593, 155–176. DOI: 10.1016/j.ins.2022.02.003

Oksana, Z. (2024, Jan 25). *Opening the Black Box: How to Create AI Transparency and Explainability to Build Trust*. Retrieved Aug 15, 2024, from https://shelf.io: https://shelf.io/blog/ai-transparency-and-explainability/

Orantes, M. (2018). Leveraging Machine Learning and Artificial Intelligence to Combat Human Trafficking (Master's thesis, Utica College).

Osmani, N. (2020). *The Complexity of Criminal Liability of AI Systems*. Masaryk University Journal of Law and Technology., DOI: 10.5817/MUJLT2020-1-3

OVIC. (2023). *Artificial Intelligence and Privacy – Issues and Challenges*. Retrieved Aug 10, 2024, from https://ovic.vic.gov.au: https://ovic.vic.gov.au/privacy/resources-for-organisations/artificial-intelligence-and-privacy-issues-and-challenges/

Owoc, M. L., Sawicka, A., & Weichbroth, P. (2021). *Artificial Intelligence Technologies in Education: Benefits, Challenges and Strategies of Implementation*. Springer., DOI: 10.1007/978-3-030-85001-2_4

Palanively, V., & Vasanthi, B. (2020). Role of artificial intelligence in business transfromation. *International Journal of Advanced Science and Technology* .

Pardel, J. (1992) *Droit penal. introduction general, droit penal general*, 8eme Cujas, Paris.

Park, S., & Ko, H. (2020, August 1). Machine Learning and Law and Economics: A Preliminary Overview. *De Gruyter*, 11(2), 20200034. Advance online publication. DOI: 10.1515/ajle-2020-0034

Partington, S. T. (2017). *Age, imprisonment and social re-entry: Exploring the needs and experiences of older offenders following release and resettlement from prison* (Doctoral dissertation, University of Huddersfield). https://eprints.hud.ac.uk/id/eprint/34149/

Patel, S., & Garcia, L. (2022). Chatbots in legal services: Enhancing client engagement and accessibility. *AI & Society Journal*, 21(2), 143–160.

Paul, V. (2023, Apr 20). *Accountability and Responsibility in AI: Assigning Responsibility in the Age of Autonomous AI Systems*. Retrieved Aug 19, 2024, from https://www.linkedin.com: https://www.linkedin.com/pulse/accountability-responsibility-ai-assigning-age-systems-paul-veitch/

Paulson, P. (2013). The Role of Community Based Programs in Reducing Recidivism in Ex-Offenders. https://library.stkate.edu/archives/sophia

Pearlman, R. (2018). *Recognizing Artificial Intelligence (AI) as authors and inventors under U.S intellectual property law*. Rich. J. L. & Tech.

Pedro, F. (2020). Applications of Artificial Intelligence to higher education: possibilities, evidence and challenges. https://iulresearch.iuline.it/index.php/IUL-RES/article/view/43, 61-76.

Perlin, M. W., Dormer, K. J., Hornyak, J. M., Schiermeier-Wood, L., & Greenspoon, S. A. (2014, March 25). TrueAllele Casework on Virginia DNA Mixture Evidence: Computer and Manual Interpretation in 72 Reported Criminal Cases. *PLoS One*, 9(3), e92837–e92837. DOI: 10.1371/journal.pone.0092837 PMID: 24667531

Petrescu, R. V. (2019, January 1)... *Face Recognition as a Biometric Application.*, 3(1), 237–257. DOI: 10.3844/jmrsp.2019.237.257

Pham, Q. V., Nguyen, D. C., Hwang, W. J., & Pathirana, P. N. (2020). Artificial Intelligence (AI) and Big Data for Coronavirus (COVID-19) Pandemic: A Survey on the State-of-the-Arts.

POIROT-MAZERESDU. I. (2013). Chapitre 8. Robotique et médecine: quelle(s) responsabilité(s)? *Journal International de Bioéthique*, Vol. 24, No. 4.

Praveen, M. (2024, Feb 27). *AI And The Legal Landscape: Embracing Innovation, Addressing Challenges*. Retrieved Aug 03, 2024, from https://www.livelaw.in: https://www.livelaw.in/lawschool/articles/law-and-ai-ai-powered-tools-general-data-protection-regulation-250673

Predicting crime, LAPD-style. (2023, February 6). https://perma.cc/2FEC-4TCS

Predictive Policing Technology. (2012, March 9). https://www.predpol.com/technology

PredPol is LAPD's Racist Predictive Policing Program. (2019, October 11). https://freerads.org/2019/10/11/a-guide-to-predpol-and-dismantling-it/

Pudjihartono, N., Fadason, T., Kempa-Liehr, A. W., & O'Sullivan, J. M. (2022). A review of feature selection methods for machine learning-based disease risk prediction. *Frontiers in Bioinformatics*, 2, 927312. DOI: 10.3389/fbinf.2022.927312 PMID: 36304293

Qiao, Q., Yunusa-Kaltungo, A., & Edwards, R. E. (2022). Feature selection strategy for machine learning methods in building energy consumption prediction. *Energy Reports*, 8, 13621–13654. DOI: 10.1016/j.egyr.2022.10.125

Qu, K., Xu, J., Hou, Q., Qu, K., & Sun, Y. (2023). Feature selection using Information Gain and decision information in neighborhood decision system. *Applied Soft Computing*, 136, 110100. DOI: 10.1016/j.asoc.2023.110100

Rajab, M., & Wang, D. (2020). Practical challenges and recommendations of filter methods for feature selection. *Journal of Information & Knowledge Management*, 19(01), 2040019. DOI: 10.1142/S0219649220400195

Ramos, S., López, J Á P., & Abreu, R. (2020, June 1). An Analysis of the Importance of the Artificial Intelligence on the Information System of Police Forces. DOI: 10.23919/CISTI49556.2020.9141006

Rankin, S. G. (2020, January 1). Technological Tethereds: Potential Impact of Untrustworthy Artificial Intelligence in Criminal Justice Risk Assessment Instruments. RELX Group (Netherlands). DOI: 10.2139/ssrn.3662761

Ré, R M., & Solow-Niederman, A. (2019, May 19). Developing Artificially Intelligent Justice

Rehan. (n.d.). *Who owns computer generated works*. Learn and Digest. https://learndigest.blogspot.com/2014/06/who-owns-computer-generated-works.html

Reier Forradellas RF and Garay Gallastegui LM, 'Digital Transformation and Artificial Intelligence Applied to Business: Legal Regulations, Economic Impact and Perspective' (2021) 10 Laws 70

Robinson, K., & McDaniel, R. (2020). AI in law firms: Benefits, challenges, and the road ahead. *Law Firm Management Review*, 27(4), 112–130.

Rodolfa, K. T., Salomon, E., Haynes, L., Mendieta, I. H., Larson, J., & Ghani, R. (2020). Case study: predictive fairness to reduce misdemeanor recidivism through social service interventions. In *Proceedings of the 2020 Conference on Fairness, Accountability, and Transparency* (pp. 142-153). DOI: 10.1145/3351095.3372863

Rodriguez, A., & Gomez, M. (2021). The automation of legal document drafting: Benefits and challenges. *Legal Technology Review*, 29(4), 45–67.

Rokad, B., Karumudi, T., Acharya, O., & Jagtap, A. (2019). Survival of the Fittest in PlayerUnknown BattleGround. *arXiv preprint arXiv:1905.06052*.

Roll, I., & Wylie, R. (2016). Evolution and Revolution in Artificial Intelligence in Education. *International Journal of Artificial Intelligence in Education*, 26(2), 582–599. DOI: 10.1007/s40593-016-0110-3

Rosen, J., & Lyman, D. (2019). Predictive analytics in the legal sector: Use cases and impact. *Journal of Data Science and Law*, 30(3), 95–118.

ROSS. (2023). *ROSS's AI Search*. Retrieved Aug 10, 2024, from https://www.rossintelligence.com: https://www.rossintelligence.com/what-is-ai

Rowena, R. (2020, December). Legal and human rights issues of AI: Gaps, challenges and vulnerabilities. *Journal of Responsible Technology*, 04, 100005. Advance online publication. DOI: 10.1016/j.jrt.2020.100005

Russell, S., & Norving, P. (2009). *Artificial Intelligence - A Modern Approach* (3rd ed.). Prentice-Hall.

Rwrsilany, S., Cleice De Pontes, B., Adriana, B. N., & Rogerio, P. D. (2023, Nov 10). THE ROLE OF JURIMETRICS AND PREDICTIVE ANALYSIS IN JUDICIAL DECISIONMAKING: A CURRENT PANORAMA. *SemeAd*, 01-21. Retrieved Jul 30, 2024, from https://login.semead.com.br/26semead/anais/arquivos/925.pdf?

Saarela, M., & Jauhiainen, S. (2021). Comparison of feature importance measures as explanations for classification models. *SN Applied Sciences*, 3(2), 1–12. DOI: 10.1007/s42452-021-04148-9

Saghiri, A. M., Vahidipour, M., Jabbaarpour, M., Sookhak, M., & Forestiero, A. (2022). *A Survey of Artificial Intelligence Challenges: Analyzing the Definitions, Relationships, and Evolutions. Applied Sciences. Abbot, R. (2017). Research Handbook on Intellectual Property and Digital Technologies*. Edward Elgar Publishing Limited.

Sag, M. (2012). Orphan Works as Grist for the Data Mill. *SSRN*, 27, 1503–1550. DOI: 10.2139/ssrn.2038889

Saha, P., Garimella, K., Kalyan, N. K., Pandey, S. K., Meher, P. M., Mathew, B., & Mukherjee, A. (2023). On the rise of fear speech in online social media. *Proceedings of the National Academy of Sciences of the United States of America*, 120(11), e2212270120. DOI: 10.1073/pnas.2212270120 PMID: 36877833

Salah, A. A. A. (2021). AI bugs and failures: How and why to render AI-algorithms more human? In Verdegem, P. (Ed.), *AI for Everyone?* (pp. 161–180). University of Westminster Press., https://www.jstor.org/stable/j.ctv26qjjhj.12

Salcedo-Sanz, S., Cornejo-Bueno, L., Prieto, L., Paredes, D., & García-Herrera, R. (2018). Feature selection in machine learning prediction systems for renewable energy applications. *Renewable & Sustainable Energy Reviews*, 90, 728–741. DOI: 10.1016/j.rser.2018.04.008

Samsuddin, S., Shah, Z. A., Saedudin, R. R., Kasim, S., & Seah, C. S. (2019). Analysis of attribute selection and classification algorithm applied to hepatitis patients. *International Journal on Advanced Science, Engineering and Information Technology*, 9(3), 967–971. DOI: 10.18517/ijaseit.9.3.5041

Sánchez-Maroño, N., Alonso-Betanzos, A., & Tombilla-Sanromán, M. (2007). Filter methods for feature selection–a comparative study. In *International Conference on Intelligent Data Engineering and Automated Learning* (pp. 178-187). Berlin, Heidelberg: Springer Berlin Heidelberg. DOI: 10.1007/978-3-540-77226-2_19

Sanctis, F M D. (2021, March 23). Artificial Intelligence and Innovation in Brazilian Justice. Cambridge University Press, 59(1), 1-10. DOI: 10.1017/cri.2021.4

Saqr, W. (2021). Criminal liability for artificial intelligence crimes, "a prospective analytical study.". *Spirit of Laws*, 33(96), 1–156. DOI: 10.21608/las.2022.121777.1050

Sarkar, S. (2021, August 5). *India recognises AI as co-author of copyrighted artwork*. Managing IP, https://www.managingip.com/article/2a5czmpwixyj23wyqct1c/exclusive-india-recognises-ai-as-co-author-of-copyrighted-artwork

Scheuerman, M. K., Jiang, J. A., Fiesler, C., & Brubaker, J. R. (2021). A framework of severity for harmful content online. *Proceedings of the ACM on Human-Computer Interaction, 5*(CSCW2), 1-33. DOI: 10.1145/3479512

Schlanger, M. (2017). Prisoners with disabilities. https://repository.law.umich.edu/book_chapters/114/

Schwab, K. (2017). *The Fourth Industrial Revolution - A Book in Minutes* (In Arabic), summaries of international books, published by the Mohammed bin Zayed Knowledge Foundation, Dubai, UAE, 2017.

Schwartz, R., Down, L., Jonas, A., & Tabassi, E. (2021, June 22). A Proposal for Identifying and Managing Bias in Artificial Intelligence. DOI: 10.6028/NIST.SP.1270-draft

Scott, R., Rich, C., & Tréa, L. (2024, Jul). *What is GDPR? Compliance and conditions explained*. Retrieved Aug 11, 2024, from https://www.techtarget.com: https://www.techtarget.com/whatis/definition/General-Data-Protection-Regulation-GDPR

Selbst, A. D. (2017, January 1). Disparate Impact in Big Data Policing. RELX Group (Netherlands). DOI: 10.2139/ssrn.2819182

Shah, N., Bhagat, N., & Shah, M. (2021, April 29). Crime forecasting: A machine learning and computer vision approach to crime prediction and prevention. *Visual Computing for Industry, Biomedicine, and Art*, 4(1), 9. Advance online publication. DOI: 10.1186/s42492-021-00075-z PMID: 33913057

Shand, R. A. (1996). Pre-release/transition: Inmate programs and support upon entry, during incarceration, and after release. *Journal of Correctional Education*, •••, 20–40. https://www.jstor.org/stable/23292010

Shank, D., & DeSanti, A. (2018). Attributions of morality and mind to artificial intelligence after real-world moral violations. *Computers in Human Behavior*, 86, 401–411. DOI: 10.1016/j.chb.2018.05.014

Sheeba, N. (2023, July). Artificial Intelligence's Effects on the Legal Sector: Transforming Legal Practice. *International Journal for Legal Research & Analysis*, 02(07), 1–21. Retrieved August 12, 2024, from https://www.researchgate.net/publication/372343835_Artificial_intelligences_effects_On_the_legal_sector_transforming_Legal_practice

Shivani, T. (2024, Apr 02). *Smart Contracts Explained: Understanding Their Functionality on the Blockchain*. Retrieved Aug 10, 2024, from https://www.spydra.app: https://www.spydra.app/blog/smart-contracts-explained-understanding-their-functionality-on-the-blockchain#:~:text=Smart%20contracts%20are%20digital%20agreements,agreement%20are%20enforced%20by%20code

Simmons, R. (2018, January 1). Big Data, Machine Judges, and the Legitimacy of the Criminal Justice System. RELX Group (Netherlands). DOI: 10.2139/ssrn.3156510

Singh, B. (2023). Blockchain Technology in Renovating Healthcare: Legal and Future Perspectives. In *Revolutionizing Healthcare Through Artificial Intelligence and Internet of Things Applications* (pp. 177-186). IGI Global.

Singh, B., & Kaunert, C. (2024). Harnessing Sustainable Agriculture Through Climate-Smart Technologies: Artificial Intelligence for Climate Preservation and Futuristic Trends. In *Exploring Ethical Dimensions of Environmental Sustainability and Use of AI* (pp. 214-239). IGI Global.

Singh, B., & Kaunert, C. (2024). Revealing Green Finance Mobilization: Harnessing FinTech and Blockchain Innovations to Surmount Barriers and Foster New Investment Avenues. In *Harnessing Blockchain-Digital Twin Fusion for Sustainable Investments* (pp. 265-286). IGI Global.

Singh, B., & Kaunert, C. (2024). Salvaging Responsible Consumption and Production of Food in the Hospitality Industry: Harnessing Machine Learning and Deep Learning for Zero Food Waste. In *Sustainable Disposal Methods of Food Wastes in Hospitality Operations* (pp. 176-192). IGI Global.

Singh, B., Jain, V., Kaunert, C., & Vig, K. (2024). Shaping Highly Intelligent Internet of Things (IoT) and Wireless Sensors for Smart Cities. In *Secure and Intelligent IoT-Enabled Smart Cities* (pp. 117-140). IGI Global.

Singh, B., Kaunert, C., & Vig, K. (2024). Reinventing Influence of Artificial Intelligence (AI) on Digital Consumer Lensing Transforming Consumer Recommendation Model: Exploring Stimulus Artificial Intelligence on Consumer Shopping Decisions. In *AI Impacts in Digital Consumer Behavior* (pp. 141-169). IGI Global.

Singh, B., Vig, K., & Kaunert, C. (2024). Modernizing Healthcare: Application of Augmented Reality and Virtual Reality in Clinical Practice and Medical Education. In Modern Technology in Healthcare and Medical Education: Blockchain, IoT, AR, and VR (pp. 1-21). IGI Global.

Singh, B. (2023). Unleashing Alternative Dispute Resolution (ADR) in Resolving Complex Legal-Technical Issues Arising in Cyberspace Lensing E-Commerce and Intellectual Property: Proliferation of E-Commerce Digital Economy. *Revista Brasileira de Alternative Dispute Resolution-Brazilian Journal of Alternative Dispute Resolution-RBADR*, 5(10), 81–105. DOI: 10.52028/rbadr.v5i10.ART04.Ind

Singh, B. (2024). Evolutionary Global Neuroscience for Cognition and Brain Health: Strengthening Innovation in Brain Science. In Prabhakar, P. (Ed.), *Biomedical Research Developments for Improved Healthcare* (pp. 246–272). IGI Global., DOI: 10.4018/979-8-3693-1922-2.ch012

Singh, B. (2024). Lensing Legal Dynamics for Examining Responsibility and Deliberation of Generative AI-Tethered Technological Privacy Concerns: Infringements and Use of Personal Data by Nefarious Actors. In Ara, A., & Ara, A. (Eds.), *Exploring the Ethical Implications of Generative AI* (pp. 146–167). IGI Global., DOI: 10.4018/979-8-3693-1565-1.ch009

Singh, B. (2024). Social Cognition of Incarcerated Women and Children: Addressing Exposure to Infectious Diseases and Legal Outcomes. In Reddy, K. (Ed.), *Principles and Clinical Interventions in Social Cognition* (pp. 236–251). IGI Global., DOI: 10.4018/979-8-3693-1265-0.ch014

Singh, B., & Kaunert, C. (2024). Salvaging Responsible Consumption and Production of Food in the Hospitality Industry: Harnessing Machine Learning and Deep Learning for Zero Food Waste. In Singh, A., Tyagi, P., & Garg, A. (Eds.), *Sustainable Disposal Methods of Food Wastes in Hospitality Operations* (pp. 176–192). IGI Global., DOI: 10.4018/979-8-3693-2181-2.ch012

Singh, B., Kaunert, C., & Vig, K. (2024). Reinventing Influence of Artificial Intelligence (AI) on Digital Consumer Lensing Transforming Consumer Recommendation Model: Exploring Stimulus Artificial Intelligence on Consumer Shopping Decisions. In Musiolik, T., Rodriguez, R., & Kannan, H. (Eds.), *AI Impacts in Digital Consumer Behavior* (pp. 141–169). IGI Global., DOI: 10.4018/979-8-3693-1918-5.ch006

Sivaranjani, N., & Jayabharathy, J., & M., S. (2019). A Broad View of Automation in Legal Prediction Technology. *3rd International Conference on Electronics and Communication and Aerospace Technology, ICECA 2019* (pp. 180-185). Coimbatore: Institute of Electrical and Electronics Engineers Inc. DOI: 10.1109/ICECA.2019.8822019

Skowrońska, J. (2023). *A range of legal obligation for operators of Artificial Intelligence Systems in the context of Criminal Law*. Humanities & Social Sciences Reviews., DOI: 10.18510/hssr.2023.1151

Smialowski, P., Frishman, D., & Kramer, S. (2010). Pitfalls of supervised feature selection. *Bioinformatics (Oxford, England)*, 26(3), 440–443. DOI: 10.1093/bioinformatics/btp621 PMID: 19880370

Smuha, N A. (2021, January 2). From a 'race to AI' to a 'race to AI regulation': regulatory competition for artificial intelligence. Taylor & Francis, 13(1), 57-84. DOI: 10.1080/17579961.2021.1898300

Smuha, N. A. (2019). The EU Approach to Ethics Guidelines for Trustworthy Artificial Intelligence. *Computer Law Review International*, 97-106.

Solorio-Fernández, S., Carrasco-Ochoa, J. A., & Martínez-Trinidad, J. F. (2020). A review of unsupervised feature selection methods. *Artificial Intelligence Review*, 53(2), 907–948. DOI: 10.1007/s10462-019-09682-y

Spolaôr, N., Cherman, E. A., Monard, M. C., & Lee, H. D. (2013). ReliefF for multi-label feature selection. In *2013 Brazilian Conference on Intelligent Systems* (pp. 6-11). IEEE. DOI: 10.1109/BRACIS.2013.10

Sreelatha, A., & Gyandeep, C. (2023, Sep). *Exploring The Use of AI In Legal Decision Making: Benefits and Ethical Implications.* Retrieved Aug 15, 2024, from https://woxsen.edu.in: https://woxsen.edu.in/research/white-papers/exploring-the-use-of-ai-in-legal-decision-making-benefits-and-ethical-implications/

Srinivasan, S. (2014). The Rights of Prisoners: An Overview. https://papers.ssrn.com/sol3/papers.cfm?abstract_id=2704761

Srinivasan, S. (2021). Health problem faced by Elderly inmates' in Central prisons India. https://papers.ssrn.com/sol3/papers.cfm?abstract_id=3962980

Srinivasan, S. (2021). Mental Health problems faced by Aged Inmates due to Overcrowding of Central prison in Tamil Nadu.

Srinivasan, S., & Ilango, P. (2015). The Elderly Inmates in the Indian Prisons–A Psychosocial Perspective. In *The 2nd International Social Work Conference*. https://papers.ssrn.com/sol3/papers.cfm?abstract_id=2704808

Steiner, E. (2003). Early release for seriously ill and elderly prisoners: Should French practice be followed? *Probation Journal*, 50(3), 267–276. DOI: 10.1177/0264550503503013

Stevovic, I., Kirin, S., & Bozić, I. (2021). Artificial Intelligence And Nature-Inspired Optimization On Integrative Capacity Of Renewable Energy In The Western Balkan. *Contemporary Materials*, 12(2). Advance online publication. DOI: 10.7251/COMEN2102226S

Stoykov, K., & Chelebieva, S. (2019, October 1). Legal data extraction and possible applications. *IOP Conference Series. Materials Science and Engineering*, 618(1), 012037–012037. DOI: 10.1088/1757-899X/618/1/012037

Strubell, E., Ganesh, A., & McCallum, A. (2019). *Energy and Policy Considerations for Modern Deep Learning Research.* AAAI Special Programs.

Subramaniam, M., Kathirvel, A., Sabitha, E., & Anwar Basha, H. "Modified Firefly Algorithm and Fuzzy C-Mean Clustering Based Semantic Information Retrieval", Journal of Web Engineering, Vol. 20 1, 33–52, 2021b. Publisher: © River Publishers, 15 Feb 2021, ISSN: 1540-9589 (Print Version). ISSN: 1544-5976 (Online Version), https://doi.org/DOI: 10.13052/jwe1540-9589.2012

Sudha, D., & Kathirvel, A. An Intrusion Detection System to Detect and Mitigating Attacks Using Hidden Markov Model (HMM) Energy Monitoring Technique. Stochastic Modeling an Applications, 26(3) (January – June, Special Issue 2022 Part – 9), 467-476, 2022a. ISSN: 0972-3641.

Sudha, D., & Kathirvel, A. The effect of ETUS in various generic attacks in mobile ad hoc networks to improve the performance of Aodv protocol. International Journal of humanities, law, and social sciences, Kanpur philosophers, Vol. 9 Issue 1, 2023b, N0.1, 467-476, 2022. ISSN: 2348-8301.

Sudha, D., & Kathirvel, A. The performance enhancement of Aodv protocol using GETUS. International Journal of Early Childhood Special Education (INT-JECSE), Vol. 15, Issue 2, 2023a. Pp. 115-125. ISSN: 1308-5581. DOI:DOI: 10.48047/IN-TJECSE/V15I2.11

Sugianela, Y., & Ahmad, T. (2020, February). Pearson correlation attribute evaluation-based feature selection for intrusion detection system. In *2020 International Conference on Smart Technology and Applications (ICoSTA)* (pp. 1-5). IEEE. DOI: 10.1109/ICoSTA48221.2020.1570613717

Surden, H. (2019). Artificial intelligence and legal analytics: New tools for lawyers. *Harvard Journal of Law & Technology*, 32(1), 85–124.

Susskind, R. (2020). *Tomorrow's lawyers: An introduction to your future*. Oxford University Press.

Swetapadma, S., Subudhi, R N., & Chattoraj, P. (2023, August 7). Are reporting and investigation of rape cases victim friendly? Responses of the police from a cross-sectional study conducted in three states of eastern India., 30, 576-595. DOI: 10.1177/02697580231185156

Tan, D. (2023, November 29). Generative AI and Copyright Part 1 Copyright Infringement. *Singapore Academy of Law*https://journalsonline.academypublishing.org.sg/Journals/SAL-Practitioner/Intellectual-Property-Law/ctl/eFirstSALPDFJournalView/mid/597/ArticleId/1921/Citation/JournalsOnlinePDF

Tasioulas, J. (2022). Artificial intelligence, humanistic ethics. *Daedalus*, 151(2), 232–243. https://www.jstor.org/stable/48662038. DOI: 10.1162/daed_a_01912

Tayumi Ishiy, K., & Marcondes Ramos, J. R. (2023). Access to justice and the new technologies applied during the implementation of prison sentences.

Thesaurus, C. A. (2024). *Definition of artificial intelligence.*

Thomas, K., Kelley, P. G., Consolvo, S., Samermit, P., & Bursztein, E. (2022, April). "It's common and a part of being a content creator": Understanding How Creators Experience and Cope with Hate and Harassment Online. In *Proceedings of the 2022 CHI conference on human factors in computing systems* (pp. 1-15).

Thomas, A. (2024). Exploring the power of AI-driven decision making in the judicial domain: Case studies, benefits, challenges, and solutions. In *Using Traditional Design Methods to Enhance AI-Driven Decision Making* (pp. 337–351). IGI Global., DOI: 10.4018/979-8-3693-0639-0.ch015

Thomas, K., Akhawe, D., Bailey, M., Boneh, D., Bursztein, E., Consolvo, S., & Stringhini, G. (2021, May). Sok: Hate, harassment, and the changing landscape of online abuse. In *2021 IEEE Symposium on Security and Privacy (SP)* (pp. 247-267). IEEE. DOI: 10.1109/SP40001.2021.00028

Tim, B., & William, D. (2017). Correctional Offender Management Profiles for Alternative Sanctions (COMPAS). In D. G. Jay P. Singh, *Handbook of Recidivism Risk/Needs Assessment Tools,* (pp. 49-75). Wiley Online Library. DOI: 10.1002/9781119184256

Tonry, M. (2022). Punishments, politics, and prisons in Western countries. *Crime and Justice*, 51(1), 7–57. DOI: 10.1086/721278

Travis, J., Solomon, A., & Waul, M. (2001). *From prison to home.* The Urban Institute., https://d1wqtxts1xzle7.cloudfront.net/53679164/FROM_PRISON_TO_HOME20170627-4007-5rbnzk-libre.pdf?1498577786=&response-content-disposition=inline%3B+filename%3DFrom_Prison_to_Home.pdf&Expires=1723569654&Signature=N5esnCFuwnkIGupnufzk3FKoTw~wpW1RcAlqc774a~peCLXke0ynvXZAtdTBGV5IAIluhJZEHIXi8O9xaJxHeQWhaUEXYuvJcNdubScO4PM0ZZdsAjJ2d1bRCNW6iybVylJrbQjIR33JhPcQJd25Fmwfay-Ud4obGyCtzBjTnAfLtcsKW-uOwHWep-x2EXwYYGdBseG6InVyAY3llhUVfmqOsOmHZsw~tHhqH3TohfTn2tpjABv2EAjAvUCfyyYSOk9UO6a6oIlsI2fhcM6Q8qrlekrks4iJpmDZ665QHOwH~tB75WAVMJavR9HIXkYSDJ1q7AmAc6O6Xpsb00lZ2w__&Key-Pair-Id=APKAJLOHF5GGSLRBV4ZA

Tsiros, M., & Mitchell, A. (2021). AI and the legal profession: Transformations and challenges. *Legal Innovation Quarterly*, 29(1), 22–39.

Tsou, J.-C., Hsieh, K.-Y., Huang, C.-H., Shih, Y.-A., Yu, H.-C., & Fan, Y.-C. (2022). Extracting Crime Prosecution Elements based on Neural Machine Reading Comprehension Model. *IEEE International Conference on Big Data, Big Data 2022* (pp. 3329 - 3335). Osaka: Institute of Electrical and Electronics Engineers Inc. DOI: 10.1109/BigData55660.2022.10020404

Türk, V. (2024, 08 24). HIGH LEVEL SIDE EVENT OF THE 53rd SESSION OF THE HUMAN RIGHTS COUNCIL.

Tyxhari, G., Gorishti, A., & Marku, M. (2023). Technology progress unveiled: Performance indicators in developed vs. developing Western Balkan Countries. *Journal of Southwest Jiaotong University.*

UK Parliament, (2016). Robotics and artificial intelligence, Report of the Committee on Science and Technology, Published 12/10/2016.

Ullmann, S., & Tomalin, M. (Eds.). (2023). *Counterspeech: Multidisciplinary Perspectives on Countering Dangerous Speech.* Taylor & Francis. DOI: 10.4324/9781003377078

UN WIPO. (1886, September 9). *Berne Convention for the Protection of Literary and Artistic Works,* No. 11850.

United Nations Congress on Crime Prevention and Criminal Justice (UNCCPCJ), (2020). Current Crime Trends, Recent Developments, and Emerging Solutions, especially New Technologies as Means of Committing Crime and Tools for Combating Crime, Workshop at the Fourteenth Congress held in Kyoto, Japan, 20-27 April 2020.

ÜNVER. H. A. (2024). *Artificial intelligence (AI) and human rights: Using AI as a weapon of repression and its impact on human rights.* Brussels: European Union.

Vaissnave, V., & Deepalakshmi, P. (2019, December 30). An Artificial Intelligence based Analysis in Legal domain. Blue Eyes Intelligence Engineering and Sciences Publication, 9(2S2), 1046-1051. DOI: 10.35940/ijitee.B1113.1292S219

Valvoda, J., Thompson, A., Cotterell, R., & Teufel, S. (2024, June 02). The Ethics of Automating Legal Actors. *Transactions of the Association for Computational Linguistics*, 12, 700–720. DOI: 10.1162/tacl_a_00668

Varshney, K. (2016). Engineering safety in machine learning. *IEEE*, 1-5.

Vezina, B., & Moran, B. (n.d.). *Artificial Intelligence and Creativity: Why We're Against Copyright Protection for AI-Generated Output.* Creative Commons. https://creativecommons.org/2020/08/10/no-copyright-protection-for-ai-generated-output/

Villasenor, J., & Foggo, V. (2020). Artificial Intelligence, Due Process and Criminal Sentencing. *Mich. St. L. Rev.*, 295. https://heinonline.org/HOL/LandingPage?handle=hein.journals/mslr2020&div=11&id=&page=

Visentin, A., Nardotto, A., & Osullivan, B. (2019). Predicting judicial decisions: A statistically rigorous approach and a new ensemble classifier. *31st IEEE International Conference on Tools with Artificial Intelligence, ICTAI 2019* (pp. 1820-1824). Portland: IEEE. DOI: 10.1109/ICTAI.2019.00275

Visher, C. A., & Travis, J. (2003). Transitions from prison to community: Understanding individual pathways. *Annual Review of Sociology*, 29(1), 89–113. DOI: 10.1146/annurev.soc.29.010202.095931

Visser, J. (2006, March 1). Jurimetrics, safety and security. Taylor & Francis, 20(1-2), 123-133. DOI: 10.1080/13600860600580801

Wachs, S., Gámez-Guadix, M., & Wright, M. F. (2022). Online hate speech victimization and depressive symptoms among adolescents: The protective role of resilience. *Cyberpsychology, Behavior, and Social Networking*, 25(7), 416–423. DOI: 10.1089/cyber.2022.0009 PMID: 35639126

Wachs, S., Wright, M. F., & Gámez-Guadix, M. (2024). From hate speech to HateLess. The effectiveness of a prevention program on adolescents' online hate speech involvement. *Computers in Human Behavior*, 157, 108250. DOI: 10.1016/j.chb.2024.108250

Wahidin, A., & Cain, M. E. (Eds.). (2006). *Ageing, crime and society*. Cullompton: Willan. 10.4324_9781843925729_previewpdf (1).pdf

Wah, Y. B., Ibrahim, N., Hamid, H. A., Abdul-Rahman, S., & Fong, S. (2018). Feature selection methods: Case of filter and wrapper approaches for maximising classification accuracy. *Pertanika Journal of Science & Technology*, 26(1).

Wanbil, W. L., Wolfgang, Z., & Henry, C. (2016, Dec 24). *An Ethical Approach to Data Privacy Protection*. Retrieved Aug 09, 2024, from https://www.isaca.org: https://www.isaca.org/resources/isaca-journal/issues/2016/volume-6/an-ethical-approach-to-data-privacy-protection

Warner, M., Strohmayer, A., Higgs, M., & Coventry, L. (2024). A Critical Reflection on the Use of Toxicity Detection Algorithms in Proactive Content Moderation Systems. *arXiv preprint arXiv:2401.10629*.

Watiktinnakorn, C., Seesai, J., & Kerdvibulvech, C. (2023). Blurring the lines: How AI is redefining artistic ownership and copyright. *Discover Artificial Intelligence*, 3(1), 37. DOI: 10.1007/s44163-023-00088-y

Wazir, A. (2008). *Explanation of the Penal Code - General Section, The General Theory of Crime*. Dar Al-Nahda Al-Arabiya. (In Arabic)

WENG. (2015, February). Y-H. SUGAHARA, Y. HASHIMOTO, K. TAKANISHI, A. (2015). Intersection of "Tokku" Special Zone, Robots, and the Law: A Case Study on Legal Impacts to Humanoid Robots. *International Journal of Social Robotics*.

Will Douglas, H. (2020, Jul 17). *Predictive policing algorithms are racist. They need to be dismantled.* Retrieved Aug 15, 2024, from https://www.technologyreview .com: https://www.technologyreview.com/2020/07/17/1005396/predictive-policing -algorithms-racist-dismantled-machine-learning-bias-criminal-justice/

Williams, B., & Abraldes, R. (2007). Growing older: Challenges of prison and reentry for the aging population. In *Public health behind bars: From prisons to communities* (pp. 56–72). Springer New York., DOI: 10.1007/978-0-387-71695-4_5

Wilson, J., & Daugherty, P. (2018). How humans and AI are working together in 1,500 companies. Harvard Business Review, July-August. Retrieved August 13, 2018, from https://hbr.org/2018/07/collaborative-intelligence-humans-and-ai-are -joining-forc. *Harvard Business Review, July-August.*

Winkler, R., & Sollner, M. (2018). Unleashing the potential of chatbots in education: A state-of-the-art analysis. *Proceedings - Academy of Management*, 2018(1), 1–40. DOI: 10.5465/AMBPP.2018.15903abstract

Wright, L., & Schauer, F. (2023). Expanding access to justice: AI-powered platforms and legal aid. *Journal of Access to Justice*, 25(1), 59–82.

Wu, M., & Wang, Y. (2015). A feature selection algorithm of music genre classification based on ReliefF and SFS. In *2015 IEEE/ACIS 14th International Conference on Computer and Information Science (ICIS)* (pp. 539-544). IEEE. DOI: 10.1109/ ICIS.2015.7166651

Wu, Y. (2018, January 1). Research On the Mechanism Innovation Of The Cultivation Of Rule Of Law Talents In the View Of Big Data. DOI: 10.2991/asssd-18.2018.63

Wu, Y., Liu, Y., Lu, W., Zhang, Y., Feng, J., Sun, C., & Kuang, K. (2022). Towards Interactivity and Interpretability: A Rationale-based Legal Judgment Prediction Framework. *Conference on Empirical Methods in Natural Language Processing, EMNLP 2022* (pp. 4787 - 4799). Abu Dhabi: Association for Computational Linguistics (ACL). DOI: 10.18653/v1/2022.emnlp-main.316

Yang, J. (2021, March 1). Analysis and Application of Judicial Data Based on Machine Learning. *Journal of Physics: Conference Series*, 1846(1), 012027–012027. DOI: 10.1088/1742-6596/1846/1/012027

Yan, Q. (2023). *Legal Challenges of Artificial Intelligence in the Field of Criminal Defense.* Lecture Notes in Education Psychology and Public Media., DOI: 10.54254/2753-7048/30/20231629

Yasmin, N., & Pandey, R. (2018). Prospective memory, working memory, planning, and attention in schizophrenia and bipolar disorder: A comparative study. *Applied Cognitive Psychology*, 32(4), 487–498. DOI: 10.1002/acp.3423

Yimam, S. M., Dementieva, D., Fischer, T., Moskovskiy, D., Rizwan, N., Saha, P., . . . Mukherjee, A. (2024). Demarked: A Strategy for Enhanced Abusive Speech Moderation through Counterspeech, Detoxification, and Message Management. *arXiv preprint arXiv:2406.19543*.

Yoshija, W. (2024, February 26). Managing the race to the moon: Global policy and governance in Artificial Intelligence regulation—A contemporary overview and an analysis of socioeconomic consequences. *Springer Link*, 04(14), 14. Advance online publication. DOI: 10.1007/s44163-024-00109-4

Yulia, R., & Sergiy, R. (2021, April 29). Justice in the Digital Age: Technological Solutions. *Hidden Threats and Enticing Opportunities.*, 4(2), 104–117. DOI: 10.33327/AJEE-18-4.2-a000061

Zarefsky, J., & Koonin, S. (2020). Legal document automation: Impact and future directions. *Stanford Technology Law Review : STLR : An Online High-Technology Law Journal from Stanford Law School*, 23(2), 89–112.

Zha, J. (2020). AI in Agriculture. *Jounal of Physics*.

Zhao, Q., Gao, T., & Guo, N. (2023, September). LA-MGFM: A legal judgment prediction method via sememe-enhanced graph neural networks and multi-graph fusion mechanism. *Information Processing & Management*, 60(05), 103455. Advance online publication. DOI: 10.1016/j.ipm.2023.103455

Zhao, Z., Zhang, Z., & Hopfgartner, F. (2022). Utilizing subjectivity level to mitigate identity term bias in toxic comments classification. *Online Social Networks and Media*, 29, 100205. DOI: 10.1016/j.osnem.2022.100205

Zhong, H., Xiao, C., Tu, C., Zhang, T., Liu, Z., & Sun, M. (2020, January 1). How Does NLP Benefit Legal System: A Summary of Legal Artificial Intelligence. DOI: 10.18653/v1/2020.acl-main.466

Zia, T., Akhter, M. P., & Abbas, Q. (2015). Comparative study of feature selection approaches for Urdu text categorization. *Malaysian Journal of Computer Science*, 28(2), 93–109.

Zivanai, E., & Mahlangu, G. (2022). Digital prison rehabilitation and successful re-entry into a digital society: A systematic literature review on the new reality on prison rehabilitation. *Cogent Social Sciences*, 8(1), 2116809. DOI: 10.1080/23311886.2022.2116809

About the Contributors

Halim Bajraktari, Highest Degree Earned: Assoc. Prof. Dr. Institution that Awarded It: University "Ukshin Hoti" Prizren. Current Position and Affiliation: Professor at the Faculty of Law, University of Prizren “Ukshin Hoti” Summary of Past Academic Contributions: International Human Rights Law: Professor Bajraktari has made significant contributions to the field of international human rights law. His research and teaching focus on the protection of fundamental rights and freedoms at the global level. International Criminal Law: He has also delved into international criminal law, examining issues related to accountability for serious crimes such as genocide, war crimes, and crimes against humanity. European Union Law: Professor Bajraktari’s expertise extends to European Union law, where he explores legal harmonization, integration, and the impact of EU policies on national legal systems. Kosovo’s Challenges and Reforms: His work includes analyzing Kosovo’s political, economic, and legal challenges in the context of European integration. He has written extensively on Kosovo’s journey toward EU membership. Cybersecurity and Terrorism: Professor Bajraktari has investigated cyber warfare and terrorism in Kosovo, emphasizing the legal implications and security challenges posed by these emerging threats. Human Rights Advocacy: He actively engages in promoting human rights and good governance, particularly in identifying hate crimes on social networks. Environmental Effects of Foreign Investment: His research also covers the social and environmental impacts of foreign investment in Kosovo. Professor Halim Bajraktari’s dedication his commitment to advancing knowledge in various legal domains make him a valuable contributor to academia and the legal community.

***

Dafina Abdullahu, is an teaching assistant in the Faculty of Economics at the University “Ukshin Hoti” Prizren. She received her master’s degree (MSc) in Accounting and Auditing in the University of Prizren. Currently, pursuing a PhD in

Management at the University of Osijek- Croatia. She has contributed to research papers in scientific journals and conferences, and she has proficiency in Microsoft Office, Spss, Stata and Pro- Data Finance. She is a member of SCAAK since 2020 and has received scholarship during bachelor studies. For 3 years she worked at the bank as a credit analyst.

S.M. Aamir Ali is an Assistant Professor of Law at Symbiosis Law School, Pune, Symbiosis International (Deemed University) Pune, Maharashtra, India. He is pursuing his Ph.D from West Bengal National University of Juridical Science (WBNUJS), Kolkata. He has completed his LL.M from National Law School of India University (NLSIU), Bengaluru, specialising in Human Right Laws and B.A. LL.B (Hons.) from Aligarh Muslim University, Murshidabad Campus. Along with his education and academic roles, he has also published over 27 academic research papers in National and International Peer Reviewed Journals, including 10 Scopus Indexed journals such as Novum Jus, Journal of Intellectual Property Rights (JIPR), Brazilian Journal of International Law, Manchester Journal of Transnational Islamic Law and Practice, Brazilian Journal of Alternative Dispute Resolution, Economic Political Weekly (EPW) etc. Furthermore, he has contributed to Book Chapters with Internationally reputed publishers such as IGI Global, Springer Nature, Thompson Reuter, etc. He has also presented papers and participated in National and International Seminars, Workshops, and Online Faculty Development Programmes.

Kathirvel Ayyaswamy, acquired, B.E.(CSE), M.E. (CSE) from Crescent Engineering College affiliated to University of Madras and Ph. D (CSE.) from Anna University. He is currently working as Professor, Dept of Computer Science and Engineering, Panimalar Engineering College, Chennai. In-charge for CSE Cyber Forensics Research Group. He is a studious researcher by himself, completed 18 sponsored research projects worth of Rs 103 lakhs and published more than 110 articles in journals and conferences. 4 research scholars have completed Ph. D and 3 under progress under his guidance. He is working as scientific and editorial board member of many journals. He has reviewed dozens of papers in many journals. He has author of 13 books. His research interests are protocol development for wireless ad hoc networks, security in ad hoc network, data communication and networks, mobile computing, wireless networks, WSN and DTN. He is a Life member of the ISTE (India), IACSIT (Singapore), Life Member IAENG (Hong Kong), Member ICST (Europe), IAES, etc. He has given a number of guest lecturers/expert talks and seminars, workshops and symposiums.

Nitesh Behare is an accomplished author with a wealth of knowledge and 15 years of experience in the academic field. He currently holds the position of

Associate Professor at the Balaji Institute of International Business (BIIB), Sri Balaji University Pune (SBUP). Throughout his career, Dr. Behare has made significant contributions to the academic world through the publication of numerous research papers and book chapters, establishing himself as a recognized authority in his field.

Mayura Prakashrao Borde is a versatile experienced person and is currently associated with Yashwantrao Chavan Law College, Pune. Her academic accolade includes B.Sc.(Physics), LL.M. Ph.D., SET, NET (JRF) M.A.(Political Science) DIPR, DCL. She has a teaching experience of 14 years. She has organised and participated in various State, National and International Conferences, Workshops and FDPs. She has authored 30 Research publications in reputed National and International Journals having high impact factor. She has participated and presented research papers in 20 National and International Seminars and Conferences. Along with the doctoral research, she has contributed through several articles and papers in conference proceedings, newspapers, 2 Book chapters and a case study. She is associated with various professional and social organizations. Her areas of interest are Constitutional Law, Criminal Law, Intellectual Property Rights, Law of Contract.

Amir Ahmad Dar is the Faculty in the Department of Mathematics at Lovely Professional University Punjab. The area of interest: Financial mathematics, financial economics, statistics and business mathematics.

Ramy El-Kady is a Full Professor of Criminal Law at the Police Academy and holds the position of Head of the Criminal Law Department. He was rewarded with the State Encouragement Award in Legal and Economic Sciences, Citizenship and Human Rights Branch, on the topic of "the right of persons cooperating with justice for protection in international conventions and national legislation. He graduated from the Police College in 1999. He obtained a postgraduate diploma in criminal sciences and public law, which is equivalent to a master's degree in criminal law, in 2003. He obtained a PhD in criminal law from the Faculty of Law, Cairo University, on the topic of (Mediation as an Alternative to a Criminal Case: A Comparative Study. He currently teaches criminal law subjects to college students. He supervised numerous studies submitted for doctoral degrees and higher diplomas and authored a host of research in the criminal law field. He has previously judged numerous research papers in a number of refereed regional scientific journals. He published a host of research in refereed and indexed periodicals and took part in a number of international and local conferences and symposia.

Anuttama Ghose is an Assistant Professor of Law and Program Co-ordinator of BA LLB (Hons.) Program at the School of Law, Dr. Vishwanath Karad MIT World Peace University, Pune, India. She is also presently Heading the Centre for

Innovation Incubation and Intellectual Property Laws (CIIIPL) at MIT WPU School of Law. She has completed her B.A LL.B (IPR Hons.) from the School of Law, KIIT University, Bhubaneshwar and LL.M with specialisation in the field of Intellectual Property Laws from Symbiosis Law School, Pune, India. She has completed her PhD in the field of Protection of Non-Conventional Trademarks from School of Law and Justice, Adamas University, Kolkata. She has previously worked as Vice-Principal and Assistant Professor of Law at Indian Institute of Legal Studies, Darjeeling, West Bengal. Apart from being an IPR enthusiast, she is a very keen researcher and has over 25 academic publications in National and International Journals to her credit. Her scholarly contributions extend to well-regarded Scopus Indexed Journals and Book Chapters with Internationally reputed publishers such as IGI Global, Springer Nature, Thompson Reuter, etc.

Rakshita Gouri, LLB, B.Tech | Registered Advocate and dedicated legal professional and practitioner with over two years of experience in legal consultancy..

Christian Kaunert is a Professor of International Security at Dublin City University, Ireland. He is also Professor of Policing and Security and Director of the International Centre for Policing and Security at the University of South Wales. Previously, he served as an Academic Director and Professor at the Institute for European Studies, Vrije Universiteit Brussel, a Professor of International Politics, Head of Discipline in Politics, and the Director of the European Institute for Security and Justice, a Jean Monnet Centre for Excellence, at the University of Dundee. He was awarded a large Horizon 2020 research grant on Terrorist Radicalisation processes – Mindb4Act, a large Horizon Europe Marie Curie Doctoral Network EUGLOCTER, and a Jean Monnet Network EUCTER, alongside several Jean Monnet Chairs, Centres, Modules, and TT.

Madhavi More is an experienced educator with a wealth of experience spanning over 11 years in the field of legal education and currently associated with CHRIST deemed to be University, Lavasa. His academic accolades include BALLB, LLM NET. She holds a prestigious Doctorate degree in law faculty from Savitribai Phule Pune University, Pune, a testament to her perseverance and academic achievements. Dr. More's academic interests are diverse, with a particular focus on subjects such as Environmental Law, Constitutional Law, ADR Laws, and Legal research.He has organised and participated in various State & National seminars and Faculty Development Programmes in the field of socio legal studies. She has authored research papers in national and international journals having high impact factors. Beyond her academic pursuits, Dr. More is deeply committed to social causes, showcasing her passion via University Women's Association, Pune as a Youth

Convener. Her multifaceted approach to academia, coupled with her humane endeavours, demonstrates her holistic commitment to education, research, and social furtherance.

Valeri Qatani, currently a researcher at University "Ukshin Hoti" in Prizren, focusing on career development and scientific research in the field of legal studies. Significant publications indexed in Scopus that examine various legal and social issues, reflecting its commitment to advancing knowledge and improving academic discussion. Moreover, it's equipped with many certificates from international conferences in various fields, which have been held in many countries of the world.

R. Rajeshkanna is an accomplished academic with over 16 years of experience in the field of computer science and information technology. He holds a Ph.D. from Bharathiar University, Coimbatore, and an M.Phil from Vinayaka Missions University, Salem. He also earned his MCA from Periyar University, Salem. Currently, Dr. Rajeshkanna serves as an Assistant Professor in the Department of Computer Science at CHRIST (Deemed to be University), Bangalore, a position he has held since July 2022. Prior to this, he was the Professor and Head of the Department of Information Technology at Dr. N.G.P Arts & Science College (Autonomous), Coimbatore. His tenure at this institution, spanning from January 2020 to June 2022, followed a series of progressive roles, including Associate Professor and Head of the Department, and earlier, as an Assistant Professor. Dr. Rajeshkanna has made significant academic contributions through his research and scholarly activities. He has published 35 papers in reputed international journals with high impact factors and has contributed 16 book chapters through IGI Global Publications.

Nicamil Sanchez is a prominent figure in the fields of social work, research, and technology development. With a distinguished career spanning various domains, Dr. Sanchez has made significant contributions to academia and society. With a PhD in Social Work from Australian Catholic University (ACU), Dr. Sanchez stands as the first Filipino to have completed such a doctoral degree and returned to his homeland to serve. His academic achievements have been recognized internationally, earning him the prestigious Australian Leadership Awards and Outstanding Alumni of Australian Catholic University. Currently, he is also an Adjunct Research Faculty of University of the Philippines, Man

Samrudhee Shah is a legal professional with 5 years of overall experience, currently serving as an Assistant Professor at Dr. D.Y. Patil Law College, Pimpri, for the past 1.5 years. Her academic contributions include the publication of a research paper on Whistle blowing mechanisms in the Pimpri Law Review and her role as an editor at the International Journal on Legal Development and Practice. Samrudhee's experience extends to moot court judging, having evaluated an intra moot court competition at Army Law College and the International Client Counseling Competition at Manipal University, Jaipur. She recently coordinated the International Conference on Product Safety and Consumer Advocacy, further showcasing her organizational skills in the academic realm. She holds a master's degree from Sandip University, Nashik, and is also CS Professional aspirant, reflecting her commitment to continued professional development in law and corporate governance.

Atmaram F. Shelke is working as an Associate Professor at Symbiosis Law School, Pune a constituent of Symbiosis International (Deemed University). He has been awarded two gold medals for achieving first position in LL.M. at Symbiosis International University, Pune (India). His PhD research focused on Intellectual Property Rights Violation in Cyberspace. Dr. Shelke specialises in IPR Violation in Cyberspace, Constitutional Law, Administrative Law and Research Methodology. The fields of his research interest are IPR Violation in Cyberspace, Constitutional Law, Administrative Law, Criminal Law. He participateed in "DAAD–New Passage to Indian Programme" in Germany from 2nd to 14th May, 2014, Bulgaria under EURASIA project in December, 2018 and under EURASIA project in September, 2019. With over 16 years of teaching experience, he has instructed students in BA/ BBA LL.B. (Hons.), Master's degree programs, PhD coursework, and EU Value Added Courses such as E-Justice in the EU and Data Protection and Data Privacy in the EU. He has also been involved in teaching European students visiting India under the umbrella of Symbiosis International (Deemed University). Dr. Atmaram Shelke is regularly invited to review articles of Journal of Intellectual Property Rights (JIPR); Christ University Law Journal (CULJ), ISSN 2278-4322 and International Invention Journal of Medicine and Medical Sciences (IIJMMS). He has contributed to the "Project on Indian Penal Code" sponsored by Shri. Ram Jethmalani, Sr. Advocate, Supreme Court of India; project on 'Critique on Indian Legal Framework for Addressing Sexual Abuse, Exploitation and Trafficking of Children (Special focus on male child)'; a project on problems of foreign prisoners in Pune; project on legal aid with City University of New York. Additionally, he worked as a co-investigator on 'Report on Transformation of the Criminal Justice System in India' submitted to the Ministry of Home Affairs, Government of India in April, 2020; worked as a member of committee on recommendations on Digital Courts Vision & Roadmap (Phase III of the e-courts Projects) in May, 2021. He also guided 13 projects on various aspects of the criminal justice system with CID, Pune. He has more than 20 publications on his account. He worked as a member of the outcome report of Round Table Discussion on "Draft Guidelines for Conducting Preliminary Assessment under Section 15 of The Juvenile Justice (JJ) Act, 2015" organised by SLS, Pune in January, 2023, report has been submitted to NCPCR. Previously, he served as the Deputy Director (Administration) at Symbiosis Law School, Pune for 3 years. He also worked as one of the editors of 11th International Annual Research Conference on Rule of Law in Context: Globalisation and Indian Resonances to Sustainable Development Goal, published by Taylor and Francis in 2024. He has been invited as a resource person to over 40 national and international conferences, programmes, workshops etc. He has completed Advanced Course in Copyrights and Related Rights (ACCRR-WIPO Academy) in 2008, General Course on Intellectual Property Rights (GIPR-WIPO Academy) in 2008, Diploma in Crop Science (Amaravati University, India) in 2001, Diploma of Library Assistant, Library Director, Maharashtra State, 2003 and Certificate Course on Cyber Law and Security (Gujarat National Law School, India), 2012.

Bhupinder Singh working as Professor at Sharda University, India. Also, Honorary Professor in University of South Wales UK and Santo Tomas University Tunja, Colombia. His areas of publications as Smart Healthcare, Medicines, fuzzy logics, artificial intelligence, robotics, machine learning, deep learning, federated learning, IoT, PV Glasses, metaverse and many more. He has 3 books, 139 paper publications, 163 paper presentations in international/national conferences and seminars, participated in more than 40 workshops/FDP's/QIP's, 25 courses from international universities of repute, organized more than 59 events with international and national academicians and industry people's, editor-in-chief and co-editor in journals, developed new courses. He has given talks at international universities, resource person in international conferences such as in Nanyang Technological University Singapore, Tashkent State University of Law Uzbekistan; KIMEP University Kazakhstan, All'ah meh Tabatabi University Iran, the Iranian Association of International Criminal law, Iran and Hague Center for International Law and Investment, The Netherlands, Northumbria University Newcastle UK,

Mohana Priya T is Assistant Professor at CHRIST(Deemed to be University), Bangalore, India. She Holds a PhD degree in Computer Science in Machine learning at Bharathiar University, Coimbatore, India. Her research areas are Machine Learing and medical image analysis. She is acted as Coordinator for curriculum development cell and Software development cell.She published 10 Journal articles in various international peer reviewed journals, 2 Book publications and 15 presentations in various international level conference held in india and abroad.. She can be contacted at email: drtmohanapriya @gmail.com

Srinivasan S. is an accomplished Assistant Professor (Research) in the Department of Humanities and Social Science at Graphic Era (Deemed to be

University), Dehradun. He has previously contributed as Guest Faculty (Social Work) at Bharathidasan University, Tiruchirappalli, Tamil Nadu, where he served for two years. Mr. Srinivasan holds a Master of Philosophy degree from the Central University of Pondicherry, Pondicherry, India. His academic journey is marked by the publication of numerous research papers that cover a broad spectrum of subjects. His expertise spans across various areas including migration, aging, women's and children's issues, public health issues, tuberculosis, correctional administration, public policy, gender issues, artificial intelligence, and machine learning. Mr. Srinivasan's diverse research interests reflect his commitment to addressing complex social issues through an interdisciplinary lens, making significant contributions to both the academic and practical realms of social science.

Shrikant Waghulkar is a seasoned educator with a wealth of experience spanning over 10 years in the field of management education. He holds a prestigious Doctorate degree in management faculty from Savitribai Phule Pune University, Pune, a testament to his dedication and scholarly achievements. Dr. Waghulkar's academic interests are diverse, with a particular focus on subjects such as Research Methodology, Personal Management, Rural Marketing, and Digital Marketing. Beyond his academic pursuits, Dr. Waghulkar is deeply committed to social causes, showcasing his passion for community upliftment. He is actively involved in philanthropic endeavors and serves as a leading figure in a charitable trust dedicated to advancing the educational prospects of farmer's children. Through this initiative, he aims to provide better educational opportunities to underserved communities, thereby contributing to their social elevation and empowerment. Driven by his passion for both academia and social welfare, Dr. Waghulkar also harbors a keen interest in marketing research. His multifaceted approach to academia, coupled with his altruistic endeavors, exemplifies his holistic commitment to education, research, and societal betterment.

Index

A

C

D

E

F

G

H

I

J

L

M

www.ingramcontent.com/pod-product-compliance
Lightning Source LLC
LaVergne TN
LVHW081350300926
849161LV00008B/2116